READINGS IN MORAL THEOLOGY NO. 5:
OFFICIAL CATHOLIC SOCIAL TEACHING

READINGS IN MORAL THEOLOGY
No. 5:

Official Catholic Social Teaching

Edited by
Charles E. Curran
and
Richard A. McCormick, S.J.

PAULIST PRESS
New York/Mahwah

Acknowledgements
The articles reprinted in *Moral Theology No. 5* first appeared in the following publications and are reprinted with permission: "The Rights and Duties of Labor and Capital" from *The Papal Ideology of Social Reform* by Richard Camp, E.J. Brill; "Toward a New Society" by George Higgins; "The Drafting of Quadragesimo Anno" by Oswald von Nell-Breuning, S.J., *Stimmen der Zeit;* "Forty Years Later: Reflections and Reminiscences" by John Cronin, S.J. from *American Ecclesiastical Review,* 1971, Catholic University of America Press; "The Option for the Poor" from *Pope John XXIII—A New Direction?* by Donal Dorr, Orbis; "Human Rights in Roman Catholicism" by John Langan, S.J. in Summer 1982 edition of *Journal of Ecumenical Studies;* "Looking Back on Populorum Progressio" by Barbara Ward in *Doctrine and Life,* St. Savior's Press; "Action for Justice as Constitutive of the Preaching of the Gospel: What Did the 1971 Synod Mean?" by Charles Murphy in *Theological Studies,* Vol. 44, 1983, pp. 298–311, Georgetown University; "Development of Church Social Teaching" by John Coleman, in *Origins,* June 4, 1981, Vol. II, No. 3, Paulist Press; "The Changing Anthropological Bases of Catholic Social Ethics" by Charles Curran, April 1981, *Thomist;* "Laborem Exercens and Social Morality" by Richard McCormick, S.J. in *Theological Studies* 43 (1982), 92–103, Georgetown University; excerpts from John Paul II's Encyclical on Labor by Gregory Baum, Paulist Fathers, Inc.; "Laborem Exercens: Toward a New Solidarity" by Bartolomeo Sorge, *Theology Digest,* Spring 1984; "John Paul II: Continuity and Change in the Social Teaching of the Church" by J. Bryan Hehir in *Co-Creation and Capitalism,* University Press of America, Inc.; "The Popes and Politics: Shifting Patterns in Catholic Social Doctrine" by Peter Hebblethwaite, *Daedalus;* "Methodological Differences" in *Barriers to Ecumenism* by Thomas Sieger Derr, Orbis; "The Problem of Poverty and the Poor in Catholic Social Teaching" by József Lukács, in *Concilium* V, 104, Paulist Press; "From Catholic 'Social Doctrine' to the 'Kingdom of Christ on Earth' " by James Schall in *Communio 3* (1976), 284–300, Gonzaga University; "The Bias Against Democratic Capitalism" from *The Spirit of Democratic Capitalism* by Michael Novak, Simon & Schuster, Inc.; "Economic Systems, Middle Way Theories, and Third World Realities" in *Co-Creation and Capitalism* by John Houck, University Press of America; David Hollenbach, S.J., "Global Human Rights: An Interpretation of Contemporary Catholic Understanding," in *Human Rights in the Americas: The Struggle for Consensus;* edited by Alfred Hennelly, S.J. and John Langan, S.J., Georgetown University Press; "From Rerum Novarum to Laborem Exercens: Toward the Year 2000. A United States Perspective" by Thomas R. Donahue, first appeared in *Rerum Novarum, Laborem Exercens 2000 Symposium,* Pontifica Commissio Justitia et Pax 1982; "Feminist Themes and Laborem Exercens" by Andrea Lee and Amata Miller in *Co-Creation and Capitalism,* John Houck, ed., University Press of America, Inc.; Christine Gudorf, "Major Differences: Liberation Theology and Current Church Teaching" in *Catholic Social Teaching on Liberation Themes,* University Press of America, Inc.

Contents

FOR MSGR. GEORGE G. HIGGINS

ON HIS SEVENTIETH BIRTHDAY

Foreword

This fifth volume of our series *Readings in Moral Theology* deals with commentaries on official Catholic social teaching. The purpose and format of this series is to gather together significant studies on a particular aspect of moral theology. To insure an in-depth and scholarly presentation the topic must be suitably limited. This volume is concerned with the area of Christian social ethics, but such a topic area is much too broad. Official Catholic social teaching is the focus of the present volume. This collection presupposes a general knowledge of these documents and attempts to offer significant commentaries to analyze and criticize this important body of social teaching.

Official Catholic social teaching refers to that body of documents containing the teaching of recent Popes and the Catholic bishops of the world. Most observers point to the encyclical letter of Pope Leo XIII, *Rerum novarum* in 1891, as the beginning of this social teaching. This encyclical marked the response of the Pope to the problems created by the industrial revolution and emphasized both the need for the state to intervene to protect the rights of a particular class and the rights of workers to organize. Subsequent Popes often took advantage of the anniversary of *Rerum novarum* to issue new encyclicals and letters on the social issues facing the Church and the world at that particular time. Thus in 1931 Pope Pius XI issued *Quadragesimo anno* whose very title indicates its commemoration of the fortieth anniversary of *Rerum novarum*. In 1961 Pope John XXIII wrote *Mater et magistra* which was followed two years later by *Pacem in terris*. The Second Vatican Council (1962–1965) dealt with these questions in a number of documents but especially in *Gaudium et spes*, the Pastoral Constitution on the Church in the Modern World. Pope Paul VI emphasized the worldwide nature of the social question in *Populorum progressio* in 1967. In 1971, the eightieth anniversary of *Rerum novarum*, Pope Paul VI wrote his letter *Octogesima adveniens* while the Second General Assembly of the Synod of Bishops issued *Justitia in mundo*. Pope John Paul II has written extensively on social questions, but the primary document is *Laborem exercens* which appeared a few months after the anniversary of *Rerum novarum* because of the attempted assassination of the Pope. Many of these documents are available in two different collections: *The Gospel of Peace and Justice: Catholic Social Teaching since Pope John*, ed. Joseph Gremillion (Maryknoll, NY: Orbis Press, 1976) and *Renewing the Earth: Catholic Documents on Peace, Justice, and Liberation*, eds. David J. O'Brien and Thomas A. Shannon (Garden City, NY: Doubleday Image Books, 1977).

This book is divided into three parts. The first part treats the historical development of this social teaching beginning with the background to *Rerum novarum* and including discussions of the contributions of the different Popes down to Pope Paul VI (d. 1978). The second part presents overviews which point out the developments that have occurred within this teaching and the contemporary discussions dealing especially with the approach of Pope John Paul II. The third part contains commentaries on this body of teaching from many different perspectives— Protestant, Marxist, third world, labor, conservative, liberal, feminist, and liberationist.

The topic of official Catholic social teaching provided the primary criterion for the selection of contributions to this collection. There are no studies dealing primarily with a particular topic such as peace. In addition it would have broadened the topic too much to include official Catholic teaching proposed by the bishops of the United States. There are many excellent books and articles dealing with social ethics and its methodology within a Catholic perspective which are not included in this volume because they did not focus on the official Catholic social teaching as such.

In keeping with the spirit and practice of this series we tried to make sure that all differing viewpoints are found in this volume. We obviously have our own positions, but this volume tries to give a faithful representation of the many different approaches that have been taken to Catholic social teaching. Also we tried to provide selections from those who have often written on this topic.

We are grateful for the permission to include here these articles which were originally published elsewhere. A special word of thanks goes to Kenneth Hallahan, a doctoral student at the Catholic University of America, for his assistance in preparing this volume.

Charles E. Curran
Richard A. McCormick, S.J.

PART ONE:
HISTORICAL DEVELOPMENT

The Catholic Social Movement: Historical Aspects[1]

Edward Cahill, S.J.

This article originally appeared in *The Framework of a Christian State*, 1932.

ART. 1—ITS NATURE

A Reaction Against Anti-Christian Forces

In the earlier chapters of the present work we have given a short sketch of the Church's action up to the 16th century in building up the fabric of European civilization. As already shown, the decay of that civilization, which is so marked a feature of European society to-day, began with the Protestant revolt in the first half of the 16th century. Rationalism, political and economic Liberalism, Freemasonry, unchristian Capitalism and Socialism, which are now undermining the foundations of the old Christian organisation of Europe, are the natural consequences of that revolt. The modern Catholic social movement, which began about the middle of the last century, represents the vital reaction of Christianity against these principles and tendencies. It aims at repairing or reconstructing Christian civilization where it has been injured or destroyed.

Such a movement is not a new phenomenon in the life of the Church. The Catholic faith is a living force, which tends to affect profoundly, and even to transform the character of the individual or the society that has adopted it. Hence Catholic Action, of which a Catholic social movement is the result, or rather the embodiment, is as old as the Church itself. It is in fact the main source of all that is best in European civilization.

The Church, [writes Pius X], while preaching Jesus crucified
. . . has been the first inspirer and promoter of civilization.
She has spread it wherever her apostles have preached, preserving and perfecting what was good in ancient pagan civilizations; rescuing from barbarism and raising to a form of
civilized society the new peoples who took refuge in her ma-
ternal bosom [viz., the Teutonic invaders of the period between the fourth and sixth centuries A.D.], and giving to the
whole of human society, little by little, no doubt, but with a
sure and onward march, that characteristic stamp which it still
everywhere preserves.[2]

Scope and Aims

The movement, although inspired by religion, and carried on under
the immediate guidance of the Pope and the Catholic hierarchy, is not
confined to the religious and moral interests of the people. Besides these
it includes in its scope all that may affect their social, intellectual and
material well-being; and it seeks to promote these by means which are
in harmony with Catholic tradition, and the moral and dogmatic principles of Christianity.

No practical solution, [writes Leo XIII], of this question [viz.,
the modern social question] will be found apart from the intervention of religion and the Church. . . . The Church im-
proves and betters the condition of the workingman by means
of numerous organizations; she does her best to enlist the services of all classes in discussing and endeavouring to further
in the most practical way the interests of the working classes;
and considers that for this purpose recourse should be had in
due degree to the intervention of the law, and of State authorities.[3]

Hence the immediate objects of the movement are:

I. To disseminate among the masses of the people a better knowledge of Catholic social principles and ideals.

II. To reorganize the public life of the nation in accordance with Catholic standards, and

III. To counteract by suitable measures, in harmony with the teachings of the Church, the poverty, insecurity and material misery of the labouring population.

Essential Characteristics[4]

(a) Active Participation of the Laity

A special characteristic of the movement is the active co-operation of the laity (of both sexes), under the guidance of the Bishops, in the social activities of the Church. This trait is in large part an outcome of the Church's traditional policy of accommodating her methods as far as possible to the customs and ideals of the society in which she is operating. In contrast with the civic organization of mediaeval times, when the political power was mostly in the hands of one class, the mass of the people now take an active part in the duties of legislation and administration. Hence the Church, adapting herself to this democratic tendency, invites, and indeed urges, the laity of all classes, and of both sexes, to take an active part in the work of building up again the shattered fabric of Christian civilization.

> Catholic action, [writes Pius XI], does not merely consist in each one striving after one's own Christian perfection, although this, it is true, is everyone's primary and principal duty, but it means a very real apostolate, in which Catholics of every rank and order take part. In this work the outlook and activities of each and all are linked up with and borrow their character from certain central institutions duly constituted with episcopal sanction, which supply the guiding principles, and direct and co-ordinate the varied activities.[5]

Further down in the same letter occurs the well-known phrase in which Catholic Action is authoritatively defined as "the participation and collaboration of the laity with the Apostolic Hierarchy."

On the same subject the late Cardinal Vaughan writes:

The Catholic layman has, perhaps, a more distinguished part to play now in the service of Christ than at any former time. . . . He is invited by the authorities of the Church to co-operate in a hundred ways and to take part in a hundred works, which are essentially and intimately connected with public life and with the salvation of souls. Rich and poor, learned and unlearned, are united in groups and associations which aim at securing the claims of Christianity and souls.[6]

(b) Unity and Endless Variety

The movement, which has now spread into every country that has a notable Catholic population, embraces an endless variety of organisations, and aims at influencing the moral, intellectual and social lives of the people in almost every detail. Yet, amid all its various aspects and manifestations, the whole movement is marked by a wondrous unity of spirit and of aim, and is besides in perfect harmony with the traditional principles and aims which have inspired Catholic Action for almost two thousand years.

The principle of this essential unity is, in the first place, the moral and dogmatic teachings of the Church, upon which the whole movement is founded, and which never vary. Thus, in every phase of the movement, religion, justice, charity and piety are accorded primacy of place among the forces that are to solve the social question. Again, in dealing with the material miseries of the people, all Catholics are united in opposition to the exaggerations and false principles of Liberalism, Collectivism, Communism and the ultra-nationalistic and secularist aspects of Fascism. Catholics seek a solution in harmony, at the same time, with the instincts of human nature and the exalted ideals of Christianity.

A second source of the uniformity of which we speak is the fact that all the Catholic social activities of which the movement is composed are carried on under the guidance of the Bishops and the Supreme Pontiff, so that, in all its phases and organisations, it is directed by the same guiding hand. The recent Encyclicals of Pius XI on *Marriage* and *Christian Education,* and, above all, the Encyclical on the *Social Order (Quadragesimo Anno,* 1931) are outstanding examples of the authoritative and unifying guidance of the Sovereign Pontiff.

(c) Solidarist Ideal

This last Encyclical was issued, as is expressly stated in the document itself,[7] to secure this unity especially among Catholic writers on social science. The Encyclical practically embodies the principles and conclusions of the present day German Catholic School of Sociology and Social Reform. The writers of this school include such names as Pesch,[8] Nell-Breuning, Otto Schilling and Gundlach. These and other workers in the same field have elaborated the system known as *Solidarismus*, which in reality is nothing else than the concrete expression of the Catholic traditional ideals as applied to modern conditions. The central idea of the Solidaristic social philosophy is the *organic* conception of the State functioning in accordance with the dictates of Legal Justice and Charity as contrasted with the "individualistic" ideal of the Liberals, the "class-war" of the Socialists, and the excessive bureaucracy of Socialists and Fascists alike. This organic conception is realised by means of local units such as municipalities and professional corporations (including both employers and employed), all enjoying each within its own sphere a large measure of autonomy.[9]

(d) Strictly Non-Political

The movement, although sometimes termed "Christian Democracy" (a name which has received the official sanction of Leo XIII and Pius X),[10] is strictly non-political. In other words, like the Church itself (which is affiliated to no political party, and has no special predilection for any particular form of government, provided only that the functions of government are duly fulfilled), the Catholic movement is outside and above all party politics. It may and does aim at promoting legislation and administration in accordance with Christian principles, and even may, when necessity arises, use pressure for that purpose on governing authorities; but it is never allied to or identified with any political party. On this subject Leo XIII writes:

> Although Democracy, by its very name and by philosophical usage, denotes popular rule, yet in this application it must be employed altogether without political signification. . . . For

the precepts of the natural law and the Gospel, for this very reason that they transcend the chances of human existence, must necessarily be independent of any form of civil government and adapt themselves to all, *so long as these are not opposed to what is right and just.* They are, therefore, and remain in themselves completely outside party rivalries and political changes. . . . This has ever been the morality of the Church; by it Roman Pontiffs have constantly dealt with States, what ever might be their form of government.[11]

This direction of Leo XIII has been formally confirmed by Pius X, who writes:

Christian democracy ought never to mix in party politics; and ought never to be made use of for party purposes or political objects; that is not its province; but it should be a beneficient activity in favour of the people, founded on the natural law and the precepts of the Gospel.[12]

We shall now sketch briefly the rise and development of the Catholic social movement in the Catholic countries of Europe. In a separate article a brief account shall be given of some of the more important and characteristic organisations which have taken shape under its influence.

ART. 2—HISTORICAL SKETCH

Precursors—Taparelli and O'Connell

Father Aloysius Taparelli, S.J. (1793–1862), a native of Turin, and for many years Rector of the Roman College of the Society of Jesus, may be considered as the precursor of the modern Catholic social movement, especially in its doctrinal or theoretical side. His works have had a profound influence upon Catholic social teaching and Catholic action for the past eighty years. His main work, *Theoretical Essay on Natural Right from the Historical Standpoint,*[13] which appeared about ninety years ago, still remains as one of the best expositions of Catholic principles and ideals regarding social and civic organisation.

Again, the career and work of Daniel O'Connell in Ireland, and the great popular movement of which he was the leader, had great influence in Continental countries; and inspired ideas which prepared the way for a Catholic popular revival.

Ketteler, Windthorst and the Catholic Movement in Germany

The actual movement, however, began in Germany, and Baron Von Ketteler (1811–1877), Bishop of Mainz, was its real founder. Ketteler recognized the danger to the Church from the apathy of the wealthier Catholics, and even of large numbers of the clergy, in face of the misery and material degradation of the labouring population. In 1847 appeared the *Communist Manifesto* of Marx and Engels, heralding the birth of the Socialist movement. Ketteler was one of the few men of his generation that recognized its significance; and to him belongs, in the words of another great Catholic leader, Gaspard Decurtins, "The undying honour of having met the manifesto of the Communists with a programme of Christian social reform that stands unsurpassed to this day."[14]

It was at the first Catholic Congress held at Mainz, 1848, two years before Ketteler's consecration as Bishop of Mainz, that he delivered the famous address which was really the beginning of the Catholic social movement in Germany. "The task of religion, the task of the Catholic societies in the immediate future," he said, "has to do with social conditions. The most difficult question—one which no legislation, no form of government has been able to solve—is the *social question*. The difficulty, the vastness, the urgency of this question fills me with the greatest joy!" The cause of the joy he explains to be the fact that "It must now become evident which Church bears within it the power of divine truth. The world will see that to the Catholic Church is reserved the definite solution of the social question; for the State, with all its legislative machinery, has not the power to solve it."[15]

It was largely as a result of Ketteler's labours and incessant exhortations, continuing over a period of nearly thirty years (1848–77), that German Catholics were stirred into vigorous action on the social question. Since his time the Catholic clergy of Germany have taken a prominent part in social reform, and have produced from their own ranks a succession of able writers and social leaders. Among these latter may be mentioned Canon Moufang, who succeeded Ketteler in the leadership of the movement, and later on, Canon Hitze, who succeeded Moufang.

Besides Ketteler's numberless sermons and addresses, pamphlets and books poured from his pen. Even to-day his two books, *Liberty, Authority and the Church*[16] and *Christianity and the Labour Question,*[17] as well as his work published under the title of *A Christian Labour Catechism,*[18] remain a classical expression of the Church's position.

When, in 1870, the German Centre Party was formed under the leadership of Ludwig Windthorst (1812–91), to oppose Bismarck's *Kulturkampf,* the promotion of the Catholic social programme became a central item in its policy. After the death of Bishop Ketteler in 1877, Windthorst became the predominating figure at every one of the great German Catholic Congresses.[19] He fitly closed his great career with the founding of the *Volksverein*—The People's Union for Catholic Germany—the constitution of which he drafted on his death-bed. We shall refer to it again.

Precursors of the Social Movement in France[20]

In the first seventy years of the nineteenth century many French Catholic publicists and economists of different political views wrote strongly in favour of social reform legislation, and advocated also Catholic organisation to combat the evils resulting from industrial liberalism. Among these may be mentioned Chateaubriand, author of the *Le Génie du Christianisme* (1802); Philip J. B. Buchez (1796–1865); Louis Veuillot (1813–1883); Lacordaire (1802–1861), the great Dominican preacher; Vicomte J. P. A. Ville-neuve-Burgemont (1784–1850); Vicomte Arnauld de Melun (1807–1877); and Frederick Ozanam (1813–1853).

Ozanam, besides writing a good deal on social subjects and on the great rôle played by Christianity in promoting social well-being,[21] is perhaps best remembered as the founder of the Society of St. Vincent de Paul. This work, and indeed Ozanam's whole life, might be regarded as a reply, and not a wholly unconscious reply, to the well-known challenge to the Holy See which Saint-Simon, the Socialist writer, puts into the mouth of Luther.

Your predecessors, [he says in a supposed address to the Holy Father], have sufficiently perfected the theory of Christianity; they have sufficiently propagated that theory. . . . It is the general application of that doctrine must now be your concern. True Christianity should make men happy not only in heaven but also on earth. . . . The clergy will always exercise a predominant influence on the temporal institutions of all nations when it sets to work in a positive manner to ameliorate the condition of the poorer class, which is always the most numerous class of the community.[22]

Frederick le Play[23] (1806–1882) and Henry C. X. Perin (1815–1905), Professor of Law in the Catholic University of Louvain, both wrote extensively on social subjects; and both exercised great influence on French Catholic thought during the third quarter of the 19th century. Their views, however, were more conservative than those of the Catholic writers of the preceding generation and of the school of social thought that arose after 1870. Unlike both these latter groups they were opposed to State interference in the relations between employers and workmen.

Count Albert de Mun

The real founders, however, of the Catholic social movement in France were two young Catholic noblemen, officers in the French army, who made each other's acquaintance while prisoners of war (1870) in the German internment camp at Aix-la-Chapelle. These were Count Albert de Mun and the Marquis Réné de la Tour du Pin.

De Mun tells the whole story in his memoirs, which were published thirty-seven years later (1908).[24] He and his companion, returning to France after their release from prison, witnessed the dreadful scenes of the Paris Communist insurrection in 1871, and took part in the operations against the insurgents. When the fighting was over and De Mun and others were shocked by the ruthlessness of the measures adopted against the defeated Communists, a certain Vincentian lay-brother, Maurice Maignen, with whom De Mun accidentally came into contact, made a deep impression on him. Maignen one day pointed dramatically to the charred ruins of some of the great palaces, declared with emphasis that it was

12 / Edward Cahill, S.J.

the rich and noble and not the proletarian insurgents who were fundamentally responsible for the ruined streets and the charred and mangled corpses with which they had been so recently strewn.

> It is you, [he said], who have amused yourselves within these palaces now in ruins; you who pass by without seeing the people, without knowing them or their character or thoughts, or caring for their needs and their sufferings, it is you who are the real culprits.[25]

Catholic Workingmen's Clubs

Towards the end of the year 1871 the foundations of the new movement were laid, when De Mun, Maignen, La Tour du Pin, and several other leading Catholic gentlemen of Paris issued the famous "Appeal to Men of Good Will," and sketched their social programme. The latter included such items as the multiplication of Catholic Workingmen's Clubs on a huge scale (*Oeuvres de cercles Catholiques d'Ouvriers*):

> To subversive doctrines [the appeal continued] and dangerous teachings, we must oppose the holy teachings of the Gospel; to materialism the notion of sacrifice; to the cosmopolitan spirit the idea of country; to atheistical negation Catholic affirmation. . . . The privileged classes have duties to fulfil towards their brethren, the workingmen; and society, though it has a right to defend itself with arms, must know that shot and shell do not cure, and that other measures are needed.[26]

De Mun and his party relied too much on the leadership and patronage of the wealthier and better educated classes, and did not believe in associations made up exclusively of the working classes, which Leo XIII later on and his successors have so strongly recommended. However, the Association of Catholic Workingmen's Clubs expanded rapidly, and in 1884 had 400 Committees, with 50,000 members. But its importance and significance were out of all proportion to its actual numbers, for it was the means of initiating a national movement, which aroused the Catholic upper classes to a sense of their social obligations.

It also became, through De Mun himself and the political party called the Popular Liberal Party (which he founded in 1899 in conjunction with Piou and others), an important factor in influencing social legislation.

Another outcome of this Association was the Catholic Association of French Youth (*Association Catholique de la Jeunesse Francaise*), which was founded by De Mun in 1886 as a kind of preparatory school for the Catholic workingmen's clubs. The Association of French Youth has now over 140,000 members,[27] and serves as a recruiting bureau for the Action Populaire (of which we shall speak later), and the other social popular organisations which sprang up later on.

In France, as in Germany and Belgium, Bishops and priests threw themselves whole-heartedly into the social movement. In France especially there is a very voluminous social literature written mostly by the priests.[28]

De Mun and the Socialists

Perhaps it was the Chamber of Deputies that witnessed De Mun's greatest efforts. There he fought, with all his great oratorical powers, during a period of some thirty years, for remedial social legislation. The definiteness of the programme which he consistently but all too unsuccessfully advocated formed a striking contrast to the vague demands of the Socialists. Hence he could declare, as he did during a debate on April 30th, 1894, addressing Millerand, the Socialist leader:

For twenty years past I have demanded, here in this tribune, the most precise social reforms. It is not my fault if hardly a single one of them has been achieved. My responsibility is absolutely cleared. It is yours that is in question. You teach the people to expect nothing, to hope for nothing from the progress of ideas, of institutions, of laws, and to seek in their labour organizations, not the means of defending their rights, but a weapon of combat, preparing by means of continual violence for civil war. . . . I say, with profound conviction, you have cruelly betrayed the cause of the people.[29]

The Movement in Switzerland, Belgium, etc.

From Germany and France the Catholic movement gradually spread into all the countries of Western and Central Europe, including Switzerland, Belgium, Holland; and later on Italy, Spain and England. The beginnings of the movement in Switzerland are associated with the names of Cardinal Mermillod and Gaspar Decurtins. Mermillod filled in Switzerland somewhat the same position as Ketteler in Germany. Decurtins was a disciple of Ketteler and a friend of Cardinal Manning. It was he who, like De Mun in France, led the political agitation for social reform.

It was under Decurtins' auspices, too, that the first "International Federation of Catholic Social Workers" was formed, in 1884, at Fribourg, under the presidency of Cardinal Mermillod. The social code and programme which was drawn up as a result of the conferences of the Federation was presented by Cardinal Mermillod to Leo XIII in 1888, and was probably one of the causes that finally resulted in the publication of the *Rerum Novarum* three years later.

The Malines Union

The Fribourg Union discontinued its sittings after 1891. Another international Union on a wider basis was established at Malines in 1920 under the presidency of Cardinal Mercier. The Malines Union, which is called "The International Union for Social Studies," includes in its membership several of the most distinguished Catholic scholars in the social and economic sciences, drawn from all countries of Western Europe, France, Germany, Belgium, Holland, Italy, Spain, and England. After the death of Cardinal Mercier in 1924, his place as president of the Union was taken by Archbishop Van Roly, his successor in the See of Malines. The most important achievement, so far, of the Malines Union has been the issue, in 1927, of a compendium of Catholic principles and conclusions applicable to the present post-war conditions in Europe and America.[30] This little book summarizes and brings up to date the conclusions and recommendations of the best Catholic authorities concerning contemporary social problems.

The Movement in other Countries

Space will not permit us to follow the developments of the Catholic movement in the different countries of Europe and America. In Italy Catholic action is very highly organised, and is under the immediate patronage of the Pope himself. There are regularly recurring local and national congresses, and a network of diocesan and national councils, which control associations of various kinds, covering almost every phase of human activity. Spain, in which the movement is organised partly on the model of Italy, held its first Catholic congress in 1929, under the presidency of the Cardinal Archbishop of Seville. [31]

In Holland the movement is particularly strong and is very highly organised, being under the guidance of a number of priests specially devoted to the work, under the leadership of Mgr. Poels, a dignitary of the diocese of Limburg. It was the Catholic organisations that were mainly instrumental in saving Holland from the Bolshevist peril in 1919. Even in the United States of America, in which the Catholics form less than twenty per cent of the population, the beginnings of a strong Catholic movement have appeared.

The Movement in Ireland

In Ireland a Catholic social movement in the ordinary sense was practically impossible up to very recent times. The land struggle, the fight for educational freedom, the national contest, the work of church building and religious organisation, engaged the energies of the priests and people during the nineteenth and the first quarter of the twentieth century. It is certain, however, as Nitti acutely observes, [32] that it was principally owing to its Catholic faith, and the strenuous efforts and leadership of the Catholic clergy, that the Irish nation has been so far saved from destruction.

The time has now, however, arrived, when a movement for social reconstruction on a definitely Catholic basis is possible. That such a movement is urgently needed is admitted on all hands; and in several different ways efforts are being made to promote it. Thus a regular course of social study has been inserted by the Irish Bishops in the programme of Religious Knowledge for the secondary schools. A whole series (nn. 233–249) of the Decrees of the Maynooth Synod of 1927 are devoted to the subject of "Catholic Action." The Society of St. Vincent de Paul, which is year by year becoming more active, especially in the principal towns, is now carrying on several activities of a social reconstructive character. The number of Catholic social activities of different kinds, rescue societies, boys' clubs, etc., is increasing.[33] The work of professional organisation on definitely Catholic lines has been begun. Thus the "Irish Guild of Catholic Nurses," founded in 1922, has received the formal approbation of the Bishops (1927).[34] The "Legion of Mary," a union of Catholic women for social work, which was founded in Dublin in 1925, is gradually extending over the whole country. The "Catholic Boy Scouts" was founded in 1928, under the patronage of the Bishops, and is growing fast. The foundations of a Catholic press are being gradually laid. *An Rioghacht* (the League of the Kingship of Christ) was founded in Dublin on October 1st, 1926 (the first celebration of the Feast of Jesus Christ the King), with the object of promoting social study and Catholic social propaganda and initiating social reconstruction. Efforts are also being made to reunite and co-ordinate for similar purposes the already existing "Catholic Young Men's Societies." The Central Catholic Library, founded in Dublin (1921), and the growing activities of the Irish Catholic Truth Society are all evidences of a nascent national movement for Catholic social reconstruction.

In England

In England Cardinal Manning wrote strongly during the second half of the 19th century in favour of social reform. In innumerable letters to the Press and in articles and periodicals he supported the workers in their demands for protective legislation.[35] His efforts were ably seconded by Bishop Bagshawe, of Nottingham, who advocated a programme of social reform even more thorough than that of Cardinal Manning. In reality, however, Manning as well as Bagshawe had more lasting influence on the Continent than in England itself where a Catholic movement on a large scale was at the time scarcely possible.

The foundation of the Catholic Social Guild, in 1909, by a group of Catholic social workers, of whom Father C. Plater, S.J., was the leading spirit, marked the beginning of a definite movement which continues to make steady progress. The main activities of the Guild are the establishment over the whole country of circles of social study, the publication of handbooks for the students, the organisation in Oxford of a Catholic Workers' College, for the higher education of carefully selected men of the working class, with a view to further propagandist work among workingmen; and the conducting of an annual summer school in Oxford. The organ of the Guild is *The Christian Democrat,* which appears monthly.[36]

The Popes and the Catholic Movement

The German associations which marked the definite beginnings of the modern Catholic movement, were called *Piusvereine* after Pius IX. It was due in no small part to his great influence with the people that the widespread Catholic consciousness was formed, which led gradually to a reaction against Liberalism, and to the general movement towards Catholic reconstruction which we have described.

The Encyclicals of Pope Leo XIII, and especially the Encyclical *Rerum Novarum* (1891) on the condition of the working classes, began a new phase in the history of the Catholic social movement. These pronouncements of the Supreme Pontiff, which have since been confirmed and enforced by the Encyclicals of Pius X and our present Holy Father Pius XI on the same subject,[37] besides containing the strong and cordial approval of the Holy See for the movement, are essentially an authoritative exposition of the Church's teaching on social matters. They are full of urgent appeals to the Bishops, the clergy and the faithful, to devote themselves zealously to the great work of Catholic social reconstruction.[38] Above all, the Encyclicals of Pius XI and the new phase of the movement which has developed under the name of Catholic Action, as a result of his influence, have given fresh life and renewed vigour to the Catholic Cause.

It is due mainly to the exhortations and guidance of the Sovereign Pontiffs that the movement has steadily gathered strength for the past forty years, and has spread so widely, while still preserving its unity of character and aim.

Art. 3—The Catholic Organisations

As it is outside our present scope to follow out in detail the several phases and developments of the Catholic Social Movement, we shall only indicate briefly some of the principal organisations to which it has given rise, and to which it mostly owes its steady progress.[39]

German Catholic Congresses

The German Catholic Congresses had their origin in the society called the *Piusverein,* already referred to, founded by Professor Kaspar Riffel and his friend Lennig for the defense of religious liberties.[40] A general meeting of the delegates from the various centres was arranged to take place at Mainz in 1848. This was the first of the great Catholic congresses. It was at this gathering that Bishop Ketteler delivered his historic address, previously mentioned, which began the great social movement in Germany and in Europe. In 1858 not only were representatives of local branches of the *Puisverein* invited, but also representatives of other Catholic associations, as well as leading Catholic journalists, publicists, and professional men, so that the meetings took on the character of a Catholic parliament.

Their Utility

These general meetings of Catholic Germany were found to have extraordinary utility in encouraging and co-ordinating the efforts of the Catholic social workers and propagating Catholic thought. They encouraged Catholic workers by giving them a sense of solidarity, and bringing home to each individual worker the fact that he had tens of thousands of fellow labourers in the same cause. The congresses were an encouragement, too, in another way. Where the Catholics of a particular district needed strengthening, there the congress went to strengthen them, as happened at Neisse, in Silesia (1899). Local effort was stimulated by the presence, for a whole week, of the picked forces of all Catholic Germany. The Catholics, disheartened, perhaps, by the sneers of their Socialist fellows, could thus again hold up their heads and glory in their faith.

Again, the congresses co-ordinated Catholic endeavour. Windthorst called them the "Autumn Manoeuvres," and a hostile paper referred to them as "The Review of the Catholic Troops." Practically all the German Catholic institutions are now represented at these congresses, and many take the opportunity supplied by the congress to hold their annual meeting and publish their reports. Different societies profit by thus getting into touch with one another, learning local needs and essaying fresh developments. Thus the efforts, aims, methods and results of the various associations are made known to the whole country, and when fresh needs arise the congresses call into being new organisations to meet them.

Especially as a Means of Propaganda

Finally, the congresses propagate Catholic thought. In the first place wide publicity is given to the proceedings of the congresses by an army of reporters, representing every newspaper of standing, including non-Catholic papers. An illustrated volume is always published, giving a full account of the meetings, including those of the various societies represented at the congress. Besides all this, the congress issues a number of resolutions embodying some Catholic principle suited to the time. These resolutions are repeated by the Press, and serve as mottoes for Catholic speakers. They form the watchwords, for the year, of the Catholic associations, and so create a sound public opinion on questions of the day.

It was in no small measure due to these congresses that Catholic Germany stood so firm under the pressure of the Kulturkampf. There was even an advance in some directions. For, whereas, before the Kulturkampf, there were but four or five Catholic papers in Prussia, the number had increased, in 1873, to one hundred and twenty, including many dailies.[41]

The Volksverein

Of the permanent Catholic organisations of Germany, the *Volksverein*, or "People's League," is the most important. Father Plater, S.J.,[42] has described it as the most successful association ever devised for the promotion of the social sense among a people. Founded by Windthorst in 1890 to defend the Catholic position against the Social Democrats, the society spread very rapidly. In 1904 it had 400,000 members, and in 1924, after the havoc wrought by the war, it had again attained to 588,902, of whom 130,000 were women. The Volksverein has evolved a definite social programme, and educated the people in Catholic social principles. Besides its social teaching and propaganda, it also provides the people with an abundance of excellent yet cheap literature on Christian Apologetics.

The Central Bureau is at München-Gladbach. Here thirty-five men are employed. Of these, nine are scientific and literary collaborators, some being ecclesiastics and doctors in theology, others laymen and doctors in political economy. There is also a publishing-house with a press; a section for lantern-slides; a library of Social Science and Apologetics (70,000 volumes); a service of social information. In the country there are seven branch libraries, sixteen regional secretariates with nineteen employees, of whom ten are university graduates.

The *Volksvereinsverlag* publishing-house at München-Gladbach has published over 700 books and pamphlets; and countless leaflets have been distributed free. Every two months there appear *Der Volksverein*, a review for men; *Die Frau im Volksverein*, a review for women; *Führerkorrespondenz*, a review for directors of organisations. Then there is a bulletin for representatives, a bulletin for propagandists or "Confidence-men"; and the *Sozialpolitische Korrespondenz*, which appears every three weeks and is sent free to 350 Catholic newspapers.[43]

Besides this abundance of excellent literature which comes pouring out from the München-Gladbach every year about 5,000 popular meetings are held where lectures are given on topical subjects. In various districts special courses are given in practical sociology, lasting from eight to fifteen days. At the central headquarters there are vacation courses of eight days; special courses for workmen, artisans, business-men, agriculturists, commercial employees, school-masters, etc., social and apologetic courses for propagandists as well as for the leaders of Catholic and interdenominational professional organisations. This is but a very imperfect outline of one of the fifty-eight great Catholic organisations of Germany.

The *"Semaines Sociales de France"*

In France the *Semaines Sociales*[44] are the national congresses of the Catholic social movement. Even seventeen years ago a French publicist could truly write:

> All courses and all classic works treating of economic doc-
> trines give a large space to the study of social Catholicism.
> And all signalise the *Semaines Sociales* as the most character-
> istic and most notably scientific manifestation of this socio-
> logical school.[45]

The *Semaines Sociales* are sessions of social study which take place in a different French city every year, gathering the directors of organisations around the most eminent masters of Catholic social science. "To attend as a student," says a contemporary writer, "is no sinecure. From eight in the morning until eleven at night, the student has hardly time to breathe. In the morning, he attends two lecture courses, each lasting an hour and a half; after lunch, he is taken to visit neighbouring factories, co-operative societies, trade unions, or workingmen's gardens; late in the afternoon there is another lecture course; and finally, in the evening there is a general lecture, open to a more popular audience as well as to real students."[46]

Their Activities and Affiliated Organisations

During the fifteen sessions which took place between 1904, the year of foundation, and 1923, more than 100 professors or lecturers have delivered over 300 courses or lectures, of which the reports *in extenso* are a store-house of learning.

Besides their own direct work, the *Semaines Sociales* have led to the creation of several organisations destined to extend their field of influence. Among the more important of these are: *Les Semaines Sociales Regionales* ("Local Social Weeks"), *Les Semaines Rurales* ("Rural Weeks"), and the *Union d'Etudes des Catholiques Sociaux* ("Catholic Social Study Unions").

The second of these organisations is of special interest to Irish social students. The purpose of the "Rural Weeks" is the education of social leaders for the rural districts. In a house of retreats, a monastery, or a school during the holidays, suitable young persons from 18 to 30 years of age are brought together. For a week religious courses are held, as well as courses of agricultural technique, but, above all, social courses (treating of such matters as trade unions, co-operation, rural credit, mutual insurance). In 1923 more than twenty "Rural Weeks" were held in various regions of France.[47]

The *"Action Populaire"*

If the *Semaines Sociales* of France correspond somewhat to the German Catholic congresses, the *Action Populaire,* which is conducted by the Jesuit Fathers, corresponds to the *Volksverein,* and was, in fact, inspired by it. It was founded in 1902, and up to the European War had its headquarters at Rheims. During the War all its books, documents, etc., were lost owing to the bombardment of Rheims, and other causes. It resumed work in 1919, establishing its new headquarters in Paris.

The *Action Populaire* is an editorial and distributing centre for social literature, as well as an information bureau and a centre for organising study courses and popular conventions. Thus it is in a manner the heart and centre of the Catholic social movement in France. Even in 1912 the central office at Rheims employed sixteen editors—ten priests and six laymen—besides twenty-seven secretaries. A large staff kept busy sending out the mass of literature daily dispatched from the bureau. This literature, produced by the most prominent Catholic social writers and by non-Catholic economists, is sold very cheaply. The association has recently brought about the foundation of a Joint Stock Company ("Edition Spes," Paris), which includes a publishing office, and has charge of the distribution of the pamphlets and other publications of the association.

Its Publications

From the outset the *Action Populaire* has been publishing a series of thirty-page pamphlets (called *Brochures Jaunes*) on such subjects as old age pensions, co-operative associations, labour unions, mixed industrial boards, housing problems, accident compensation, socialism, workingmen's gardens, child labour, etc. To this series was added later on another called *Les Actes Sociaux,* which is a very cheap edition of the principal laws, papal pronouncements, and other documents on social matters. A third series, *Les Plans et Documents,* comprise documentary and doctrinal monographs, designed for social study clubs. A very notable publication is the *Année Sociale Internationale,* which is a monumental work of reference on the whole social movement.

The *Action Populaire* has also six periodicals. Of these we may mention *Dossiers de l'Action Populaire,* a fortnightly review, composed of detachable articles for study, documentation and action; *Peuple de France,* a monthly review for popular education; and *L'Action Populaire,* a quarterly of social and religious propaganda.

Its Other Activities and Departments

Again, the *Action Populaire* is an information bureau, where thousands of inquiries are answered every year. These inquiries are on all sorts of religious and social questions—how to found a mutual aid society; what employment young girls leaving their home village should seek; what authority should be consulted on social insurance, etc.

Finally, the *Action Populaire* has engaged increasingly in the work of organising study courses, participating in social conferences, organising popular conventions, etc.[48]

The Belgian "Boerenbond" (Farmer's Union)

Of very special interest to the Irish reader is the Belgian *Boerenbond.*[49] It was founded in 1890 by M. L'Abbé Mellaerts (a parish priest of a rural parish in Flanders), assisted by M. Helleputte and M. Schollaert. To-day it is a social force of the first order among the Flemish peasants, answering in the highest measure to the needs of the farming population. It caters principally for small cottiers whose holdings consist usually of some ten statute acres.[50]

The union comprises about 1,200 guilds, each guild including about 150 cottiers. The parish priest is usually the hon. secretary of the guild; and he with a few of the more intelligent and better educated of the peasants form the local executive committee. Every member must be a practising Catholic. The president of the union is a priest—a dignitary of the Archdiocese of Malines. In the head office at Louvain about 500 men are employed, of whom about seventeen are priests. All these are paid officials. The officials of the local guilds are not paid.

Its Activities

The functions of the Union are to watch over the interests of its members in the public legislature and administration, and to supply them with all the services (and many more) which are in other countries committed to a State Department of Agriculture. Amongst the advantages which the member enjoys the following are noteworthy:

(a) All that the peasant requires to buy, such as seeds, artificial manures, implements and machinery, etc., may be procured through the *Boerenbond* depôt. The most important advantages of this privilege are that the farmers are ensured the best quality of seeds and manures, and when selling the produce are assured a just price.

(b) An excellent, cheap and safe system of insurance of cattle, hay, etc., as well as of life insurance, is brought within reach of all the members through the *Boerenbond* Insurance Department. This belongs to the farmers themselves and is self-contained.

(c) Every guild has a local bank which is affiliated to the Central *Boerenbond* Bank at Louvain. This latter is one of the strongest and most important banks in Belgium. Thus the union has complete control of its own financial affairs; and can accommodate its members with loans at a very cheap rate. Advances are made to the individual cottier on the recommendation and *guarantee* of the local guild to which he belongs.

(d) Some forty inspectors are employed for the help of the members. All of these are skilled in organising and each is besides a specialist in some particular branch of agricultural science or work, such as Veterinary Science, Engineering, Building, etc.

(e) Several journals and reviews are published for the education of the members in agricultural and other matters.

The *Boerenbond* has transformed the whole agricultural life of West Flanders; and since its rise the cottiers have become quite independent and prosperous. Associations like the *Boerenbond,* combined with the excellent social legislation of the Catholic government that held power for so many years previous to the War (1884–1914), places Belgium in a foremost position in social reform.[51]

Press Organisations

Another class of Catholic social organisation which has been making much headway in Catholic countries since 1920 is the Catholic Press Association. The object of this association is to organise and propagate amongst the people reading matter of good quality, treating of all subjects of interest, including religion, education, politics, economics, finance, sport, etc., but handling them from the Christian standpoint, and with a Catholic tone and outlook. The Catholic Press is thus meant to supplant the unchristian capitalistic Press, or at least to counteract its influences.

Some fifteen different Press Associations belonging to Germany, France, Italy, Spain, Holland, Hungary, etc., are enumerated[52] as existing in 1923. The number is probably very much greater at present. Some of these, such as the *Oeuvre du Franc de la Presse*[53] (founded in Paris, 1919, by Canon Couget), aim at providing funds for the founding of Catholic papers or for subsidizing those already in existence. The object of others is to unify and co-ordinate the activities and efforts of all the Catholic newspapers and pressmen of the country. Others again aim at forming a body of zealous workers who would devote their energies to extend the circulation of the Catholic Press.

"Ora et Labora"

The object of the *Institucion Internacional Ora et Labora,* which was founded in the Pontifical Seminary of Seville, 1905, and has now a membership of over 15,000, is to train seminarists for Catholic propaganda in all its forms; to carry on a crusade on behalf of the Catholic Press; and to propagate among all the nations the institution of the "Press Day."[54] It has sections in seventy-four Spanish seminaries, and correspondents in most of the chief cities of the world.

The *"Maison de la Bonne Presse"*[55]

The *Maison de la Bonne Presse* of Paris is the most powerful institution for Press propaganda that exists in France. It is organised as a Joint Stock Company, and unites in a single establishment a mass of newspapers, magazines, books and writings of all kinds, including works of information and organs of propaganda of the first order of excellence. It has special staffs for all its papers and magazines, which numbered thirty before the war. It has branches and committees over all France, and a governing administration in Paris.[56]

Conclusion

The associations which we have briefly described are a few typical examples of the multitudes of social organisations which exist and continue to increase. Very many of the people's needs in such matters as education, insurance, banking, agricultural and industrial training, public libraries, the Press, etc., which in other countries are provided by the State at great expense, and too often very inefficiently, or are in the hands of non-Catholic or neutral bodies, to the injury and peril of Catholic interests, are in many continental Catholic countries now supplied by these Catholic associations.[57]

Notes

1. Cf. *La Hierarchie Catholique et la Problème Social,* compiled by the Malines "Union Internationale D'Etudes Sociales" in 1931, and published by the "Edition Spes" of Paris. This invaluable work, issued on the occasion of the fortieth anniversary of the *Rerum Novarum,* is a bibliography and summary (specially referred to by Pius XI in the *Quadragesimo Anno*) of Pontifical and Episcopal pronouncements on the Social Question made between the years 1891 and 1931. Cf. also Leo XIII, *Rerum Novarum* (1891), pp. 147–166; *Graves de Communi* (1901), pp. 169 ff; Pius X, *Fin Dalla Prima* (1903), pp. 182 ff, and *Il Fermo Proposito* ("Christian Social Action") (1905), pp. 189–201; Pius XI— *Ubi Arcano* (1922) (*see* Ryan—*Encyclicals of Pius XI,* pp. 2 ff, Herder, London, 1927), and *Quas Primas* (1925), instituting the Feast of Our Lord Jesus Christ the King (*see Ib.,* pp. 129 ff); *Quadragesimo Anno* (1931) (The Social Order: Its Reconstruction and Perfection. *See* C. T. S. pamphlet, London, 1931); *Quae Nobis* (Nov. 13th, 1928), Apostolic Letter to Cardinal Bertram on the Fundamental Principles of Catholic Action (cf. the *Irish Ecclesiastical Record,* Feb., 1929, pp. 212 ff); Plater, S.J.—*The Priest and Social Action* (Longmans, London, 1914), pp. 1–150, and *Social Work in Germany* (Sands, London, 1909); Ryan and Husslein—*The Church and Labour* (Harding and Moore, London, 1920) (*see* pp. 207–219 for a reprint of the *Pastoral Letter of the Irish Bishops on the Labour Question,* Feb., 1914); Antoine, *op. cit.,* chap. x; Nitti—*Catholic Socialism* (translated from the Italian, *Il Socialismo Catholico,* Turin, 1890) (Macmillan, New York, 1895), chaps. vii-xii (Nitti uses the word *Socialism* in a sense now obsolete, as including Catholic social reform. He traces the Catholic movement up to 1890); Metlake—*Ketteler's Social Reform* (Dolphin Press, Philadelphia, 1912); Moon—*The Labour Problem and the Social Catholic Movement in France* (Macmillan, New York, 1921); McEntee—*The Social Catholic Movement in Great Britain* (Macmillan, New York, 1927); Crawford—*Switzerland To-day—a Study in Social Progress* (Sands, London, undated, *circa* 1913); Monti—*International Handbook of Catholic Organisations,* published in the five principal European languages by the International Office of Catholic Organisations, Rome ("Edition Spes," Paris, 1924), chaps. ii to vii.

2. *Il Fermo Proposito* (1905), p. 190. Cf. also Leo XIII—*Immortale Dei* (1885), p. 54.

3. *Rerum Novarum,* pp. 141–148.

4. Cf. A useful booklet—*L'Action Catholique,* by Chanoine L. Picard— one of the series entitled *Etudes Religieuses,* published by "La Pensée Catholique" (Quai Mativa, 38 Liège, Belgium).

5. *Quae Nobis* (1928). (Cf. *Irish Ecclesiastical Record, loc. cit.,* p. 213).

6. Cited in Plater—*The Priest and Social Action,* pp. 22 ff.

7. See *Quadragesimo Anno* (C. T. S. edition, London, 1931), p. 70.

8. Cf. H. Pesch, S.J.—*Lehrbuch der Nationalökonomie* (5 vols.) (Herder, Fribourg, 1915–23), and *Neubau der Gesellschaft* (Flugschriften der Stimmen (edition 1919); Teschleder und Weber—*Socialethik* (2 vols.) (Münster, 1931).

9. *Quadragesimo Anno,* pp. 38–41. For a very brief outline of this traditional Catholic conception of civil organisation, *see infra,* chap. xx, art. 5; chap. xxii, arts. 5 and 6; chap. xxvii, arts. 2 and 3; and chap. xxvi and xxvii.

10. Cf. Leo XIII—*Graves de Communi* (1901), pp. 170–172, and Pius X—*Fin Dalla Prima* (1909), pp. 185–186.

11. *Graves de Communi,* p. 172.

12. *Fin Dalla Prima,* pp. 185, 186. The same direction is again strongly insisted on by our present Holy Father Pius XI (*Quae Nobis,* 1928. Cf. *Irish Ecclesiastical Record, loc. cit.,* pp. 213, 214), and again still more definitely in the Encyclical on Catholic Action—*Non Abbiamo Bisogno* (1931) (C. T. S. edit., pp. 15–17).

13. *Saggio Teoretico di Diretto Naturale Apogiatto Sul Fatto* was first published about 1840. An abridgement of the book, entitled *An Abridged Course in Natural Right,* appeared in 1860, of which a French translation was published in Paris (1864). Among Taparelli's other works, one of the most important is his critical examination of Representative Government in Modern States (*Esame Critica degli Ordini Representativi della Societa Moderna,* Rome, 1854). Cf. *supra,* "Introduction."

14. Metlake, *op. cit.,* p. 31.

15. *Ib.,* p. 26.

16. Metlake, chap. ix.

17. *Ib.,* chap. x.

18. *Ib.,* chap. xii.

19. Plater, *op. cit.,* p. 59.

20. Cf. Moon, *op. cit.,* pp. 13–120.

21. His best work is *La Civilisation Chrétienne Chez les Francs* ("Christian Civilization among the Franks").

22. Cited in Moon, *op. cit.,* p. 26, from Saint Simon's book, *Le Nouveau Christianisme* (1852). We may note in passing that although earthly happiness is not the object aimed at by Christian morality, the nation that is true to its precepts normally obtains the largest measure of true happiness that earthly life can afford (*see* chap. xxix, art. 3, *infra*).

23. Le Play's most remarkable works are *Les Ouvriers Européens* (1855) and *Le Reforme Sociale en France* (1864). The former work, which is of permanent interest and importance, is a series of thirty-six monographs on the social condition of the working class families in as many different countries of Europe

through which he had travelled for the purpose of investigating social conditions. Cf. Moon, *op. cit.*, p. 421. For an account of Perin and his writings, cf. *Ib.*, pp. 59 ff and p. 422.

24. *Ma Vocation Sociale* (Paris, 1908).

25. *Ib.*, p. 62 (cited in Moon, *op. cit.*, p. 82).

26. *Ma Vocation Sociale,* pp. 67–75 (Moon, p. 83).

27. Cf. Moon, *op. cit.*, pp. 347 ff.

28. Cf. Plater, *The Priest and Social Action,* chap. v.

29. Cited in Moon, *op. cit.*, p. 199. Cf. *ib.*, pp. 113–120, for a very interesting and suggestive account of Leon Harmel, and the remarkable Catholic industrial guild (in which the mediaeval Catholic principles are successfully adapted to modern needs) formed by the Harmel family at the Harmel Cotton Mills at Val-des-Bois. *See* also the two volume *Vie de Leon Harmel,* par Père Guitton, S.J. ("Edition Spes," Paris, 1927).

30. *Code Social* ("Edition Spes," Paris, 1927). An English edition entitled *A Code of Social Principles* has been published by the Catholic Social Guild, Oxford, 1929.

31. What may be the effects on the *Catholic Movement* of the Spanish Revolution of 1931, and about the same time the Fascist attack upon the Catholic societies in Italy, is not yet known (1931). Cf. the Encyclical of Pius XI—*Non Abbiamo Bisogno,* 1931 (C. T. S. edition).

32. *Catholic Socialism,* p. 330.

33. Cf. The booklet published by the St. Vincent de Paul Society, entitled *Handbook for Catholic Social Workers in Dublin* (1929), for a full list of these.

34. Cf. *The Irish Nursing News,* published monthly, which is the official organ of the Guild. A Catholic Guild of Medical Doctors, to be called the "Guild of SS. Luke and Damien," is also in process of formation, as well as a Catholic Guild of Chemists (1931).

35. Cf. McEntee, *op. cit.*, pp. 68 ff, and Nitti, *op. cit.*, chap. ii.

36. Cf. McEntee, *op. cit.*, pp. 173 ff. *The Christian Democrat* (a very valuable publication for all interested in the Catholic movement) is published by the Catholic Social Guild, Oxford.

37. Most of these are published in English in *The Pope and the People* (new edition, 1929). Cf. also *The Great Encyclicals of Leo XIII* (Benziger Bros., New York, 1903), and *The Encyclicals of Pius XI,* edited by J. H. Ryan (Herder, London, 1927). The Encyclical *Quadragesimo Anno,* 1931, of Pius XI is, with the *Rerum Novarum,* the most important document hitherto published on the Catholic Social movement. This Encyclical and those on Marriage and the Christian Education of Youth, which are not contained in the collections just referred to, are each published in booklet form by the English Catholic Truth Society.

38. Cf. Leo XIII—*Rerum Novarum,* 1891, pp. 141–148; Pius X—*Fin*

Dalla Prima, 1903, pp. 193 ff; Pius XI—*Ubi Arcano,* 1922, pp. 247 ff, and, above all, *Quadragesimo Anno,* 1931 (C. T. S. edit.), pp. 61–70.

39. Besides the reference already given, cf. *Catholic Encyclop.,* vol. iv, pp. 242–251, art. "Congresses, Catholic."

40. Plater—*Social Work in Germany,* p. 39.

41. Plater, *op. cit.,* p. 60.

42. *Ib.,* p. 81.

43. *International Handbook of Catholic Organisations,* p. 65.

44. The institution of *Semaines Sociales* has been extended to other countries, such as Belgium, Canada, Chile, Spain, Italy, Holland, Poland, Switzerland, Uruguay, etc.

45. *Revue Hebdomadaire* (Aug., 1913), pp. 522–531.

46. Moon, *op. cit.,* p. 342.

47. *International Handbook,* pp. 62–63.

48. Cf. *International Handbook,* p. 61; also Moon, *op. cit.,* pp. 321–339.

49. The Head Offices are in Louvain (Rue des Recollets 24).

50. On this farm the Boerenbond peasant now keeps five or six milch cows (whose average annual yield of milk is at present 800 gallons each), rears two or three calves, keeps a sow and some fat pigs and much poultry.

51. Cf. Vermeersch, S.J.—*Manuel Social,* for an account of the great series of laws for social and industrial reform passed by the Catholic Government of Belgium during these thirty fruitful years.

Among the several other types of Catholic associations which now flourish in Belgium the Association of Catholic Youth ("Association Catholique de la Jeunesse Belgique," or "A. C. J. B.") holds a foremost place. These include associations of boys, of girls, of boys of the labouring class ("Jeunesse Ouvrière Catholique" or "J. O. C."), of boys of the agricultural class ("J. A. C."), etc. Cf. Picard and Hoyois—*L'Association Cath. de la Jeunesse Belgique,* published at the Secretariat General de l'A. C. J. B., 126 Rue de Tirelemont, Louvain, 1924; also *Les Documents de la Vie Intellectuelle* (Monthly Review), Sept. 20th, 1931, published at 11 Rue Quentin-Bauchart, Paris viii[e].

52. Cf. *International Handbook,* chap. iii. An excellent and very comprehensive account of the Catholic Press as it was twenty years ago, will be found in the *Catholic Encyclopedia,* art. "Periodical Literature, Catholic," vol. xi, pp. 369–396.

53. The title in English would perhaps be *"Society of the Press Shilling."*

54. The "Press Day," which takes place all over Spain every year on the feast of SS. Peter and Paul, is celebrated by a General Communion, a solemn ceremony in the church, including a sermon on the Apostolate of the Press, and a collection for the Catholic Press. The collection yields over £6,000 a year (1931).

55. The Head Office is at 5 Rue Bayard, Paris viii^e.

56. Cf. *International Handbook,* p. 23.

57. If the framework of the social organism in Ireland is to be refashioned in accordance with Catholic ideals (and only such a refashioning can save the Catholic nation of Ireland from extinction) a strong Catholic Press must be built up, and a network of Catholic associations, such as we have described, gradually formed under the guidance of the Church. A strong and widespread movement for such a purpose is probably at present the country's most urgent need.

The Rights and Duties of
Labor and Capital

Richard L. Camp

This originally appeared in Camp's *The Papal Ideology of Social Reform: A Study in Historical Development*, 1969.

> The greatest scandal of the nineteenth century was the fact that the Church lost the working class.
>
> Pius XI

> At the factory, I dare not say that I am a Christian; at church, I dare not say that I am a worker.
>
> Quoted by Adrien Dansette

Even the most bitterly antisocialist of popes understood that denunciation and refutation of socialist doctrines, however thorough, would not suffice to keep the working classes out of the enemy camp. The appeal of socialism to the masses was less a product of rational assent than it was the result of the intense bitterness felt by many workers because of their conviction that they had been abandoned by the guardians of the traditional social order. Even the Church, to which they had once given at least nominal allegiance, seemed to them now only a force for social oppression, a force which had contemptuously abandoned them to the mercies of their employers.[1] Beginning with Leo XIII, the papacy tried to convince the working classes that the Catholic Church had not forgotten them, that it wanted to reform their condition, and that it knew what measures were needed and how far they should go.

LEO XIII: "THE POPE OF THE WORKINGMAN"

Many measures were taken in Leo XIII's period, for a modest improvement in the workingman's standard of living was achieved in these years. The most advanced nations in this respect were the two most advanced industrial powers of Europe: England and Germany. The English workers by 1900 had gained much from their masters in terms of higher pay, shorter hours, and more sanitary conditions in home and factory, although the eight hour day still eluded them. By the end of the century, their average purchasing power had risen 80 percent above that of 1850. They were no longer on the verge of starvation; they were becoming well-organized, they were being educated, and they were saving money.[2]

In Germany, the laborers benefited from their nation's unique social insurance program[3] as well as rising wages and shorter hours. Their unions grew rapidly after 1900, and their educational level rose sharply.[4] By contrast, the pope's native land lagged far behind the advanced countries in labor reform, as it did in general economic development. Throughout the century, the Italian workers were forced to endure a high level of unemployment, an equally high rate of illiteracy, and squalid working conditions. But, by the end of Leo XIII's reign, their average working day had declined to about ten or eleven hours, and their real wages had made a modest advance.[5]

The growth of labor organizations was at least partly responsible for these improvements although less so perhaps in Italy than in England, Germany, and France. Again England took the lead with the development of powerful, well-organized, and well-financed trade unions which were thoroughly moderate and nonrevolutionary in their aims. They won many important strikes and were still growing in 1900 when their membership stood at two million.[6] The German unions were smaller than the British, were established later, and were more ideologically committed. By 1902, the socialist and Christian unions together had one million members out of a total work force of eight million. They called few strikes but had made noticeable progress in collective bargaining over wage scales.[7]

French and Italian unions also developed later than the English. The French organizations did not acquire full legal status until 1884 and were not established on a permanent basis until the 1890's. Like the German unions, they were not so large nor so highly institutionalized as were those in England; as a rule, they had neither full-time officials nor welfare funds. The ideological program of the French union leaders was given the name, "anarchosyndicalism," for the unionists shunned political activity and hoped instead to bring about the destruction of capitalism by the "direct action" of union militants. This action was to take the form of wave after wave of strikes leading to a final, cataclysmic general strike that was to overthrow the old order. After this had been accomplished, they dreamed of creating an anarchist paradise in which the workers in each factory would form the basic unit of whatever government was required.[8]

The Italian labor movement was also influenced by the anarchists but only in rural areas. Among the industrial workers, the unions began a rapid period of growth in the 1880's and the 1890's and shunned the anarchism of some of the agricultural laborers. Although they claimed to be nonpolitical, their members were generally loyal to the Socialist Party and its radical, Marxist ideology.[9]

Leo XIII understood the reason for such loyalty—in Germany and later on in France as well as in Italy—better than had most other Catholics. He was not bemused, as others often were, into thinking that radicalism among the workers represented the opinion of only a small minority who could be rendered harmless by vigorous government repression. Nor did he agree with the followers of Périn, some of whom said that the poverty of the masses was necessary so that the rich could have the opportunity to practice the duty of charity![10] The most effective weapon against socialism, he came to say, was to eliminate poverty altogether, not merely by the temporary expedient of charity but by a permanent readjustment in the workers' standard of living and their position in society.

He was not alone in these convictions, nor was he the first to give expression to them. The social Catholics had been urging reform for years without much response or cooperation from either clergy or laity. Part of their ineffectiveness was of their own doing. Many social Catholics were disciples of Ketteler and were corporatists who doubted that the working class could ever receive social justice under modern capitalism. When they proposed labor reform, they viewed it as a mere prelude to a corporatist transformation. Some thought it a weapon against the capitalist order itself. As could be expected, such a vision had little appeal to the many Catholics who had a more realistic attitude towards the longevity of the capitalist system.

Yet there was more to the social Catholic program than naïve dreaming. Many social Catholics had constructive reforms to propose. Among these was Prince Löwenstein of Germany who gathered together Catholics of many countries in the 1880's for a series of labor conferences on his estate in Haid. A series of "Haiden Theses" was approved in these meetings among which was the demand for a minimum "family wage" and a regulation of the labor contract for the good of the whole community.[11]

Another, better known effort was the "Union of Fribourg," a succession of international Catholic social conferences called by Bishop Mermillod at his residence in the Swiss city of Fribourg. Beginning in 1884 and meeting annually until Mermillod's death in 1892, the Union also proposed, among other things, a "just wage" sufficient for the laborer's family. The pope was deeply interested in their work and asked for a report in 1888.[12]

He also noticed the recommendations of other social Catholics who divorced reform entirely from dreams of reviving the medieval corporate system. To men such as Cardinal Manning of England and Cardinal Gibbons of the United States, labor reforms would give the workers their God-given rights within the capitalist, industrial economy, not bring about another type of economic system. When they demanded such things as higher wages, better working and living conditions, and protective associations for the workers, they did so with a confidence that modern capitalism could provide them and prosper in so doing.[13]

Leo XIII was of the same persuasion. He was not a man who willingly took sides, for he owed much to all branches of social Catholicism. His own writings were not so much the beginning of Catholic social theory as they were the culmination of the work of many others, including the corporatists. Yet, much as he respected men such as Ketteler, he could not share their hatred of the capitalists and their belief that capitalism could never truly reform itself.

His own view to the contrary began to emerge in messages that served as a prelude to *Rerum Novarum*. In an address to a pilgrimage of French workers on October 20, 1889, he proclaimed that the remedy for the social ills of modern life was the fulfillment by all classes of their duties. For the employers, these included treating their workers as brothers, giving them conditions of work as favorable as possible, and always observing the demands of justice and equity. Their employees had to be resigned to a life of labor and its consequences and had to respect their masters.[14] A few months later, he told Kaiser William II of Germany:

> Religion will teach the employer to respect the worker's human dignity and to treat him with justice and equity. It will inculcate into the conscience of the worker the sentiment of duty and fidelity and will render him moral, sober, and honest.[15]

Rerum Novarum was a hundredfold development of these thoughts and was the first detailed program for the reform of labor conditions ever to come from the Holy See. It was also a vindication for social Catholics of all factions and gave them an impetus to continue their labors. It began with a statement taken from Ketteler[16] which acknowledged how much reform was still needed:

> Public institutions and laws set aside the ancient religion. Hence, by degrees it has come to pass that working men have been surrendered, isolated and helpless, to the hard-heartedness of employers and the greed of unchecked competition. . . . To this must be added that the hiring of labor and the conduct of trade are concentrated in the hands of comparatively few; so that a small number of very rich men have been able to lay upon the teeming masses of the laboring poor a yoke little better than that of slavery itself.[17]

The remedy? For the workers, it was neither class struggle nor victory in a class war against the capitalists, for this would only make their situation more abominable:

> The great mistake made in regard to the matter now under consideration is to take up with the notion that class is naturally hostile to class, and that the wealthy and the working men are intended by nature to live in mutual conflict. So irrational and so false is this view that the direct contrary is the truth. Just as the symmetry of the human frame is the result of the suitable

arrangement of the different parts of the body, so in a State is it ordained by nature that these two classes should dwell in harmony and agreement, so as to maintain the balance of the body politic. Each needs the other: capital cannot do without labor, nor labor without capital.[18]

Each therefore had duties to the other, the fulfilling of which would go far to solve the labor problem. For the workers, these included furnishing without hesitation the labor agreed upon in contracts freely and equitably drawn up. They could, in justice, harm neither the wealth nor the person of their employers, and their claims had to be free from violence and sedition.[19] The employers, in turn, were forbidden to treat their employees as if their status as wage earners deprived them of human dignity and the right to a decent, honorable living. Labor was not a disgrace for those who performed it; it was an honor, because it furnished an honest means of sustaining life. "But to misuse men as though they were things in the pursuit of gain," he added, "or to value them solely for their physical powers—that is truly shameful and inhuman."[20]

Such a disgrace could be avoided if the capitalists honored the many particular duties which arose out of the general obligation to respect their employees' human dignity. The workers had to be preserved from influences dangerous to their morals and had to be encouraged to look after the welfare of their families. Work could not be demanded of them which was beyond their strength or incompatible with their age or sex. Workers could not be subject to acts of violence, fraud, or "usury" which struck at their savings.[21] Nor could they be deprived of the right to receive a "just wage."

This concept of wages made no sense to the many Europeans of the nineteenth century, Catholic and otherwise, who accepted liberal economic principles. Only the market, these people replied, could set wages, as it determined prices. To allow other considerations to enter in was naïve and unscientific. Some liberals realized that non-market factors, such as tariffs and government subsidies, influenced prices heavily, but they were still unalterably opposed to government tampering with wage levels.

Leo XIII and most other social Catholics could not accept this type of double standard. Even those who were not corporatists had, for the most part, rejected liberal assumptions about the need for economic freedom and were quite willing to make alterations in the free market economy if these were necessary for the sake of social justice. Regarding wages, Leo XIII agreed with most other social Catholics that, free market or no free market, there was a certain level below which a worker's compensation could not justly go. The level had to be flexible and in line with modern economic realities. The factors entering into its calculation were complex and subject to change, but this did not alter the basic Christian principle that to pay less than a just minimum was to exploit the poverty and misery of the humble and to rob them of a fair return on their labor.[22]

Even a free and legal contract did not make unjust wage levels acceptable. Leo XIII was not willing to accept as absolute the liberal principle of the freedom of the labor contract if the salary scale written into it was abnormally low:

> Let the working man and the employer make free agreements, and in particular let them agree freely as to the wages; nevertheless, there underlies a dictate of natural justice more imperious and ancient than any bargain between man and man, namely, that wages ought not to be insufficient to support a frugal and well-behaved wage-earner. If through necessity or fear of a worse evil the workman accept harder conditions because an employer or contractor will afford him no better, he is made the victim of force and injustice.[23]

Why? Because labor had a double aspect to the pontiff. First, it was personal in that it was inherent in the particular force of each worker and belonged to him alone. But it was also necessary, because the wage earner usually had no other means of sustaining himself, and this was a requirement of nature itself. When this other aspect of labor was recognized, salaries could never be purely a matter of individual bargaining between the laborer and his employer even if both freely consented to the result. Individual freedom had to be subordinated to the higher moral law which was the guiding light of man's earthly activities.[24]

The ultimate goal of the wage policy which that law decreed was to make the workers less dependent upon wages themselves. If the working classes were ever to live at a decent material level, they would have to be given the chance, through a just wage, to lift themselves into the ranks of the owners of property:

> If a workman's wages be sufficient to enable him comfortably to support himself, his wife, and his children, he will find it easy, if he be a sensible man, to practice thrift, and he will not fail, by cutting down expenses, to put by some little savings and thus secure a modest source of income. Nature itself would urge him to this. We have seen that this great labor question cannot be solved save by assuming as a principle that private ownership must be held sacred and inviolable. The law, therefore, should favor ownership, and its policy should be to induce as many as possible of the people to become owners.[25]

In short, the labor reform program of Leo XIII was precisely the opposite of socialism. Rather than making everyone a wage earner by eliminating private property, Leo XIII wanted to generalize the property institution. Marx and Engels argued that the masses were turning into an undifferentiated horde of propertyless, unskilled laborers.[26] Leo XIII wanted the reverse by means of higher salaries and workers' savings; ultimately he envisioned the "deproletarization" of the working classes. Such a reform, he hoped, would redistribute the wealth more justly and would help the working class identify itself with the capitalists instead of with the ideals of socialism.

Nothing in this program was inconsistent with Catholic traditions, he repeatedly asserted. If the Church now called upon factory owners to improve the lot of their employees as a matter of justice, this was only an extension of its traditional teaching that property could never be used for the benefit of the owners alone but had to be subordinated to the general welfare. If the papacy called for a redistribution of wealth in favor of the working class, it was only reaffirming the traditional doctrine that the rich had the duty of giving their superfluous wealth, through charity, to the poor.[27]

But did these various duties include the obligation to pay higher than normal salaries to workers with large families? Most social Catholics were sure it did and earnestly supported the principle of the "family wage" in every labor contract.[28] *Rerum Novarum* was more ambivalent. It expressed the hope that wages would be large enough for the workers to support their families but did not request an extra allowance for wage earners with more children than the average. Its caution was understandable. Had the family wage been accepted as a basic principle in the labor contract, which it has not been, it might have worked against the family man himself; in times of unemployment, management might have been reluctant to hire a laborer with a large family because of the extra expense involved. Even if this difficulty could have been overcome, the technical problems of implementing such a policy were more than enough to keep Leo from declaring it as absolute. He felt competent to discuss only the underlying moral principles for the redemption of labor, not the techniques for bringing it to fruition.

Rerum Novarum was the last of his writings to examine these principles at length, but his later work showed that he did not lose interest in them. To Gaspard Descurtins, an active social Catholic, he said that the Vatican championed the cause of the workingman, because it did not want such a large and useful multitude abandoned to an exploitation which transformed the fortunes of a few into the misery of the masses.[29] In *Graves de Communi,* one of his last encyclicals, he complimented the social Catholics on their desire to make the workers' lot more tolerable and their future more secure. It was praiseworthy, he said, to defend their rights and prevent them from being treated like animals.[30]

Encouraging as his praise must have been to social Catholics, it could not conceal the weaknesses inherent in Leo XIII's approach to the labor problem. Part of his faulty analysis was due to the influence of the social Catholics themselves, for their clichés about capitalism were often written into Leo's great encyclical. Among such clichés was the contention, surprisingly similar to one of Marx's doctrines, that capitalism had enabled a few to monopolize the wealth and reduce the many to pauperism:

> The result of civil change and revolution has been to divide cities into two classes separated by a wide chasm. On the one side there is the party which holds power because it holds wealth; which has in its grasp the whole of labor and trade; which manipulates for its own benefit and its own purposes all the sources of supply, and which is not without influence even in the administration of the commonwealth. On the other side

there is the needy and powerless multitude, sick and sore in spirit and ever ready for disturbance.[31]

That this was a distorted, surrealistic vision of industrial capitalism is more easy to perceive now than it was for many well-meaning people in the 1890's. The extreme anticapitalists on both left and right thought this a fairly accurate picture of nineteenth century society, and perhaps many others did as well. For some reason, they did not notice the marked improvement in the living standard of the masses which the new economy had already made possible in nations such as England and Germany. They also ignored the creation of new types of small business and the development of new middle classes, larger and richer than the old, that made a fantasy of the anticapitalist dogma that the wealthy were turning the masses into impoverished wage slaves. Perhaps the pontiff should be forgiven for making the same mistakes, since his statement in *Rerum Novarum* was at least a recognizable description of his native land.

Yet that nation's problems only illustrate the deficiency of *Rerum Novarum*'s approach as well as that of social Catholicism in general. Italy was oppressively poor in the nineteenth century, not because she was capitalistic, but because she was not capitalistic enough. Italy had failed to develop modern industry rapidly enough to meet the needs of her expanding population, and the masses therefore suffered not so much from a concentration of wealth but from a system that produced it too slowly to provide sufficient stable and well-paid employment.[32]

Rerum Novarum did not consider this side of the question. Instead, like the social Catholics, it tended to blame industry and industrialists for the suffering of the working class and concentrated exclusively on schemes for distributing the wealth more equitably rather than being concerned about how to produce more of it. Leo XIII never seemed to realize that the former might be meaningless without the latter.

Yet few could say from the perspective of the twentieth century that distribution was not a serious problem in Leo's era and fewer still would contend that the workers' place in society or their share of the national wealth was satisfactory in even the most advanced nations. *Rerum Novarum* met these issues directly and proposed a balanced, pragmatic blueprint for the regeneration of the proletariat within existing economic institutions which could enable the laborer to take his place as a respected and dignified member of society. In so doing, its author showed the vision and courage which the papacy had lacked up to his time. He saw the need for the Church to speak to the workingman, and he inspired Catholics to make the laborer's cause their own. Had he done nothing else, his place in history as a great pope would still have been secure.

Pius X and Benedict XV: Labor's Exaggerated Hopes

The reforms which Leo XIII and his followers so earnestly desired were realized slowly after 1903 and did not succeed immediately in giving the working class a substantially greater share of the national wealth. In most nations, small gains in purchasing power were made before 1914 along with considerable improvements in social welfare benefits, but many of these were swept away by the First World War and the economic dislocations which followed it. Yet, by 1922, the workers in France, Germany, England, and Italy had all received the forty-eight hour week, the recognition of union rights and the acceptance of collective bargaining.[33]

The unions could take much credit for winning these reforms and gained a great deal in terms of both prestige and membership because of it. In England, the trade unions continued to develop both their economic and political power, the latter through the newlyfounded Labor Party. Their strikes were successful only part of the time, but their membership increased in spite of this from 2,000,000 in 1900 to 4,000,000 in 1914 to a peak of 8,000,000 in 1920.[34] German unions also flourished; they grew from 700,000 members in 1900 to 3,000,000 in 1914 and then exploded to 9,000,000 in 1922. Most of them were still loyal to the Social Democratic Party and were still guided by it, but they became increasingly moderate and tended to influence the party in the same direction.[35]

No such moderation could be found in the unions of France and Italy except for the minority sponsored by Catholics.[36] In France, most unions were affiliated with the "General Confederation of Labor" (C.G.T.) which grew from about 100,000 effectives in 1900 to 600,000 in 1912 and then to 1,800,000 by 1919. Anarchosyndicalism was still its official policy, and the destruction of capitalism its ultimate goal. In the early years of the twentieth century, called by some the "heroic era," the C.G.T. attempted to realize its revolutionary goal by calling numerous, unsuccessful strikes. After 1910, these futile tactics were gradually abandoned, and the more moderate "reformists" gradually assumed control of the movement.[37]

Italian unionism closely imitated the French pattern except for the anarchist ideology of the latter. It was established in modern form only in the twentieth century and tended to lag behind the Germans and the English both in effective membership and in organization. Most unions belonged to the "General Confederation of Labor" (C.G.L.) which was not organized until 1906 and had only 320,000 members in 1914. As in the labor confederations of other countries, the C.G.L. experienced a huge increase in membership after the war reaching a peak of 2,000,000 in 1920 with another 1,000,000 affiliated with other unions. It was never so revolutionary as the Socialist Party was but retained a close relationship with it and allowed the party to drag it into revolutionary strike movements, especially after 1918. This only increased the fears of the middle classes and helped to bring the fascists to power.[38]

Despite such ups and downs, it was clear that the wage earners of Western Europe were learning how to work together and how to make their demands respected over a broad segment of the economy. For the first time in history, their organizations became nation-wide in scope and were a challenge both economically and politically to the power of the capitalists. More significantly still, their attitudes, at least in Germany and France, were changing. Like the English, they were losing their desire for revolution and were more and more willing to accept a gradual improvement of their condition within the existing order. They were overcoming their conviction that the capitalist system offered them nothing but misery and were now trying to make this system better serve their needs.

Pius X did not quarrel with that objective. He was not inherently hostile to the cause of elevating the material status of labor for all of his conservatism. In his early years especially, he took an interest in labor problems, partly because they were at this time the subject of so much debate among Catholics in Italy. Throughout his reign, he encouraged the efforts of social Catholics to aid the workers and to combine material relief with moral and spiritual betterment. Yet he was more cautious and more negative in his approach than was Leo XIII and wrote nothing comparable to *Rerum Novarum* in which he tried to develop the universal significance of Catholic labor doctrine. He confined his remarks to occasional letters, and what he said in them convinced many observers that he was not basically interested in reform, because he thought social problems were primarily a matter for charity.[39]

Such a conclusion was not entirely fair. It would have been more just to say that Pius X felt social Catholics were neglecting the role of charity too much in their zeal for reform, and he wanted to right the balance. He never rejected reform itself as a goal for Catholics as long as it was kept within the bounds of Catholic teaching and tradition. This was clear in his early encyclicals such as *E Supremi Apostolatus* (October 4, 1903) in which he took as his motto "The Restoration of All Things in Christ" and applied it to the social field. The Catholic Church was interested, he said, not only in the spiritual welfare of peoples but in their material prosperity as well. In a world restored to Christ, the wealthy would be both just and charitable to the humble, and the latter would endure in patience the privations of their less fortunate condition.[40] In another encyclical, he declared that the teachings of Jesus gave support to the material well-being of individuals and families in society. In so far as the clergy and laity were trying by just and charitable means to improve the economic condition of the masses, they were performing a religious duty.[41]

He became more specific when he attempted to define, for the benefit of Italian social Catholics, the rights and duties of both labor and capital. Italian Catholics were as divided on the issue of labor policy as they were on most other subjects in the early twentieth century. The main battle was, as usual, between the Christian democrats and the conservatives. The issue in this case was whether the working class needed to be guided by the "ruling classes" in seeking reform, as the conservatives wanted, or whether the Christian democrats were correct in insisting that the very object of reform was to make the working class independent of any outside control.[42] In an effort to settle the conflict, Pius X wrote a *motu proprio* published on December 18, 1903, in which he summarized certain teachings of Leo XIII.

Among these teachings were the requirements for labor and capital as expressed in *Rerum Novarum*. The wage earners were to furnish faithfully and completely the work upon which they freely and equitably agreed. They could never threaten either the person or the property of their employers, nor could they use violence even in the defense of their legitimate claims. The capitalists, for their part, had to pay a just wage to their workers and could not endanger their "just" savings either by violence, or fraud, or "usury" whether open or hidden. Their employees had to be given the chance to perform their religious duties and were to be protected from vice and immorality. Their spirit of thrift and family loyalty were to be encouraged by their masters, and the work demanded of them could not be too heavy for their physical capacity, their age, or their sex.[43]

Since there was no mention of the issue of working class autonomy, this did nothing to resolve the clash of opinion which gave rise to its writing in the first place. It was nothing more than a repetition of *Rerum Novarum,* except that it made no mention of any program to distribute the wealth more equitably or to transform the proletariat into property owners. Where *Rerum Novarum* said nothing about the questions raised by the Christian democrats, the pronouncement of Pius X was also silent.

The letter to the *Sillon* of 1910 was in a different category. No silence greeted the French Christian democrats concerning their peculiar social doctrines as it had the Italians seven years before; instead, the *Sillonists* were served a thundering anathema. The letter began mildly enough with the pope praising the men of the *Sillon* for wanting to elevate the workingman and promote more perfect justice and charity in labor relations. But the *Sillon* was not satisfied with this, the pontiff continued. It hoped to revolutionize society by redistributing the economic authority of the capitalists to the workers in such a way as to give each laborer the "soul" of an employer.

Such a program contradicted the teaching of Leo XIII that authority and inequality were necessary in society, Pius continued. It implied that existing social patterns had to be abolished before the laboring man could gain his rights. It paved the way for radically new measures which would transform the present labor-management structure beyond recognition. How different was truly Christian labor reform! The latter taught that justice could be achieved within the existing order and that social problems would be well on their way to solution if both the great and the small thought less of their rights and more of their duties. If this were not enough, if the worker could not achieve justice because of "dishonest forces" around him or because of conflicts of interest, Catholics were permitted to use protective measures but not those leading to radical change. This, rather than the program of the *Sillon,* proclaimed Pius X, was what *Rerum Novarum* stood for.[44]

Leo XIII's encyclical may have been closer to the goals of the *Sillon* than the Pontiff realized. Pius X was incorrect in his accusations. The *Sillon* did not wish to abolish the authority of employers or achieve radical social revolution; it wanted only to achieve more justice and equality for workers.[45] Perhaps the author of *Rerum Novarum* would have been reluctant to endorse some of the more naïve enthusiasms of the *Sillon*, but he might also have hesitated to approve the notion, implied by Pius X, that the authority of capital over labor was as essential to the social organism as that of Church, government, or family. Leo almost certainly would have contested Pius's theory that social injustice was only an exception to the rule that virtue and patience were all the working class needed; *Rerum Novarum* was nothing if not a proclamation that the violation of workers' rights was widespread through no fault of their own.

Benedict XV may have been more sympathetic to Leo XIII's point of view than was Pius X, but he was similar to his immediate predecessor in other ways. His pronouncements showed the same combination of desire for social justice, lack of original ideas on how to achieve it, and suspicion that the workers' claims were too extreme. He was also certain, as was Pius X, that the working class should be satisfied with the existing economic structure and not be deluded into thinking that labor reform could be achieved better in some other system. Neither pope went even so far as Leo XIII did in denouncing the abuses of the bourgeois society, and neither seemed so influenced by anticapitalist thought.

But this did not mean that Benedict XV had no interest in the workers' needs nor sympathy for their plight. Both of these were more than evident in his first encyclical, *Ad Beatissimi*, in which he deplored the "poisonous" spirit of class hatred which he thought was spreading throughout the society of his day. With the fervor of *Rerum Novarum*, he proclaimed that cooperation, unity, and mutual affection between rich and poor were absolutely necessary if the social order were to function properly. In this, the rich had as much of a duty as the poor; they had to reach out to the humble and treat them not only in strict justice, which was their minimum obligation, but with good-will, and kindness, and consideration as well. He roundly condemned what he thought to be the desires of all classes for purely material riches which led to an insane competition that only stimulated the hatred of the poor for those above them. In the final stages of such a competition came all-out class war with one side determined to satisfy its wants regardless of the means for so doing, and the other side equally bent on keeping what it had.[46]

He continued to deplore such divisions after the war and continued to encourage Catholics to help the proletariat. In a declaration of March 10, 1919, on *Rerum Novarum,* he said that the social classes would never truly cooperate until justice and charity triumphed. *Rerum Novarum* contained a true understanding of both of these, he thought. The workers had a special interest in Leo XIII's encyclical, because it spoke not only of the workers' duties and employers' rights but the converse as well. The workers did not need to ignore their rights, and employers dared not forget their responsibilities.[47] In 1920, he told the Bishop of Bergamo that Catholics were not forbidden to ameliorate the material condition of the masses; the clergy needed to take an interest in economic and social action because of the importance it had for the Church's own religious and moral interests and because of its significance for the general welfare.[48]

Yet he was certain that the general welfare could never be served if the workers expected too much, and he feared that they did. This fear, doubtless stimulated by the acrimonious labor-management relations in Europe and especially in Italy at this time, overshadowed his interest in labor reform and made its mark on his pronouncements. His hostility to working class radicalism was evident in *Ad Beatissimi* where he sharply criticized the proletariat for its strikes and insurrections and for its hatred of the wealthy. If the workers agitated against the rich as if the latter had stolen their property, the laborers were not only violating justice and charity; they were acting contrary to good sense, since they could ameliorate their condition by honest labor if they so desired.[49] Considering the social and economic conditions of 1914, when this encyclical was written, one could doubt that "honest labor" was sufficient for a real improvement in the status of labor.

The pope himself seemed increasingly to have reservations about it and wondered whether any substantial improvement was possible. In the same postwar message in which he told Catholics to ameliorate the lot of the poor, he added:

Whatever amelioration they bring to their situation, whether by their personal efforts or with the help of others, there will always remain for them, as for other men, a heavy heritage of suffering. If they have this exact vision of reality, they will not exhaust themselves in useless efforts to elevate themselves to a level above their capacities, and they will endure unavoidable evils with the resignation and courage which gives the hope of eternal riches.[50]

More startling than what this said was what it left unsaid. The improvements already made by and for the working class, the higher real wages, the shorter hours, the more tolerable working conditions, and the arbitration machinery which held so much promise for the settling of the strikes Benedict deplored were all passed over in silence. Even if he did not feel that an extension of these reforms was likely in the near future, he might at least have taken cognizance of the progress already made, *how* it was made, and its implications for the status of the working class. Surely, this would have been more relevant than vague, pessimistic admonitions to be content with suffering—no matter how much suffering was still to come.

Notes

1. The attitude of the French workers towards the Church is movingly described in Dansette, *Destin du catholicisme français*, pp. 40–45.

2. Cole, *Short History of the British Working Class Movement*, pp. 265–70; Ashworth, *op. cit.*, pp. 192–213.

3. See below, p. 139.

4. Clapham, *op. cit.*, pp. 329–38.

5. Clough, *Economic History of Modern Italy*, pp. 140–44, 382.

6. Cole, *Short History of the British Working Class Movement*, pp. 237ff.

7. Clapham, *op. cit.*, pp. 329–33; Landauer, *op. cit.*, pp. 311–16.

8. Dolléans, *op. cit.*, Vol. II, pp. 23–52; Lorwin, *op. cit.*, chapter iii.

9. Horowitz, *op. cit.*, pp. 37–47.

10. Georges Jarlot, S. J., "Les Avant-Projets de *Rerum Novarum*," *Nouvelle Revue Théologique*, Vol. LXXXI (1959), pp. 70–71.

11. Ritter, *op. cit.*, pp. 81–84.

12. Giovanni Hoyois, "Aux Origines de *Rerum Novarum:* l'Union de Fribourg," *Les dossiers de l'action social catholique,* May, 1951, pp. 322–30.

13. Abell, *op. cit.*, pp. 55–71; Georgiana McEntee, *The Social Catholic Movement in Great Britain* (New York: Macmillan, 1927), pp. 23–33, 84–87.

14. *Acta (Leo XIII),* Vol. IX, pp. 300–301.

15. Letter of March 14, 1890, *ibid.,* Vol. X, p. 97.

16. Cf. Robert Kothen, "Monseigneur Guillaume-Emmanuel von Ketteler, 1811–1877," *Les dossiers de l'action sociale catholique,* May, 1951, p. 314.

17. Gilson, *op. cit.*, pp. 206–207.

18. *Ibid.*, p. 214.

19. *Ibid.*, p. 215.

20. *Ibid.*

21. *Ibid.*, pp. 215–16. In this same encyclical, he delivered the first condemnation of usury made by a pope since 1745 ("The mischief has been increased by rapacious usury, which, although more than once condemned by the Church, is nevertheless, under a different guise, but with like injustice, still practiced by covetous and grasping men."), *ibid.*, p. 206. But he did not elaborate on what this "different guise" was, nor did he try to revive the usury laws of the Middle Ages as a weapon against capitalism, as some of the corporatists wanted. Cf. John T. Noonan, *The Scholastic Analysis of Usury* (Cambridge: Harvard University Press, 1957), pp. 389, 402.

22. Gilson, *op. cit.*, pp. 215–16.

23. *Ibid.*, pp. 229–30.

24. *Ibid.*, p. 229. His conclusion from all this was that the state could intervene in cases of unjust contracts whenever necessary, but that it was preferable for the workers' associations to try to solve the problem first. See below, chapters v & vi.

25. Gilson, *op. cit.*, p. 230.

26. Marx, *The Communist Manifesto,* pp. 26–36.

27. Gilson, *op. cit.*, pp. 217–18.

28. Fogarty, *op. cit.*, pp. 49–50.

29. Letter of August 6, 1893, *Actes de Léon XIII,* Vol. III, p. 215.

30. Jan. 18, 1901, *ibid.,* Vol. IV, pp. 213–15.

31. Gilson, *op. cit.*, p. 230. The reader may notice that this is similar to the passage from the same encyclical quoted above, p. 81. In addition, it is almost identical to one of the major theses in *The Communist Manifesto,* pp. 18–38.

32. Cf. Clough, *Economic History of Modern Italy,* pp. 57ff.

33. Cole, *Short History of the British Working Class Movement,* pp. 283,

369–70, 376–77, 388–89; Ashworth, *op. cit.*, pp. 201–13, 240–53; Dolléans and Dehove, *op. cit.*, Vol. II, pp. 11–19; Clough, *Economic History of Modern Italy*, pp. 161–63, 382; Horowitz, *op. cit.*, pp. 137–42; Gustav Stolper, *German Economy*, 1870–1940 (New York: Reynal & Hitchcock, 1940), pp. 210–17.

34. Cole, *op. cit.*, pp. 326, 369–70, 384–86.

35. Landauer, *op. cit.*, pp. 312–14, 358, 369–70.

36. This minority will be discussed in more detail in chapter v. See below, p. 117.

37. Dolléans, *op. cit.*, Vol. II, pp. 117ff; Lorwin, *op. cit.*, pp. 23–30, 43ff.

38. Horowitz, *op. cit.*, pp. 58–94, 128–53.

39. Cf. Scoppola, *op. cit.*, p. 93; and Dansette, *Histoire religieuse de la France contemporaine*, Vol. II, p. 398.

40. *Actes de Pie X*, Vol. I, p. 47.

41. *Il Fermo Proposito*, June 11, 1905, *ibid.*, Vol. II, pp. 92–94, 99, 102–103.

42. Gambasin, *op. cit.*, pp. 544–49.

43. *Actes de Pie X*, Vol. I, pp. 109–10.

44. *A.A.S.*, Vol. II (1910), pp. 608–21, 630–31.

45. Breunig, *op. cit.*, p. 236.

46. *A.A.S.*, Vol. VI (1914), pp. 649–54.

47. Full text in Georges Guitton, *1891, une date dans l'histoire des travailleurs* (Paris: Editions Spès, n.d.), pp. ix–xi.

48. *Actes de Benoît XV*, Vol. II, pp. 127, 130.

49. *A.A.S.*, Vol. VI (1914), p. 652.

50. Letter to the Bishop of Bergamo, *Actes de Benoît XV*, Vol. II, p. 129.

Toward a New Society

George G. Higgins

This article appeared in *The Catholic Mind*, 1956.

May 15 was a great day for the Church. The occasion was the sixty-fifth aniversary of Pope Leo XIII's encyclical *Rerum Novarum* (English title: *On the Condition of Labor*) and the twenty-fifth anniversary of Pope Pius XI's *Quadragesimo Anno (On Reconstructing the Social Order)*. Both of these great Pontiffs had chosen the same day—forty years apart—on which to give us timeless social principles to guide us in our life in society.

The very fact that the anniversary of these two great social encyclicals was publicly commemorated in the United States by fifteen or twenty diocesan social action committees and by an even larger number of colleges, universities and local Catholic organizations is evidence that the two encyclicals have had a considerable influence in our nation at least to the extent of making people aware of the moral aspects of economic life and conscious of their moral responsibilities as individuals and as members of economic groups.

Back in 1891, and even as recently as 1931, relatively few Americans, Catholics included, were thinking in terms of the morality or immorality of economic systems and practices. Fewer still, perhaps, were prepared to admit that the economic order, in all things connected with the moral law, comes within the jurisdiction of the Church. Economic Liberalism or individualism, which demands that there be no moral or social controls over economic life—and which was so roundly condemned by both Leo XIII and Pius XI—was the dominant philosophy of American economic life.

Considerable progress has been made, however, since 1931. Economic Liberalism, at least in certain mitigated forms, still exercises a certain amount of influence in the United States, but more and more Americans in these latter days find themselves agreeing with Pope Pius XI when he says that "even though economic and moral science employs each its own principles in its own sphere, it is, nevertheless, an error to say that the economic and moral orders are so distinct from and alien to each other that the former depends in no way on the latter."

This is progress, symbolized by the widespread observance of the anniversary of the two encyclicals and by the ever- growing number of social education programs being sponsored by Catholic organizations and schools.

PROGRESS MADE

But how much progress have we made in the practical application of the moral directives of the two encyclicals?

To answer this question, we have to distinguish between the "reform" of economic life and the long-range "reconstruction" of the economic order. Many specific measures of "reform" are advocated by the two encyclicals, but the English word "reform," as the late Monsignor John A. Ryan suggested shortly after Pius XI's encyclical was issued, "is too weak to characterize adequately the Holy Father's proposals for the remaking of industrial society. The term 'reconstruction,' in other words, rebuilding, is the only adequate expression. What the Pope demands is a new kind of society, a new social order, an industrial organization which will differ radically from the economic arrangements which have existed for the last 150 years."

We have made a great deal of progress in carrying out the specific "reforms" of the encyclicals, but considerably less in promoting this long-range "reconstruction."

The principal measures of "reform" advocated by Leo XIII and Pius XI are *legislation* and *organization*. Progress has been made in both fields, although certain gaps remain to be filled.

Since 1891, and more particularly since 1931, the Federal Government, reversing a very bad tradition of *laissez faire,* or "hands off," has gradually come to merit the praise that Pius XI bestows upon those nations in which "a new branch of law, wholly unknown to the earlier time, has arisen from the continuous and unwearied labor to protect vigorously the sacred rights of the workers that flow from their dignity as men and as Christians.'' These new types of law, the Holy Father continues, ''undertake the protection of life, health, strength, family, homes, workshops, wages and labor hazards, in fine, everything which pertains to the condition of wage workers, with special concern for women and children.''

In all of these fields and in others left unspecified in this particular passage of the encyclical, the Federal Government, however belatedly and experimentally, has enacted legislation more or less in harmony with the teaching of Leo and Pius.

THE BISHOPS' PROGRAM

In 1919, long before the Federal Government had seriously begun to ''protect . . . the sacred rights of the workers,'' the American Bishops recommended eleven major types of governmental action which in their own opinion were badly needed at the time. This ''Bishops' Program of Social Reconstruction'' was more or less ignored during the twenties, but happily the preface to the twentieth anniversary edition of the ''Program'' was able to report that by 1939, of eleven proposals, all but one had been either wholly or partially translated into fact. And additional progress has been made since then.

There are still some serious gaps in federal legislation and even more serious deficiencies in the social legislation of the individual states, some of which have been scandalously recreant in their duty to ''protect the sacred rights of the workers.'' In general, however, we may conclude that considerable progress has been made since, and to a certain extent because of the influence of the two great social encyclicals.

Both Leo XIII and Pius XI vigorously defended the right of labor to organize into unions of their own choosing and wholeheartedly gave their approval to unionism as a necessary measure of reform in modern economic life. Leo's endorsement of unionism was notoriously disregarded in the United States, even by certain influential Catholics, so much so that by the time of Pius XI's encyclical, forty years later, only two or three million American workers were members of bona fide unions. But if you lived through the Great Depression, you know that considerable progress has been made since 1931. Labor's natural right to organize was given more or less effective legal protection—for the first time—in 1935 with the passage of the National Labor Relations Act. Today, in spite of the many retrogressive features of the Taft-Hartley Act and in spite of even more reprehensible laws in certain states, approximately fifteen million workers are organized. Progress, yes. But the organization of agricultural and so-called white collar workers must be carried forward as rapidly as possible.

These two types of "reform"—legislation and organization, including of course the organization of farmers, employers and professional people—are aimed at implementing what might be called the central principle of the two encyclicals, namely, that ownership and work are both individual and social in character and therefore must be made to serve the interests not only of individuals but of society as well. Legislation and organization have done much to bring about this necessary balance between the individual and social aspects of economic life, but they are not the final answer. They are, or should be, merely steps in the right direction.

What is needed, if we are to avoid the dictatorship of wealth on the one hand or the dictatorship of government on the other, is an overall reconstruction of the social order along the lines of the so-called Industry Council system. It is "most necessary," as Pius XI tells us, that there be established a "juridical and social order which will, as it were, give form and shape to all economic life," an order "which public authority ought to be ever ready effectively to protect and defend."

TWIN DANGERS

Protective and "reform" legislation is necessary; so is organization. But legislation, if relied upon too heavily, can innocently lead us into statism; and organization alone—along class lines—can easily result in an all-out struggle for domination between or among contending economic power groups.

Our task for the future, while continuing to fill in the gaps in federal and state legislation, and while continuing to organize the unorganized, is to encourage existing organizations of labor, management, agriculture and the professions to co-operate as much as possible—under government supervision, but free from government domination—in a federated system of industrial and professional councils specifically designed to facilitate the practice of social justice by consciously promoting the general welfare or the common good. And even as we are working toward the establishment of such a system, it is most necessary that there be the fullest possible cooperation between government and private organizations. Otherwise we may become totalitarian ourselves in opposing totalitarianism in other parts of the world.

A gradual but steady growth into a system of agencies of cooperation for the common good must be accompanied by serious efforts to extend the ownership of productive property as widely as possible not only in farming but in city industry. The widespread ownership of property is basic to a sound economy and a good social order. This period of change, of transition from the present system into something better, can be used to induce ownership by employees of the companies in which they work. Profit-sharing in which the people working in the company participate in ownership seems a reasonable method of distributing productive property. Since small stockholders are individually helpless, it may be mutually advantageous for an employees' stockholders' association to represent the rank-and-file of the worker-owners. This is an unusual proposal, but we ask the unions and all interested parties to give it thoughtful consideration.

INDUSTRY COUNCIL PLAN

This program of social reconstruction which is outlined in Pope Pius XI's encyclical, *Quadragesimo Anno,* is commonly referred to in the United States today as the Industry Council Plan. Many people—including some of us who use it most frequently—are not at all satisfied with the name. The name, however, is relatively unimportant; the all-important thing is the program itself.

The encyclical program—call it what you will—is based upon the principle that an organized *economic* society is as natural and as necessary as an organized *political* society. In the absence of a properly organized political society we have either anarchy or dictatorship. By the same token, in the absence of a properly organized economic society we have either uncontrolled competition (which is economic anarchy) on the one hand, or economic dictatorship (concentration of ownership and economic control) on the other. And, as Pius XI reminds us, the former inevitably and "of its own nature" produces the latter.

But what is a properly organized economic society? It is one in which "men have their place, not according to the position each has in the labor market but according to the respective social functions which each performs."

This means that all of the people engaged in a given industry or profession (workers and employers alike) are intended by nature (and not simply because the Popes have said so) to cooperate with one another for the good of their own industry or profession and for the good of the whole economy. Nature itself intends them to organize for this purpose—to "form guilds or associations" and through these "self-governing associations" to regulate economic life according to the requirements of social justice. Each industry forms a separate "order" (or "guild" or "occupational group" or "industry council") and the various industries, thus organized, are to work together for the common good. Together they form the Social Order whose function it is, in cooperation with the government, to "give form and shape to all economic life."

These "orders" are not the creatures of government. They are natural organizations and, to the greatest possible extent, they are to be self-governing—subject, however, to the over-all supervision of the State, which has the final responsibility for coordinating the activities of all subordinate groups in the interest of the common good.

It is very important to emphasize that this organized system of cooperation among the various self-governing "orders" is not a distinctively Catholic program, but rather one which is based upon the natural law—upon the nature of man and the nature of society—and therefore one which ought to recommend itself to all right-thinking Americans, whatever their religion. It is encouraging to note that the program is recommending itself to an ever increasing number of Americans, irrespective of their religious beliefs.

There have been a dozen or more non-Catholic authors, who, within the last two or three years, have independently advocated a program of social reconstruction similar in its essential details to the Industry Council program advocated by the encyclicals.

A LOOK AT THE RECORD

But you may say: "Well and good. But that's all very theoretical. What I want to know is whether or not there is any progress being made in practice as opposed to theory." Well, let's take a look at part of the record.

The U. S. Department of Commerce recently published an enormous directory, *National Associations of the United States,* giving detailed information on approximately 4,000 trade, professional, civic, labor, religious and other organizations, the majority of which are national in scope. Indispensable as a convenient reference book for busy executives, it also serves a very useful purpose for economists and sociologists, and, in general, for all those who are interested in the reconstruction of the social order along the lines of the Industry Council Plan.

One of the more common objections to the Industry Council program used by some persons can be summarized as follows: The Industry Council program presupposes that employers and workers are already highly organized into their own voluntary associations. But, while workers are partially organized at the present time, employers are unorganized and wish to remain unorganized. Therefore the Industry Council program, however desirable in theory, is impractical as far as the United States is concerned, at least for the foreseeable future.

This objection fails to take into account the information contained in the new directory of the Department of Commerce. Actually American businessmen are very highly organized, much more so, as a matter of fact, than the workers are. Economists have known this for a long time, but even they will probably be surprised at the sheer quantity of statistical evidence provided in the new directory.

Fifteen hundred national trade associations and an additional 300 associations made up predominantly of businessmen are listed. We are told that the 1,500 trade associations have a paid staff of 16,000 persons and a gross membership of over 1,000,000 business firms. Including locals and branches, it is estimated by the editors of the directory that there are 12,000 trade associations and 4,000 Chambers of Commerce, to say nothing of 15,000 civic service groups, luncheon clubs and similar organizations of business and professional men and women.

These figures are extremely encouraging. They indicate that Americans are really not as individualistic as they sometimes pretend to be.

Most important of all, they indicate that the groundwork for the Industry Council Plan is already fairly well established. Neither labor nor management is completely organized, of course, but both are certainly well enough organized to warrant our giving thought to the establishment of the Industry Council program.

The organization of the unorganized, particularly of unorganized workers, ought to continue to have a high priority on the agenda of social reconstruction. At the same time, however, we can be reasonably optimistic about the progress already made in this direction. Also, we can begin to concentrate on the all-important problem of persuading our existing organizations of labor and management to cooperate with one another on behalf of the common good instead of being preoccupied almost exclusively with their separate and more selfish interests.

If you read the Catholic press regularly, you will remember that the Bishops of the United States called attention to this problem in 1948 in their annual statement, *The Christian in Action*. They clearly recognized that economic individualism, which is so often said to be characteristic of the United States, is more of a myth than a fact. American economic individualism, they implied, has been transformed into "group individualism"—if we may use a rather contradictory phrase.

"Today we have labor partly organized," the Bishops said, "but chiefly for its own interests. We have capital or management organized, possibly on a larger scale, but again for its own interests. What we urgently need, in the Christian view of the social order, is the free organization of capital and labor in permanent agencies of cooperation for the common good."

The new directory of the Department of Commerce, as we have already indicated, generously supports the Bishops' conclusion that our national economy is already very highly organized.

The evidence is overwhelming—634 pages of names and addresses of national organizations, including 1,500 national trade associations and 200 national unions. Ten years from now, perhaps, the Department of Commerce will be able to publish another directory indicating that some of these trade associations and some of these unions, while preserving their own autonomy and their separate identity, have come together in "permanent agencies of cooperation for the common good." Let us hope so. Let us hope and pray that more and more of our trade associations and unions will take to heart the words of Pope Pius XI in his encyclical, *On Reconstructing the Social Order:* "And may these free organizations [trade associations and unions among others], now flourishing and rejoicing in their salutary fruits, set themselves the task of preparing the way, in conformity with the mind of Christian social teaching, for those larger and more important guilds, Industries and Professions [Industry Councils], which we mentioned before, and make every possible effort to bring them to realization."

*   *   *

SOUND SOCIAL ECONOMY

Then only will the social economy be rightly established and attain its purposes when all and each are supplied with all the goods that the wealth and resources of nature, technical achievement, and the social organization of economic life can furnish.

The Drafting of Quadragesimo Anno

Oswald von Nell-Breuning, S.J.

This article originally appeared in *Stimmen der Zeit*, 1971.

"Quadragesimo anno (expleto)" or "Forty years have gone by", ran the opening words of the encyclical that Pius XI issued to the world on the 40th anniversary of Rerum Novarum. Meanwhile, another 40 years have passed since that encyclical. For a number of years now, I have been the only one still living of those who cooperated on it. Records from which the story of how QA came about or from which the history of its development could be learned scarcely exist. I destroyed my own papers during the 1930's in order to keep them out of the hands of the Gestapo. So it may be high time to write down a little of what still remains in my memory. Perhaps it is not without interest to draw a comparison between the way I, at 40 years old, saw my duty then, and how as an 80 year old I see it today in retrospect. The change that I discern in myself only reflects the change that the prevailing concept of ecclesial teaching authority generally and of Catholic social teaching in particular has experienced in the same space of time.

The most important statements on the actual course of events at the initiation of QA were already published in my article "The Konigswinter [Rhine town] Group and their share in QA" in the Götz Briefs Commemorative Book of 1968. I add here a little about my personal share.

With the intent of publishing a new encyclical on the 40th anniversary of the encyclical Rerum Novarum, Pius XI, bypassing all Vatican offices, (only the Cardinal Secretary of State knew about it) entrusted its preparation to Fr. Wlodimir Ledochowski, Superior General of my order, who enjoyed his highest confidence. The Pope remarked that the German fathers would have to do most of the work. Fr. Ledochowski in turn gave me the assignment of preparing a draft in strict secrecy, according to the custom of that time. Neither my house superior nor my provincial superior knew what work I had to do for the General. Since no one could be let in on the secret, I could not consult anyone and was left wholly on my own. Where did I get the courage, I ask myself today, to take on such a task, which was altogether too much for me?

When the job was given me, I had already been a few years in the disputes that at that time split the social Catholicism of the German speaking districts, that is, in the south German and Austrian regions. And I was able, although self-taught, to consider myself, without presumption, one of the spokesmen in the science of political economy. In 1928 I obtained a doctorate in theology with a dissertation on the morality of the stock exchange. At the beginning of 1930, I gave a short lecture, recently reprinted, on morality and the reform of laws on stocks. It anticipated the requirements that were in part enacted in the German stock law of 1965. So I possessed a certain name, in the Catholic labor movement in western Germany and even beyond.

In the Konigswinter Group already mentioned, to which men like Theodore Brauer and Götz Briefs belonged, I was accepted as a participant in their discussions. All of this gave me a certain self-confidence. In addition, there was my confidence in the education in abstract thinking bestowed in the regular Jesuit course of training. This education conferred a superiority similar to that which the educated Marxist possessed toward his opponent.

The deciding confidence however, was given by my trust in the teaching office of the Church, in whose service I was to work. If you were trained at that time, you could simply not conceive that the teaching office, specifically when it spoke through the Pope, its head, could err sometime and make an unfounded statement, this even when you were clearly aware that the statement was in no way covered by infallibility. You were also convinced that the Holy Spirit was there to permit no false teaching even where He did not give the guarantee of infallibility. As I once expressed it: the Spirit would if necessary protect the Pope against his advisers. So every teaching statement was considered as undoubtedly true. To criticize one, to doubt its correctness seemed to be so misleading that a person who had hold of himself would not allow such a thought to arise. You put a similar confidence in the certainty of natural law deductions. That I was not a social philosopher, but an economist and a student of law, I was thoroughly aware; but I did not experience this as a defect, since the social and philosophical thought of my brother priest, Gustav Gundlach, that I soaked up like a dried out sponge, seemed to offer the solution or at least the key to the solution of all relevant questions. I decided to incorporate his contributions unshortened into the draft of the encyclical. QA is in fact well saturated with Gundlach's thought and so I could, if I wanted to speak about its authorship, point to the continuous help of Gundlach and coin the phrase; he has in QA set up for himself a lasting monument.

Accordingly, my trust was decisive. The presence of the Holy Spirit would protect the Pope. No error of mine could get into the official teaching statement.

I was with Pius XI just a single time, at the beginning of the work. Without going into details, he called the draft good; it should be worked up further. To my horror, they had given him my first draft, single spaced and done with a worn out ribbon in the typewriter. I recall exactly only his remark, "You have a poor typewriter." Whether he had actually read through the whole thing remained unclear; he turned the conversation to other matters. He did at least examine sufficiently much the greater part of subsequent revisions—there were eight—as the corrections prepared by him of typing errors demonstrated. Only a few remarks on the subject were prepared by him. Changes that he required were mostly of a different sort. That Pius had himself worked on the many technical problems treated in the encyclical, seemed to me unlikely; how could he now take the time for it? Naturally, Fr. Ledochowski, at the many audiences he had with the Pope, did not neglect to draw his attention to the bases for controversial points, so that Pius XI knew the range of what was to be published in his name.

Shortly before the conclusion of the project, he sent a note on fascism, written in Italian in his own hand, that was to be inserted in the appropriate place (91–96). Fr. Ledochowski gave it to me with the remark, the Holy Father asked me to say that we should see where the note can best be inserted. He continued in a very firm tone: "But if you have any doubts, you have the duty to inform me." In view of the esteem that he enjoyed with Pius XI, he could be confident that if necessary he could prevail upon the Pope to alter his note. I read it and was convinced that here the Holy Spirit really was guiding the Pope's pen. I was enthusiastic and notified Fr. Ledochowski that I had already found the place where the note fitted in smoothly. It needed only to be translated into Latin (the

Italian translation of QA contains the original draft of the note—one of the few cases where the text of an encyclical was edited by the Pope himself). This my first opinion did not last very long.

What Pius XI wrote Cardinal Schuster (Milan) about fascism aroused doubts in me as to whether Pius XI really understood the phenomenon of fascism. Today I am firmly convinced that he did not understand it, that he was not acquainted with the social and political character of fascism. This doubt, like my present conviction, leaves the official declaration undisturbed, just as it in no way disparages Pius XI's great accomplishment, the resolution of the Roman question in 1929.

It is clear to me today that the insertion of Pius XI's comments on fascism bears the chief blame for the total misunderstanding of the picture of order, or rather outline of a social order, developed in QA, which in the German translation is called by the unhappy word 'occupational' and in French by 'corporatism'. This is no excuse for the inadequate delineation; that was my responsibility exclusively. On the contrary, I blame myself. I became confident because the Pope did not complain in any way about my exposition; and I blame myself far more because I approved the supplement to it written by him. I lulled myself into a false sense of security and undertook no further reflections.

Despite the warning of Fr. Ledochowski, no doubts stirred in me as to whether the paragraphs written by the Pope would combine with my text into a significant whole. Nor did I consider whether my text, in order to be made unmistakable alongside the Pope's lines—written in a quite different style—would need either to be recast or completely rewritten.

But the other question I had to ask myself and still ask today; did I for my part understand rightly the Pope's note? Already in my Commentary of 1932 and later, I continually interpreted these statements of Pius XI as diplomatic irony and I could refer to Mussolini for the correctness of this interpretation. He understood the encyclical as such an unfavorable criticism of him that he unleashed his anger over it against the Italian Catholic youth organizations. The Pope complained that Mussolini reacted so spitefully to the 'benevolent nod' that he had given him. I believed this complaint was to be understood as diplomatic talk and I still would like to understand it as such. Naturally, I do not possess an account of how the Pope understood his statements or wanted them understood.

When, three years later, Pius XI expressed high appreciation of the 'QA state' allegedly established in Austria through the Constitution of May, 1934, I was completely dismayed. For in my understanding of the social order picture of the encyclical, the term 'QA state' is a direct self contradiction; in any case inexplicable. Citizens of a state are expressly given, referring to Leo XIII, the right to choose freely the form of state (86).

The encyclical wants to establish no specific form of state; the state should merely be relieved of tasks that are not its business. What should be curbed is capitalistic class society, centered on the labor market; it should be converted into a class free society (a pity that this apt phrase had not yet then been coined!). The structures of this society are regulated by the services of the various social groups, contributing to the common good of the whole.

It can be, naturally, that Pius XI, convinced of the good will of the Austrians, also assumed the goodness and correctness of their plans or their work. More likely, it seems to me, that he—thinking in terms of Roman law—regarded what they tried to undertake as the realization of the QA picture of social order.

In Austria it is still presumed (occasionally even the determined assertion emerges) that the section on the 'occupational order' goes back to the influence of the Vogelsang school or may lead back to Chancellor Ignaz Seipel. No Austrian cooperated on the development of QA. In my work, no article coming from Austria came to my attention. However surprising it may sound, these QA thoughts arose exclusively from the Monchengladbach instituted Konigswinter Group, chiefly—as Erich Streissler recently determined—from the 'extremely liberal' thinking of Gustav Gundlach. His was the expression used by Nuncio Pacelli at the Freiburg Catholic Convention of 1929, "From the confrontation between classes to the harmonious cooperation of professions." (QA 81) on which this whole section of the encyclical is 'suspended'. Fr. Ledochowski was not prepared, without further consideration, to introduce these thoughts into the encyclical. I had to intercede strongly for it. I recall chiefly his doubting question, "How long do you think it will take to achieve this?" and my disarming reply, "It will never be achieved; it is much too sensible for people ever to do it."

When I consider today, that this heart of the encyclical (for that it is, without any doubt) has brought about misunderstandings and has been disparaged in the widest circles of Catholic social teaching as 'statist' or 'restorative' or 'reactionary', etc.,—quite apart from the political decisions referring to it and their consequences (Austria, Portugal)—then the thought is for me oppressive that without my insistence this section would surely not have been included in the encyclical. What I wanted to say in it and what I am convinced it does say unambiguously, I considered afterwards as before to be progressive, liberal, definitely democratic, against individualism and against statism; in short, correct. And this, despite all the unclearness of the unhappy phrase 'according to occupational status' used in the German version for lack of a better term.

Basically, I am of the opinion that the expounding of an official document should depend exclusively on what the wording means, according to ordinary rules of interpretation, and not on what the author of the draft, or on what the teaching authority presumed it meant. In the case of enacted laws, arising from the deliberations of a legislative body, it is clear that what an individual representative thought a law meant doesn't matter. The same holds even for the monarchial or monocratic legislator and likewise for the bearer of teaching authority; the message does not depend on his view of it, but exclusively on his statements.

My commentary on QA interprets the lines of the encyclical in the sense that, in my plan, they were to bear, and that in my conviction, they actually do bear. To what extent Pius XI understood them as, in my belief, they should be understood, is beyond my knowledge. An exchange of views, where any possible misunderstanding or unclearness could have become apparent and cleared up, did not, as I said, ever take place. In general, I credit myself with the ability to express my thought in distinct and adequate language, and so I believe that the statements of QA are the adequate expression of the ideas that I wanted to put into it, apart from a few exceptions, where the Latinist was able to prevail against me.

In the drafting of the Vatican Council II Constitution Gaudium et Spes, there arose a dispute over the interpretation of QA. In the section of the Constitution treating of co-determination, there is at 68, footnote 7, the expression 'curatio', management, taken from the Latin text of QA. The question was raised, what this expression means at this place in QA and how the reference there to the inclusion of social law elements into labor relations is to be understood. They wanted to know what I thought of this at the time, what I conceived by 'curatio'. To this I can only repeat my basic explanation; it is not at all a question of what I thought or conceived; it is only a matter of what the text and the context convey.

That I am inclined to project back into this section of QA my later acquired insights, doubtless already present germinally at that time, is obvious. For just this reason, I am aware that here I must distrust myself. Whether the choice of the word 'curatio' was mine or the Latinist's, I can no longer determine, since I no longer have any records. So I can only refer you to Latin dictionaries, where you can look up what the word curatio ordinarily means.

Similarly, I can say no more about the pair 'vel' and 'aut', that is, 'or' and 'or' in the same sentence with curatio, than that, linguistically, it is possible to interpret the first 'or' in such a weakening way that 'sharers in management' approaches so near to 'sharers in ownership' that you can consider the first as identical to or as flowing out of the second. Against this, the statement as a whole makes this meaning seem forced; there may be a simpler reason for the pairing. [The whole sentence runs: 'In this way wage-earners are made sharers in some sort in the ownership, or the management, or the profits.']

The German version of QA that I prepared and for which I am responsible lets you recognize unambiguously that it understands 'sharers in ownership' and 'sharers in management' as two different concepts, clearly distinguished from each other, and that for me, 'sharers in management' means sharers in administration. And yet it is not a question of my understanding of the sentence, neither my understanding then nor now, but solely of what the sentence means objectively.

Despite the duty imposed on me of maintaining secrecy, my membership in the Konigswinter Group offered me the priceless opportunity of bringing up, at the meetings, the subjects which, in my view, should be discussed in the encyclical. Only, I could not give any hint of the use I planned to make of the benefit deriving from this exchange of ideas. So later, the Group noticed to their astonishment how many of their stock of ideas reappeared in the encyclical. They regretted that they had not previously published their results, that were then receiving, through the encyclical, a confirmation that was, by the standards of that time, extraordinarily impressive. Without doubt, the Konigswinter Group had, even if unknowingly, a great share in QA. For me it meant a great support in being able to make myself ever more secure through the exchange of ideas in this group of specialists.

Nonetheless, the responsibility remained chiefly on me. True, my order General gave me at times a fellow priest (professor at our order's School of Commerce in Antwerp) as a partner at my side. But my influence prevailed in all passages that I believed should be emphasized. The teaching part of the encyclical did include everything that I wanted to introduce into it, but—apart from a few lines—nothing else was included that was not my intellectual property.

On occasion, a few brother priests who enjoyed in their own countries a certain respect on questions in the social field were consulted, not regularly, but just when a favorable opportunity arose. So they could only express their opinions on the questions that seemed especially pressing to them. I did not, so far as I recall, have in a single case to judge between conflicting opinions, with reasons and counter reasons.

But the final say as to what was to be incorporated in the encyclical could, in the circumstances, be made only by Fr. Ledochowski, the man appointed by the Pope. He accepted my material and as a rule agreed to my proposals. When, as an exception, he denied his approval, it was not because he was of another opinion on the subject and thought he understood it better, but as a matter of expediency. He did not want to awaken sleeping bears, (whether Vatican or fascist) needlessly. An encyclical on the 'social question', a question that, under the fascist government, just as later under the nazis, officially no longer existed (!) would provoke the wrath of Mussolini. This was naturally realized by both Pius XI and Fr. Ledochowski; they considered it adviseable not to stir him up unless that was unavoidable.

Formally, the whole responsibility lay with Fr. Ledochowski, though in fact he depended on me in technical questions. When I think back on it today, it seems to me that such a procedure, that allowed the whole bearing of an official document to be determined by a consultant—in order not to say by an editorial secretary—without establishing any counter check worth mentioning, seems frighteningly irresponsible.

As to how far the overtrustfulness went, consider the following illustration. The sections that I had sketched in rough Latin then ran through the hands of three Latinists, one after the other, who recast it in increasingly smoother Latin. With such linguistic retouching, there is inevitably the danger that the sense will be altered, or at least that fine points will be lost and essential distinctions distorted. This all the more, as the material was unfamiliar to the Latinists, and their whole concern was for elegance of language. No one except me was appointed to examine the final wording for correctness.

The German translation, naturally, came wholly from my pen. No one reviewed it; it went to press at the Vatican Press without anyone else having examined it. In contrast, I was given the job of checking translations prepared by others: French, English, Italian, and—despite my minimal knowledge of Spanish—even the Spanish translation. I carried out the task as well as I could and as the time allowed. In those days, all this did not impress me too much. What is distressing for me now is the thought that even today, apparently, if the occasion arose, they would proceed in a manner similar to that for QA. But currently, the world is more demanding.

Today, people expect that announcements of the highest Church authorities—on questions in which the profane sciences also have a voice—be on just as high a level as that of scientific statements of the most qualified international bodies. This presumes that an international group of recognized specialists in the science participate in the elaboration and assume the technical scientific responsibility for such new announcements.

Forty Years Later:
Reflections and Reminiscences

John F. Cronin, S.S.

This article originally appeared in *The American Ecclesiastical Review*, 1971.

When Pius XI issued his magisterial social encyclical on May 15, 1931, it was often called *Forty Years Later,* a title based on the opening words of the Latin original. Another forty years have passed, and I have been asked to reflect on the reactions of American Catholics to this historic document. But this article will contain much more than reminiscences. It is impossible to savor the climate of the 1930's without adverting to the tremendous strides, both economic and theological, taken in the four-decade interval.

Pius XI wrote at a time when the world was suffering its most severe economic depression. The economy in the United States was literally on the brink of collapse. Within two years the President of the United States was to close down the nation's banking system, reorganize securities markets, and begin a six-year program of widespread social reform. This was the time of the sit-down strikes, the Wagner Act, and the rise of industrial unionism. During these years millions of Americans tuned in each Sunday on Father Charles Coughlin whose magic voice combined a plea for social justice with monetary theories reminiscent of William Jennings Bryan's "Cross of Gold" speech.

The encyclical itself was printed in full by *The New York Times,* an unusual event in a nation which but a few years before witnessed anti-Catholic sentiment in a Presidential campaign. Pamphlet versions were quickly brought out. Later the NCWC was to sponsor a more accurate translation based on the original Latin rather than the Italian version. Study groups were organized around the country, encyclical courses were offered in colleges and even high schools, and the Catholic social action movement began to flower. In 1940, the Catholic bishops of the United States issued a long document, mainly authored by Bishop Alter (later to become Archbishop of Cincinnati), explaining the encyclical to the American Catholic public.

To one American priest the encyclical was a personal vindication. Monsignor John A. Ryan was then Professor of Moral Theology at Catholic University and Director of the Social Action Department, NCWC. His best-known book at that time was entitled *Distributive Justice*. But in 1905 he had written a doctorate dissertation published the following year as *A Living Wage*. Ryan was a controversial figure, considered radical because of his espousal of labor unionism and his claim that a family living wage was a moral imperative binding upon the conscience of the employer. Ryan indeed insisted that such a wage had the first call on business income, prior to profits, interest, and rent charges.

After the publication of Leo XIII's encyclical in 1891, *On the Condition of Workers*, theologians had debated about the concept of a living wage. Many defined it as a claim by the worker alone for a wage adequate to his basic needs. Others, Ryan included, insisted that the family be encompassed in this moral demand. The debate continued until 1931, when Pius XI defined a living wage in terms of the needs of a worker and his family.

I had the good fortune to be studying under Ryan at the time and can remember his quiet satisfaction resulting from papal support for his position. Ryan went further and interpreted encyclical passages as endorsing the view that wages were the first claim upon business income. It was easy to move from here into the stance that the employer who could not pay a family living wage should go out of business (this was discussed as a possibility in the encyclical). During this period the Social Action Department, NCWC, was sponsoring Catholic Industrial Conferences—tripartite local meetings of business, labor, and government officials discussing the implications and applications of the encyclical. Many Catholic businessmen left such sessions furious after being denounced as exploiters, unfaithful to the social teachings of their Church. Usually, however, they received consolation from their pastors, many of whom were economic conservatives, blissfully unaware of the social teachings of the magisterium.

By now many readers may have sensed a certain theological and economic naiveté in the Catholic social action movement of the thirties. This will be developed later, since it comes up as a key point in certain later parts of our narrative. At the present, it will be useful to note another major part of the encyclical which had a deep impact upon Catholic social thinking and social action. Pius XI advocated as one of the main remedies for the class struggle and social injustice the establishment of joint employer-worker councils to impose social controls upon industrial life. The pontiff made such industrial structures a demand of a natural moral law. It was considered the central point in Catholic social economic teaching in the United States.

This was understandable since Pius XI repeated his insistence six years later in an encyclical on Atheistic Communism. It was retained unchanged during the pontificate of Pius XII, who time and again made this the key to social reform. (John XXIII treated it briefly in 1961, and Vatican Council II did not mention it at all in 1965.) The industry-council idea was based on the solidarism of Heinrich Pesch, whose pupils, Oswald Von Nell-Breuning and Gustav Gundlach, were generally considered the redactors of the encyclical. Their names will reappear in this narrative.

A few years after the issuance of the encyclical, President Roosevelt asked Congress to pass a National Industrial Recovery Act, generally known as NRA. This law, until stricken down by the Supreme Court, permitted and even mandated price-fixing and other controls upon American industry. Ryan and his followers quickly seized upon the NRA as the embodiment of the social teaching of Pius XI. After the Court killed the law, Ryan called for a constitutional amendment which would give the federal government the power to establish industrial councils. The Industry Council Plan, the title adopted by the Catholic social movement, was supported by the Congress of Industrial Organizations (CIO) under Philip Murray.

Within the Church there was debate as to the exact form that these councils should take. Ryan, Monsignor Francis J. Haas (later Bishop of Grand Rapids), and Father Raymond McGowan (assistant to Ryan in the Social Action Department, NCWC) generally insisted that the Plan called for total social controls, including price-fixing. Some of us, however, doubted the economic wisdom of this interpretation of the encyclical and expressed this thought in our teachings and writings. Ryan, although a theologian by profession, had a competence in economics and apparently began to have second thoughts. At least, when this writer went to see him at his death-bed in 1944, Ryan told him to continue his independent ways. Later I wrote to Father Von Nell-Breuning about the controversy and received a reply that the Catholic Social Movement in the United States had totally misinterpreted a key encyclical thought. This was later explained at length in 1951 in a personal interview in Frankfurt.

A few years later this writer had the opportunity to visit, in Rome, Father Gustav Gundlach, by then the drafter of the socio-economic messages of Pius XII. Gundlach waxed vehement on the theological naiveté of American social Catholicism. He taxed us for interpreting encyclicals like biblical fundamentalists. He also said that we were foolish to be expecting new leads from Rome every year or so, instead of developing our own social analysis which could guide Rome in its thinking. Particularly he found it unbelievable that complex social documents would be studied at the high-school level.

There was more correspondence with Von Nell-Breuning. In 1957, an English Catholic economist, Professor Michael P. Fogarty, wrote a strong attack upon the present writer's treatment of the economics of a living wage. I discussed this by mail with the great German Jesuit and came to the conclusion that Fogarty was right. In my theological innocence, I had taken literally the statement of Pius XI that the living wage was due in strict justice and hence was an obligation of the individual employer. This led to some weird economic consequences which I tried to evade by casuistry. Fogarty insisted that the living wage was primarily a matter of social justice.

The methodology of this particular blunder was interesting. My approach was quite simple; to take the magisterium for moral teaching on social issues and then to use economic analysis to apply this to the American scene. Where the magisterium was ambiguous, as in details of the so-called Industry Council Plan, there was no difficulty in asserting economic common sense, even against the prevailing understanding in the Catholic social movement. But the encyclical seemed so clear in making the living wage a matter of strict justice that it was taken as a moral given, with the unfair demands upon individual employers shunted aside under the axiom that these were, in the circumstances, a moral impossibility.

Today, with a more sophisticated hermeneutic, I would have

avoided several methodological errors. One would be to avoid concentrating upon a single phrase, clear as it seemed, without considering the context of the encyclical as a whole, with its strong emphasis upon social justice. Another would have been to consider the entirety of the magisterium, since Pius XI in *Casti Conubii* took primarily a social-justice approach to the living wage. Finally, there should have been a warning that sound morals and sound economics should not clash, so some backtracking on premises was indicated.

Nell-Breuning, as I recollect our correspondence, handled the problem deftly. He said that the primary obligation for a living wage was in social justice. This means the reorganization of economic society so that a worker could in fact produce the economic equivalent of such a wage. Only at this stage would it be possible to assert that an employer, in justice, was obliged to pay such a stipend. Also social justice would confront the fact that some workers, either because of the depressed state of their industries or because of personal handicaps, could never produce enough to warrant such a wage. For them, social supplements would be necessary, such as a family allowance system or President Nixon's proposal for guaranteed income.

There is no point in elaborating this issue at length. It was used primarily to illustrate the difficulties faced by those who were advanced and liberal in their economic views, yet limited and fundamentalist in their ecclesiology. We knew quite a bit about the history of Catholic social thought, yet we failed to realize how the magisterium reached conclusions on social matters and how these were to be interpreted. It never occurred to us that these documents were both historically and culturally conditioned. We realized that the encyclical was clearly addressed to the major industrial nations of the world. But it did not occur to us how much of the mind-set was Italian and Germanic. Most of us never heard of form criticism. Probably we would not have dared to use it on documents of the magisterium, even had we known what it meant.

It would be misleading to concentrate, with twenty years hindsight, upon the mistakes we made in handling the encyclical of Pius XI. There were notable positive points which we seized upon and used to good effect. One of these was the concept of social justice, an innovation in terms of papal teaching and an idea almost equally new to theologians. The latter spoke of general or legal justice, to which they added distributive and commutative. The great John A. Ryan approached social problems primarily in terms of distributive justice (an approach rather sharply disavowed by Pius XII in 1950) and legal justice (social legislation). But social justice is a new concept that defies being categorized in the Thomistic concepts of justice.

Social justice almost has to be approached phenomenologically if we are to express adequately the ideas of Pius XI. It is broader than legal justice, since it can be practiced by individuals and groups other than organs of civil society. Father Bernard Dempsey called it contributive justice, pairing it with distributive. It involves the embedding of moral ideals in the laws, customs, institutions, and structures of society and this to promote the common good. There is a middle ground between justice as practiced by the individual and as practiced by the state. When a group of people voluntarily band together to bring about racial housing integration in their neighborhood, they practice social justice. When an individual, such as Morris Milgrim, devotes his life to promoting forms of integrated housing, he is a living example of social justice. Labor union contracts can embed the concept of social justice.

Pius XI also made quite clear that the Church's defense of private property against socialism and communism was not a condoning of exploitive abuses of property rights. Like Leo XIII he was vehement in condemning gross disparities in income and wealth. He went beyond Leo in making a sharp distinction between the individual and social aspects of ownership (an idea not foreign to Aquinas). It would not be difficult currently to use this idea as a theological basis for our concerns over ecology.

Encyclical concern for labor's right to organize preceded by a few years an historic organizing campaign by the Congress of Industrial Organizations. This impelled a number of the clergy, later called "labor priests," to campaign actively for union recognition. Since the Catholic Church in the United States has always been close to the worker and to the poor, this aspect of the encyclical received rather wide support. Even the more conservative clergy, not temperamentally attuned to addressing union groups, at least permitted Church halls to be used for organizing meetings.

In this area also our theological innocence asserted itself. Because the pope called for Christian unions, or at least parallel Christian organizations, we had an Association of Christian Trade Unionists and a proliferation of Church-run labor schools. There labor history, labor law and parliamentary procedure were taught side-by-side with the inevitable encyclical course. Such schools eventually were dropped when we realized that papal warnings were based mainly upon historical and cultural conditions proper to certain Latin nations of Europe. Rome itself quietly dropped the idea under John XXIII.

Another phenomenon which reveals something about the Church in America was the disparate reception given to three major encyclicals of Pius XI. These dealt with Christian marriage (1930), social order (1931), and atheistic communism (1937). The first gave occasion for many sermons and speeches on birth control. The third reinforced an already strong American Catholic position against communism. The second alone failed to generate any wide and deep reaction, either favorable or unfavorable, among American Catholics. True the bishops funded the Social Action Department, NCWC, staffed by Ryan, McGowan, Miss Bresette, Miss Garrity, and Miss Schaefer. But the whole question was considered as something for specialists only (as was race relations until 1958 or perhaps 1962). The Department itself was heavily oriented toward labor organization and social legislation, although it did have sections on social education, race relations, and peace (headed by the ladies named above).

Why this disparity in reaction? So far as birth control was concerned this appeared at the time a relatively simple, clear-cut moral issue. The magisterium had spoken and good Catholics would obey, no matter what the cost in terms of marital suffering. Communism likewise appeared as an unmitigated evil, aiming at stamping out freedom, religion, morality and other equally sacred human values. By contrast, such ideas as industry councils and a living wage brought in complex economic issues far beyond the competence of the average prelate or priest.

Was there also an element of selective disobedience? Pius XI in his 1937 encyclical complained about pressures in certain countries against the dissemination of the 1931 document. It would not be surprising that social conservatism here was a factor in the rather specialized reception of the encyclical on social order. There is always a temptation towards selective obedience, endorsing authority when it conforms to our views and ignoring it when our views are opposed.

But this point should not be labored too much. The strong focusing in on race relations by the Roman Catholic bishops and clergy, beginning in 1958, shows our willingness to face complex moral issues, once they are properly presented. Likewise our growth in areas connected with war and peace has been phenomenal in recent years. Before both areas were considered to be highly specialized apostolates, reserved for the few. But the right charismatic leader (or the appropriate historical circumstances) arrived, and suddenly the whole Church in the United States made difficult decisions of conscience.

Interest in the encyclical and in social action began waning in the United States during the 1950's. The rather sustained surge in economic growth after World War II and the Korean War left many of us with the illusion that our major problems were solved. When the issue of poverty in an affluent society surfaced in the 1960's, thanks to Michael Harrington and other writers, the nation was surprised. Although the primary focus of social action at the time was upon racial discrimination, there was enough concern about poverty to launch President Johnson's war on poverty in 1964. Today the economic aspect of racial discrimination is more and more stressed.

About 1966, there developed a sudden and dramatic turning away from the traditional methods of Catholic social teaching and social action. Encyclical courses were dropped from colleges and seminaries. Even updated books based on the social magisterium ceased to sell. This trend was so evident by 1968, that the Catholic Economic Association devoted a session to the problem at its annual meeting. A recent article in *The Critic* noted the demise of the older forms of social action.

Today the tendency is to learn by doing and not by reading. Involved clergy and religious go to Selma or even go to jail for acts of civil disobedience. Values are sought directly from the Scriptures, not through the mediation of the magisterium. Prediction is hazardous, but it seems that the golden era of Catholic social thought, beginning in 1891, has ended by 1971. There is a loss here. For all its limitations, it was a noble example of truly Christian concern for the wretched of the earth.

Pope John XXIII—
A New Direction?

Donal Dorr

This article was originally published in *Option for the Poor: A Hundred Years of Vatican Social Teaching*, 1983.

It is generally agreed that Pope John made a major contribution to the social teaching of the Catholic Church. My purpose in this chapter is to examine the overall effect of his stance on social questions, rather than considering the details of what he had to say about such matters as private property or international aid. This should help one to see whether, or in what sense, he gave a new direction to Catholic social teaching. There are two sections in the chapter. In the first section I hope to show that in one sense his position was by no means a radical one, nor did it represent any major departure from the direction set by earlier popes, especially by Pius XII. In the second section I shall suggest that, despite what has just been said, Pope John had, in another sense, a major role to play in turning the Catholic Church in quite a different direction on social issues.

SECTION ONE:
A SUPPORTER OF THE STATUS QUO?

There was an extraordinary freshness about Pope John XXIII, both in his manner and in his two major encyclicals on social issues—*Mater et Magistra*[1] and *Pacem in Terris*.[2] Those who like to categorise every-body as either a liberal or a conservative have little difficulty in seeing 'good Pope John' as a liberal, in sharp contrast to his predecessor. This is of course an over-simplification but as a journalistic generalisation it contains a good deal of truth, especially in so far as it refers to the *style* of the pope; for it is in his teaching that one can find much more continuity with Pius XII. The trouble with these labels is not so much their inaccuracy as the assumption that between them they are exhaustive. In fact, however, there is room for at least one other label—'the radical'— which cannot be reduced to either 'liberal' or 'conservative'. The word 'radical' has been given a remarkably wide variety of meanings in history;[3] but as used here it refers to the readiness to work for a fundamental change in the structures of society. The radical may be liberal on some issues, conservative on others; but in many cases the radical has an entirely different outlook, one which shows up just how much the liberal and the conservative have in common.

On social issues Pope John was *not* a radical. In regard to the fundamental re-structuring of society his approach was not very different from that of Pius XII; and in some ways Pius XI was more radical than either of them. The similarities and the differences between Pius XII and John XXIII can be found in a significant passage near the end of *Pacem in Terris,* written shortly before John died:

> There are, indeed, generous souls who . . . burn with desire to put everything right and are carried away by such an ungovernable zeal that their reform becomes a sort of revolution.
>
> To such people we would suggest that it is in the nature of things for growth to be gradual and that therefore in human institutions no improvement can be looked for which does not proceed step by step and from within. The point was well put by Our predecessor Pius XII: 'Prosperity and justice lie not in completely overthrowing the old order but in well planned progress. Uncontrolled passionate zeal always destroys everything and builds nothing. . .'[4]

Pope John's remarks lack the acerbity of his predecessor's. He shows understanding and sympathy for the 'generous souls' who are not satisfied with a step-by-step reform. But, despite this, he in fact reaffirms the gradualist approach of Pius XII. This is no mere verbal acceptance made in the interests of assuring a kind of doctrinal continuity. Pope John really believed that the necessary improvements could come 'step by step and from within', without any radical disruption of the system. He was an optimist.[5]

Optimism about the World

This optimism of John XXIII has to be teased out, so as to disentangle various elements in it. First of all it represents a new theology of the world. It would perhaps be more accurate to speak of a new spirituality of commitment to the world, a spirituality that contains the seed of a new theology. During the Second Vatican Council this seed sprouted very rapidly indeed. The new spirituality can be detected mostly as a difference of tone; to document it, one would have to note what John omits more than what he says. What comes through is the fact that he is not afraid that commitment to the world and its values will cause people to neglect the highest spiritual values. One significant point in *Mater et Magistra* is the way in which the pope speaks about human work[6] and especially about agricultural work.[7] Two years later, in *Pacem in Terris*, the new approach is rather more explicit, especially in the pope's call for a 'synthesis' between scientific and spiritual values,[8] an 'interior unity' between religious faith and action in the temporal sphere.[9]

One important element in Pope John's conception of the world is his understanding of how people work together for the common good and how this process is to be facilitated by the civil authorities. On this point there is a clear doctrinal continuity between what he says and the teaching of Leo XIII; but nevertheless there is a difference of tone which has important practical implications. Like his predecessors, John XXIII insists that human authority is derived from God. But, significantly, he immediately adds a text from St John Chrysostom which shows that it is not that a particular ruler is appointed by God but rather that the authority exercised is from God.[10] So already in this first paragraph of his teaching on the question, Pope John is distinguishing between authority and the office-holder. In the next paragraph he insists that human authorities are subject to a higher authority.[11] He goes on to say that civil authorities can impose an obligation in conscience only in so far as their authority is intrinsically linked to the authority of God.[12] If civil authorities make demands contrary to the moral order, or fail to acknowledge human rights, their authority no longer exists and so the citizen is not bound to obey.[13] The whole purpose of political authority is the promotion of the common good.[14] The denial by a government of the right of the individual to an area of personal freedom is branded by Pope John as 'a radical inversion of the order of human society'.[15] These statements indicate that he is emphasising a very different aspect of authority from that stressed by Leo XIII. The latter was afraid of anarchism so he put the emphasis on the right of human authorities to make demands on citizens with the authority of God himself; only reluctantly and minimally did he take note of the cases where human authorities forfeited the right to unquestioned obedience. John XXIII, like Pius XII, was more concerned lest individual freedom be stifled by authoritarian rulers or bureaucracies. So he paid more attention to the duty of authorities to fulfil their proper role, the service of the common good; human authority ceases to be real authority when it fails in this regard. Quite clearly this approach leaves much greater scope for the individual to assess whether those in power are in fact exercising a lawful authority; and there is a wider gap where dissent may enter. Pope John is not of course encouraging political dissent, still less any kind of organised resistance. But evidently his conception of human society is that of a community of persons who voluntarily submit to civil authority in order to attain the common good. He does not hold that democracy is the only valid form of government[16] but the values he promotes are those to which democracy at its best is committed and which it should embody.

The general optimism of Pope John about the world finds expression in his teaching about political organisation and authority. He believes people can cooperate successfully not only at the local and national levels but also at the international level.[17] The whole presupposition of his two great social encyclicals was that people needed only to be encouraged and animated to cooperate more fruitfully. He presumes not merely the ability to cooperate but the fundamental willingness of people and nations to cooperate even at the cost of personal, sectional, or national sacrifice. This presupposition might easily be overlooked. But it is important to note it. For it explains why John XXIII addressed himself mainly to the question, *what* improvements are needed in economic, social, and political affairs in order that people may live with greater human dignity. He did not concentrate on another question which may be equally or more important: *how* can these changes be brought about, especially where many of those who hold power are reluctant to accept reforms that would curb their power?

Optimism about the Modern World

John XXIII was not just optimistic about the world in general. His optimism and hopefulness were directed specifically to the *modern* world—meaning the kind of society that had emerged in the Western world as a result of rapid economic growth. Here his tone is notably different from that of Pius XII. He speaks with ringing hope and challenge of this age of the atom and of the conquest of space as 'an era in which the human family has already entered on its new advance toward limitless horizons'.[18] He asks whether the modern developments in social relationships will entangle people in a maze of restrictions so that human freedom and responsibility will be eliminated; and his answer is a firm 'no'.[19] The 'modernisation' of society can, he believes, have more advantages than disadvantages, if it is properly controlled and directed.[20]

In a moving passage in *Mater et Magistra* the pope expresses his distress about the plight of poverty-stricken workers of many lands and whole continents. He adds that one of the reasons for this poverty is the fact that these areas are still underdeveloped in terms of modern industrial techniques.[21] In a later paragraph he says that usually an underdeveloped or primitive state of economic development is the fundamental or enduring cause of poverty and hunger.[22] Clearly he has no serious doubts about the need for 'modernisation' and 'development' as the way in which the world must make progress. He is of course aware that this kind of 'development' can create social problems[23] and even economic difficulties.[24] He also realises that the modern situation offers opportunities for a new kind of elitism. So he warns against abuses of power by the new class of managers of large-scale enterprises—and he makes the important point that such abuses can occur both in private business and in public bodies.[25] Furthermore he notes two causes of poverty which are particularly important in this modern world—the arms race[26] and the squandering of money by governments on prestige projects.[27] But all of this he would see as an argument for control and balance, not a reason for questioning the whole direction of modern 'development'.

Optimism about Capitalism

We have seen that Pope John's optimism is not just about the world but about the modern world, including the processes of 'modernisation' and 'development'. Now it must be added that the optimism extends even further—to the capitalist system which is most conspicuously associated with 'modernisation'. (Of course Communist countries are also dedicated to economic development; but the West, including the Vatican, has tended to assume that the link between capitalism and 'development' is more natural and more successful.)[28] There are indications that Pope John took a rather optimistic view of what might be expected from capitalist society in the future. Not that he ignored its deficiencies and abuses, or repudiated the condemnations of capitalism by Leo XIII and Pius XI. But he seemed to believe that before too long and without too much trouble the system could be effectively humanised.

One of the more significant and controversial paragraphs in *Pacem in Terris* draws a distinction between 'false philosophical theories' and the 'historical movements' which are inspired by these theories.[29] It is commonly and correctly assumed that Pope John was referring here primarily to those left-wing movements which, historically at least, draw their inspiration from Marx.[30] But the pope would no doubt also apply the distinction to capitalism: the capitalist ideology remains incompatible with Catholic social teaching; but capitalist society in its actual historical development can be viewed rather more optimistically by Pope John.

Already in his 1959 encyclical *Ad Petri Cathedram* the pope had remarked that class distinctions were less pronounced than before.[31] He went on to say: 'Anyone who is diligent and capable has the opportunity to rise to higher levels of society.'[32] This statement shows the extent to which he accepted one aspect of the free enterprise ideology, namely, the assumption that it gives most people a reasonably equal chance of 'getting on', i.e. of moving upwards in society. The implication of this belief is that, by and large, the rich and powerful have 'earned' their privileged place in society, while the weak and the poor are in some sense responsible for their 'failure'. Needless to say, the pope did not accept this implication. But there are indications that he did not question the free enterprise ideology very thoroughly.

One such indication is to be found in an important paragraph of *Mater et Magistra* where Pope John insists on the need for a wider distribution of property of various kinds.[33] Like his predecessors, John XXIII was aware of the tendency of capitalism to concentrate wealth in the hands of the few. What is significant from our present point of view is that the pope maintains that now is a particularly suitable time for countries to adjust their social and economic structures so as to facilitate a wider distribution of ownership. Why *now*? Because, says Pope John, it is a time when an increasing number of countries are experiencing rapid economic development. This statement suggests that John accepted the common assumption that rapid economic growth offers the easiest way to overcome the problem of the unequal distribution of wealth. No wonder; for, on the face of it, this approach seems almost self-evidently correct. Instead of having to face the difficult task of taking wealth from the rich to re-distribute it to the poor, why not create sufficient *new* wealth to enable the poor to become reasonably well-off? But despite its apparent obviousness this line of thinking can in practice play a part in bringing about the very opposite to what it aims at. This is what in fact has happened in large parts of the world. So it will be useful to look more closely at the process.

How best can rapid economic growth be promoted in a society which follows the 'free enterprise' approach? Both the theorists and the real-life capitalists claim that the only effective way is to allow the entrepreneurs and investors an adequate return for their contribution. What it means in practice is that this group must be allowed a major share of the new wealth in the form of profits and inducements. The argument is that the 'national cake' must first be enlarged even at the cost of some delay in redistributing the shares of the 'cake'. So a lower priority is given to equitable distribution of wealth than to creation of wealth. Once that pattern is established it becomes exceptionally difficult to change it. There never comes a time which seems right for a more fair distribution. Various 'compelling' objections disguise the fact that those with wealth have the power to retain it. Their power is exercised both politically and through the moulding of opinion in society. Consequently the best hope left to the poorer and less powerful people is that growth will be so great that they will become better off in absolute terms, even though the gap between them and the rich continues to widen. This is what happened in many Western countries during the 1950s and 1960s. But in a world of limited resources it is increasingly unrealistic to expect that *all* countries can attain such a degree of growth.

The belief that the best way to solve social problems is to speed up economic growth is not confined to Western countries. Most, but not quite all, Third World countries are convinced that their best hope of eliminating poverty lies in rapid growth. And Communist nations also put great emphasis on rapid growth; indeed their leaders have at times imposed almost intolerable sacrifices on the people in order to achieve 'growth'. But there is an important difference between socialist and capitalist societies on this question. In a centrally planned economy increased growth and equitable distribution are not incompatible goals. When failures occur they are mostly due to authoritarianism, or bureaucracy, or to a pandering to some power elite. In a capitalist society, however, the relationship between growth and equitable distribution is complex and particularly interesting:

—First, capitalism is committed to growth not merely for practical reasons but also ideologically. At a practical level an ever-increasing demand seems to be necessary if the whole system is not to collapse. Hence the need for an ideology of growth; this is promoted in various ways, notably by the advertising industry. The belief is fostered that there is no foreseeable limit either to human needs or to the ability of a free enterprise system to meet these ever-expanding 'needs'.

—Secondly, the growth that actually takes place tends, as we have seen, to concentrate wealth in the hands of a minority rather than leading to a more equitable distribution.

—But, thirdly, another part of the ideology of capitalism masks this lack of equity. It promotes an image of free enterprise where all have a fair opportunity to use their talents profitably. Hard work and initiative are correlated with success and prosperity. The implication is that poor distribution of wealth is to be explained more in terms of the laziness and lack of ability of some rather than any lack of opportunity imposed by the system.[34] Furthermore, the idea is fostered that the new wealth will soon 'trickle down' from the richer to the poorer sectors of society. These beliefs are illusions which protect the interests of a particular group by hiding the truth.

Needless to say, Pope John did not set out to promote such misleading ideas. But they must have had some effect on him. This is shown by his statement (quoted above) that anybody who is diligent and careful can rise to higher levels in society. The fact that the pope uncritically accepted this belief suggests that there was a certain blind spot in his outlook. This blind spot becomes more evident when one adverts to the gap between the end he was hoping for and the means he proposed to achieve it. The end-result he wanted was a wider distribution of property.[35] The means by which he hoped this would come about was a gradual reform of the existing structures and the introduction of controls designed to reverse the tendency of capitalism to concentrate wealth in the hands of a few. But Pope John seems to have been unduly optimistic in thinking that this could be brought about fairly easily. Perhaps he was unrealistic in seeing the current time of rapid growth as the best occasion for a relatively painless reversal of this 'normal' pattern. Tampering with the system is never easy—and, ironically, it may be especially difficult when the system is working smoothly as it was at the time *Mater et Magistra* was written.

But surely the pope was correct when he supported his case by noting the progress towards wider ownership made in some economically developed countries?[36] His facts were correct but it is doubtful whether they should be used as the basis for a generalisation. Undoubtedly the years between 1945 and 1961 saw a considerable growth in prosperity for most workers in Western countries. But this was part of a wider reality—the increased wealth of Western nations as a whole vis-à-vis the Third World. This imbalance was in turn related to the extravagant use by industrialised countries of energy and raw materials, much of which came from poorer countries at a very cheap price. So whatever improvement occurred within the Western countries must be seen in the context of an increasingly lop-sided distribution of wealth on the international (or intercontinental) level.

Furthermore, there is a certain ambiguity in the pope's call, at this point in the encyclical, for a wider distribution of ownership of property. What exactly is the end-result that he is looking for here? Is he asking that whatever wealth is available should be distributed more equally? Or is he merely asking that more people (especially those who are poor) should become owners of property? This second position would be compatible with a widening of the gap between rich and poor. It is quite likely that John XXIII did not advert to this possibility. It would seem that he was simply following in the footsteps of Leo XIII by insisting on the importance of more people becoming owners of property (the first position)—and tacitly assuming that this would involve a narrowing of the gap between rich and poor (the second position). But the history of Western countries since World War II shows that this assumption is not justified. There is reason to believe that the gap between the richer and the poorer sectors of Western society has widened during the very period when more and more ordinary workers were becoming owners of the kind of property mentioned by the pope (e.g. a house and garden). Is this the situation that the pope is setting up as a model for the rest of the world? The answer should be, 'no', because in two earlier paragraphs of the encyclical he had insisted very strongly on the central importance of equitable distribution of wealth.[37] Following Pius XII, he even went so far as to say: 'the economic prosperity of any people is to be measured less by the total *amount* of goods and riches they own than by the extent to which these are *distributed* according to the norms of justice.'[38]

One must conclude that, in terms of his own principles, Pope John was not entitled to present as a 'success story' those 'nations with developed social and economic systems' where ownership has become more widespread.[39] These Western countries can certainly be cited as proof that in certain circumstances rapid economic growth under a free enterprise system is compatible with, and perhaps even gives rise to, wider ownership of possessions. But they should not be cited as proof that it is possible in practice to reverse the inherent tendency of capitalism towards an inequitable distribution of wealth and power. This is not to say that John XXIII was wrong when he said that private ownership had increased in some 'developed' countries. But what he said could leave one with a wrong impression, namely, that the present free enterprise system of the Western world requires only gradual and moderate reform in order to become a system that would bring social justice on a world scale.

The Welfare State

This issue of whether Western countries serve as a model for a humanised version of capitalism is vitally important. So it is appropriate to say something here about the Welfare State approach adopted in several Western European countries in the years after World War II. It is true that the expanding social services that were offered could scarcely have been provided without the rapid economic growth of those years. (And as growth has slowed down in recent years the social services have come under strain partly through shortage of funds and partly for ideological reasons.) But it would appear that the determination to cope with poverty through national social welfare programmes came *prior* to most of the economic growth. It is arguable that the fundamental change in structures and attitudes involved in the Welfare State owes more to the chaos at the end of the war than to the success of a revived capitalism. Workers were determined never again to face the deprivations of the depression years; and the breaking of the moulds that came during and after the war offered the chance to give political expression to this determination. The point is that basic changes in social structures are more likely to be associated with the *failure* than with the 'success' of a growth-oriented free enterprise model of society. This suggests that it is illusory to expect raw capitalism to develop naturally, organically, and painlessly into a system characterised by equitable distribution of wealth and effective care for the weaker sectors of society.

It is well to note also the limited aims of the Welfare State approach. It did not set out overtly to bridge the gap in *ownership* between rich and poor by wholesale nationalisation or redistribution of capital goods; in other words it is not to be equated with a full programme of socialism. Rather it presupposed the continuance of a free enterprise economy with its inherent tendency towards imbalance and concentration of wealth. It sought to cope with the resultant poverty and deprivation i.e. with the effects rather than the causes. In some European countries the Welfare State approach was combined with a limited type of socialism which set out to redistribute ownership through the imposition of very high levels of taxation on income and profits. But in other countries it was not linked to any serious effort to redistribute ownership. So the Welfare State approach is not necessarily socialistic. In fact its comparative success was due largely to the fact that it was supported also by people who were opposed to socialism. Not that it was universally accepted; there were many champions of a rugged free enterprise philosophy who fought against any build-up of a comprehensive programme of state welfare. But, faced with the ideological struggle between left and right, the ma-

jority of voters in Western Europe settled for the Welfare State as a kind
of compromise—a way of combining social compassion with the efficiency and respect for initiative of the free enterprise system. The Welfare State was seen by many as a way of giving 'a human face' to a
society built on a capitalist economy.

Twenty years ago this approach seemed to be working well. It
seemed to offer a direction which could be taken further in the future,
not merely in Europe but in the wider world. So the scenario for the future envisaged by many concerned people, including, most probably,
Pope John and at least some of the drafters of *Mater et Magistra,* would
have been along the following lines: a healthy ever-expanding economy,
primarily free enterprise in character but including some degree of State
capitalism, combined with expanding public welfare programmes (supplemented by the welfare programmes of voluntary agencies, especially
the Churches) to mitigate the deficiencies and cope with the casualties
of such an economic system. The intervening years have made this scenario increasingly problematical. First, an indefinite period of rapid economic growth can no longer be presumed: there are severe limits to the
amount of cheap energy and raw materials that are available to make this
possible; and furthermore the inherent problems of a capitalist order
(problems of prediction, credibility, cycles, protectionism, etc.) have
proved far more intractable than expected. Secondly, it is now more evident that the 'development' of the West depended on the availability of
cheap resources from the Third World so it cannot be seen as a model
which can be repeated all over the world. Thirdly, the Welfare State approach has itself run into serious difficulties in Western Europe: the expansion of the 'national cake' has slowed down but the demands of the
stronger groups in society have increased; the result is that there is less
left for the poorer segment of society, which in some Western countries
now comprises about a quarter of the population. Finally, government
efforts to stimulate the economy are costing the tax-payer a great deal;
the heavy tax burden offers a convenient opportunity for opponents of
State welfare to renew their ideological attack on the social services as
wasteful and as an encouragement to idleness and parasitism. And in
such an atmosphere it becomes quite unrealistic to hope that something
analogous to the Welfare State will emerge at the *international* level,
with the rich nations providing adequate help for the poor ones.

The conclusion that emerges from what has been said is that Pope John, like many of his contemporaries, including notable economists and social scientists, showed a rather uncritical optimism in relation to Western-style democratic capitalist society. Most of the scholars and religious leaders of more recent times (including Pope John Paul II) would be far more cautious; they would be slow to assume that national and international social justice can come about through a gradual and relatively painless reform of the capitalist order of society.[40]

Option for the Poor?

Pope John's social encyclicals played a major part in bringing the Catholic Church into a more open relationship with modern society. But was this at the cost of an acceptance of the Western *status quo,* subject only to gradual and relatively minor reforms? Did his openness to existing Western society imply a playing down of the Church's challenge to the world? More specifically, did it involve a failure to make an effective option for the poor? These questions call for a carefully nuanced response.

The first thing to note is that Pope John himself clearly did not see himself as having to choose between on the one hand an option for the poor and on the other hand an acceptance of capitalist society. He believed that the latter could be tempered and adapted in such a way as to ensure that the poor really were looked after. His encyclicals appeared at a time when the Western economic model seemed to be working well and seemed to be amenable to the kind of reforms he was looking for. It was not a time when many Church leaders or scholars saw the issue in terms of a clash between capitalism and social justice. To present the issue in terms of such a stark choice is to see it more as it was seen thirty years earlier (at the time of Pius XI's *Quadragesimo Anno*) or as it is seen by a significant number of Church leaders today, twenty-two years after the appearance of *Mater et Magistra.*

Another important point to note is the fact that John XXIII consistently adopted the 'spoonful of honey' approach, avoiding condemnations as far as possible, praising what he could, and inviting people to make improvements. The fact that he is less critical than his predecessors in matters of social injustice is no indication that he had abandoned their concern about the exploitation of the poor. Nor does it prove that he had become an enthusiastic convert to the capitalist system. There seems to be a considerable degree of over-statement in the conclusion of the scholar Camp that Pope John saw capitalism 'as a positive good'.[41]

Nevertheless, John XXIII differed from the popes who went before him in so far as he seems to have approved of the general direction in which the world was moving. Camp is broadly correct in judging that Pope John 'did not want a change of institutions. Rather, he frankly admired what was already being done and wished an expansion of its benefits to more people.'[42] The pope did, however, want *some* changes. He thought gradual reforms could make the world a more just and humane community of people and peoples. But in proposing such gradual reform he was at the same time implicitly giving a considerable measure of endorsement to the existing free enterprise system. From the point of view of their formal teaching the social encyclicals of John XXIII show no very radical departure from the tradition of social teaching of his predecessors. But there are subtle differences in tone and emphasis which give these encyclicals a different effect when seen as interventions by the pope at this particular time. Pope John did not demand a radical reconstruction of society such as Pius XI had proposed. It is significant that the summary of *Quadragesimo Anno* given in *Mater et Magistra* omits all reference to Pius XI's account of Italian corporatism.[43] It also preserves a careful vagueness in the way it uses such terms as 'vocational groups' and 'intermediate bodies'.[44] So, despite the continuity with the past from a 'doctrinal' point of view, the net effect of the social teaching of Pope John was rather different from that of Pius XI. It was to give a certain approval and legitimation to the Western economic approach, provided this is taken in conjunction with the democratic reformist and socially conscious currents of the thought of that period.

Whether John XXIII's position is considered to be an improvement on that of Pius XI depends of course on the stance of the person making the judgment. A fairly typical evaluation of *Mater et Magistra* is that which was given by John F. Cronin who was assistant director of the Social Action Department of the conference of U.S. bishops. He held that the encyclical was 'realistic, moderate, and progressive'.[45] Obviously he saw this as high praise. It is a useful exercise to 'translate' his words into more descriptive and neutral language:

—'Realistic' means that the encyclical does not call in question in any radical way the economic order existing in Western society and dominating most of the world.

—'Moderate' means that the reforms it calls for would not seriously disrupt this order either in their extent or by the speed with which they are to be introduced.

—'Progressive' means that the encyclical fits comfortably into the more 'enlightened' strand of Western thinking, sharing the values of the liberals—provided one has in mind not the hard economic liberalism of the nineteenth century but the socially conscious liberal thinking of more recent times. Understood in this way, Cronin's words can be applied not only to *Mater et Magistra* but to Pope John's social teaching taken as a whole.

In the light of the clarifications just given, it is now possible to offer a fairly brief answer to the question whether John XXIII failed to make an effective option for the poor. He was deeply concerned about the plight of different categories of poor people; and he proposed a variety of measures designed not merely to provide relief but to prevent imbalances in society.[46] Nevertheless he did not commit the Catholic Church to an option for the poor if one takes that in the very specific sense in which it is frequently used today—namely, a radical challenge to the capitalistic structures that prevail in Western countries and largely determine the international economic order. On the contrary, the effect of his interventions in social issues was to give a certain sanction and support to these structures, provided they are supplemented and restrained in ways that limit their harmful social effects.

SECTION TWO:
A NEW DIRECTION

It would be misleading and unjust to stop at this point in the evaluation of the effect of Pope John's encyclicals. For there is a sense in which his teaching made a major contribution towards putting the Church on the side of the poor. More accurately, one might say he removed from the rich and the powerful an exceptionally important weapon which they could use to maintain injustice in society. To explain how he did so it is necessary to look closely at his teaching about 'socialisation'.

Socialisation

Probably the most important single passage in *Mater et Magistra* is the following:

> One of the main features which seem to be characteristic of our time is undoubtedly an increase in the number of social relationships. Day by day people become more interdependent and this introduces into their lives various kinds of associations which are generally recognised in contractual or public law. . . . These developments in social life are both a sign and a cause of an increasing degree of State intervention in matters of considerable importance and risk since they have to do with the intimate life of the person.[47]

The first English translation of this passage followed the Italian version in using the word 'socialisation' where the Latin text speaks of an increase in social relationships.[48] But the more widely used English versions avoid this word very deliberately,[49] either for the purely linguistic reason that it is not used in the Latin text or on the grounds that its omission from the Latin was a significant correction of the original unofficial working text in Italian.[50] It was felt by some that to use the word 'socialisation' in the English translation might give the impression that Pope John had abandoned the papal tradition of being opposed to socialism. In fact some sectors of the media did interpret the encyclical as proposing some version of socialism. Consequently, Church spokes-persons were kept busy explaining that as used in the working text 'socialisation' did not really mean the introduction of socialism—and that it didn't even mean what Pius XII meant when he used the word. (For him it meant, mostly, nationalisation.)[51] They explained that the word was being used in a technical sense to describe a recent development in Western industrialised society. The main features of this development may be described as follows:

People are now more closely inserted in a web of relationships where the actions of each individual affect many others. This gives rise to the need for greater control. Many aspects of daily living which used to be seen as personal or family matters are now organised or at least regulated on a larger scale. So the individual and the family have to rely more on, and use the services of, large institutions. Some of these are, technically, private institutions—trade unions, for instance, or non-State insurance schemes. But many are new organs of the public authorities—from local councils up to national governments and even international agencies.

The originality of John XXIII lies not so much in his noting of this fact of modern life as in his response to it. He holds that it would be not merely pointless but positively wrong if the Christian were just to bemoan and resist this development, pining for the simple life of the past.[52] Of course the pope admits the dangers it poses—especially the risk of excessive interference with personal responsibilities[53] and an undue degree of bureaucratisation. In this he was taking account of the preoccupations of Pius XII. But Pope John evidently considers the positive aspects of the process to be more important: it promotes the personal welfare of individuals in many ways; and it can also enable people to live, work, and play more as a community.[54] So he believes that the process is not inherently destructive of humanity.[55] But on the other hand it is not to be seen as automatically beneficial either. In fact it is not a process whose outcome is pre-determined at all.[56] Everything depends on the people involved; it is they who are responsible for the direction it takes.[57]

So much for John XXIII's account of 'socialisation'. But what is so significant about his approach? In order to answer this question it is necessary first of all to look closely at the accident of history which makes of resistance to 'socialisation' a policy associated with 'traditional conservatism'. Twentieth-century conservatives in Europe and America see themselves as standing in defence of the *traditional* independence of the individual against the encroachments of society in the form of the State. But how traditional is it for the individual to have a high degree of independence from society? It is not a tradition that goes back very far. It finds its high point in America at about the time the United States came into existence; and the U.S. constitution enshrines and defends various rights of the individual. But the notion of the independence of the individual as a traditional value is largely a myth. In fact traditional societies tend to leave very little room for individual independence; most of a person's behaviour is prescribed and enforced by the community (though not by written laws and regulations of the modern type). So there is a certain irony in the fact that conservatism should be associated with rugged individualism. The more normal type of conservatism would be that which resists individualism in favour of socially determined behaviour.

So the important thing to note is that the 'socialisation' of which Pope John is speaking is a feature of modern Western society, to be understood in the light of *Western* history. It would appear that one of the early effects of Western modernisation and urbanisation was to weaken many traditional social relationships and the obligations attached to them. The result was greater independence for individuals. There was a period when the more fortunate and more ruthless of the new generation seemed to have the best of two worlds. On the one hand they had a high degree of freedom from social constraints, allowing them a wide scope for initiative (and at times for opportunism and even exploitation). On the other hand they could still rely on patterns of obedience, respect, and cooperation inherited from the past. The less fortunate people at the bottom of the social ladder had, correspondingly, the worst of two worlds. The decline in social restraints left them open to new forms of oppression. But their efforts to protect themselves were resisted by the rich who justified themselves by invoking a myth they had built around the values of untrammelled freedom and rugged individualism.

Whatever about the myth of independence for the individual, the reality was that before long there emerged an obvious need for new and different forms of social institutions and restraints. Society could no longer 'free-wheel' on the traditionally ingrained patterns of cooperation. There had to be new social systems to look after security, welfare, public health, education, economic development, etc. And as society became more concentrated in urban areas, less centred on small community units, these needs expanded. No wonder then that Pope John felt it was pointless and wrong to resist the expansion of such social institutions. Rather they should be intelligently planned and controlled. The aim should be to retain as much as possible of the values of personal freedom while protecting the common welfare. But neither was it any wonder that there should be strong resistance to the new restraints. Precisely because they are needed to prevent the exploitation of the weak by the strong, they are experienced by the powerful as unwarranted limits to their freedom. And one of the most powerful weapons used to resist these restraints is the invocation of the myths of the defence of the 'traditional values' of personal initiative and freedom, and old-fashioned rugged independence.

The Newness of Mater et Magistra

Against this background one can understand the position of John XXIII and the reaction to it. It is a carefully nuanced position. Pope John preserves a clear continuity with his predecessors in his teaching about the values that are to be preserved and the means of doing so. Like them he stresses the principle of subsidiarity.[58] Following them he insists on the importance of vocational groupings and similar intermediate organisations which are not organs of the State itself.[59] He maintains that intervention by government or other public authorities should be limited to those cases where it is really necessary.[60]

On the other hand, John XXIII differs from Pius XI and Pius XII in his judgment about where *in fact* such State intervention is required. It is here that the newness of *Mater et Magistra* becomes very evident. Retaining continuity with previous social teaching from a 'doctrinal' point of view, it is startlingly different in its net effect. For in fact it proposes a programme of action that might well have been borrowed from the manifesto of a moderate socialist political party! The real issue then is not whether the *word* 'socialisation' is the correct translation of the Latin text. Rather the issue is whether the pope is moving the Catholic Church away from its suspicion of such 'socialistic' notions as that of the Welfare State. When one provides a literal translation of the Latin text of the encyclical one loses not only the word 'socialisation' but also its overtones; and these overtones might have conveyed more accurately what Pope John was referring to. Nobody is likely to object to 'an increase in social relationships'. But the problems begin when one starts to spell out the implications. So it is opportune to look at some of these implications as envisaged in the encyclical.

Pope John develops and extends the teaching of Pius XI,[61] and by-passes the reservations of Pius XII,[62] when he says that in some circumstances employees may be entitled to a share in the companies where they work[63] and to a say in management both at the level of the individual firm[64] and in determining policy at various levels, even on a national scale.[65] Again, the State must exercise strict control over managers/directors of large businesses.[66] An increased amount of State ownership is justified by the needs of the common good in the modern situation.[67] It must also be recognised, says the pope, that in fact the State and public authorities have taken on a greatly expanded role in coping with social problems.[68] Indeed Pope John proposes just such a role for them in dealing with the special difficulties of those working in agriculture[69]—and he goes into considerable detail in regard to tax assessment,[70] credit facilities,[71] insurance,[72] social security,[73] price support[74] and price regulation,[75] and even the directing of industry into rural areas.[76] All this is necessary because in modern Western life human interdependence is possible only by going beyond one-to-one relationships and those of the small community; life is lived on a scale that requires the massive apparatus of the State to be actively involved in directing and controlling the economic and social life of the people. Even when a nation keeps this State involvement as low as possible by respecting the principle of subsidiarity (as Pope John asks), still the common good nowadays requires far more State 'interference' than was needed in the past. *Mater et Magistra* gives a mandate for this extra involvement by the State; and the result begins to look like an encouragement to 'socialisation' in the popular sense of the word.

Now one can see why some right-wing American Catholics reacted to the encyclical by saying '*Mater si, Magistra no*'. Their opposition is a confirmation of the fact that there really is a distinct change of emphasis in Pope John's social teaching—even when one makes allowance on the one hand for exaggerations of its socialising tendency and on the other hand for its considerable degree of continuity with the teaching of Pius XII. One is hardly likely to find socially conservative Catholics objecting to the teaching of Pius XII—even though there are echoes of that teaching in even the most 'advanced' parts of *Mater et Magistra*.[77] Probably the most important effect of the encyclical, seen as an intervention in the continuing debate about social issues, was that it began the process of breaking the long alliance between Roman Catholicism and socially conservative forces.

With the issuing of Pope John's encyclical in 1961 it began to seem credible, for the first time in the modern era, that Catholicism might have more in common with 'the left' than with 'the right'. There is a certain irony in the fact that *Mater et Magistra* should in this sense be more radical than even *Quadragesimo Anno*. For, as pointed out above, Pope John was no radical. He was looking for moderate and gradual reforms in the capitalist order, while Pius XI was asking for a much more fundamental restructuring of society. But the corporatist ideals of Pius XI were somewhat right-wing, at least in their background and overtones: some strands of corporatism were drawn from a conservative nostalgia for the guilds of the past; others were drawn from aspects of the fascist model of society. Corporatism was strongly opposed to socialism; and Pius XI rejected even a mitigated form of socialism. Pope John, on the other hand, while continuing to insist on the importance of private initiative,[78] private property,[79] and intermediate non-State vocational groupings,[80] put forward an ensemble of practical proposals that was far more congenial to 'the left' than to 'the right'. He seems to have realised that the Church's traditional defence of private initiative and private property had come to be used in an ideological way; and he was determined to put an end to this.

A whole body of social teaching had evolved as a vindication of the dignity of the individual against a totalitarian type of collectivism or socialism. But this teaching had come to be seen as a support for a rather individualistic type of free enterprise, and for the private interests of individuals or groups over against the public interest. It is important to see how this had come about. There was no time at which the Church's social teaching could seriously be accused of giving sanction to capitalism in the form of ruthless big business. But capitalism has another face, a more attractive one. It is what might be called 'frontier free enterprise', typified in the small-town entrepreneurs who use local resources and their own initiative and skill to meet local needs and provide employment in the area. Different popes wanted to encourage this kind of initiative and to protect it against bureaucracy. And their defence of the latter could be used as giving a measure of support to capitalism in all its forms.

Public opinion in Western countries—and especially in the

U.S.A.—is subject to the same confusion. The idealised image of free enterprise is used to give respectability to capitalism in its less acceptable forms. Frequently this takes place unconsciously, simply because people have not had the opportunity or education to make the necessary distinctions. But it is not at all uncommon to have a deliberate manipulation, a campaign to justify capitalism in its more unacceptable forms through a glamorisation of the ideal of free enterprise. One feature of this campaign is the reduction of all the various possible options to just two. People are presented with a stark choice between two alternatives: on the one hand is free enterprise with its respect for personal initiative and responsibility; on the other is a massively bureaucratic State socialism which is centralised, inflexible, and inefficient. (The books and television programmes of Milton Friedman provide examples of this kind of over-simplification.)

This background helps one to understand what is meant by the claim that the Church's social teaching had come to be used in an ideological way to defend sectional interests. In most cases this was not the result of some sinister plot but an unfortunate accident of history. In the political sphere Catholics were among the strongest opponents of socialism. So it is quite understandable that a lot of emphasis was put on those parts of papal teaching most strongly opposed to socialist tendencies. Meanwhile papal reservations about capitalism were rather under-played—except for the relatively short period when the corporatist proposals of *Quadragesimo Anno* were taken seriously as providing a workable alternative model of society.

In the social sphere there was a similar process. As 'modern' life patterns came more and more to replace the traditional ones there was an ever-increasing loss of the former support-systems for the individual and the family. The anonymity of modern urban-style living did not lend itself easily to the development of new *voluntary* support systems to replace the extended family and the local community. So there was a great need for the State or other public authorities to provide the individual and the family with supports in social, cultural, and economic affairs. Without a great increase in public welfare programmes of all kinds—and the taxes to pay for them—only the very wealthy could live a dignified human life in this 'modern' world which had emerged. But Catholic social teaching had not taken sufficient account of this new situation. Church authorities tended to be opposed to socialised health care programmes. They were also opposed to giving the State a monopoly in the area of education and culture. Traditional papal teaching was that the State should not intrude itself unduly into the economic sphere; therefore nationalisation of industry or of the economic services such as banking should never go beyond what was proved to be strictly necessary.

The effect of all this was that almost by accident the Church came to be allied with certain sectional interests. It seemed to be more concerned with the defence of the rights of private groups than with the public interest and especially the needs of the poorer classes of society. That was not its intention nor its ideal. The principles proposed in the Church's social teaching were put forward as a defence of people against bureaucracy and totalitarianism. But the way in which they were being applied in practice was now causing the Church to be allied to the opponents of welfare programmes badly needed by the poor. Similarly, the Church's defence of private property—intended to protect the dignity of the person—was now invoked to justify resistance to land reform. Even the payment of the heavy taxes needed to support social welfare programmes for the poor could be opposed on the grounds that they were an undue interference in private ownership and a step towards socialism.

The link between sectional interests and Catholic social teaching was further strengthened by the fact that dioceses and religious congregations were themselves the 'private' owners of many schools, colleges, hospitals, and other property. They felt themselves threatened by anything that seemed like a move towards nationalisation or a State monopoly of such services. This gave them a certain common interest with the more privileged groups in society. For instance, in many Western countries the medical profession jealously guards its privileged position and resists the expansion of public health schemes designed to help the poor. It is all too easy to find situations where Catholic social teaching was invoked to justify such stances and where the Church found itself allied to a conservative group resisting the kind of changes that would make for a more just society. In the sphere of education the situation was rather similar. There were some Catholic schools designed specifically for the wealthy; so it was not surprising that they should find common cause with other 'elitist' institutions. But more interesting is the situation of the great majority of Church-run schools where it was the policy to charge very low fees so as to be available to the less well-off. Nevertheless those who sent their children to such schools tended to be middle-class people or people with middle-class aspirations. Consequently these schools were inclined to propagate middle-class values. The school authorities were not usually seen as favouring the type of change in educational structures that would lessen the inequalities in society.

The general image of the Church was therefore that of a socially conservative force giving ideological and 'political' support to those who were opposed to left-wing changes. All this happened despite the fact that the original purpose of most of the educational and medical institutions of the Church was to serve the poor. It even happened when these institutions continued to be at the service of poor people. For they worked *within* the existing system. Originally they had represented a challenge to the current structures of society. But as time went on they became incorporated as parts of the system. In so far as these institutions required a legitimation for their existence this was provided by Catholic social teaching. And so, the social teaching of the Church seemed in practice to be offering support for the *status quo* rather than calling prophetically for structural changes in the interests of the poor.

What has been outlined so far is an unfortunate but almost accidental process by which Catholic social teaching came to justify conservative social stances, as against efforts to minimise the gap between the different sectors of society. But at times this process has been taken further by a *deliberate* harnessing of the social teaching of the Church to make it serve a political function. This may have taken place in some of the American campaigns against anything that could be labelled 'communist' or even 'socialist'. But the most obvious and blatant example is the way in which right-wing authorities in Latin America seek in the Catholic faith an ideological support for their attitudes. They resist land reform and a more equal division of wealth, in the name of the sacrosanctness of private property. They also invoke Church teaching about obedience to authority and about non-violence as support for their resistance to the changes demanded by social justice. The social teaching of Pope John is a major step towards the prevention of such an ideological use of Church teaching and towards the recovery of its original purpose.

A Shift to the Left

There are two passages in *Pacem in Terris* which express a key insight of John XXIII:

> One of the fundamental duties of civil authorities . . . is so to co-ordinate and regulate social relations that the exercise of one man's right does not threaten others in the exercise of their own rights. . .[81]
>
> The common good requires that civil authorities maintain a careful balance between co-ordinating and protecting the rights of the citizens on the one hand, and promoting them, on the other. It should not happen that certain individuals or social groups derive special advantage from the fact that their rights have received preferential protection.[82]

There is of course nothing very startling in these as general statements. But the pope seems to have had in mind actual situations where the entrenched rights of some were the main obstacle to the exercise of the rights of others—especially of the poor. In the modern situation social justice required the recognition of new rights for the people at the lower end of the social scale. But the recognition and promotion of these rights was being hindered, either deliberately or uncritically, by the invocation of Catholic social teaching on the right to private property and the right to personal initiative. This amounted to an ideological use of this teaching, i.e. its use as a cover and legitimation for resistance to the changes needed to promote social justice. So the passages just quoted were intended to prevent such an abuse.

Already in *Mater et Magistra* Pope John had set out to lessen the chances that such things could happen. By means of that encyclical he had publicly and clearly put the weight of the Church on the side of a policy of social reforms in favour of the poor and deprived, both within each country and at the international level. *Mater et Magistra* advocated a considerable degree of control by public authorities over the activity of individuals and groups. It also recommended certain initiatives to be undertaken by the State to help those who are disadvantaged in society. The traditional and philosophical basis for such State control and initiative can be found in this passage: 'Our predecessors have constantly taught that inherent in the right to have private property there lies a social role and responsibility.'[83] Leo XIII can certainly be cited as insisting on the importance of property owners using their wealth responsibly.[84] Pius XI insisted that 'the right to own private property has been given to man . . . both in order that individuals may be able to provide for their own needs and those of their families, and also that by means of it the goods which the Creator has destined for the whole human race may truly serve this purpose.'[85] Pius XII gave priority to the universal purpose of the goods of the earth and saw the institution of private property as a means for the attainment of this purpose.[86] Quite evidently there is a pattern here: each of these popes in turn lays greater stress than his predecessor on the social obligations attaching to private property. In *Mater et Magistra* John XXIII built on the foundation laid down just twenty years earlier by Pius XII. John's own contribution consisted mainly in drawing the obvious practical conclusions. He saw clearly that quite often private ownership was not in fact serving the purpose for which Pius XII had said it had been instituted. So he proposed a variety of measures to ensure that its social function should be attained. By the very fact of owning property a person incurs social responsibilities. Pope John was not content with encouraging property owners to take these responsibilities seriously; he envisaged that they should be compelled by law to do so.

As we have seen, Pope John was not looking for a radical restructuring of the present order of Western society. Given that order, he accepted the need for State intervention in social and economic affairs to an extent well beyond what would have been advocated by Catholic leaders in the past. Perhaps even more important was the fact that he eliminated a good deal of the suspicion of State control and State initiatives, a suspicion which had been a central feature of the Catholic social outlook. In this sense it is not inaccurate to see in *Mater et Magistra* a certain 'opening to the left' (*apertura a sinistra*) in the socio-economic sphere. How closely that was related to an opening towards the left in the political sphere remains open to debate. Certainly, *Pacem in Terris,* issued two years after *Mater et Magistra,* contains a very significant passage referred to earlier.[87] In it the pope distinguished between false philosophical theories and the historical movements that are inspired by such theories; the latter, says the encyclical, can change profoundly and may contain positive and praiseworthy elements. This statement provided a justification for a significant change in the attitude of the Vatican in the political field. It was an irenic gesture directed mainly towards left-wing movements at the national and international level. It left the door open for practical political cooperation between the Catholic Church and communist governments and parties. But it is important not to focus attention on the political question to an extent that plays down the significance of the move towards the left that had already taken place on social and economic matters in *Mater et Magistra*. Perhaps the most accurate way to sum up the effect of that encyclical, and of Pope John's social teaching in general, would be to call it not so much an opening to the left as a decisive move away from the right.

This helps one to understand why *Mater et Magistra* contains detailed directives on such specific matters as the two kinds of insurance needed by farmers.[88] The pope scarcely imagined that his proposals were so original and compelling that governments would immediately adopt them! Rather it must be presumed that John is speaking not to governments or political parties or civil servants as such but to those to whom the encyclical is officially addressed—'the . . . bishops, clergy and faithful of the Catholic world'.[89] He feels the need to go into specific details because the approach he is advocating is quite different from the prevailing interpretation of Catholic social teaching, especially as regards its practical applications. One may show, as Bolté does quite effectively,[90] that there is considerable continuity between Pope John's teaching and that of his predecessors. One can conclude quite correctly that he was within a developing tradition. But this continuity applies at the level of 'doctrine' and general principles. In the application of the principles and in the practical implications for the stance of the Christian on social questions the discontinuity is more obvious. It would be wrong to exaggerate this discontinuity, to speak as though Pope John were advocating socialism. But it must be said that *Mater et Magistra* stands as a turning-point in Catholic social teaching.

The extent to which the encyclical was a turning-point has emerged more clearly in recent years. It stands at the source of two important developments whose full implications could hardly have been foreseen at the time. The first of these is in the area of theory, though it has many practical effects. *Mater et Magistra* opened up cracks in what had been a rather monolithic body of social teaching. It raised doubts about attitudes that had not previously been questions—for instance the attitude of suspicion about State intervention and a conviction that it ought to be kept to a minimum. Before long there was considerable questioning of many other parts of the traditional social outlook. Furthermore, the encyclical was controversial and was subject to a variety of interpretations. This gave rise to fragmentation at the practical level: there was no longer a clear, universally accepted Catholic 'line' on many socio-economic issues. It was not long before the very concept of a 'social doctrine' was called into question.[91]

The second development was that the encyclical began the process by which the Catholic Church got new allies and new opponents. This was perhaps the most important effect of the encyclical—at least for those who recognise that social teaching arises from, and relates back to, social praxis. The speed at which this development has occurred varies from place to place and even from continent to continent. Latin America is the region where one can see most clearly what may be involved. The 'option for the poor' which the Church is making in many parts of that continent could never have taken place unless the Church had ceased to be an ally of the rich and powerful. The refusal to provide a legitimation for the privileges of the 'elite' was a major factor in enabling the Church to opt for solidarity with the poor and oppressed. The Church of course sees itself as having a message for all of humanity and every sector of society. But many Latin American Church leaders became convinced that they must at times give a specific answer to the question: 'Whose side are you on?' In regard to basic issues of social justice they felt that they could not plead neutrality. So they committed the Church to making what came to be called 'a preferential, but not exclusive, option for the poor'. For the ability to see the need for such an option, the Church owes much to John XXIII and especially to the social teaching of *Mater et Magistra.*

Notes

1. *Mater et Magistra,* dated 15 March 1961 but actually issued just two months later. *AAS* 53(1961) 401–64. There are at least five English versions, of which the most widely used at present seems to be that of W.J. Gibbons for the

Paulist Press. This text is available in Joseph Gremillion (ed.), *The Gospel of Peace and Justice: Catholic Social Teaching Since Pope John*, Maryknoll (Orbis: 1976) 141–200; also in David J. O'Brien and Thomas A. Shannon (ed.), *Renewing the Earth: Catholic Documents on Peace, Justice and Liberation*, Garden City (Doubleday Image: 1977) 50–123. J.R. Kirwan made an interesting translation which often succeeds in expressing the underlying meaning of the text much better than the other versions, but is occasionally unacceptable. It can be found together with some helpful comments by Kirwan, in the *The Social Thought of John XXIII*, Oxford (Catholic Social Guild: 1964). A very careful French translation is to be found in Paul-Emile Bolté, *Mater et Magistra: texte latin, nouvelle traduction, index et analytique*, Montréal (Univ. de Montréal: 1968). As a companion to his translation, Bolté has produced a four-volume commentary on the text: Paul-Emile Bolté, *Mater et Magistra, commentaire,* Vol. I 1964, Vol. II 1966, Vol. III 1967, Vol. IV 1968, Montréal (Univ. de Montréal). References to the text of *Mater et Magistra* will be given by citing the paragraph number preceded by the initials MM.

2. *Pacem in Terris,* dated 11 April 1963, *AAS* 55(1963) 257–304. There are a number of English versions, some of which differ from each other only in minor respects. The easiest to read is that of Henry O. Waterhouse, available in *The Social Thought of John XXIII*, Oxford (Catholic Social Guild: 1964); but it seems rather less accurate in some important places than the version of Donald R. Campion available in Joseph Gremillion (ed.), *The Gospel of Peace and Justice . . .* , (see note 1 above) 201–41. References to the text of *Pacem in Terris* will be given by citing the paragraph number preceded by the initials PT.

3. See Raymond Williams, *Keywords: A vocabulary of Culture and Society,* Glasgow (Collins Fontana: 1976) 209–11; cf. Joe Holland and Peter Henriot, *Social Analysis: Linking Faith and Justice,* Washington D.C. (Center of Concern: 1980) 13–9.

4. PT 161–2 (Waterhouse version, adapted).

5. Cf. John F. Cronin, 'A Commentary on *Mater et Magistra'* in John XXIII, *The Encyclicals and Other Messages of John XXIII,* Washington D.C. (T.P.S. Press: 1964) 242.

6. MM 107.

7. MM 149.

8. PT 150 (Campion version).

9. PT 152 (Campion version).

10. PT 46.

11. PT 47.

12. PT 49.

13. PT 51, 61.

14. PT 84.

15. PT 104 (Campion version).

16. PT 52.

17. MM 155–65, 170–7; PT 80–145.

18. PT 156 (Campion version).

19. MM 62. Bolté makes the interesting suggestion that the '*negandum*' of the Latin text should be translated not as 'it will not happen' but as 'it must be resisted' i.e. not allowed to happen. This translation would certainly fit in better with what the pope says in the following two paragraphs; but neither the Italian text nor the letter of the Holy See to the French Social Week (the text of which seems to have been the original source for the passage in the encyclical) is open to this interpretation; see Bolté's commentary referred to in note 1 above, I, 289.

20. MM 67.

21. MM 68. See Bolté, op. cit. II, 376–7 for the nuances of the translation.

22. MM 163; cf. MM 154 which speaks of primitive and obsolete methods of agriculture.

23. MM 124–5.

24. MM 154.

25. MM 104, 118.

26. MM 198, 69, 204; PT 109.

27. MM 69.

28. On 'development' in relation to capitalism and socialism see Jean-Yves Calvez, *The Social Thought of John XXIII: Mater et Magistra*, London (Burns and Oates: 1964) 64–6.

29. PT 159. The translation of the passage is itself a matter of controversy. I have taken the phrase 'false philosophical theories' from the Waterhouse version since it is clearer than the Campion version which uses the word 'teachings' instead of 'theories'. But I have used the phrase 'historical movements' from the Campion version in preference to Waterhouse's vague phrase 'practical measures'. The translations into other European languages speak of 'movements' (see Bolté, op. cit. II, 613); and the latter part of the paragraph clearly refers to developments within such movements.

30. Cf. Arthur Fridolin Utz, *Die Friedensenzyklika Papst Johannes XXIII: Pacem in Terris*, Freiburg (Herder: 1963) 136, note 47; Jeremiah Newman, *Principles of Peace*, Oxford (Catholic Social Guild: 1964) 199–201. The following remark by Cronin sums up the position: 'It is widely held that they apply to contacts with the Communist world . . . But the principles as given in the encyclical are general in nature, and we cannot quarrel with those who also see in them reference to anti-clerical movements in Europe and Latin America, or the "opening to the left" in Italian politics, Spanish fascism or any similar accommodation with historic antagonists'.—John F. Cronin, 'A Commentary on *Pacem in Ter-*

ris' in John XXIII, *The Encyclicals and Other Messages of John XXIII*, Washington D.C. (T.P.S. Press: 1964) 325.

31. *Ad Petri Cathedram*, 29 June 1959, *AAS* 51(1959) 497–531. English text in John XXIII, *The Encyclicals . . .* (note 30 above) 33; cf. MM 48.

32. Ibid.

33. MM 115.

34. Cf. Harold Brookfield, *Interdependent Development*, London (Metheun: 1975) 38.

35. MM 113–14.

36. MM 115.

37. MM 73–4.

38. MM 74 (my translation, with emphasis added). The sentence quoted is not a direct quotation from Pius XII but a summary of an important part of a radio message he gave—see Pius XII, *La solennità della Pentecoste,* 1 June 1941, *AAS* 33(1941) 200–1.

39. MM 115 (Gibbons version).

40. See Chapter Ten below—especially the treatment of *Redemptor Hominis*.

41. Richard L. Camp, *The Papal Ideology of Social Reform: A Study in Historical Development 1878–1967*, Leiden (E.J. Brill: 1969) 159.

42. Ibid. 160.

43. *Quadragesimo Anno*, paras. 91–7.

44. Bolté, op. cit. II, 321–5. (Note that Bolté's numbering of the paragraphs of *Quadragesimo Anno* differs from that of the English text.)

45. John F. Cronin, 'Significance of John XXIII' in Benjamin L. Masse (ed.), *The Church and Social Progress: Background Readings for Pope John's Mater et Magistra,* Milwaukee (Bruce: 1966) 44.

46. MM 124, 150, 154, 157–74, 185; PT 88, 95, 96, 101, 103–7, 121–5.

47. MM 59–60 (my translation). For the nuances of meaning see Bolté, op. cit. I, 231–57; cf. the note by J.R. Kirwan to his translation in *The Social Thought of John* XXIII (note 1 above) 90–3; and publisher's note, ibid., (v); cf. also Jean-Yves Calvez, op. cit. (note 28 above), publisher's note, (v)-(vi), and 102, footnote 13 to Chapter I. In the English version given above I have translated *ius privatum* as 'contractual law' in order to give some approximation to what the pope has in mind—see Bolté, op. cit. I, 247–8.

48. '*Socialium rationum incrementa*'; equivalent Latin phrases are used in each of the paragraphs from 59–67 inclusive; in each of these nine cases the Italian text uses '*socializzazzione*'. Many translations in other European languages used words equivalent to the Italian word; but one authoritative German version and Bolté's later, careful, French text gave a more literal translation of the Latin.

49. The Gibbons version speaks of 'the multiplication of social relation-

ships'; that of Kirwan gives 'the development of the network of social relationships.'

50. Kirwan sees it as quite significant that the official Latin text 'rejected the term' (op. cit. 92); Bolté (op. cit. I, 241) inclines to the opposite view—that the reason the word was omitted was simply to avoid a Latin neologism.

51. See Address of 11 March 1945, *AAS* 37(1945) 68–72; and radio message to Austrian *Katholikentag* 14 Sept 1952, *AAS* 44(1952) 792.

52. Cf. John F. Cronin, 'Significance of John XXIII' (note 45 above) 44.

53. MM 62.

54. MM 60.

55. MM 62.

56. Calvez, op. cit. (note 28 above) 8–9.

57. MM 63; cf. Calvez, op. cit. (note 28 above) 14: 'Socialisation has no meaning in reality save as . . . a "should" of personal freedom.'

58. MM 53, 117, 152.

59. MM 65. J.R. Kirwan, op. cit. (note 1 above) 93–4, points out that the terms used echo those of *Quadragesimo Anno*. For a careful study of the relationship between the words used in the two encyclicals see Bolté, op. cit. I, 317–25.

60. MM 117, 152.

61. *Quadragesimo Anno,* para. 65.

62. Pius XII, Address of 3 June 1950, *AAS* 42(1950) 487.

63. MM 75.

64. MM 92–3, 97.

65. MM 97.

66. MM 104.

67. MM 116–7.

68. MM 120.

69. MM 128–41.

70. MM 133.

71. MM 134.

72. MM 135.

73. MM 136.

74. MM 137.

75. MM 140.

76. MM 141.

77. Bolté's very comprehensive study at times gives the impression that his discovery of such parallels has led him to play down the difference in approach between Pius XII and John XXIII; for instance, on the question of 'socialisation', op. cit. I, 246.

78. MM 51, 55.

79. MM 109.

80. MM 65.

81. PT 62 (Campion version).

82. PT 65. The Campion text quoted here is preferable to the Waterhouse version which does not bring out the contrast in the first sentence (Latin: '*tum . . . tum*').

83. MM 119 (my translation). The phrase '*munus . . . sociale*' is very difficult to translate accurately. Kirwan gives 'social function' and the Italian and French texts use a corresponding phrase. But in English this is too vague. The Gibbons text gives 'social responsibility'; this is excellent except that it only conveys one of the two aspects of the meaning of '*munus*'. I have added 'role' to express the second aspect.

84. *Rerum Novarum*, para. 19.

85. *Quadragesimo Anno*, para. 45.

86. *La solennità della Pentecoste, AAS* 33(1941) 198–9.

87. See notes 29 and 30 above. It has been noted that Pope John's 'opening to the left' was actually a belated response of the Vatican to the overtures of the Italian Communist Party, led by Gramsci and Togliatti—see Carl Marzani, 'The Vatican as a Left Ally?', in *Monthly Review,* July/August 1982, 14–6.

88. MM 135. See also the details referred to in notes 70–6 above.

89. MM title.

90. Bolté, op. cit. I, 245–6.

91. E.g. M.-D. Chenu, *La 'doctrine sociale' de l'Église comme idéologie,* Paris (Cerf: 1979). This issue will be discussed below, in Chapter Ten.

Human Rights in Roman Catholicism

John Langan, S.J.

This article originally appeared in *Journal of Ecumenical Studies,* 1982.

I

The central and classical document for the doctrine of human rights in the Roman Catholic tradition is *Pacem in terris* (Peace on Earth), the encyclical letter which Pope John XXIII issued in 1963. It represents a moment of equipoise, of creative assimilation and synthesis, which comes after a long period of struggle and tension but which in turn gives rise to further questions and challenges, many of them unforeseen and unintended by the fashioners of the synthesis. *Pacem in terris,* together with the decrees of Vatican II, is the resolution of a crucial stage of Roman Catholicism's long struggle with the modernizing and secularizing culture of the West. In this struggle the issue of religious freedom was central, but the notion of human rights included a much wider range of concerns than simply religious freedom, and it provided a basis for the transformation of Catholicism from an ally and ward of traditionalist regimes to a critic of repression by both reactionary and revolutionary regimes.

Pacem in terris proceeds in a serene and irenic manner which conceals much of the struggle that raged during the preceding 200 years on both the philosophical-theological and the social-political fronts. John XXIII began with the necessity of human rights for the good order of society: "Any human society, if it is to be well-ordered and productive, must lay down as a foundation this principle, namely, that every human being is a person, that is, his nature is endowed with intelligence and free will. By virtue of this, he has rights and duties, flowing directly and simultaneously from his very nature. These rights are therefore universal, inviolable and inalienable."[1] This passage reveals a great deal about the standard form of Catholic human-rights theory as it is presented in the official social teaching of the Church.

First, it employs two key notions which are presented as harmonizing with each other, namely, the personal character of the human being manifested in intelligence and freedom, and the nature which is the source of rights and duties. This combination of two different patterns of thinking about humanity distinguishes the Catholic tradition from those forms of idealism and existentialism which set a fundamental distinction between the realm of natural law and the realm of personal freedom, and also from those tendencies in the empiricist and positivist traditions which would reduce the personal to the natural interpreted as the scientifically knowable. Human-rights theory in Catholicism works from an anthropology which is fundamentally realistic in its account of human knowing and of human moral endeavor and which stresses both the unity of the human person as a being in the world and the necessary orientation of the person to society and community. This anthropology is compatible with and takes inspiration from such central Christian theological doctrines as the Incarnation and the creation of human beings "in the image and likeness of God" (Gen. 1:26),[2] but it is not presented as accessible only to those who accept these theological beliefs. It is nourished by the Christian view of the unfolding of salvation in history and by the more specifically Catholic sense of the ecclesial community as one in space and time and by the Catholic form of sacramental imagination.[3] As a result, Catholic proponents of this anthropology and its application to human rights will often seem most distinctively Catholic to those who come from other religious and intellectual traditions when they take themselves to be simply delineating the contours of the universally human.

Second, the doctrine aims to be universal and not particularistic in both its foundation and its application.[4] The foundation of human rights and of the principles of order for human society generally is to be found "where the Father of all things wrote them, that is, in the nature of man."[5] The role of divinely revealed truth in discovering these norms is essentially confirmatory.[6] The basing of human rights on natural law provides a link with the central Catholic theological tradition, particularly Thomas Aquinas; it also provides a parallel to the move made by Western revolutionaries in the eighteenth century in appealing beyond the complexities, irrationalities, and injustices of positive law and the institutions of the old regime to a "higher law," which affirmed natural and God-given rights. The desire for a foundation for human rights which would be universally accessible is also interwoven with the contemporary desire of the Church to address the modern world in its own terms.[7] But it may be doubted whether a natural-law foundation for human rights really enhances communication with either secular liberals or Reformed Christians. A very good case can be made that the appeal of human rights norms themselves is really far broader than the appeal of any philosophical or theological foundation which may be offered for them.[8] Thus there has been a tendency in more recent Catholic teaching to put less explicit reliance on natural-law categories, even though there is no sharp change in the underlying anthropology. This tendency is also, in part, a consequence of the desire to present more of the Church's teaching in biblical terms.

The universality envisaged in Catholicism's approach to human rights also involves the range of application of such claims. Thus *Pacem in terris*, as we have seen, affirms that human rights are "universal, inviolable, and inalienable."[9] These are to be protected by law,[10] and special programs to ensure the rights of "the less fortunate members of the community," who are "less able to defend their rights," are commended by the encyclical.[11] John XXIII explicitly noted the increasing participation of women in public life and their growing sense of their human dignity which impelled them to claim "the rights and duties that befit a human person."[12] He also affirmed the equality of all human beings "by reason of their natural dignity" and argued from this that racial discrimination cannot be justified[13] and that all political communities have equal natural dignity.[14] Neither sex nor race nor economic class can, then, form a basis for denying or restricting the rights of human persons.

Human rights not only apply to all groups, even those most oppressed in the past, but they are also moral claims which are more binding than the enactments of states. Thus, John XXIII held that "if any government does not acknowledge the rights of man or violates them, it not only fails in its duty, but its orders completely lack juridical force."[15] It is important, however, to note that here he did not accept interpretations of universal human rights which would overturn such customary institutions of Western society as the family, the private ownership of property, the nation-states, and ethnic communities.[16] In the papal approach, rights claims are normally advanced within an ongoing framework of social institutions. These institutions are obliged to respect and promote human rights in various ways, but the destruction or enfeebling of these institutions would serve neither the common good nor, in the long run, the cause of human rights. There is room, then, for considerations which might justify the restriction or overriding of human rights claims, even though the details of such justification are not worked out. The encyclical does not attempt to prescribe one particular form or constitution for states on the basis of human rights considerations.[17] It acknowledges the diversity of historical circumstances but strongly commends both the separation of powers and the advantages of citizen participation in government.[18]

Third, the content of human-rights doctrine in *Pacem in terris* is comprehensive. The encyclical gives what David Hollenbach in his valuable study of the Catholic human rights tradition, *Claims in Conflict*, called "the most complete and systematic list of . . . human rights in the modern Catholic tradition."[19] It includes both what are commonly referred to as civil and political rights (of the sort listed in Articles 1–21 of the Universal Declaration of Human Rights[20] and social and economic rights (Articles 22–28 of the Universal Declaration), but it does not enumerate rights on the basis of this common but often perplexing categorization. The encyclical also offers an explicit, though qualified, endorsement of the Universal Declaration of Human Rights, which it calls "an important step on the path toward the juridico-political organization of the world community,"[21] precisely because of its acknowledgment of the dignity of all human persons.

The encyclical consciously juxtaposes items from different ideological traditions in its enumeration of rights. Thus it lays down as the starting point of its enumeration "the right to life, to bodily integrity, and to the means which are necessary and suitable for the proper development of life"; these means include "food, clothing, shelter, rest, medical care, and finally the necessary social services."[22] The position laid down in this one paragraph can be appealed to in criticism both of regimes which practice judicial murder and the "disappearance" of dissidents and of societies which fail to provide the things necessary for the survival for all their members. So, also, when John XXIII spoke of rights within the economic sphere, he affirmed that "human beings have the natural right to free initiative in the economic field and the right to work."[23] Here he picked up the concern of liberal capitalism for promoting freedom of entrepreneurial activity, the free disposition of private property, and freedom of choice in market situations, even while he also endorsed the obligation affirmed by socialist and social democratic movements of providing all citizens with an opportunity to exercise their right to work. These juxtapositions illustrate the tendency in the major documents of the church's social teaching to find a middle way between laissez-faire capitalism and Marxist socialism.

A fourth characteristic tendency of Catholic presentations of human-rights doctrine is the concern for moral and religious values. *Pacem in terris* includes a strong affirmation of the right of human beings to "honor God according to the dictates of an upright conscience" and to profess one's "religion privately and publicly."[24] This affirmation is still based on our obligation to serve God rightly and on the church's right to liberty; in some respects it falls short of the formulation employed by Vatican II in its declaration on religious freedom, which holds that, even in cases where there is an establishment or special legal recognition of one form of religion, "it is at the same time imperative that the right of all citizens and religious bodies should be recognized and made effective in practice."[25] Part of what is being worked out in *Pacem in terris* is the problem of reconciling the rights to freedom of belief and expression with the obligatory aspects of such values as truth, the common good, and the moral virtues—a problem which continues to trouble liberal democracies.[26]

What the Catholic tradition was able to do in the discussion of religious liberty leading up to Vatican II was to work out a nonrelativistic, nonagnostic foundation for religious freedom. In this approach, the human obligation to seek truth in religious matters is to be understood in accordance with the "dignity of the human person and his social nature";[27] it is, therefore, to be free and dialogical. Vatican II was then able to affirm the obligation to follow conscience and to respect both conscience in others and, what had often been in practice the more difficult point, the right of religious groups to be constituted, to gather, and to worship in public and private. The council also argued for religious freedom on the basis of the freedom of the act of faith and contended that respect for religious freedom was in accordance with the example and teaching of Jesus.[28]

Pacem in terris manifests the concern of the Catholic human-rights tradition to set specific rights into a moral context which includes, in addition to the distinct values of truth and the moral virtues, the more immediately linked network of rights and duties, both those attaching to the person who is the subject of a particular right and those attaching to other persons who may affect or be affected by the subject's exercise of her or his right. This concern is generalized in the two principles of the correlation of rights and duties in the individual subject and between persons. John XXIII illustrated the first type of correlation with the following examples: "The right of every man to life is correlative with the duty to preserve it; his right to a decent standard of living, with the duty of living it becomingly; and his right to investigate the truth freely, with the duty of pursuing it ever more completely and profoundly."[29] The basis of this first correlation of rights and duties is a recognition that the goods with which both are concerned are essential to human flourishing and are, at least in their most fundamental and universal forms, not optional for human beings.[30] The consequence of this first correlation is that the individual is not in a condition of pure liberty and discretion with regard to these goods but remains under moral obligation. There is not, once this correlation is granted, a simple division between freedom and law as Hobbes supposed in his remark that "Law and Right differ as much as Obligation and Liberty; which in one and the same matter are inconsistent."[31]

The second correlation which is proposed is the more familiar one that obtains between persons: "To one man's natural right there corresponds a duty in other persons: the duty, namely, of acknowledging and respecting the right in question."[32] Those who claim rights for themselves without acknowledging the rights of others are guilty of a fundamental inconsistency. The practice of claiming and exercising rights is not merely an instrument for protecting and advancing self-interest, though it can be that, but it can itself be obligatory as an expression of respect for one's human dignity. John XXIII wrote, "He who possesses certain rights has likewise the duty to claim those rights."[33] This clearly is not intended to rule out all cases of waiving one's rights, but it makes a point against sacrificial conceptions of Christian morality.

The mutual acknowledgment of rights and duties in society is also seen as a kind of *preparatio evangelica,* since it brings human beings to awareness of a world of values such as "truth, justice, charity, and freedom" and brings them to "a better knowledge of the true God, who is personal and transcendent."[34] Here one finds the possibility of a political theology which takes as its starting point not the struggle of the oppressed in a radically unjust society, but the active involvement of persons in exercising rights and fulfilling duties in a society which provides at least the possibility of meeting the demands of justice and attaining the common good through its institutions and practices. There is positive religious value in the advancing and weighing of claims, in the organization and advocacy of groups of citizens working for a cause, and in the characteristic activities of a society which is participatory rather than hierarchical in its understanding of order and fulfillment. This marks a large and important shift in Catholicism's vision of human society.

In summary, the Roman Catholic understanding of human rights in its classical form differs from the dominant varieties of liberalism, especially in Anglo-American culture, in its distrust of individualism and its emphasis on community. This is a matter of both the underlying anthropology and the moral restraints that affect the exercise of freedom in society. It differs from Protestant approaches in its mode of argumentation and presentation, which relies on philosophical rather than theological or biblical categories in dealing with basic issues of political and legal theory. Catholic human-rights doctrine emerges as a comprehensive and generous structure within which religious believers can both share and address the moral dilemmas of a religiously pluralistic and increasingly secular world and which, while not without some internal points of tension and incompleteness, is able to offer shelter to those who are repelled both by the neglect of social and economic rights for the disadvantaged in liberal societies and by the repressiveness of authoritarian and totalitarian regimes. But it would be misleading to look at the Catholic human-rights tradition only in its classical moment of synthesis. It is necessary to look both backward to the struggles of its past and forward to the potentialities and problems of its future.

II

If one moves back 100 years before *Pacem in terris* in the history of papal teaching on society, one comes to the *Syllabus of Errors* of Pius IX (1864). Among the positions *condemned* in this celebrated list are the following:

55. The Church should be separated from the State and the State from the Church.

77. In this age of ours it is no longer expedient that the Catholic religion should be treated as the sole State religion and that any other forms of religious worship should be excluded.

78. Hence those States, nominally Catholic, who have legally enacted that immigrants be permitted to have free exercise of their own particular religion, are to be praised.[35]

Pius IX was struggling to preserve a privileged or even a monopoly position for the Catholic religion. In so doing, he was continuing the opposition to religious freedom which Pius VI, in the face of the French Revolution's Declaration of the Rights of Man, had enunciated as early as the brief *Quod aliquantum* of 1791, which singled out for criticism the articles calling for freedom of opinion and communication.[36] Catholicism's institutional sympathies during most of the nineteenth century were with a conservatism which had its roots in the *ancien regime*. It is important neither to conceal nor to overstate these sympathies. The Church, especially in France, experienced the proclamation of human rights in 1789 as a very cold and hostile wind, and it cannot claim for itself a significant place in either the theoretical or the practical struggle for human rights in the eighteenth and nineteenth centuries. Human-rights theory in an explicit and politically dynamic form confronted Catholicism as an alien force, and it has taken Catholicism a long time to appropriate it.

If it is true, as Wolfgang Huber has argued, that "the consciousness of human rights arose in the context of confrontation with the principle of absolute sovereignty,"[37] it has to be recognized that the church, even in its most conservative and supine phase, always felt the responsibility to oppose the principle of absolute sovereignty, whether exercised by Louis XIV or Napoleon. The necessity of this opposition arises from the church's concern for its own liberty in proclaiming the gospel, in carrying on its sacramental life, and in ordering its communities. Catholicism gave a convinced but not unconditional support to the old order, a support which was reinforced by the anti-clericalism of many proponents of the new doctrines. The Church feared for its privileged position and its property, but also for its place in the hearts of the faithful and its freedom to be itself. This fear was naturally greatest where the Church had most to lose (that is, the traditionally Catholic lands of Europe and Latin America), and least strong where the Church had adjusted to competitive or even repressive conditions (as in North America, Holland, Ireland, and Poland).[38] Catholicism has always had the intellectual and moral instruments (if not the political will or courage) to condemn the gorier excesses of tyranny and barbarism, which are at the same time violations of human rights. The major exceptions to this have also involved the denial of religious freedom, as in various crusading and inquisitorial activities.

The first stage in the development of Catholic human-rights doctrine can be located in the reign of Pius IX's successor, Leo XIII, who, in 1891, issued his famous encyclical on the condition of the working class in industrial society, *Rerum novarum*. Along with a vehement affirmation of the natural rights of property[39] and a denunciation of the Marxist notion of class struggle,[40] Leo affirmed "the natural right" of each person "to procure what is required in order to live."[41] Leo XIII himself used this as part of his argument for a just or living wage and against an unrestricted freedom of contract between employers and workers. But we can also see this as the nucleus of a theory of subsistence rights, that is, social and economic rights to those things which are necessary for survival. These rights are prior to any particular political, legal, or economic order: "Man precedes the State, and possesses, prior to the formation of any State, the right of providing for the sustenance of his body."[42] Hollenbach observes that Leo's stress on the primacy of the personal was more creative for the Catholic Church's teachings on economic rights than in the political and cultural spheres, where Leo continued "the classical association of Catholic thought with a hierarchical and traditionalist model of social organization."[43] The papacy was, in fact, more ready to challenge economic liberalism and the practices of laissez-faire capitalism than to endorse egalitarian democracy.

The second stage is not marked by one central document but consists in Catholicism's acceptance of the values, procedures, and norms of Western constitutional democracy as the appropriate framework for modern societies. This is the result of a painful process of learning from the great European civil war of 1914 to 1945 and its aftermath in the Cold War. Put simply, it is the church's movement from the time of Franz Josef to the time of Konrad Adenauer, through the time of Adolf Hitler. During this period the last hopes for a return to the values and practices of the old regime were destroyed; the evils of racism and totalitarianism were made manifest on a colossal scale; and the Western constitutional democracies emerged as relatively humane victors and as the de facto protectors of Catholicism against communist advances in Europe.

Two aspects of this process should be mentioned, one practical and the other theoretical. The first is the emergence of Christian Democratic parties which gave the church and the world an experience and an example of political life that was both religious and democratic and that could be trusted with the exercise of power in ways which did not infringe on human rights. The second is the work of Jacques Maritain in developing from Thomistic foundations an understanding of natural law and the common good which included as a vital and constitutive element the rights of the human person.[44] This was an important reaction to totalitarian ways of interpreting common good which would allow the destruction of persons for the sake of preserving or enhancing the power of the state.

The end of this second phase of Catholic development coincided with the internationalization and universalization of human rights in the declarations of the Allies, in the moral reflections provoked by the war-crimes trials, and ultimately in the Universal Declaration of Human Rights in 1948. It also coincided with the decisive beginnings of the process of decolonization in Asia and with the move to universal application of the Wilsonian principle of national self-determination. These processes meant the end of Western hegemony over the non-European world and opened the way for a less Eurocentric way of conceiving both human rights and Catholicism, which became manifest in Vatican II and in the social teaching of Paul VI with its focus on problems of development.

One very important aftermath of the global extension of the notion of human rights and of greater realization of the evils of racism was that the struggle for human rights took as one of its central and paradigmatic forms the struggle against discrimination.

The third phase of the development we have already seen in *Pacem in terris* and in Vatican Council II. With regard to religious liberty, the church found considerable difficulty in accepting human-rights norms which had formed part of enlightened opinion since the late eighteenth century. Whereas the affirmation of most human rights is a lesson which the church teaches its faithful and the world, the affirmation of religious freedom is a lesson which the church itself must learn. The church even in its modernized form is more comfortable in conceiving itself as a moral teacher proposing norms than as a moral agent whose actions are to be bound by norms. The eventual acceptance of the principle of religious freedom owed much to the experience of Catholicism in the United States and to the theological work of John Courtney Murray, S.J., in explicating that experience in terms which did not imply relativistic indifferentism or secularism.[45] What was required was not merely a theoretical argument, but also an encouraging example of Catholicism flourishing in an open society, an example which could overcome the fears and the defensiveness shown by the church in earlier phases of human-rights development. The decisive removal of equivocation on the issue of religious freedom by Vatican II was a major, though belated, accomplishment which both preserved the credibility of the Catholic Church's teaching on human rights and opened the way to fuller and richer relationships with other religious traditions.

III

Few major accomplishments, however, are without problematic consequences. Few syntheses remain unchallenged; few classic moments are undisturbed. Let us then look, briefly, at the relatively recent past since the end of Vatican II in 1965 and at the challenges of the near future. There are, I suggest, four of these which bear watching.

First, there are still unresolved elements in the church's struggle with modern individualism and liberalism. At a fairly deep level within Catholicism there lives a desire for a more unified, more cohesive, and more disciplined form of society than prevails in the secularized West. There is also a view that liberalism errs in giving too much room to individual freedom at the expense of the common good and the needs of the disadvantaged, that its doctrine of rights leads to a neglect of duties, that liberal societies have lapsed into a resentful and self-protective consumerism, and that liberalism involves both the denial of a normative structure of goods for human beings in society and serious errors in anthropology. All this is, of course, apt material for future debate and dialogue. It does not indicate that Catholicism will abandon its human-rights doctrine; the doctrine now has the weight of authority and argument behind it. But it does indicate that institutional Catholicism and Catholic political movements and actors may make significantly different choices about which human rights to struggle for in the political arena and which rights to accord priority to. One manifest example of this is the characteristically but not exclusively Roman Catholic concern for the right to life of the unborn. Catholic human-rights theorizing and advocacy will probably continue to be distinctively Catholic, even as they attempt to grasp the contours of the universally human and natural.

Second, there is an unresolved question about the preferred shape of society from the standpoint of human-rights theory. If one espouses a comprehensive human-rights theory including both civil and political rights and social and economic rights, as Catholicism does, what form of economy and polity will enable a society to meet this complex set of moral demands and constraints? This question is directly related to Catholicism's search for a middle way between Marxist socialism and what John Paul II calls "rigid capitalism."[46] Certain answers are clear. The state must acknowledge the rule of law. Its power must be limited, not absolute. It must respect the right to life and religious freedom. This rules out both communist regimes and national security states of the type which have developed in the Southern Cone of Latin America since 1964. The promise of liberal democracies with regulated capitalist economies to satisfy social and economic rights is weak, and their performance is uneven. But the record of professedly socialist societies with regard to both social and economic rights and civil and political rights is discouraging. Some form of social democracy or of chastened and humanized socialism seems to be indicated.

But this is a long way from giving a concrete answer to the basic question about the preferred shape of the future society, an answer which might motivate political action and guide political choices. It is a basic limitation of human-rights theory that it is more helpful in enabling us to denounce violations of human dignity than in guiding us in the design of institutions which will promote that dignity.[47] However, efforts to enlarge human-rights theory to deal with fundamental questions of political and economic order and to provide the basis for a political program run the double risk of breaking the moral consensus about human-rights violations which is capable of transcending standard political and ideological divisions and of producing an overly moralistic and legalistic approach which may be inappropriate to the deeper problems of economic development and world order.

Third, there is the question of a shifting foundation for Catholic human-rights theory. In the key documents of the 1960's, particularly *Pacem in terris* and *Gaudium et spes,* which is Vatican II's pastoral constitution on the church and the modern world, there is a polarity between neo-scholastic and biblical approaches to the bases of Christian human rights, between what Hollenbach called "universalist and particularist warrants for human rights theory."[48] He noted the turn away from a rationalistic neo-scholastic philosophical approach on the basis of natural law to a more flexible theological approach which is sensitive to the processes of history and the diversity of cultures. This is simply one aspect of the general movement in contemporary Catholicism away from the once dominant and mandatory system of neo-Thomism.

While the turn to a more biblical and less *a priori* approach to human-rights theory creates new possibilities for dialogue with other religious traditions, especially Protestantism, it leaves a gap between the historical and theological categories of biblical revelation and the philosophical, legal, and practical categories of human-rights theory and action. This gap is not particularly difficult to overcome when it is a matter of appealing to religious symbols in order to motivate. But the difficult questions of the weight and interconnection of different types of rights and the necessity of collaborative work and reflection with secularists and people of radically different religious traditions mean that some systematic positions in ethics, political philosophy, and jurisprudence will have to be brought back into the argument, smuggled in under cover of theological darkness. I have already argued both that the anthropological basis is essential to the elaboration of Catholic human-rights theory and that it cannot be divided neatly into philosophical and theological segments. However, the recognition of the importance of historical process and cultural diversity is an important corrective to premature rationalistic systematizations of the sort that neo-scholastic philosophy was only too ready to perpetrate.[49] One happy byproduct of this double foundation for human-rights theory in Catholicism is the opportunity it creates for a wider range of dialogue with people from a diversity of religious and intellectual traditions.

A fourth area of future challenge and development is to be found in the internal life of Roman Catholicism itself. The Church uses human-rights doctrine to proclaim a message of justice and peace to the world, but the applicability of the doctrine to the Church itself remains unclear.[50] Thus, there is no significant use of human-rights doctrine in the proposed revision of the Code of Canon Law. But the problems are more extensive and more troubling than this lacuna suggests. For it has been argued that rights to participation and to self-determination on the part of the laity are not effectively exercised and protected, that the exclusion of women from ordained ministry and from most positions of power in the Catholic Church is a discriminatory violation of rights to equal treatment and equal respect, that ordained ministers are denied the right to marry, that theologians are restricted in their rights to freedom of inquiry and expression, that lay employees of the Church are often denied rights to organization and to social benefits, and that due process procedures for the protection of rights are weak or nonexistent.[51]

Not all these issues are "live" issues in all parts of the Catholic Church; in fact, the list just given reflects characteristic concerns of North Atlantic Catholicism, particularly those parts of it influenced by Anglo-American legal culture. This is the heartland of human-rights theory, and so its concerns, while not universal, are particularly revealing. One should also note the different character of the different issues. Some involve matters of theological principle (e.g., the ordination of women), or fundamentals of church discipline (e.g., marriage of the clergy and modes of lay participation). Some involve more-or-less widespread abuses (e.g., denial of the right to form unions). Some may involve both. It seems to me unfair and unwise to treat those who have honest disagreements on matters of principle as favoring either the violation of human rights or the overthrow of church discipline.

There are three main strategies open to the Church for dealing with this family of issues. The first would be to interpret canon law and ecclesiology on the basis of papal teachings on "the universal, inviolable, and inalienable" rights which are to be acknowledged by "any human society, if it is to be well-ordered."[52] This view would, if adopted comprehensively, assimilate the Church to the state and other political, economic, and social organizations to the extent that the same human-rights norms would apply. Implementation of such a view would require extensive changes in the church and might well alter the social character of Catholicism in ways which cannot easily be foreseen. In some parts of the world, it may be at odds with the "enculturation" of the local church. The application of universal norms in the transformation of societies and institutions is a difficult business, even in the best of times. But such an approach, which would amount to restructuring the Church along the lines of an egalitarian universalism, has the attraction of directness and simplicity and would meet the moral demands of many.[53]

A quite different response would be for the Catholic Church to maintain that the principles which rightly apply to human societies in general do not apply to the church because of its divine institution, its supernatural end, its specific objectives and practices, and its dependence on Scripture for its basic norms and structure. This is an approach which would maintain most of the institutional structure and the social style of traditional Catholicism; it would involve a sharp dualism between the norms applying to a participatory, egalitarian, and democratic secular society and the norms applying to a hierarchical and authoritarian religious society.[54] This dualism does not seem to be psychologically untenable, if we look at the historical experience of American Catholicism. It may well be vulnerable to historical arguments to the extent that certain traditional practices and norms have not been universal in the Catholic past and so may be subject to human alteration and development. It also raises questions about how we are to understand the convergence between the development of human society and the fulfillment of humanity in God, a theme which figures prominently in *Gaudium et spes* of Vatican II. For instance, Vatican II affirmed:

> Modern man is on the road to a more thorough development of his own personality, and to a growing discovery and vindication of his own rights. Since it has been entrusted to the Church to reveal the mystery of God, who is the ultimate goal

of man, she opens up to man at the same time the meaning of his own existence, that is, the innermost truth about himself.[55]

Are we to suppose that human development proceeds along radically different lines once we enter the ecclesial sphere—and that the innermost truth about humanity is at odds with the development of human personality and human rights?

A variant response which might be offered to support this dualistic view of church and society is to argue that the church is a voluntary association, that its members waive certain rights, and that no injustice is done them when the opportunity to exercise these rights is either denied or not provided. This response involves a highly voluntaristic conception of society and law, which is at variance with the mainstream of Catholic social thought and does not correspond fully to the Church's sense of itself as the "universal sacrament of salvation."[56] But it does have the merit of reminding us of the difference in scale and kind between human-rights issues in the church and the brutal and massive violations of the most basic rights which have occurred in the political life of our times. Also, the voluntaristic view serves to provide the church and its members with the protection of rights which human-rights theory ascribes to all voluntary associations, and it protects the church from judicial and political regulation of a sort which would be burdensome and offensive. The voluntaristic view has more plausibility in justifying the discipline of clerical celibacy and other practices where one can point to an act of consent bearing directly on the practice.

The various issues on the current agenda of the Church which have a human-rights component in them may well have to be treated with different strategies, and their resolution may take quite a long time. It is a sign of the vitality, the relevance, and the ambition of Catholic human-rights doctrine that it leads us to many of the most fundamental and most perplexing social issues of our time. The tension between what a sound human-rights theory seems to demand and what the church does may produce problems of governability within the church and a reaction of incredulity in the face of its teaching. But Catholics can also take courage in the reassuring words of Vatican II:

Since the Church has a visible and social structure as a sign of her unity in Christ, she can and ought to be enriched by the

development of human social life. The reason is not that the
constitution given to her by Christ is defective, but that she
may understand it more penetratingly, express it better and adjust it more successfully to our time.[57]

The precise shape of the church after it has fully assimilated human-
rights theory and the eventual effect on society at large of the Catholic
proclamation of human rights and human dignity will be a major part of
the history of religion in our time.

Notes

1. John XXIII, *Pacem in terris/Peace on Earth* (New York: America
Press, 1963), par. 9.

2. Ibid., par. 3.

3. For a presentation of the relevance of sacramental imagination to issues
of social justice, see David Hollenbach, "A Prophetic Church and the Catholic
Sacramental Imagination," in John Haughey, ed., *The Faith That Does Justice*
(New York: Paulist, 1977).

4. The formulation of human-rights doctrine in the standard English translation of *Pacem in terris* used here may seem to go against this claim and to be
particularistic in an objectionable way, i.e., sexist. This problem of formulation
(as contrasted with possible problems of content) arises from the English translation and not from the official Latin version.

5. John XXIII, *Pacem in terris,* par.6.

6. Ibid., par.10.

7. This desire is manifest particularly in *Gaudium et spes,* the Constitution of Vatican II on the Church and the Modern World (1965).

8. Foundational proposals, however, retain the values of showing ways
to integrate human-rights norms into the various religious, intellectual, and political traditions and of clarifying their relationship to major philosophical and
theological issues. Evidence for the greater appeal of human-rights norms independent of foundations can be seen in the Universal Declaration of Human
Rights itself, which makes no foundational claim; in the near-universal reluctance of governments of all ideological hues to admit that they violate human

rights; and in the general public response to the work of Amnesty International and similar organizations.

9. John XXIII, *Pacem in terris,* par.9.

10. Ibid., par. 79.

11. Ibid., par. 56.

12. Ibid., par. 41.

13. Ibid., par. 44.

14. Ibid., par. 89.

15. Ibid., par. 61.

16. See Ibid., pars. 16, 21, 48, 55, 92, 100.

17. Ibid., par. 67.

18. Ibid., pars. 68, 74.

19. David Hollenbach, *Claims in Conflict: Retrieving and Renewing the Catholic Human Rights Tradition* (New York: Paulist Press, 1979), p. 66.

20. See pp. 105–109, below.

21. John XXIII, *Pacem in terris,* par. 144.

22. Ibid., par. 11.

23. Ibid., par. 18.

24. Ibid., par. 14.

25. Vatican II, Declaration on Religious Freedom, *Dignitatis humanae,* par. 6.

26. The current wave of controversy in the United States over such disparate "moral" issues as pornography, school prayers, and abortion can serve as evidence of both continued dissatisfaction with the form of liberalism dominant in the juridical system and of the difficulty of stating the issues in a form acceptable to both sides in the disputes.

27. Vatican II, *Dignitatis humanae,* par. 3.

28. Ibid., pars. 10, 11.

29. John XXIII, *Pacem in terris,* par. 29.

30. See John Finnis, *Natural Law and Natural Rights* (New York: Oxford University Press, 1980).

31. Thomas Hobbes, *Leviathan,* ed. C. B. Macpherson (Baltimore: Penguin, 1968), p. 189.

32. John XXIII, *Pacem in terris,* par. 30.

33. Ibid., par. 44.

34. Ibid., par. 45.

35. Pius IX, *Syllabus of Errors*, in *Church and State through the Centuries,* trans. and ed. Sidney Ehler and John Morrall (London: Burns and Oates, 1954), pp. 284–285.

36. See Bernard Plongeron, "Anathema or Dialogue? Christian Reactions to Declarations of the Rights of Man in the United States and Europe in the Eigh-

teenth Century,'' trans. Lawrence Ginn, in *The Church and the Rights of Man,* Concilium 124, ed. Alois Muller and Norbert Greinacher (New York: Seabury, 1979), p. 41.

37. Wolfgang Huber, "Human Rights—A Concept and Its History" in *The Church and the Rights of Man,* trans. Martin Kitchen, Concilium 124, p. 5.

38. Plongeron, in "Anathema," pp. 40–42, makes this point specifically for the period of immediate reactions to the French Revolution, but I think it is more generally relevant.

39. Leo XIII, *Rerum novarum,* pars. 5–10.

40. Ibid., pars. 15–17.

41. Ibid., par. 34. In taking this position, Leo XIII was following the teaching of Thomas Aquinas, *Summa Theologiae,* II-II, 66,7.

42. Leo XIII, *Rerum novarum,* par. 6.

43. Hollenbach, *Claims in Conflict,* p. 49.

44. See especially his works of the war and post-war years: *The Rights of Man and Natural Law,* trans. Doris Anson (New York: Scribner's, 1945); *The Person and the Common Good,* trans. John Fitzgerald (New York: Scribner's, 1947); and *Man and the State* (Chicago: The University of Chicago Press, 1951).

45. John Courtney Murray, *We Hold These Truths* (New York: Sheed and Ward, 1960).

46. John Paul II, *Laborem exercens,* par. 14.

47. One interesting effort to move beyond this limited result in the direction of normative principles for policy is found in Hollenbach, *Claims in Conflict,* chap. 5, especially pp. 195–207.

48. Hollenbach has an excellent treatment of this polarity in relation to secular philosophical and Protestant styles of ethical theory in his *Claims in Conflict,* pp. 108–118.

49. For some telling conservative criticisms of the misuse of the concept of nature in later scholastic moral theory, see Finnis, *Natural Law,* p. 102.

50. The focus of concern here is those members and nonmembers of the Church whose rights are affected by the ministry and the governance of the Church and its institutions. It was also possible for Church officials, when they exercised significant economic and political power, to be involved in violations of human rights, but such violations present no special doctrinal or ecclesiological problem.

51. The listing of human-rights issues here is drawn from James A. Coriden, "Human Rights in the Church: A Matter of Credibility and Authenticity," in Muller and Greinacher, *The Church and the Rights of Man,* pp. 70–71.

52. John XXIII, *Pacem in terris,* par. 9. I owe this suggestion to a conversation with James Donlon.

53. Egalitarian universalism as a comprehensive norm for nonecclesial societies occupies a central place in *Laborem exercens*.

54. For a further treatment of this sort of dualism, see John Langan, "Order and Justice under John Paul II," *The Christian Century* 97 (April 30, 1980): 496.

55. Vatican II, *Gaudium et spes*, par. 41.

56. Ibid., par. 45.

57. Ibid., par. 44.

Looking Back on
Populorum Progressio

Barbara Ward

This article originally appeared in *Doctrine and Life*, 1978.

The year of 1977 was a particularly appropriate occasion to be thinking about the tenth anniversary of *Populorum Progressio* and what it means for our society today because, in one sense, so much has changed. If we look back to 1967, it is almost like looking back to another period in history. Yet, at the same time, we can now see in much clearer perspective how many of the analyses, how many of the facts given, almost for the first time in *Populorum Progressio,* are more relevant today than they were when they were actually written. In fact, one can almost say that they represent a sort of prophetic vision, a far clearer idea of what was going to happen in our planet than the ideas contained in many of the extremely learned economic treatises written at the time— some of them, alas, written by me.

MORE PAINFUL AND CHALLENGING

When we look back to the 1960s, we can see most of us caught up in the euphoria of economic growth. It seemed clear that, thanks to the Keynesian revolution of 'demand management', developed societies had virtually solved their problems. We would gallop forward to the society of high consumption, there to enjoy its felicities—whatever they might prove to be. At the same time, behind us would follow the developing world by 'stages of growth', and the wealth created in the process would inevitably trickle down until it reached the poorest. *Pop-*

ulorum Progressio might think otherwise. As Pope Paul VI put it: 'It is not sufficient to increase overall wealth for it to be distributed equitably. It is not sufficient to promote technology to render the world a more human place in which to live'. But we knew better. Within a reasonable amount of time, everyone would be rich, everyone would enjoy high consumption and everyone might or might not be happy—we did not even discuss that. But this was a picture of an almost automatic transfer of the development process, and it was against this background that, in 1967, Pope Paul published an analysis which warned us that this optimism, this euphoria were, in fact, misplaced. What was to come would be much more painful, much more difficult and infinitely more challenging to the Christian conscience than anything that was being more generally discussed at the time.

I would like just to pick out one or two of the things which *Populorum Progressio* underlined, perhaps for the first time. As we have seen, it did not believe in 'trickle down'; on the contrary, it foresaw the continued massive destitution of millions of people. It did not see easy movement forward through development into the felicities of high consumption. The Pope had seen people in their favelas and bustees and ruined farms; he had seen them as they were in existential fact—in Latin America, in Bombay. There is no allusion in *Populorum Progressio* to easy transfers or easy exchanges; Pope Paul had seen the fact of destitution and he cried out against it. He cried out to the Christian people of the world to realize what a responsibility faced them day by day. The death of children, the misery of families in growing illiteracy, the fact of unemployment and, behind it all, the increasing risk that people would be unable to feed themselves, and that malnutrition, and at times starvation, could become the way of the world as it developed—that was the vision *Populorum Progressio* set against the euphoria of the day.

Another point which was made, literally, I think for the first time, was to put people on guard against the degree to which a straightforward acceptance of modern industrial technology, unless carefully adapted to local cultural needs, could create the destruction of essential institutions or of essential values before there was anything else to take their place. It is very interesting to compare our assumption that the technology transfer would take place easily with the Pope's warning about what might be lost by the adoption of new industrial techniques and little respect for local cultures. As *Populorum Progressio* puts it, the developing nations should see to it 'that there be no interference in their political life or subversion of their social structures'. (Par. 56).

PEOPLE MUST BE INVOLVED

Another extremely important point, underlined in *Populorum Progressio* in a way that very few—if any—development economists at the time were emphasizing, is the fundamental point that there is no true development unless the people are involved in their own development. Quoting Père Lebret, the great Dominican economist, who was closely associated with the preparation of *Populorum Progressio,* the Pope wrote:

> Development cannot be limited to mere economic growth. In order to be authentic, it must be complete: integral, that is, it has to promote the good of every man and of the whole man. As an eminent specialist has very rightly and emphatically declared: 'We do not believe in separating the economic from the human, nor development from the civilisations in which it exists. What we hold important is man, each man and each group of men, and we even include the whole of humanity.'(par. 14)

In other words it was no answer for aid agencies or charities to visit the destitute masses and give them a little 'food for peace' or a touch of technical assistance. No, Pope Paul pointed out that true development is the development of the people by themselves, by their own work, by their own productivity, by their own involvement in their own decision-making, by the full human rights which go with the right to become, in fact, a fully participating, responsible citizen in a modern economy. It is very striking reading *Populorum Progressio* again, to note how much this sense that *people* are at stake, dominates the Encyclical; the reminder that development is for people, and, unless they are the actors in their own drama, there can be no true development. Another vital point brought out by *Populorum Progressio* was, of course, known to economists back in the Sixties. As the result of the long colonial period, 30% of the world's people living in the North, particularly in the North Atlantic region, are enjoying 70% of the world's goods and services, 80%

of its trade and new investments, over 90% of its industry and nearly 100% of its critical capacities for advanced research. But what I think *Populorum Progressio* made clear at a very early stage was the deeper consequences of this imbalance. Since 1967, the insight has become one of the foundations of the search for the New Economic Order; its importance cannot be overestimated for our present decade. But Pope Paul was one of the first to analyse the consequences.

UNEQUAL BARGAINERS

He pointed out that, if you are bargaining in a market (the market is not to be negated; the market is a very good tool, though a very bad master) and if the inequality between the bargainers is too great, then every single bargain that is struck will help the rich and not the poor. The words are striking for they show the continuity of the Church's teaching on this point:

> The teaching of Leo XIII in *Rerum Novarum* is always valid: if the positions of the contracting parties are too unequal, the consent of the parties does not suffice to guarantee the justice of their contract, and the rule of free agreement remains subservient to the demands of the natural law. What was true of the just wage for the individual is also true of international contracts: an economy of exchange can no longer be based solely on the law of free competition, a law which, in its turn, too often creates an economic dictatorship. Freedom of trade is fair only if it is subject to the demands of social justice.' (par. 59)

This clearly, until the oil crisis, was the position in the field of world trade. Virtually the whole of the benefit of the bargain lay with those who produce the manufactured goods, 93% of whom are still the countries of the North. The nations who provide the raw materials have been getting the worst of almost every bargain. Prices of manufactures tended upwards. Agricultural raw materials had all the instabilities of harvests, especially devastating to single crop economies. They had competition from synthetics. Above all, the earnings which flowed from the processing of their commodities were whisked off into the industrial North. All of what the economists called 'value added' remained with the rich nations with sometimes a share for a small local, wealthy, trading elite.

To this very day, the figures are extraordinary. Take, for example, about a dozen of the major primary exports of the developing world: the producing nation gets paid between 20 and 30 billion dollars for the product, be it a banana, a bean of coffee or whatever. But by the time it reaches the developed world consumer, its cost is 200 billion dollars. That is what has been added for the rich industrialists and middlemen and that, in a nutshell, is how the bargain works. All this is set out with the utmost clarity in *Populorum Progressio* and is taken back to its fundamental root which is the simple and basic one, first underlined by Pope Leo XIII. In the open market, the strength and the power of the bargainers will determine the outcome. This is not a blanket 'collectivist' condemnation of the market as such. A market is an admirable method of serving all the diverse needs of the community, provided there are not too great differences in economic power, provided, too, that people can enter into that market with income to spend, provided, in fact, that there is some sort of balance. If there is not, the market system itself becomes a means of reinforcing the poverty of the very poor, and reinforcing the wealth of the very wealthy.[1] It is not a Marxist economist but the sober statisticians of the World Bank that have pointed out that in some Latin American countries in the 1960s, all the gains from rapid economic growth—sometimes 10 per cent a year—were engrossed by the top 10 per cent of the people. The poorest were actually poorer still.

VIOLENT CONSEQUENCES

This analysis of the 'unequal bargain' in *Populorum Progressio* is not only a key issue in today's new economic order. It is something much more fateful. Pope Paul went on to remind his readers that if such conditions were to continue, if such destitution were to be left without recourse and without hope, the kind of instabilities in the world could only lead to violence. In the words of the Encyclical:

There are certainly situations whose injustice cries to heaven. When whole populations destitute of necessities live in a state of dependence barring them from all initiative and responsibility, and all opportunity to advance culturally and share in social and political life, recourse to violence, as a means to right these wrongs to human dignity, is a grave temptation. (par 30)

Nor is this local violence. Hatred and fear between the nations, breeding the arms race (which was already high and dangerous in the Sixties but nothing like what it has become since) would be exacerbated by the failure of the world community to come to grips with this basic problem of profound social imbalance and injustice. Pope Paul said in opening the Encyclical that 'the social issue has now become world-wide'. (par 3) And the consequence of leaving social conflict to develop throughout world society would be to leave humanity with so little solidarity, so little sense of brotherhood and community that finally it could do nothing but confront this injustice with anger and hatred, confront total poverty with the violence of despair. In that kind of world, the threat of war, the loss of peace, the growth of arms could be an inevitable consequence.

Thus *Populorum Progressio* was a challenge certainly to the human conscience, above all to the Christian conscience. It was based upon an analysis of the human condition which contradicted a great deal of the optimism of the 1960s. At the same time, it threw a challenge directly to the religious communities of the world, above all to the Christians who, to a very large degree, inhabit the North and are thus the rich who have the means, if not the will, to act. It was a challenge to them to take up fundamental social tasks, to get engaged in the justice of the great 'global bargain', and to see to it that the terrible risks of the continuance of injustice, destitution and despair were in fact set aside by a new, more hopeful, more loving and a more Christian approach.

ALL ANALYSES CONFIRMED

That was ten years ago. We look back. Then we look where we are. And what do we have to say? I think the first thing to say is that the Pope's analysis has been borne out with a speed and such a degree that even Père Lebret—God rest his saintly soul!—would have been astonished. The speed with which the Pope's picture of planetary reality has become the basic fact on which we have to build our common life is clear. Every single analysis of *Populorum Progressio* has been confirmed in the last ten years. Let me repeat the point. It is not some crackpot radical, it is the Chairman of the World Bank, who reminds us that the poor are getting poorer, that the whole process of development is not reaching the masses. We have even invented in our typical jargon a new phrase—the MSA—the 'most seriously affected'—for these poorest of the poor. It reminds me of the word 'under-privileged'. Under-privileged! For heaven's sake, could we not just say 'poor'? There is some evasion in all these phrases, and I find 'most seriously affected' a most seriously affected phrase. But it does point to the fact that, in the last five years, the billion people who live on incomes of less than 200 dollars a year—a billion of our fellow-men whose numbers are increasing rapidly—are worse off than they were ten years ago.

What is more, as a result of a number of U.N. conferences—on population, on food, on settlements and on water—a much more detailed analysis of this destitution is now available to us. We know more about the facts of unemployment; we know more about the effects of the vast migration of the rural poor from the stagnant countrysides into the cities where cities of a million are growing into cities of two, three and four million and the prospects of cities of sixteen and seventeen million are only twenty years away. And most of them will be in the developing world. The World Bank tells us that in some of these cities upwards of 40% of the people are either out of work or under-employed. So the momentum of our failure to get development to the mass of the people is gathering force and speed. Now, ten years after *Populorum Progressio,* its description of destitution would have to be even more radical, even more despairing.

And what is more, because of this examination in depth which the various United Nations conferences have carried on in the Seventies, there is a far greater understanding of the structural reasons for this massive poverty. Post colonial dependence is not simply cancelled by rapid growth in an unchecked, unbalanced world market. The facts have proved Pope Paul's analysis of a decade ago and brought it to the centre of the world stage.

NEW INTERNATIONAL ECONOMIC ORDER

This brings us to one of the great 'actualities' of our day which is, of course, the New International Economic Order. Many of the ideas of this New Order have such firm roots in *Populorum Progressio* that the Encyclical might almost have been its founding document. If we examine the content of the present world dialogue—in the discussions at UNCTAD, at the 'North-South' dialogue in Paris (the so-called Conference on International Economic Co-operation), what issues do we discover? Precisely the principles laid down in *Populorum Progressio,* the whole field of a new trade bargain, stable prices, buffer stocks, the ability of the nations themselves to begin processing their own goods, an increase in the share in the world's industry in the developing nations from 7% (as it is now) to 25% by the end of the century, more investment from the North to bring this about and a new determination that the investment will be of the kind that will go to the mass of the people for their basic needs. I should add one further point which is not particularly underlined in *Populorum Progressio,* the realization that agriculture, in our years of growth euphoria and of quick technology transfer, was basically neglected and that, if we are going to reach the year 2000 with any hope of feeding mankind, we have to concentrate in a quite new way on agricultural development, on clean water, on water for irrigation, on intermediate market settlements which energize the countryside.

In addition, developing countries themselves must not claim justice and help in the agricultural and other efforts unless they are entirely ready to practise the same justice at home. When a few families own all the land and peons and landless men have no rights or security, no amount of aid will serve its true purpose. On this point, Pope Paul is quite explicit:

> If certain landed estates impede the general prosperity because they are extensive, unused or poorly used, or because they bring hardship to peoples or are detrimental to the interests of the country, the common good sometimes demands their expropriation. (par 24)

Yet even if, in general, the specifics of international aid to agriculture are not mentioned, the whole approach to international justice matched by local justice is at the core of *Populorum Progressio*. The people who have to transform agriculture are the mass of farming people themselves. Aid missions cannot come in with some pieces of super-technology and then go away again. That is not the way any reform can work. We cannot leave it either to such private instruments as large multi-national corporations because they are operating with forms of capital-intensive technology wholly unsuitable to nations with a work force growing by 2 per cent a year—and massive under-employment and worklessness in town and country alike. It was prescient of Pope Paul to realize so early that choices must be made; man must not be sacrificed to technology, industries must not be introduced which actually increase unemployment. The people themselves must be drawn into the rebuilding of their lives and develop and preserve their own values. As the Encyclical puts it:

> Developing nations must know how to discriminate among those things that are held out to them; they must be able to assess critically, and eliminate those deceptive goods which would only bring about a lowering of the human ideal, and to accept those values that are sound and beneficial, in order to develop them alongside their own, in accordance with their own genius.

What Sort of Investment?

The New Economic Order does represent new insights into the nature of the investment that the developing world really needs. It is investment in basic needs of small farmers in the countryside, in the 'bazaar economy' of big cities and in new market and service centres that have to be built if new dynamism in the countryside is to be created and sustained. The needed types of industrial and agricultural investment require especial emphasis for they alone can offer hope in the world's acute demographic crisis. As Pope Paul puts it:

> . . . too frequently an accelerated demographic increase adds its own difficulties to the problems of development: the size of the population increases more rapidly than available resources,

and things are found to have reached apparently an impasse.
(par 37)

The results can be seen throughout the developing world. The terrible
haemorrhage of people to the cities is a direct product of rural failure.
Inadequately financed, inadequately capitalized countrysides, with loss
of cheap energy, with insufficient fertilizer, with a tendency to over-
crop, all mean that we are literally 'losing ground'. We are losing soil,
the earth is eroding. The foothills of the Himalayas are becoming areas
where you go from drought to flood, from flood to drought. As a result
of this neglect and abuse of our absolutely basic resource—which is the
soil—we, in fact, are endangering not only the future of the poor, but
the future of the planet.

The encouraging fact is, as the President of the World Bank has
pointed out, that wherever investment and aid do reach the mass of the
people, population pressures begin to relax because parents are confident
that their first children will survive. But suppose the effort is *not* made?
Is this the kind of planet you think we can conduct on a sane, human and
loving basis? Is this the kind of world community in which our children
and grandchildren can live? Is this the kind of way in which our global
bargain can be struck? In theory, we regard the community of man as a
community. But, say the poor, do you, the rich, regard it as anything but
a market? Will you from your wealth provide the basic capital for this
mass investment in the needs of the poorest? Will you finance sites and
services in cities and assist self-building form homes and businesses?
Will you look at energy and fertilizer needs at the village level? Will you
take seriously the entire package of agricultural proposals put forward at
the Rome World Food Conference which included stocks to carry us over
potential famine, buffer stocks to keep food prices more stable and,
above all, investment in the rural sector? And will you bring into this
investment the farmer and the artisan as active partners so that they become, to this extent, masters of their own destiny? You have done comparable things inside your own welfare states. But do you think of us as
brothers and citizens in need of the same co-operation and help? Or do
we belong to another planet? These are the questions that are being asked
at UNCTAD, in Paris. They represent the whole thrust of *Populorum
Progressio*. But they leaped forward with infinitely greater speed than

any of us thought possible even five years ago and have to be confronted with far greater urgency.

APPALLING WASTE

Now we must ask what is the precise bargaining position of North and South today, ten years after *Populorum Progressio*? I fear we have to admit that the North is in an appalling muddle. We really believed in this beautiful simple idea of perpetual growth, kept going by mounting demand with everyone consuming more and more and the whole economy comfortably at work as a result. And we forgot quite a number of things which we now have to learn. When, in 1973, the cost of oil quadrupled, we suddenly realized that we had been running our economy in the most wasteful fashion probably ever contrived by any group of people in the whole of world history. It was a 'slosh-on', 'throw-it- away' economy *par excellence,* and some of the figures are simply fantastic. Do you know that in the late 60s and early 70s, 50% of the energy that was sold in the United States—not just created, but sold—was wasted? It was so cheap that people literally did not think of price. When the oil crisis began, they found businesses which had left on their de-icing equipment throughout the year so that on July 4th you could go through their yards and find all the underground pipes just pouring out heat into the July sun.

The waste is everywhere: houses leak heat through their windows, they leak heat through their walls, wasting precious fuel. Then we have the profound, pervasive, all powerful source of waste, the motorcar, which in a congested city can get just 6 per cent efficiency from its gallon of gasoline. In addition, and this is a subtle point but one which people are beginning to realize, we use the highest quality form of energy— electricity—for simple heating jobs where lower quality energy sources like oil or gas (or indeed the sun) would be more efficient and cheaper. Most electricity generating stations convert fuel burnt in the boiler to electricity. By the time this gets to the house or the factory, three-quarters of the energy originally produced has simply leaked out into the biosphere both within the original station or during transmission. But this has been typical of the kind of happy-go-lucky waste upon which our wealthy economies were based.

I would also just throw in, because it always seems to me one of the worst forms of carelessness, the whole idea of the throw-away container. If we re-process or re-use containers—glass or metal—we can usually save something like 70 or 80% both of the metals and of the energy. But who cares? There will always be more, there will always be enough energy, there will always be enough metal. We are not going to run out, so we live with the throw-away economy and let greed determine our wastes. As the Pope said in *Populorum Progressio,* again so presciently: 'Avarice is the most self-evident mark of moral underdevelopment'. (par 10) This society was not only a very greedy society. It was getting greedier. First, it was a problem of 'one each' for everybody: little by little nearly everybody got one car. Then there was that little question of what you did with your wife when you marooned her in the suburbs. So you had to have two cars. Then came the great movement for second homes and this seemed to entail three family cars. And if you add up this steady increase in what the developed world considered to be, not a great affluence in life, but daily necessities, we finally discover that the amount of energy, per capita, which was being consumed by the wealthy in 1973 was 15 times greater than that of the poorer people, and of that, in North America, 50% was leaking away, uselessly, into the atmosphere.

STAGFLATION

This was the kind of mentality prevailing among us when, in the 1973 boom, there occurred, on the one hand, the quadrupling of the price of oil, and, on the other, the tripling of the price of food because the Russians quickly nipped in and bought 25 million tons of grain from America's grain reserve without anyone really noticing. I have always thought that for the sons of Lenin it was an extremely clever *business* operation. I wonder how they did it because, you know, 25 million tons of grain takes quite a bit of buying and quite a bit of moving in a hurry. But they succeeded and world food prices tripled as a result. Now, at this point, a perspective began to come into our ways of thinking which is still puzzling, troubling and confusing the rich nations so that their mind is really only partially attending to the North/South dialogue, to the 'global bargain'. Fundamentally the problem is this. What do you do with unemployment if growth is accompanied by a continuous rise in prices, so that when you try to pull back your price levels by spending less, you suddenly find more people out of work?

It is thus that we have contrived a situation which we now have throughout the North Atlantic world, known as 'stagflation'. This is inflation continuing and the level of unemployment and stagnation in the economy continuing as well. Frankly, I doubt if there is an economist at the moment who really believes he knows what to do about it. We have been working on the Keynesian analysis which was that sustained demand would create the entire cycle of employment and maintain steady growth. But at this point, we have discovered a new obstacle. It is quite possible that in natural terms we have been asking too much of our planet. If we let our economies 'rip' again, if we were to repeat the 6–7% rates of growth of the 60s, we might begin to run out of fossil fuels in a decade, begin to exhaust other basic resources—fertilizer, certain metals, even food and soil. Then the pressure on prices would push us back into even high inflation. So we live in a very troubled 'Northern world' that cannot come to terms with itself. And, incidentally, I see little difference here between market or planned economies. The pressure of prices, the risk of inflation affect them all.

Restraint

This malaise will slacken only when we can find some way of saying: Give us the wisdom to discover the 'philosophy of enough'. Take us off this treadmill of more and more and more. Let us have some sense of what are the decent limits, the upper limits and the lower limits of demand which a citizen can reasonably make upon the resources of his planet. Let us try to find some way in which, within our advanced industrial systems, confrontation is no longer the order of the day. Instead can we not realize that joint work and genuine productivity, coupled with decent restraint, is the only way we can achieve a functioning economy? If everybody is expecting more and more and more, and setting their standards by the pursuit of immediate and increasing wealth, inflation is a certainty and even absolute scarcities begin to be possible.

In short, we have to devise income policies, employment policies, inflation policies which balance justice with initiative and enterprise, which give people the sense of belonging to a fair community in which rewards are not grossly skewed, in which the rich do not so enormously outspend the poor that the poor are always trying to spend up to the rich. Once again, we are reminded of the Pope's words that 'avarice is the most self-evident mark of moral under-development' and his forceful repetition of the Gospel parable of the rich man whose fields yielded an abundant harvest and who did not know where to store his harvest: 'God said to him: 'Fool, this night do they demand your soul of you'' '. (par 49)

But this internal disorder is not the only difficulty for the Northern 'bargainers'. For the first time in centuries they are no longer bargaining entirely from strength. This does not mean to say that we are pressing up against absolute limits of energy and resources. But what is certainly true is that never again are developed nations likely to secure energy as cheaply as they have done in the last 25 years. That splurge is finished! Even with care, oil and natural gas will be used up in the next three to four decades. Coal will last longer, but its vast expansion could threaten the planetary atmosphere. Nuclear power not only grows more and more expensive but places unacceptable dangers—from radio-active wastes and melt-downs—on future generations. The energy spree is over. And now, today, in the dialogue with the world's poor, the cheapest, most useful fuel, petroleum, is controlled not by the North but by developing countries.

So how does the bargain look to them? They have gained great confidence from OPEC's solidarity and from the realization that for the first time in the post-colonial world, not all the power is in one place. This does not mean that countries like India, or any of the non-oil producing states, have not suffered from the increased price of energy: they have. But they have a sense of solidarity with the oil producers because they do believe that a little muscle has been introduced into their bargaining. To use the Pope's analogy of the balance of power within the market, some power has come back to the developing world. The non-oil producers have more confidence even though their situation—with fuel shortages and food risks—is actually worse. So now we come to the real danger. It is that the wealthy nations, who are confused, who do not see their way out of stagflation, who have not evolved policies for restraint to counter inflation, will come to the bargaining table determined at all cost to be evasive, to try to get the chief issues shelved until they are a little more comfortable about their own policies. But at the same time, the poor world is coming to the bargaining table with a little more confidence and saying: 'Why should we wait? We have waited year after year after year. We have waited a century. How much longer do you expect?' The dangers of confrontation are squarely there. Both the UNCTAD and the Paris conferences have given a hint of compromise. But there is no certainty of a global bargain.

Need for Our Voices To Be Heard

How does this affect us as Christian peoples, or at least as post-Christian peoples who still represent the main religious tradition of the wealthy 'Northern' states? How does this affect us as Catholics who must wish in our lives, in our influence, to follow the ideals for which Pope Paul himself has pleaded? If there is any reality and depth in our Christian commitment, it is surely at this moment that the Christian voice of Europe and North America should be raised, calling at home for restraint, for inflationary control through just and balanced income policies, for the kind of investment that not only creates jobs but helps the basic needs of the poorest citizens. In the world at large the plea should be that Europe and North America carry on the North-South 'bargain' with a genuine readiness to assist in a steady increase in industrialization in the South, for instance by a phased transfer of processing raw materials to those who, in fact, possess them. This implies a transfer of capital which should be dedicated to appropriate labour-intensive technologies and include the agricultural sector. Then, as productive capacity, training and skills rise in the developing world—as they have in Taiwan and South Korea and many parts of Latin America—arrangements for trade should include both better access to Northern markets and much more emphasis on commerce between the Southern group of states. In this way—just as much of the new oil money is being spent now in 'the North'—new productiveness and growth among the poorest states will open up new markets and take some of the strain off the United States, Europe and Japan, all now hoping to provide competitive goods—steel, machines, motor cars—for export. (The socialist states have already entered the trading process but, unhappily, their relative lack of efficiency and technical skills has already put them into some $50 billions of debt to the market economies and confident growth is inhibited as a result).

If these main issues of the 'New Economic Order'—a fairer share of wealth, a greater equality in the trade bargain—are accepted, then the dialogue of North and South can change its character. We shall begin to talk to each other as in a human community, not as rivals and enemies in confrontation. We need a voice in North America, we need a voice in Europe, crying out that these overwhelming needs of the poor people of the world can only be met by some degree of unselfishness—by some 'moral development' among the rich. And if Christians cannot say it or feel it, who in heaven's name will do instead? It is as though the good Lord were presenting us with a direct challenge to our affluence and saying: 'Look, for 25 years, you have had the prosperous years. Now come the lean years. What are you going to do to make sure that they do not become years of deepening malnutrition, famine and despair? The trends are for the poor to get poorer. They continue thus because you, the rich, have not the courage and the negotiating readiness to make these capital transfers, to secure a better trade balance, to make available the right kinds of technology and to give food production, clean water, education and employment your top priority. For although these things sound technical, I tell you, as your Lord and Master, that in the end of the 20th century, all these things are the concrete meaning of loving your neighbour as yourself'.

CHALLENGE

This is what, in fact, the tenth anniversary of *Populorum Progressio* must mean to all of us. It challenges us. Are we serious, are we in fact ready to accept from that great Encyclical the guidelines which Pope Paul laid down with such perception ten years ago, outlining for us the duty of love, the solid path of justice and real meaning of the solidarity, the fundamental teaching of the Gospel applied to our own day?

If our ears were open and our hearts ready, there is so much that we could do. First of all, we could deal with our sinful wastefulness. Every single Christian could be in the forefront in practising and demanding conservation—the conserving society—from their leaders, the sparing use of energy, for the end of the 'throw-away' mentality, for the recycling of materials, for every effort to cut out the 'squander-mania' of the last 25 years.

Next, we should be clearly and explicitly behind every effort to reduce the worst of all our wastefulness—the utterly destructive and totally inflationary world arms race. Perhaps we can help to introduce a new element beyond balanced forces and keeping 'overkill' to no more than twenty times the scale needed to destroy the whole planet. Four years ago, the Russians—with whatever tongue in whatever cheek, one does not know—proposed at the U.N. General Assembly that there should be a 10% cut in arms spending and that 10% of that should be devoted to development. Why do we not return to this proposal, increase it to the whole 10 per cent and pledge ourselves to give the capital saved from it to food, to water, to shelter and to employment? The arms bill is now running at over 300 billion dollars a year. Ten per cent of that would give us for basic investment in agriculture just about the figure which the Rome World Food Conference proposed: 30 billion dollars. This would also include the target of about 9 billion dollars needed for clean water for all by 1990. These are not impossible goals. Indeed, I suspect the capital could be secured largely from military wastes, obsolete models and possibly the bribes of the arms trade!

Now let us look at a third possibility. Why are Christians not in the forefront of those seeking to adopt a more conserving style in their own personal lives? If we are affluent, we do not really need that third television set, let alone that third car. And at lesser levels of wealth, to give us only one example, more modest eating with the balance given to private aid agencies, could save 'Southern' babies from dying and 'Northern' adults from heart attacks. If we were seriously to develop new life styles among Christians, might we not launch a movement comparable to St. Benedict who started a modest community in the Abruzzi and went on to colonize the whole of Western Europe? People would suddenly notice that something was changing. I doubt if we notice anything very different in the average Christian family at the moment. We do not seem to realize yet that there is any link between the world's divisions and disorders and our own selfishness, our easy acceptance of the consumer society and our desperate need for the 'moral development' which will make us less greedy, more conserving and more ready to demand of our leaders—this is where civic action comes in—that by the ending of waste and by conservation, we release resources for the basic needs of the poor.

TRY MORALITY FOR A CHANGE

The ridiculous thing about this blindness is that we should be better off, even in material terms, if we did try morality for a change. As I have pointed out, one of the reasons at this moment why there are such trade difficulties between Japan and Europe and North America is that their competition with each other is producing creeping protectionism which could lead to another 1931. We all suffer if ever increasing demands among the rich make inflation inevitable. But with more investment in the kind of real resources—materials and people—that exist unused in the developing world, we could build them up and take the strain off ourselves. This, in a sense, is what the United States, with half its present wealth, did with the Marshall Plan in 1947. Today, a policy of justice, a policy of collaboration, a policy which would turn the dialogue between the North and South into a real effort to build the economic base for the family of man, would turn out at the same time to be the most economically sensible thing we could do. Our prosperity for 25 years started with America's generosity. Is the model not worth trying again?

In other words, if we achieved a just and genuine 'global compact', we should not only have done what is morally right. We would find that we have followed what is just plain sensible, rational, enlightened self-interest on a global scale. God does not cheat. God does not set up for us a whole series of hurdles so that every time we jump one, we fall over another. He only asks that our self-interest be sufficiently generous and enlightened for morals to play their full part and brotherhood to be a reality, not empty rhetoric.

This is the challenge of *Populorum Progressio*. This was its foresight. There is not a page that is not relevant to where we are now. But quite simply we have not listened to the prophetic word. Today the need is for all of us to dedicate a new effort, with God's help, to greater simplicity and thrift in our own lives, and a firm determination to become a lobby for the world's poor. At no time must we allow our politicians to get up and say: 'But then, of course, there is no interest in development in my constituency. Nobody is thinking about world development in my part of the world.' Let there be everywhere at least 10% of the electorate so angrily committed to world development—and so prepared to bite the local politician's ankle—that notice is taken. Then I think the great principles could begin to work like a leaven in the mass of our world economy and out of the change could come the possibility of genuine dialogue. And from true dialogue would follow the possibility of true humanity. And from there, perhaps, would come the ultimate possibility—that we shall not destroy ourselves in a nuclear war.

Fear, says the Bible, is the beginning of wisdom. Let me end, then, not only with hope but with fear as well. In the last 25 years, there has been another great quantum jump in the scientific development of human society. We have gone beyond using nature. When we split the atom, when we create chemical compounds unknown in all evolution, when we can play about with DNA, the fundamental element of biological life itself, we can manipulate and change the basic building blocks of all existence. We have given ourselves a degree of power—for creation or destruction—of which the legends of Faust or Prometheus are all but shadows. If we have no moral restraints to this degree of power, if all we have to guide our new capacities is, on the one hand, national aggression and self-assertion, and, on the other, personal greed and moral under-development—oh! this pathetic little planet does not stand a chance.

I would say, therefore, that on our ability to conduct generously and justly the North/South dialogue, on our ability to see ourselves as a common human family, I will say it bravely—on love itself—depends the entire fate of this planet. All this is foreseen in *Populorum Progressio.* It is more relevant and immediate now than ever before. The chief question facing the Christian community—still largely 'Northern' and white—is this: Have we the courage, have we the restraint, the modesty to work together with all mankind for the creation of a true community? We have the overwhelming wealth so we have the overwhelming power to act and hence the central responsibility. This is the challenge directed to us Christians. So let us pray that in the next ten years the analysis of *Populorum Progressio* will turn into the action of *Populorum Progressio,* and that Christians can be there inspiring a true dialogue and helping the world to achieve its dream of hope and peace.

Note

1. To illustrate the degree to which philosophers have long recognized the consequences of unbalanced power, one has only to recall Thucydides, the great Greek historian's account of Athens and Melos:

"The human spirit is so constituted that what is just is examined only if there is equal necessity on both sides. But if one is strong and the other weak, that which is possible is imposed by the first, accepted by the second."

This is why since Antiquity, the symbol of justice has been a figure holding equally balanced scales.

Action for Justice
as Constitutive of the
Preaching of the Gospel:
What Did the 1971 Synod Mean?

Charles M. Murphy

This article originally appeared in *Theological Studies*, 1983.

There has been within the past century a notable growth and development in an area of church life which has come to be known as her
"social teaching." It began ninety years ago with Leo XIII's encyclical
Rerum novarum, in which the Church took up the question of the rights
of workers; it took a new turn with John XXIII's *Mater et magistra* and
the conciliar and postconciliar documents, most notably *Gaudium et spes*
and Paul VI's *Populorum progressio,* when the Church's teaching reflected a far broader and more global perspective than merely workers'
rights.[1]

A milestone in this rapidly developing area of the Church's concern
and mission, by common consent, was the document *Justice in the
World* which emerged from the second ordinary World Synod of Bishops
held in the fall of 1971. It is in this document that for the first time in a
magisterial statement of the Church the biblical concept of liberation appears.[2] The document's discussion of the personal right of social participation and the right to development conceived as the "dynamic
integration of all fundamental human rights" has been called "the beginning of a new phase of the tradition—a phase which presumes that
personal freedom is simultaneously both inescapably social and intrinsically dependent on developing social structures."[3] What has been
called the principal insight of the 1971 synod, the most notable devel-

opment to date in the history of modern social teaching, is the following sentence from that document: ''Action on behalf of justice and participation in the transformation of the world fully appears to us as a constitutive dimension of the preaching of the gospel or, in other words, of the Church's mission for the redemption of the human race and its liberation from every oppressive situation.''

We are obviously in an area where theological reflection is needed upon a vital and ongoing dimension of the Church's contemporary life. In this article, ten years after the synod, I will examine whether and to what extent the term ''constitutive'' employed by the synod clarifies the spiritual and religious basis of the Church's commitment to social justice, to human solidarity and emancipation. The sources I will draw upon are the interpretations of the synod's work provided by the principal drafters of the document, supplemented by material from the Pontifical Commission Justice and Peace and the rather complete summary of each synod's proceedings edited by Giovanni Caprile.[4]

The term ''constitutive'' is a strong, arresting term. It forces the Christian to ask the vital question whether working for justice is at the heart of the Church's mission and of the gospel itself, that is, part of the very definition of Christianity, or whether working for justice is more on the level of an ethical deduction from the central truths of the Christian message. The term ''constitutive'' confronts us with this central question for our times; as such, its theological analysis is of the greatest importance, not merely in terms of history or theory but in terms of the ongoing life of the Church and the direction she will be taking. Indeed, this sentence from the synod has been used in the United States, in Latin America, in Africa, and elsewhere as the platform and the legitimation for a whole series of new initiatives in social and political life by Roman Catholics.[5]

Some see in these new directions of involvement a loss of the Christian identity and a compromise of the gospel itself. Obviously, I cannot offer answers to all these questions, which are still very contemporary in the life of the Church, but perhaps some light will be cast by an analysis of how accurately the term ''constitutive'' represents the Church tradition thus far and even carries it forward. I will (1) begin with a description of the evolution of *Justice in the World* in the synod of 1971, (2) discuss its ''correction'' in the synod of 1974 and the apostolic exhortation *Evangelii nuntiandi* which followed it, and (3) assess the impact of the term "constitutive" on the life of the Church and the various interpretations it has received. In this last section I will attempt to supply some of the needed theological background for a fuller statement of the centrality of justice and love in the preaching of the gospel and the life of the Church.

THE SYNOD OF 1971

The synod of 1971 was the third synod since this phenomenon emerged in the contemporary Church. The synod was still at this point striving to discover its identity apart from, for example, the identity of an ecumenical council. An ecumenical council usually meets over several years, and there is the opportunity to reflect at length with wide consultation on the topics presented. A synod, however, meets for a very short period, is consultative in nature, and more recently has relieved itself of the burden of coming up with a document at the end of its sessions, preferring to give its work to the pope for further disposition. The synod of 1971 was the last to produce a full document; in fact, it produced two, corresponding to the two topics it was given to discuss: the ministerial priesthood and justice in the world.

Between October 19 and 30, during eleven "general congregations" and four days of sessions by twelve smaller study groups, the synod took up the question of justice. This was after three exhausting weeks of discussion concerning the ministerial priesthood, discussion which continued even while the synod began its deliberations about justice. On October 31 and November 1 and 2, the drafting group produced the justice statement. On November 3, the *textus prior* was presented to the full synod. Voting on this first draft, by section only, took place the next day. On November 5, the *textus emendatus* was distributed and voting on this text followed on November 6.

The head of the drafting committee, who was also the special secretary of the synod for the theme of justice, was Bishop Ramón Torrella Cascante, former auxiliary bishop in Barcelona, and the new vice president of the Pontifical Commission Justice and Peace. The sole official theologian of the synod regarding justice was Juan Alfaro, S.J., of the Gregorian University, the principal author of the eventual chapter 2, "The Gospel Message and the Mission of the Church."

Bishop Torrella proposed to the three cardinal presidents of the synod that before the intervention of the synod fathers, three lay experts be allowed to address the full assembly. The economist Barbara Ward spoke on "Planetary Justice," Candido Mendez of the University of Rio de Janeiro addressed the topic "Development and Structural Marginalization," and Kinhide Mushakoji, a Japanese expert on disarmament, gave an intervention on "The Universal Aspiration to Participation." The ideas all three expressed had considerable impact and found their way into the eventual final text. Two other members of the drafting committee were Philip Land, S.J., of the staff in Rome of the commission, and Vincent Cosmao, O.P., a member of the commission who came to Rome for the duration of the synod from Paris, where he was, and still is, associated with the Centre Foie et Développement founded by Louis Lebret. The principal author of the Introduction, in which the sentence under discussion appears, was Cosmao. The synod made two alterations in the sentence: the word "action" (*actio*) for justice replaced "struggle" (*pugna*), and "redemption" was added as a more traditional term to balance the newer term "liberation" and to avoid the danger of excessive "horizontalism." Horizontalism came up several times in criticism of the document from its earliest stages of development; it refers to the danger of reducing the gospel to a merely human project and a purely temporal goal.

The crucial word "constitutive" passed without comment or debate. The official Latin version reads "dimensio constitutiva," which is a translation of Cosmao's original French text "une dimension constitutive." The English translation is "a constitutive dimension"; the Spanish also uses the equivalent "una" but the Italian reads "la dimensione costitutiva." The Dutch and German translations use the word "essential" and not "constitutive." These latter versions would cause some difficulty in the synod of 1974.

In Cosmao's explanation of the meaning of the term "constitutive," the preaching of the gospel "occurs" by means of the action on behalf of justice: the gospel itself, taken against its Old Testament background, is the proclamation of the intervention of God for the realization of justice. The word "constitutive" was used, therefore, to make engagement for justice not merely an ethical deduction from faith but a very condition for the truth of the faith.[6] In a speech given to the French hierarchy prior to the synod, Cosmao used the same phrasing as he employed in his draft for the synod to describe the relationship between action for justice and the preaching of the gospel. "Is the participation in the transformation of the world, perceived as unjust, merely a requirement flowing from the faith and expressing itself in the works of charity, or is it constitutive of Christ's passover conceived as coextensive with human history, which is the history of human liberation?"[7]

In *Octogesima adveniens,* issued just before the synod, Pope Paul VI expressed the hope that the synod would be able to provide assistance by studying the mission of the Church with regard to justice questions. The document produced by the synod was very consistent in its development with the process for approaching these questions laid down by *Octogesima adveniens:* analysis of the social situation; reflection upon the gospel teaching in the light of the situation; judgment and action. But as the synod of 1974 opened, Paul VI stated that it was necessary that there be a "better and more subtle" definition of the relationship of evangelization as such and human striving toward progress. In the years following the synod of 1971, Pope Paul on several occasions made favorable reference to *Justice in the World* but never the passage which refers to action on behalf of justice as a constitutive dimension of the preaching of the gospel.[8]

THE SYNOD OF 1974

The term "constitutive" began to receive critical examination in the next general assembly, the synod of 1974, which was devoted to one theme, "Evangelization of the World in our Times." It was a theme which grew out of the discussions of the previous synod and laid emphasis on the religious mission of the Church. The most significant result of the 1974 synod was Pope Paul's apostolic exhortation *Evangelii nuntiandi,* which received a wide and favorable response in the Church and contributed further clarification about the relationship between the gospel and justice. It has become a foundational document in all subsequent discussion in this area.

In February prior to the opening of the synod, the Pontifical Commission Justice and Peace issued a document as its own "contribution" to the work of the synod. The *raison d'être* of the document, *Evangelization of the Modern World,* was given by Bishop Torrella in his Introduction: "It is very important that on the occasion of the coming synod action for justice and peace be reasserted in the perspective of evangelization and as one of its integral parts. Naturally, ambiguities, misunderstandings, contradictions, and confusion should be avoided."

It is apparent that some of the "ambiguities, misunderstandings, contradictions, and confusion" centered around the term "constitutive"; for Bishop Torrella goes on:

> The last synod clearly stated that action for justice . . . is a "constitutive dimension" and not a "unique dimension," as if the entire evangelization should be carried out exclusively through action for justice. But it is true that modern man is very sensitive to the values of justice, peace, and solidary love. It is a question of the credibility of the announcement of the message of salvation. It is very important to make the relation and link between evangelization and peace explicit. There can be no peace without justice, no justice without peace.[9]

It is already clear in these words of Torrella that some corrective interpretation was beginning to take place.

Torrella was still the vice president of the Pontifical Commission Justice and Peace at the time of the 1974 synod and was appointed to participate in it by the pope. His contribution to the document *Justice in the World* had been so large and significant that his interpretation of that document, and especially of the phrase "constitutive dimension," is of the greatest significance. Before the synod opened, Torrella gave an interview in which he expressed thoughts he would repeat during the course of the synod.[10] The occasion for the interview was the publication of his commission's "contribution" to the work of the synod, mentioned above. He summarized that document by saying that it is important for the synod to reaffirm the necessity of action on behalf of peace and justice within the perspective of evangelization and as an integral part of evangelization. The phrase "integral part" is important because it would be used during the synod as Torrella's explanation of what the synod of 1971 meant by the term "constitutive dimension." The Italian version of the 1971 document on justice spoke of "la dimensione costitutiva." In the interview Torrella corrected this translation: the synod meant that working for justice is but one, and only one, dimension of the preaching of the gospel. After some words about the difficulty of the gospel message acquiring credibility in the world today without the witness of action for peace and justice, Torrella asserted that the dual dangers of dichotomy and identification must be avoided.

Bishop Torrella made two interventions in the course of the synod itself. The first, on October 12, was in three parts: Justice and Evangelization; The Credibility of the Gospel Today; Challenge to Our Faith. In this intervention Torrella sought to avoid the "fatal dualism" between faith and justice of which he had spoken in his interview. He called for the present synod to provide "integration" and "synthesis" for pastoral action. His second intervention, on October 17, was made, he said, to avoid unnecessary polemics, because he had seen among the questions given to the study groups one asking for a justification of "constitutive" from the previous synod. After noting the overwhelming positive vote the whole Introduction had received with only two small emendations, he affirmed that the "mind of the synodal fathers" was that "constitutive dimension" meant "integral part," referring to the second chapter of the document regarding the love of God being made efficacious and manifest in the love of neighbor. He then explicitly stated that "essential" was not the meaning given by the synod to the word "constitutive," or at least that such could not be proven. For Torrella, constitutive defined as integral part is not so strong a term as essential; it refers to "something which accompanies, but need not be present, that is, strictly speaking, a true proclamation of the gospel could take place without action for justice."[11]

Both Land and Alfaro, however, expressed reservations about Torrella's clarifications concerning the intent of the synod. Land believes that interpreting "constitutive" as "integral" weakens the meaning of the word and confuses the issue. "If you say something is an integral part, it could be either a substantial part or an accidental part. No one wanted to say that justice is an accidental part of the gospel."[12] Alfaro saw in the 1974 synod an attempt to weaken the thrust of the 1971 synod. He believes that Torrella introduced an "unnecessary complication" in his intervention by trying to make "constitutive part" the equivalent of "integral part." Constitutive elements and integral elements are not the same, according to Alfaro. The body and soul, for example, are constitutive elements of man and woman, without which they could not exist. To assert, therefore, that in the Introduction to *Justice in the World* "constitutive" means "integral" is, according to Alfaro, "an error." "This was not the thinking of the drafting group. It is to introduce another term altogether."

Alfaro believes that the use of the scholastic term "constitutive" was unfortunate. Christianity, he maintains, as a historical reality cannot be expressed easily in such philosophical language. It would be better to use another type of vocabulary and say that in the proclamation of the gospel we cannot forget the proclamation of justice and the duty to practice justice. This at least, according to Alfaro, was the sense of the drafting group, who worked in a rather "spontaneous" atmosphere and used Cosmao's term "constitutive" not in a strict scholastic sense but in a much broader way. "Constitutive" means, for Alfaro, that justice is an essential aspect of the gospel, but not unique. Using the biblical language he prefers, Alfaro stresses that love of God and love of neighbor cannot be separated and that justice is the first requirement of love of neighbor, just as love in the Christian scheme is the motivation for justice.[13]

The "working paper" (*instrumentum laboris*) sent out prior to the opening of the 1974 synod attempted its own explanation of what the previous synod had meant to say and what it left unsaid. The working paper was in two parts: a summary of the experiences communicated by the various episcopal conferences, and a theological reflection. Part 1 noted "the intimate connection" between the work of human promotion and the Christian faith as taught by the previous synod, but asked how this work of human promotion should be carried out without losing Christian identity. Part 2 mentioned that nearly all the responses of the episcopal conferences affirmed the intrinsic connection between witness of life and evangelization ("intrinsecus ad rationem evangelizationis pertinere") as bearing upon the efficaciousness and credibility of the preaching, a witness of life especially through charity providing an experiential illustration and confirmatory sign of the truth of the gospel. According to the *instrumentum laboris,* therefore, the connection which the synod of 1971 affirmed between gospel preaching and the work of justice is one of credibility.

The "greater precision," however, about the "intimate link" between preaching the gospel and the work of justice which Pope Paul insistently called for had to await the publication of his own *Evangelii nuntiandi* one year after the synod's close.

THE APOSTOLIC EXHORTATION "EVANGELII NUNTIANDI"

In the first of the seven sections of the exhortation, Pope Paul focuses everything upon the person of Christ, who is himself the Good News, who comes to proclaim above all else the kingdom of God and His salvation. This salvation, "this great gift of God," is liberation from everything that oppresses man and woman but is above all liberation from sin and the Evil One.[14] The Church is born of the evangelizing activity of Jesus and exists in order to evangelize: this is her "deepest identity," "the grace and vocation proper to her." Paul therefore states that "It is with joy and consolation that at the end of the great assembly of 1974 we heard these illuminating words: 'We wish to confirm once more that the task of evangelizing all people constitutes the essential mission of the Church.' "[15]

Sections 2, 3, and 4, which are concerned with the definition, content, and methods of evangelization, are the most important to our discussion. Paul defines evangelization much more broadly than proclaiming Christ to those who do not know him, preaching, catechesis, and conferring baptism and other sacraments. It is "a complex process made up of varied elements: the renewal of humanity, witness, explicit proclamation, inner adherence, entry into the community, acceptance of signs, apostolic initiative."[16] Section 3 wishes to define the primary and secondary elements within the complex process of evangelization. The foundation, center, and summit of evangelization, its essential content, is the proclamation of God, revealed by Jesus Christ in the Holy Spirit, His love for the world and His offer of salvation. Secondary elements of evangelization—without which, however, evangelization would not be "complete"—are the rights and duties of every human being, family life, life in society, international life, peace, justice and development—in other words, all the gospel has to say about concrete human life, both personal and social.

The Pope then distinguishes the divine message of eternal salvation from the pastoral concern for human advancement expressed, he says, during the synod, especially by bishops of the Third World. The salvation offered through evangelization is the gift of God's grace and mercy, not an immanent salvation meeting material or even spiritual needs restricted to the framework of temporal existence and completely identified with temporal desires, hopes, affairs, and struggles. "Consequently," the exhortation continues, "evangelization cannot but include the prophetic proclamation of a hereafter, man's profound and definitive calling, in both continuity and discontinuity with the present situation: beyond time and history."[17] Pastoral concern, however, for the concrete situations of the persons and societies to be evangelized is entirely proper; for "between evangelization and human advancement—development and liberation—there are profound links." These links are of the anthropological, theological, and evangelical orders: "anthropological, because the man who is to be evangelized is not an abstract being but is subject to social and economic questions; theological, since one cannot disassociate the plan of creation from the plan of redemption which applies to very concrete situations of injustice; evangelical, which refers to charity and the justice included in it."[18]

Although it was in the form of an "exhortation" and "meditation," *Evangelii nuntiandi* in this way attempted to throw additional light on a complex and subtle relationship.

CONCLUSIONS

The document *Justice in the World* is easily the most reprinted publication issued by the Pontifical Commission Justice and Peace, and the sentence most quoted from it is far and away the one we have been discussing. This fact already provides, apart from further analysis, a hermeneutic upon the word.

Cosmao, in his significant letter to me regarding his role in drafting the document, noted the powerful impact *Justice in the World* and the word "constitutive" in particular have had in developing countries. He wrote: "I have been immediately struck most of all by the fact that the militant Churches in the Third World have recognized themselves in this phrase of the synod, which, it seems to me, once it was adopted, became a key phrase of the pontificate of Pope Paul VI."[19] Walbert Buhlmann, in his widely read book *The Coming of the Third Church,* confirms this appraisal by Cosmao regarding the strong resonance the *Justice* document achieved in Third World countries.[20] The bishops from the Third World, as we have seen, frequently alluded to it in the synod of 1974.

But the most significant contribution which the term "constitutive" has made to the life of the Church, according to Cosmao, is the remarkable reversal of perspective that took place within a period of twenty years. The Church entered the justice field originally by attempting to alleviate world hunger, acting out of a motive of charity, but then began to grasp that "her participation in the transformation of the world order is the very condition of the truth of her faith and of the relevance and meaning of the gospel she announces." This reversal of perspective was made with the justice text of the 1971 synod, so that it was a kind of pivot which has not ceased to produce its effects.[21]

The expression that working for justice is "constitutive" of the preaching of the gospel can be seen as an outgrowth of trends in earlier Church teaching. In Vatican II's pastoral constitution *Gaudium et spes,* and continuing with Pope Paul's encyclical *Populorum progressio,* the Church's involvement in the question of justice was explained not only within a framework of the natural law but more centrally from the gospel itself. We can see that the assertion we are examining from *Justice in the World* is closely allied with this evolution. *Gaudium et spes* also sought to avoid dichotomies such as church and state, speaking rather of the Church *in* the world as a participant in the struggles of mankind, sharing a common history and, by reading the signs of the times, joining with others in the search for a common solution to human problems. The Church as a people of God and a community of believers, and the intimate relationship between justice and love in Christianity, which was stressed by *Gaudium et spes,* were picked up by the Second General Assembly of the Bishops of Latin America, held at Medellin in 1968, and led quite easily to the statement made in the synod of 1971.

Although the term "constitutive" to describe the relationship of the preaching of the gospel and the work of justice is a new one, certain equivalent or approximate theological expressions from other sources can be found. Vatican II's Decree on the Laity spoke about the "saturation and perfection of the temporal sphere by the spirit of the gospel."[22] The *instrumentum laboris* of the 1974 synod referred to the "intrinsic connection between witness of life and evangelization" in terms of the efficaciousness and credibility of preaching.

The classical philosophical definition of "constitutive" is that which causes a thing to stand (the Latin roots are *cum* and *statuo*); it is that which is most fundamental and pertains to the very definition of a being, making it to be what it is. Thus Aquinas says that "filiation" is constitutive of the person of the Son in the Trinity, and rationality is said to be the "constitutive difference" of the human person.[23] "Essential" would not be an unacceptable equivalent, but "indispensable" would not seem to be adequate to communicate the force of the word.

Some, however, like Bishop Torrella, have claimed that the authentic interpretation of the word "constitutive" is "integral" and reject "essential" as too strong. Both the advocates of "essential" and of "integral" wish to stress the internal relationship between the gospel and justice, so that working for justice is not merely an ethical conclusion but pertains to the gospel itself. That internal relationship for some, however, is better expressed by "integral" because working for justice is more on the level of the credibility of the gospel in the circumstances of today than of its very essence. Neither interpretation wishes to leave the impression that justice is a mere optional aspect of the gospel, but the advocates of "integral" wish to avoid merging the divine and human contributions into one reality without keeping the proper distinctions and also to avoid the danger of reducing the mission of the Church to a "simply temporal project" and a "man-centered goal," to use the terminology of *Evangelii nuntiandi*.[24] Alfaro, on the other hand, stresses as necessary the human response to the gospel message and, operating out of a more biblical conception of what God's specific justice is and requires, defines constitutive as essential. Both meanings pick up nuances of the Church's teaching on this subtle but important point.

The heart of the ambiguity about the meaning of constitutive, therefore, seems to reside in differing conceptions of what kind of justice is being referred to. If justice is conceived exclusively on the plane of the natural, human virtue of justice as explained in classical philosophical treatises,[25] then such justice can only be conceived as an integral but nonessential part of the preaching of the gospel. But if justice is conceived in the biblical sense of God's liberating action which demands a necessary human response—a concept of justice which is far closer to agape than to justice in the classical philosophical sense—then justice must be defined as of the essence of the gospel itself. The latter sense seems to reflect better the mentality of more recent Christian social doctrine.

A decided shift took place in magisterial teaching regarding justice from John XXIII's *Mater et magistra* onward: the previous conception of an organicity through reason was placed alongside a more biblical-imaginative perspective on justice. It is within this new context that *Justice in the World* must be understood.[26]

But justice and love may be endorsed and accepted, as the past and present experience of the Church has shown, in a very otherworldly way, that is, without the inclusion within it of what is called the natural, human virtue of justice. A biblical understanding of justice is a corrective to this. *Evangelii nuntiandi* was operating within a similar unifying perspective when it spoke of the profound links between evangelization and human progress; like the Scriptures, it was presenting a single vision uniting body and soul, creation and redemption, justice and charity. This unifying, nondualistic vision of the Christian life, we know, lay behind the use of the term "constitutive."

Both Alfaro's and Torrella's definitions can be squared with the teaching contained in *Evangelii nuntiandi,* but Cosmao's is not so easily reconcilable. Cosmao believes that the preaching of the gospel occurs by means of action for justice; for him, the debate between evangelization "or" development is sterile and there can be no subordination of the one to the other. Cosmao's original draft spoke of "struggle" (*le combat*) for justice, and ten years after the synod he continues to cite the passage in his original wording. "Struggle" seems at odds with the biblical conception we have been describing of justice arising out of love, and with the general conception of *Evangelii nuntiandi.* Cosmao obviously believes that *le combat* is closer to the original intention of the term "constitutive," which was to ground the central religious value of justice in the actual everyday history of the world.[27]

The same division of opinion prevails concerning the necessity of action for justice as part of the "credibility" of the gospel preaching. Some will sharply distinguish the basic credibility of the gospel from the life of the Church, asserting that the principal sign of credibility is not the Church but Christ. Others question whether anyone could in practice accept the gospel without experience of the truth of Christian faith in the lives of the very persons proclaiming it.

The theological issues that lie behind "constitutive" are many and complex, but they ultimately converge on the question of the divine and human contributions in the economy of salvation, or, putting it in more contemporary language, "the relationship between the Christian proclamation of salvation and the emancipatory movements of our day."[28]

Here we are presented with what everyone calls an "insoluble problem."[29] The best method of approach, if not of solution, lies in the indicative/imperative modality of biblical ethics and in the vocabulary of "gift and task" employed by H. Richard Niebuhr and Walter Kasper.[30] The "indicative" is who God is and what God has done and is doing. The "imperative" is the conformity of human action to God's action. The human response is the sign and the mediation of the divine activity but does not exhaust the potentialities of God's activity. The divine significance of human activity constitutes the meaning of human history. God's grace comes first and last in that history, but the "middle" which is the human response is indispensable as the necessary response to the divine initiative.[31]

Thus the human contribution has an essential role to play in the divine "economy," the timetable based upon God's own appointed times rather than on earthly days and years. The divine economy as it unfolds includes as part of itself the human response and even lack of response, and the result is new and sometimes different initiatives on the part of God. The human response, itself the result of divine grace, is taken up into the single divine plan which is the "economy."

Preserving the divine initiative lies behind the frequent appeal by Paul VI and John Paul II to safeguard the "originality" of the Christian message by not attempting to reduce it to a human plan of action. As Paul VI said in his closing speech to the 1974 synod, anticipating what he would write in *Evangelii nuntiandi,* the "totality" of salvation is not to be confused with any liberation movement. It is God who saves us from sin and death and brings us eternal life; this is the "essential meaning" of the evangelical message. The necessity of the human response was well stated in *Gaudium et spes*: Christians should give the witness of a faith that proves itself "by penetrating the believer's entire life, including its worldly dimensions and by activating him toward justice and love."[32]

Bishop Torrella, referring to all these questions, and after much reflection, said: "You know, what we are really touching upon in the word 'constitutive' is nothing less than the relationship of the natural and supernatural." Cosmao, at the end of his letter, gives his own evaluation of the use of the term "constitutive": "I believe that today one may consider as 'received doctrine' what was said there. Perhaps it was unhappily put, but it did serve to underscore the historicity of the passover of

Christ in the sense that it calls for the building of a world in which life might be possible for everybody.''

The bishops at the 1971 synod did not wish to delve into these theological issues or break new doctrinal ground; they felt the doctrine was fairly well in place. They simply wished to issue a call for action and an appeal to conscience in response to the pleas for the witness of the Church to the cause of justice. The synod's response was the document *Justice in the World,* which by all accounts, in spite of the severe limitations under which they had to work, has proven to be the most influential statement ever coming from a synod. The reason for its influence, paradoxically, has been a strong and arresting term which at the time virtually passed without notice but remains the source of continued reflection within the Church on this most important aspect not only of her own life but the life of the whole world.

Notes

1. Pope John Paul II, in the apostolic exhortation *Laborem exercens* (1981) 2, calls attention to this shift.

2. Cf. René Laurentin, *Réorientation de l'église après le troisième Synode* (Paris: Seuil, 1972) 167–73.

3. David Hollenbach, S.J., *Claims in Conflict: Retrieving and Renewing the Catholic Human Rights Tradition* (New York: Paulist, 1979) 94.

4. *Il Sinodo dei Vescovi, 1971,* Parte Seconda (Rome: La Civiltà Cattolica, 1972), and *Il Sinodo dei Vescovi, 1974* (Rome: La Civiltà Cattolica, 1975).

5. See, e.g., the mission statements adopted by the Society of Jesus and the Maryknoll fathers and brothers respectively in 1975 and 1978.

6. Letter to the author, Paris, Dec. 18, 1980. See also two of his writings after the synod: his book *Changer le monde: Une tâche pour l'église* (Paris: Cerf, 1980), and the article "Changer le monde," *Nouvelle revue théologique* 101 (1979) 24–38.

7. "Justice dans le monde? Théologie sous-jacente au document du travail du Synode épiscopale," *Documentation catholique,* no. 1589 (July 4, 1971) 639.

8. John Paul II, however, has quoted this sentence on at least two occa-

sions. Speaking to the Third General Conference of Latin American Bishops at Puebla in 1979, he cited it but used the word "indispensable" instead of "constitutive." In his address on Feb. 27, 1982, to the provincials of the Society of Jesus, he stated that the Church considers the promotion of justice as an "integral part" of evangelization (*Osservatore romano,* Feb. 28, 1982, 3).

9. *Evangelization of the Modern World,* "Contribution of the Pontifical Commission Justice and Peace to the Synod of 1974," Feb. 1974 (Archives of the Commission) 1.

10. *Avvenire,* Sept. 18, 1974. The interview was written by Silvano Stracca.

11. Conversations with the author, fall of 1980, Rome.

12. Conversation with the author, Nov. 12, 1980, at the Center of Concern, Washington, D.C.

13. Interview, Feb. 1981, Rome. Alfaro's booklet issued just after the synod, *Theology of Justice in the World,* omits any mention of "constitutive" in explaining the teaching of the synod (Vatican City: Pontifical Commission Justice and Peace, 1973). For a fuller exposition of Alfaro's views, see *Christian Hope and Liberation of Man* (Rome and Sydney: Dwyer, 1978).

14. Paul VI, *On Evangelization in the Modern World: The Apostolic Exhortation "Evangelii nuntiandi"* (Washington, D.C.: United States Catholic Conference, 1976) no. 9.

15. Ibid., no. 14.

16. Ibid., no. 24.

17. Ibid., no. 28.

18. Ibid., no. 31.

19. Letter of Dec. 18, 1980.

20. Cf. Walbert Buhlmann, *The Coming of the Third Church* (Slough, Eng.: St. Paul Publications, 1976) 100, 103, 107, 114 ff.

21. Vincent Cosmao, *Changer le monde* 104–5.

22. *Apostolicam actuositatem* 2.

23. *Index Thomisticus,* Sectio 2, Concordantia prima, Vol. 5, 378.

24. The International Theological Commission's document "Human Development and Christian Salvation," issued in 1972, accepts "integral part" as the correct interpretation rather than "essential" because, while stressing the harmony between eschatological salvation and the human effort to build a better world, it keeps clear the distinction between the two. Cf. *Origins* 7, no. 20 (Nov. 3, 1977) 31.

25. See, e.g., John Rawls, *Theory of Justice* (Cambridge: Belknap, 1971).

26. See Marie Dominique Chenu, *La dottrina sociale della Chiesa: Origine e sviluppo, 1801–1971* (Brescia: Queriniana, 1977) esp. 52–53, and also the more nuanced view of Roger Heckel, *General Aspects of the Social Cate-*

chesis of John Paul II (Vatican City: Pontifical Commission Justice and Peace, 1980) 16–18.

27. *Changer le monde* 12, 104–5.

28. Francis Schüssler Fiorenza, "Christology after Vatican II," *Ecumenist* 18 (1980) 88.

29. Cf. Walter Kasper, *Jesus the Christ* (New York: Paulist, 1977) 240; H. Richard Niebuhr, *Christ and Culture* (New York: Harper, 1951) 10.

30. Kasper, *Jesus the Christ* 16–17; Niebuhr, *Christ and Culture* 114. John Howard Yoder, from a Christian pacifist position, suggests an offense/defense approach based upon a theology of the cross: "His [the believer's] duty is not to bring the Powers to their knees. This is Jesus Christ's own task. . . . We are to be responsible for the defense, just because He takes care of the offense" (*The . Politics of Jesus* [Grand Rapids: Eerdmans, 1972] 152).

31. Cf. L. Alvarez Verdes, *El imperativo cristiano in San Pablo: La tension indicativo-imperativo en Rom. 6* (Valencia: Constitución San Jerónimo, 1980). See also, on the Thomistic philosophical basis of this approach, D. Mongillo, "La fondazione dell'agire nel Prologo della I–II," *Sapienza* 27 (1974) 261–71.

32. *GS* 21.

PART TWO:
OVERVIEWS AND CONTEMPORARY DISCUSSIONS

Development of Church Social Teaching

John Coleman, S.J.

This article originally appeared in *Origins*, 1981.

"Would someone please tell me what is an encyclical?" These perhaps apocryphal words attributed to a much harassed Gov. Alfred E. Smith in the heat of the 1928 campaign hide a telling set of questions. Smith's query has been with me these last few months as I mused over my task this morning here at Catholic University to give some historical context for understanding Catholic papal social teaching as embodied in the social encyclicals. As we are all aware we are celebrating this year the 90th anniversary of *Rerum Novarum*, the 50th of *Quadragesimo Anno*, the 20th of *Mater et Magistra* and the 10th of *Octogesima Adveniens*, which is technically an apostolic letter rather than an encyclical, but which is usually subsumed under the list of encyclicals.

My first problems were to decide what does it mean to see the encyclicals in their historical context since, as we will see, this can have several different meanings. The second was the question, "Do I really want to run the risk of seeing the encyclicals in their historical context?" History is notoriously a relativizer of absolute values, authorities and our often cherished myths and idealizations. History is a locus of inconsistencies and compromises as often as logical coherency. To go to history is to run the risk of uncovering unpleasant facts or the equally chilling risk of debunking criticism. Would papal social teaching entirely pass the test of history?

Before attempting to probe these questions further I want us to consider first, for a moment, several of the subquestions hidden in Al Smith's plaintive cry: Would someone please tell me what is an encyclical?

In what sense are social encyclicals authoritative?

They deal, after all, with the temporal, the historically passing, with a reading of the "signs of the times" and an assessment of movements and institutions of a given age which may or may not be accurate. Thus, as one historian has noted, "the moderate reformist elements within socialism seemed to escape Leo XIII's notice entirely." He asserts also that Leo's assessment of the economic order in 1891 as involving a theory of the monopoly of the few and the pauperization of the many was not, according to economic historians, a very accurate picture even of 1891, let alone of what became of the industrial nations of Europe to whom *Rerum Novarum* was addressed.

Pius XI's complaint against "the anonymity" of property in joint stockholding companies seemed quaint even in 1931 and the pontiff nowhere suggested alternative ways for amassing investment-savings capital to increase productivity which would also guarantee potential investors against heavy risks.

It is not perhaps by chance that the first modern assault on papal encyclicals by Catholic dissenters came in response to a *social* encyclical in William Buckley's celebrated bon mot in the National Review, *Mater, si, Magistra non!* By their very nature social encyclicals depend on technical access to economic questions, disputed and controversial readings of economic trends. This raises issues about their authoritative weight.

In any event, it is clear to me that Al Smith's prior question of just what is an encyclical has to be probed and the encyclicals seen in their historical context before any answer to the question of their authoritative weight can be essayed. Presumably their authority will rest on their moral principles and insights and their theological and ethical concepts, although as we will see in a moment it is not always so clear that presumed continuities can be sustained by a historical analysis.

In what sense do the social encyclicals constitute a coherent unity of teaching?

We Catholics tend to celebrate the social encyclicals as a coherent body of unified teaching. In what sense is this assumption justified? It is interesting in this regard to contrast Catholic histories and commentaries on the encyclicals with sympathetic non-Catholic views such as those of Richard Camp and Alfred Diamant.

In general, Catholic commentaries assume a unity in the teaching, are not critical of the economic or political foundations of papal teaching and often eschew a historical for a philosophical approach. Non-Catholic commentaries find it less easy to sustain the notion that the encyclicals comprise a unity, are often, even when sympathetic, critical and see the encyclicals in a historical context. Few Catholic commentaries point up obvious difficulties in this corpus of social thought such as its relative silence on the issue of increased productivity and, in Richard Camp's words, "the naive assumption . . . that social conflict could be alleviated and perhaps eliminated by the simple expedient of bringing the social classes together in the same community."

A simultaneous reading of the encyclicals, at any rate, shows that various social teachings do not—to obedient or even servile minds and ears—entirely square with one another. Thus, to cite several of the most notable examples:

A. PROPERTY

Pius XI in *Quadragesimo Anno* corrected Leo XIII's un-Thomist understanding of private property as an almost metaphysical right and hastened to add that first occupancy as well as use constitutes a legitimate claim to property. He was responding to the Austrian medieval romanticist school of Karl Vogelsang, which maintained, drawing on its interpretation of *Rerum Novarum,* that social misuse of property or even non-use (e.g., absentee landlords) was in itself sufficient warrant for expropriation.

We are told by one historian of papal social thought that the theory of private property in *Rerum Novarum* "was first developed systematically by John Locke. In 1840 it was incorporated into the neo-Scholastic tradition by the Jesuit theologian Taperelli d'Azeglio and from there into papal social teachings."

This is a far cry from the strong insistence of John XXIII in *Mater et Magistra* that the common good and the needs of humans take priority over any right to private property, or Paul VI's remarks in *Populorum Progressio* that private property is not an absolute right, indeed is no right at all when others are in need, or John Paul II's celebrated phrase about "a social mortgage" on all property.

Clearly, in time Catholic social thought rejected Father d'Azeglio's and Leo XIII's mistaken notion that property is a direct natural right inherent in persons. Private property is of the *bene esse* rather than the *esse* of human dignity, to use the Scholastic categories. It is justified by its social consequences rather than in some inherent, inalienable right of persons. It is established by an appeal to historical experience—people show greater responsibility and initiative when they own some property or a society which fosters private property also fosters liberty—rather than by the nature of the human person as such. Private property is a derivative rather than a direct right.

In correcting Leo XIII's un-Thomist reading of private property (an irony: that the pope who revived Thomist thought in the church should have been so far from the Thomist understanding of property!), Pius XI in *Quadragesimo Anno* shifted the teaching on property without, of course, pointing out that he was correcting the mistakes of his predecessor.

B. SOCIALISM

Both John XXIII and Paul VI felicitously departed from Pius XI's puzzling, even at the time unfair, reading of mitigated socialism and distorted ahistorical essentialist definition of socialism which allowed him to assert in *Quadragesimo Anno* that "no one can be at the same time a sincere Catholic and a true socialist," even a mitigated, democratic, non-Marxist socialist who, in Pius XI's own words, has gradually come to hold tenets of mitigated socialism "no longer different from the program of those who seek to reform human society according to Christian principles."

In his encyclical *Sapientiae Christianae* Leo XIII had held that the church was not competent to adjudicate between the various forms of the state, provided only that "religion and morality are protected." Why Pius XI did not accord a similar judgment to economic systems is a mystery—although I will later suggest a historical hypothesis. Recalling the earlier Leonine assumptions of plural options for forms of the state, a leading historian of papal thought has remarked of Pius XI that "to imply that the church could not also function in a socialist society was a radical departure from tradition'' on the part of the pope.

At any event, in *Pacem in Terris* John XXIII took us back to the Leonine tradition when he asserted: ''It is, therefore, especially to the point to make a clear distinction between false philosophical teachings regarding the nature, origin and destiny of the universe and of man, and movements which have a direct bearing either on economic and social questions or cultural matters or on the origination of the state, even if these movements owe their origin and inspiration to these false tenets.'' So much for ahistorical essentialist definitions of socialism!

Gaudium et Spes, from Vatican Council II, returned to the Leonine wisdom when it asserted that ''in virtue of her mission and nature, the church is bound to no particular form of human culture, nor to any political, economic or social system.'' Evidently, under certain conditions one can now simultaneously be a sincere Catholic and a true socialist.

Nor are Pius' remarks about socialism of merely textual interest. They played a role in blocking a possible collaboration between the Catholic Center Party and the Socialists in Germany which might have forestalled Hitler's rise to power, as, earlier, Pius XI's exiling of Luigi Sturzo and disavowal of the Populari Party in Italy paved the way for Mussolini.

Gregory Baum, in his recent excellent historical study, *Canadian Catholics and Socialism,* shows how these papal judgments kept Catholics from aligning themselves with a non-Marxist, democratic Canadian socialist party which owes its origins in part to a circle of Protestant social activists and, therefore, has never been anti-religious. Cardinal Bourne of London, of course, felt compelled publicly and quickly to suggest that the papal stricture decidedly did not apply to the British Labour Party.

Because they were a misreading of the reality of the time about democratic socialist movements in Europe, Pius' remarks were unfair and unjust. They also, it would be my argument, had negative social consequences. If we look too closely into the historical context for papal social teaching, it will not always reveal to us what we want to see! Hence, as I noted earlier, there are risks in going to history.

There are other important examples of massive sea changes in the papal teaching. Thus *Quadragesimo Anno* hints at the advisability or desirability of profit-sharing and co-determination schemes in industry. In response to a *Katholiekentag* held in Bochum in Germany in 1949, Pius XII, on his part, showed a decided coolness toward the idea of workers' co-determination of industry decisions. In *Mater et Magistra* however (without mentioning Pius XII's teaching) and thereafter, co-determination (often coded under the post-Vatican II key word, workers' participation) has become a firm plank in Catholic social thought.

And what is one to make of the sheer disappearance of the central theme in *Quadragesimo Anno* of a sane, corporative order of vocational groups as the essential remedy for the reconstruction of society? Pius XII continued to stress this theme until the early 1940s, to be sure, as it was difficult for him not to so long as Father Gustav Gundlach wrote his social allocutions. Since John XXIII this very centerpiece of *Quadragesimo Anno* has been allowed to undergo a quiet and seemly death.

Obviously all the historic examples of regimes which often loudly proclaimed to be an embodiment of the encyclical's corporative idea—Seipel and Dollfuss in Austria, Vargas in Brazil, Petain in Vichy, Franco in Spain and Salazar in Portugal, the quisling Msgr. Joseph Tiso's clerico-fascist regime in Slovakia—were an embarrassment to this element of papal social teaching in the post-World War II era. To the best of my knowledge, there was never any papal disavowal that these regimes distorted the spirit and ideals of *Quadragesimo Anno,* which might have been appropriate since they claimed to embody the encyclical's main ideas.

Let me continue with some of the implications in Al Smith's question.

What is to count as the authentic corpus of papal social teaching?

Generally, the assumption is that the list should include *Rerum Novarum, Quadragesimo Anno,* various allocutions of Pius XII (with no really clear criterion of how to select from so many sources of different— in some cases dubious—perduring value), *Mater et Magistra, Pacem in Terris, Populorum Progressio, Octogesima Adveniens* and John Paul II's *Redemptor Hominis.* Usually *Gaudium et Spes* and the 1971 Synod of Bishops' document, *Justice in the World,* are also included since the ultimate promulgative authority of these documents depended on papal approval.

Why just this list? Why not also *Mirari Vos* and *Singulari Nos* of

Gregory XVI and *Quanta Cura* and the appended syllabus of errors of Pius IX? These were clearly social encyclicals, addressing the social questions of their times, albeit in a reactionary fashion. Obviously, including these will complicate our question about the authority and unity of papal social encyclicals as a corpus. Moreover, Leo XIII's other encyclicals such as *Diuturnum Illud, Immortale Dei, Libertas Praestantissimum, Sapientiae Christianae, Au Milieu de Solicitudes* and very importantly *Graves de Communi* of 1901 were also addressed to social issues. They give us a fuller picture of the papal social strategy and remind us of Leo's paternalistic view of the masses and his assumptions of a permanent hierarchical view of society. Pius XI's social encyclicals surely would include *Non Abbiamo Bisogno, Mit Brennender Sorge* and *Divini Redemptoris* on both fascism and socialism. They establish his desire to create something that was neither liberalism, fascism or socialism, the so-called third way of social Catholicism.

My purpose in raising these questions is not to debunk a treasured heritage. Surely anyone who knows me personally or my written work knows that I stand self-consciously within this tradition of social Catholicism. Rather I want to indicate what it might mean to see the encyclicals in their historic context. Perhaps—but only just perhaps—when seen against a historic backdrop we can understand or appreciate why Gregory XVI or Pius IX or later popes said what they said. Sometimes it will be the case that "to understand historically will be to forgive," as when Leo XIII in *Rerum Novarum* asserts that women are meant by nature for housework! Sometimes it will be to agree with specific historic judgments of the signs of the times, as with John XXIII's assessment that increased socialization is an inevitable social fact of life.

Sometimes, however, it will mean a calculated historical judgment that a papal assessment of societal trends and movements was simply mistaken—even for its own times and not simply from benefit of historical hindsight—or entailed socially negative consequences. Such I would argue is true of Pius XI's judgment of mitigated socialism in 1931. Such also is true of Pius X's distorted interpretation of Leo XIII when Pius asserted, in a purported authentic interpretation of *Rerum Novarum*, that the authority of capital over labor was as essential to the social organism as that of the authority of the church, government or family. This was not simply a developing understanding or a creative footnote. It is a simple inversion of Leo's famous dictum in *Rerum Novarum*, "Capital cannot do without labor nor labor without capital.'' However hierarchical Leo may have been in his general social theory, he did not extend this to his understanding of capital and labor.

What I want to suggest is that to see the encyclicals in their historical context is to run the risk of a critical reappraisal of papal social teaching—a selective acceptance but also a rejection—of certain elements of the social teaching. We will need, of course, to find some principle for this selectivity. We are appropriately and rightly celebrating here today a rich Catholic heritage in this social teaching. My purpose is not to debunk this heritage but to remind us that once we decide to see these documents in historical context, it will not be so easy to celebrate them as an absolutely unbroken coherent unity passing from papal mind to papal mind, untouched by the waves of time.

Each encyclical was the product of different minds, responded to different institutional realities and periods of history, expressed quite different worldviews and philosophical understandings. Leo XIII's ''natural law'' was not entirely the same as Pius XI's or, decidedly, John XXIII's. As I have mentioned, his natural-law understanding of private property was not even that of Aquinas.

A related shift is seen in the pre-Vatican II vs. post-Vatican II predilection, on the one hand, for philosophy and, on the other, theology, to ground the social teaching. The author of *Quadragesimo Anno,* as a good Solidarist in the line of Heinrich Pesch and Gustav Gunlach, did not think that theology belonged in direct discourse with economics or politics. The Solidarists notoriously were jealous of keeping economics from any infection by theological notions such as grace, sin, liberation as part of salvation. After Vatican II, however, explicitly theological thought strongly informs the papal teaching.

This is a massive sea change. It cannot be simply assumed—as it usually is—that a unified body of connected thought can be found to have survived that change. No one has yet, in my judgment, adequately addressed the implications of shifting from a natural-law philosophical language to theology for grounding the social teaching. One important implication of this sea change is that even moral principles from one encyclical to the next may not involve completely univocal concepts. The logical unity of the teaching still needs to be shown.

Seeing the encyclicals in their historical context will also mean that we need to look to the social consequences of papal teaching. Looking at *Rerum Novarum* and, especially, *Quadragesimo Anno,* Gregory Baum has claimed that Pius XI and Pius XII's unflinching animus against socialism meant—especially in the political context of Europe—that "while the Catholic Church recommended social reform, in actual fact it often put its weight behind the defenders of the existing economic system." This was certainly one of the consequences—perhaps unintended—of Pius XI's insistence on Catholic labor unions. They divided the unity of the working class. Baum continues, in his discussion of the so-called third way of Catholicism between liberalism and socialism, "The difficulty of Catholic social teaching was that it did not correspond to any actual historical movement . . . Catholic social teaching was idealistic in both the positive Catholic and the Marxist sense," i.e., it was anchored purely in ideas and not in real historical movements.

I am not suggesting that it is absolutely impossible to exhibit a unity in the papal teaching. I would argue that in some sense there is. But it does not always leap off the pages of the encyclicals at you! Even so sympathetic a historian of papal social teaching as Professor Alfred Diamant could claim that it includes "a diversity which has led some observers to find in it an uncritical ecclecticism or an opportunist syncretism of unrelated parts, artificially put together and polished in accordance with the interests of the church as a political instrument for the power of the papacy."

What does it mean to see the encyclicals in historical context?

The key question, however, to unravel in order to answer Al Smith's query about what is an encyclical is: "How are we to understand what it means to see the papal documents in their historical context?" What is to serve as our key to doing a historical exegesis? There are several possible keys just as there are several possible meanings to a historicizing of the encyclicals. Let me suggest a few which I will not really explore:

A. We could look at the antecedent movements to which the papal documents responded such as the Fribourg circle of Cardinal Mermillod, the workingmen's pilgrimages of the French industrialist, Leon Harmel, the disputes between the meliorists, such as Bishop von Ketteler, who accepted capitalism as a system but attacked its abuses and the romantic reconstructionists following Karl Vogelsang who rejected capitalism hook, line and sinker. This debate between "reluctant capitalists" and strong, reactionary anti-capitalists was the Catholic context for both *Rerum Novarum* and *Quadragesimo Anno*. The latter encyclical also addressed a small group of religious socialists who thought Leo's *Rerum Novarum* was too much an ideological defense of capitalism.

If we take the historical task seriously, it will not be enough, as many Catholic commentators tend to do, merely to point to antecedent groups as the source of one or other idea in an encyclical, e.g., the idea for "socialization" in *Mater et Magistra* came originally from the *Semaine Sociale* in Grenoble in 1960 or that Leo XIII was more under the influence of von Ketteler and the Fribourg circle than Vogelsang or the French monarchists. While true, these facts are trivial. What we need to do is look at the social location and milieu of these groups. Was it by chance, for example, that every other name of notables mentioned in the history books as influencing *Rerum Novarum* was a count, marquis or prince, or other member of the aristocracy or an industrialist and that no militant union organizers had any impact on the document? What was the likely or known position of these people? To do this kind of history is to see that *Rerum Novarum* was essentially a relatively conservative and paternalistic document.

B. I would also argue that we also have to do a history of the theological worldviews regnant at the time of each encyclical and compare and contrast them. What, finally, does the solidarist philosophy of the Koningswinter circle, which sustained Nell-Breuning while, all in secret, he was writing *Quadragesimo Anno,* have in common with the development economics of Lebret, so influential on *Populorum Progressio*? My simple point is that we cannot simply assume the coherence by the mere juxtaposition of congenial surface concepts from the various encyclicals. Whatever else this latter method is, it is not history.

As to a method of exegesis to understand the various documents in context, let me suggest a few possible candidates.

1) We could look mainly to the "mind" of each author of each encyclical, i.e., to the work of Oswald Nell-Breuning for *Quadragesimo Anno,* Gustav Gundlach for the allocutions of Pius XII, Pietro Pavan for *Mater et Magistra,* Lebret and Bigo and others for *Populorum Progressio.* Unfortunately, we only have Nell-Breuning among these authors who has both frankly admitted he was the single author of the encyclical and expressed, 10 years ago in an article in *Stimmen der Zeit,* what his

intentions were especially in regard to his understanding of a corporative order of vocational groups. Nell-Breuning makes very clear that he decidedly did not have a fascist, authoritarian order in mind. Just the opposite, in fact.

He also tells us that the only independent contributions of the pope to the text were sections of paragraphs 91ff, which said some ambiguously favorable things about Mussolini's fascist order as a kind of corporative order. Although the actual text of the encyclical stresses strongly that the envisioned corporative order was to be free, voluntary and not directed by the state (as should be obvious from the insistence on the principle of subsidiarity), Pius XI wanted to give a sop to Mussolini since he anticipated, correctly, great tensions with the Italian dictator when he issued his anti-fascist encyclical, *Non Abbiamo Bisogno* less than six weeks after *Quadragesimo Anno*. These papal insertions—creating unnecessary ambiguity—as well as Pius XI's imprudent public praise for the decidedly authoritarian corporatist schemes of the Catholic Engelbert Dollfuss in Austria were the historic leverage for a fundamentally mistaken reading of *Quadragesimo Anno*—at least if we follow the mind of its principal author as to what that reading should be.

2) For other encyclicals, as I have noted, we deal either with unacknowledged or, in some cases, multiple authors. A second exegetical method, suggested by Nell-Breuning himself in the *Stimmen der Zeit* article, argues that the text should simply be read for itself. I find this hard to accept, first because even from the outset a text is subject to different readings and, second, because the text is seen as an integral part of a whole papal social policy.

3) A third exegetical possibility to deal with these texts would be to look to movements, disputed questions, etc., to which the encyclical responds. Thus, we have George Jarlot's magisterial study of the antecedents of *Rerum Novarum*.

Different groups in Europe appealed to the Holy See on the social question. From France, the paternalistic monarchists, Count Albert de Mun, the Marquis Rene de la Tour du Pin and paternalistic reformers such as Le Play and Villeneuve-Bargemont showed interest in placating the lower classes and reasserting an authentic Christian aristocratic elite. Like the red Tories in England, they took up—in a paternalistic way— the cause of the workingman, harkening back to a medieval romantic view of aristocrats and a guild society. The industrialist Leon Harmel led pilgrimages of workingmen to Rome. In 1889 alone, 10,000 French members of Harmel's company unions—for that is what they were—journeyed to see the pope.

Historians tell us that the Roman Curia, hard pressed by the Roman question of papal captivity and unfriendly governments in Italy and Germany, dreamt of a new surge of barbarians who "baptized and under the tutelage of the church as the barbarians of old" would provide fresh energy for a renewed Christendom in a tired and spent Europe. Strange as this notion may seem to us, it was the backdrop metaphor of someone so realistic and basically sympathetic to modernizing the church as Ozanam.

In Germany and Austria, the frankly anti-capitalist romantics (following Vogelsang and Goerres) had appealed to the Holy See against the so-called social Catholics—meliorists like Bishop von Ketteler of Mainz—because, they charged, the latter were inciting class hatred by supporting separate unions for the workingmen. The Fribourg circle headed by Cardinal Mermillod held congresses on the social question in the late 1880s, which were deeply influential on Leo, as did the *Opera dei Congressi* in Italy.

French Christian democrats already dreamt of a Catholic democratic party. They were to be cautioned for taking *Rerum Novarum* too seriously by Leo in his 1901 encyclical *Graves de communi*. Cardinals Manning of London and Gibbons of America had also intervened with Rome in support of unions.

The questions to be adjudicated by *Rerum Novarum* included such issues as: 1) the mere existence of unions; 2) Vogelsang's claim that capitalism was inherently evil; 3) whether what was needed was the so-called mixed association of both employers and workers (an idea heavily supported by French groups) or workers' associations separate from employers; 4) whether the church should champion strict unions or mere benevolent societies for workingmen like the Kolping societies in Germany; and 5) whether Catholics could belong to a neutral, i.e., non-Catholic union.

The late 1880s was a time of deep industrial unrest and strikes in Europe and the United States. Leo XIII, basically sympathetic toward von Ketteler's meliorist approach, wrote *Rerum Novarum* in response to this social issue as well as the various Catholic movements in Europe. In it we find several persistent leitmotifs of Catholic social teaching.

Leo condemned the abuses of capitalism, but not the system itself. In fact, he suggested very little by way of institutional reform. In accepting capitalism as such, Leo opposed the Vogelsang romantic corporatists. On the other hand, he seems to espouse their fundamental theory of property in terms of grounding it in a labor theory in one place in the encyclical.

As this example makes clear, one of the difficulties in finding a coherent unity in papal social teaching is precisely the way in which such documents try to conciliate varying Catholic groups, supporting here, in part of the text, one group, there, in another part, an opposed group. One reason I suspect many of the Catholic commentaries on the encyclicals which try to show an overly neat organic growth is that they tend to neglect this principle of exegesis. The very nature of the genesis of such documents suggests that they are not always logically coherent texts to begin with.

Leo attacks especially the fact that "a small number of very rich men have been able to lay upon the masses of the poor a yoke little better than slavery itself." He espouses a principle of natural rights. "Man is older than the state." He stresses that intermediate groups are legitimate because of the social nature of human persons. He opposes the principle of class warfare.

Against both liberalism and the notion of a social contract, Leo asserts that a just wage is "more ancient than any bargain between man and man." Any justification for private property would argue to its widest distribution. "As many people as possible should become owners," he avers. Finally, he asserts a privileged option for the poor—something which, at least rhetorically, runs through the whole tradition. "When there is question of protecting the rights of individuals, the poor and helpless have a claim of special consideration. The richer population have many ways of protecting themselves and stand less in need of help from the state. Those who are badly off have no resources of their own to fall back upon and must rely chiefly upon the assistance of the state."

4) A fourth principle of historical exegesis—the one I find most congenial—would see any encyclical in continuity with the other writings, allocutions and actions of the papacy.

We know that Leo was no radical leftist, but basically a conservative reformer. From this vantage point, especially if we read Leo's letter to Kaiser Wilhelm in 1890, his letter the same year to the Italian government asserting that the church is the first and foremost of conservative forces needed to check the triumph of the left and the threat to established order, and his 1896 letter to the Hungarian bishops as well as his 1901 encyclical *Graves de communi* (which cautioned against any too radical reading of *Rerum Novarum* by French social Catholics who were stirred by it), the historian's judgment of Leo that he was a pragmatic, realistic conservative who wanted to make peace with the present is rather apt. Peter Nichols, in his book *The Politics of the Vatican,* asserts that *Rerum Novarum* "is patrician in tone, stamped more with home truths than anything so lofty as absolute truth, and it came half a century after the Communist Manifesto."

Still, the myth won the day—even then—of the pope as the champion of the workingman, although, of course, Leo remained absolutely silent about the most disputed issue of the day involved in the assertion of a right to strike and only pleaded for harmony rather than conflict. The myth, however, is fair in its own way, since Leo's words were to the left of most reigning European governments and considerably at variance with laissez-faire views of the state. Nevertheless, what Leo asserts of the state—"The state belongs to all and must guarantee actively public well-being as well as private property"—was not much different from Bismark's view on economics. In fact, the analogy of Leo with Bismark is very apt. Like Bismark, Leo wanted a conservative reform which would remove the legitimate cause of conflict by paying a just wage, thereby taking the steam out of socialism.

Most of all the myth is deserved because Leo unleashed strong movements of clergy and laity who turned to the workingman and workingmen's organizations in support and concern for justice. *Rerum Novarum* was the first and long-overdue charter for social Catholics. Finally, in the climate of widespread industrial unrest and strikes, the mere assertion of the right of workingmen to unions—although a home truth—sounded to many ears as radical as a contemporary home truth—the simple claim that the Palestinians have a right to some kind of homeland—would sound in our own day. *Rerum Novarum* certainly supported unions at a time most economic historians see as their most crucial period of early mass organization.

Quadragesimo Anno was also issued at a critical time. It had few antecedents in the many encyclicals of Pius which pre-date it (Pius XI wrote 30 encyclicals). Worldwide depression led Pius XI to speak out on economic issues for the first time in a 1931 radio address. Everywhere, in Europe and the United States, there was the expectation of the need for a new social order. The text of the encyclical, by Nell-Breuning, is a faithful version of the solidarism of his mentor, Father Gustav Gundlach.

The issues being adjudicated by the encyclical were whether capitalism was *per se* evil—to which the pope answered that capitalism was not vicious of its own nature but only in its abuses: monopoly, imperialism and the sham claims to a free market. A second lingering dispute dealt with the issue of confessional vs. mixed neutral unions. The pope clearly championed Catholic unions, allowing—subject to explicit episcopal approval—Catholic membership in neutral unions where necessary. The pope, however, urged in such cases a separate association of Catholic trade unionists within the neutral union.

As Leo supported a just wage, Pius included a just price which entailed, of course, strong state intervention for economic planning. Pius asserted the right to nationalize some property "which carries with it the opportunity of domination too great to allow it to be left in the control of individuals." Pius' famous principle of subsidiarity—be it noted neither a theological nor even really a philosophical principle, but a piece of congealed historical wisdom—affirmed the importance of social pluralism and intermediate groups. Pius' is the first social encyclical to see the need to go to a sweeping institutional reform rather than mere charity or the reform of morals to tackle the root problems of the social order.

Pius urged that the state had an obligation to create the material conditions of life, guarantee employment and take measures to protect against economic dictatorship so that "they will really affect those who actually possess more than their share of capital resources and who continue to accumulate them to the grievous detriment of others." While Pius urged a third way between socialism and liberalism, his strong animus against *any* political parties—Pius once asserted that the duty of Christians was to be above all parties as part of the grand party of God— made it difficult for any real third force to emerge. In this sense, his political conservatism tamed the economic radicalism of Nell-Breuning, who was following Gundlach, whose own teacher, Wagner, was a "socialist of the chair."

My own hunch is that the remarks on socialism in the encyclical were addressed to a small group of religious socialists in Germany and

Austria—Otto Bauer in Austria, Walter Dirks, Georg Beyer, Heinrich Mertins of the Rein-Mainische Vakzeitung—who urged collaboration between Catholics and socialists.

Pius has been described by one historian—accurately, it seems to me—as "suspicious of social radicalism and too much independence for the laity." He put his main trust in educational programs through his much loved Catholic Action. He was firm—even excessively so—on the issue of hierarchical control of the laity and the need for an insulating strategy of confessional particularism. Catholic socialists, in this context, were seen as breaking the desired Catholic unity. It was feared that they might detract from the Center Party. Gundlach wrote an article about this time suggesting as much. Nell-Breuning and Gundlach were close to members of the Center Party.

Instead of a straightforward plea for such unity however, *Quadragesimo Anno* unfairly raised the issue to high theory and ethical principle and condemned every species of socialism by appealing to an arbitrary, essentialist definition. In this respect, it is worth noting how often Catholic statements about socialism have been tied to the electoral fortunes of confessional parties in Italy (Pius XII), in Holland (the Dutch bishops' 1952 letter, *Het Mandement*) or Chile (the Chilean bishops' 1962 letter). Much of it was bent on protecting the standing Catholic party's electoral chances against defections rather than really enunciating any issue of high moral principle.

The corporative idea in *Quadragesimo Anno* seems somewhat quaint to us today, but it had other supporters in its time, perhaps the best known being the sociologist Emile Durkheim in his famous preface to the second edition of *The Division of Labor*. Joseph Schumpeter has claimed that it was a workable scheme from the point of view of economics. Political scientists, however, have been very sharp in their criticism of the naivete of multiple parliaments. It would either have led to anarchy—several parliaments without a leading role of the state—or, as in the case of fascism, too great state centralization. Even in its own time this could have been seen. The encyclical nowhere really addresses this key issue.

One notable absence in *Quadragesimo Anno* is any mention of political parties. It is said that this drew Ignaz Seipel to it in Austria. This has also leant to the idea that a corporative society is fascist. Undeserved as this is, it is the result of the peculiar amalgam at that period of history of a relatively advanced economic position joined to a fear or bias against modern parliamentary democracy. My own historical judgment is that Pius XI's political views, his distrust of any political party, made his idea of a reconstructed social order a purely idealistic notion, unanchored in any real social movement. Pius' social strategy of insulated Catholic confessional groupings guaranteed it would probably stay that way.

Still, the document—in parts, at least—was not 50 years after the Communist Manifesto. It was three years before the New Deal, five years before Leon Blum in France and almost a decade before extensive welfare-state legislation elsewhere. If we go to a cognate encyclical of Pius, *Divini Redemptoris,* we will find, as in Leo, a preferential option for the poor. Pius' words are still stirring: ''Priest go to the workingman, especially where he is poor, and in general, go to the poor.''

Finally, any account of the historical context of the encyclicals would look to the reception of the encyclicals. Here, too, history is not always kind. As Joseph Moody has remarked, ''right-wingers and left-wingers have always been able to find quotations from the encyclicals to justify the concepts of authority or of freedom, of hierarchy or of equality, of capitalism or of socialism, of corporatism or of trade unionism.''

In Austria, according to Joseph Dobretsberger, ''No one measured up to the standards of Christian ethics but everyone always quoted *Quadragesimo Anno*—even the barbers who sought legislation that only licensed barbers could shave.'' Chile's leading Catholic paper—a conservative newspaper—refused to publish *Quadragesimo Anno* on the ground that Chilean Catholics should be spared from ''the imprudences of the pope.'' The conservative economist Ludwig von Mises saw it as a cryptosocialist document. But fascists also claimed it as their own.

When *Mater et Magistra* was promulgated, both liberals and conservatives claimed to find confirmation of their position in it. While the Wall Street Journal saw *Populorum Progressio* as warmed-over Marxism, the right-wing authoritarian president of Brazil both congratulated the pope, through a telegram, for *Populorum Progressio* and claimed that his regime embodied its principles! Whatever an encyclical is, the fact that it can elicit such disparate responses seems to indicate that its unity does not leap off its pages.

If I have stressed the ways in which seeing the encyclicals in their historical context can create problems for a too easy, triumphalistic proclamation of the admittedly stirring texts of the social encyclicals, I do not think the relativities of history deserve the final say. Although I have not essayed it here, I think it is possible and legitimate to show a unity in the social teaching, if perhaps with less ease than it is usually done. David Hollenbach, in his recent book on Catholic human-rights theory, *Claims in Conflict,* shows the way toward this task (although I think that he, too, in places makes the unity stronger than the historical evidence will warrant) as has Phil Land in his splendid essay in *Above Every Name,* "The Earth is the Lord's: Thoughts on the Economic Order."

The foundation for such a unitary view, implicit in the fact that today represents the anniversaries of *four* social encyclicals, is the legitimate understanding that social encyclicals form an interconnected social charter and tradition. In that sense as the various popes—despite the different historical contexts which I have been stressing—built on one another, so it is legitimate to show the particular Catholic teaching on social issues captured, for example, in key principles and concepts such as human dignity, solidarity, subsidiarity, the right to integral development, participation, the ultimate subordination of economics and politics to human fulfillment. The writers of the social encyclicals were generally to the left of the overall social strategy of the various popes in whose reigns they were written.

Finally, as social charters, the encyclicals tended to be read, absorbed and commented on mainly by socially involved Catholics who generally gave them a more progressive interpretation than their location in historical context might have warranted. The encyclicals, then, represent in some sense a genuine unified tradition of sane and humane social thought which we both celebrate today and try to bring forward into the future.

My final judgment about the historicity of the encyclicals would be similar to my judgment about the historicity of our scripture. In the last analysis the interesting question is not "What formed scripture?" i.e., the historical antecedents for various ideas, concepts and books, but rather "What has scripture formed?" i.e., the communities, men and women of authenticity and dedication and historical movements which have grounded their being and action in scripture.

If we apply the same approach to the social encyclicals—though we may lament the fact that they are so little known, preached and acted on by the church at large and even, at times, the institutional church—they have formed over the past 90 years men and women who have found in them a charter to become concerned about institutional and structural reform, to support organization for justice, to heed the papal call to respect human dignity and to go to the poor. These men and women and the Catholic movements they have spawned are the best exegesis of the documents.

Ultimately, the future of this tradition will depend less on our ability to parrot its significant terms such as subsidiarity, a just wage, socialization, or to define in precise ways social charity, social justice or the common good, and more on our ability to read the signs of the times in fidelity to the Gospel of human dignity as Leo, Pius XI, Pius XII, John XXIII, Paul VI—with all their historical limitations, biases and failures—tried to do in their times. History will surely unveil all too well our shortcomings. May it also—as it does for this legacy of the popes—show our prophetic vision and courageous action.

The Changing
Anthropological Bases
of Catholic Social Ethics

Charles E. Curran

This article originally appeared in *Thomist*, 1981.

For one hundred years there has existed a body of official Catholic Church teaching on social ethics and the social mission of the Church. There was a social teaching within the Catholic Church before that time, but from the pontificate of Leo XIII (1878–1903) one can speak of a body of authoritative social teaching worked out in a systematic way and often presented in the form of encyclicals or papal letters to the bishops and to the whole Church. The purpose of this paper is to point out some of the changing anthropological emphases in this body of social teaching, thereby proposing an approach which can and should be employed in Christian social ethics today. The limitation of our discussion primarily to the official body of papal teaching should not be construed as failing to recognize the other theological approaches within the Catholic community. However, the teaching of the hierarchical magisterium has a special degree of authority about it and historically has served as a basis for much of Catholic social teaching during the last hundred years. Also by limiting the discussion to this particular body of teaching it is possible to place some realistic perimeters on the study.

Until a few years ago Catholic commentators were generally reluctant to admit any development within the papal social teaching.[1] The popes themselves gave the impression of continuity and even went out of their way to smooth over any differences with their "predecessors of happy memory." Often Catholic commentaries on the papal teaching were uncritical—merely explaining and applying the papal teaching.

John F. Cronin, one of the better known commentators on Catholic social teaching in the United States, while reminiscing in 1971, recognized
his failure to appreciate the historical and cultural conditionings of this
teaching and the importance of a proper hermeneutic in explaining it.[2]
In the area of Church and state relations and religious liberty the historically and culturally conditioned aspect of the papal teaching was clearly
recognized somewhat earlier.[3] In the last few years more scholars have
realized the development and change which have occurred in Catholic
social teaching.[4] Especially since the decade of the 1960s this development has become so pronounced that no one could deny its existence.

This study will concentrate on anthropology, but it will be impossible to treat all aspects of anthropology. Two anthropological aspects
will be considered in depth. The first section on the personal aspects of
anthropology will trace the development culminating in an emphasis on
the freedom, equality and participation of the person. Some of the important methodological consequences of such an understanding of the
human person will also be discussed. The second section on the social
aspects of anthropology will show the greater importance given to the
social dimensions of existence especially in terms of private property and
of the approach to socialism.[5]

I

PERSONAL ASPECTS OF ANTHROPOLOGY

Octogesima Adveniens, the apostolic letter of Pope Paul VI written
on the occasion of the eightieth anniversary of *Rerum Novarum,* proposes an anthropology highlighting the freedom and dignity of the human person, which are seen above all in two aspirations becoming ever
more prevalent in our world—the aspiration to equality and the aspiration to participation.[6] Freedom, equality and participation are the significant characteristics of the anthropology of *Octogesima Adveniens.*

The differences from the writings of Leo XIII are striking. The
Church at the time of Leo was fearful of freedom and equality and looked
on the majority of people as the untutored multitude who had to be
guided or directed by their rulers.[7]

Pope Leo condemned the "modern liberties." Liberty of worship
goes against the "chiefest and holiest human duty" demanding the wor-

ship of the one true God in the one true religion which can be easily recognized by its external signs. Liberty of speech and of the press means that nothing will remain sacred, for truth will be obscured by darkness and error will prevail. There is only a right and a duty to speak what is true and honorable and no right to speak what is false. A like judgment is passed on liberty of teaching. Finally liberty of conscience is considered. The only true meaning of the freedom of conscience is the freedom to follow the will of God and to do one's duty in obeying his commands. At best the public authority can tolerate what is at variance with truth and justice for the sake of avoiding greater evils or of preserving some greater good.[8] Leo XIII was certainly no supporter of civil liberties and the modern freedoms.

Leo XIII not only did not promote equality as a virtue or something to be striven for in society, but he stressed the importance of inequality. Inequality is a fact of nature. There are differences in health, beauty, intelligence, strength and courage. These natural inequalities necessarily bring about social inequalities which are essential for the good functioning of society. In short, the inequality of rights and of power proceed from the very author of nature. Leo had a view of society as a hierarchical organism in which there are different roles and functions to fulfill, but in which all will work for the common good of all.[9]

According to Leo:

In like manner, no one doubts that all men are equal one to another, so far as regards their common origin and nature, or the last end which each one has to attain, or the rights and duties which are thence derived. But, as the abilities of all are not equal, as one differs from another in the powers of mind or body, and as there are many dissimilarities of manner, disposition and character, it is most repugnant to reason to endeavor to confine all within the same measure, and to extend complete equality to the institutions of civil life.[10]

Inequalities and some of the hardships connected with them will always be part of human existence in this world which is marked by the presence of original sin. To suffer and to endure is the lot of people. People should not be deluded by promises of undisturbed repose and constant enjoyment. We should look upon our world in a spirit of reality and at the same time seek elsewhere the solace to its troubles.[11]

Leo XIII likewise does not call for the active participation of all in social and political life, but rather he has a very hierarchical view of civil society which follows from the inequalities mentioned above. Leo's favorite word for the rulers of society is *principes*. The very word shows his hierarchical leanings. The citizen is primarily one who obeys the divine law, the natural law and the human law which are handed down by the *principes*. Leo even quotes the maxim, *qualis rex, talis grex,* which indicates the power of the ruler over all the citizens in practically every aspect of life.[12] The citizens are called by Leo the untutored multitude who must be led and protected by the ruler.[13] At best, authority appears as paternalistic, and the subjects are children who are to obey and respect their rulers with a type of piety.[14] Leo was fearful of the liberalistic notion of the sovereignty of the people, which really meant that the people no longer owed obedience to God and God's law in all aspects of their public and private lives.[15]

In this authoritarian and paternalistic understanding, there is not the distinction between society and the state which had been present in classical thought but then lost during the period of absolutism. Leo's theory is that of the ethical society-state in which the total common good of the society is entrusted to the rulers. Society is constructed from the top down with the ruler guarding and protecting the untutored multitude from the many dangers of life just as the father has the function of protecting and guiding his children in the family.[16]

Leo's denial of liberty, equality and participation can be somewhat understood in the light of the circumstances of the times in which he lived. The pope was an implacable foe of liberalism, which in his mind was the root cause of all the problems of the modern day. Liberalism substitutes foolish license for true liberty. The followers of liberalism deny the existence of any divine authority and proclaim that every human being is a law unto oneself. Liberalism proposes an independent morality in which the human being is freed from the divine law and authority and one can do whatever one wants. Leo consequently attacks those forms of government which make the collective reason of the community the supreme guide of life in society. They substitute the decision of the majority for the rule of God. God and God's law are totally removed from society.[17]

Behind Leo's fear of equality lurks the same individualism present in liberalism. For Leo, society is an organism. Human beings are by nature social and called to join together in political society for the common good. To live in society is not a restriction on individual human freedom, for by nature all of us are social. Each one has a different function to play in the hierarchically structured organism which resembles the organism of the human body with all its different parts but each functioning for the good of the whole. Leo fears an understanding which sees society merely as a collection of equal individuals, for this would destroy any social fabric and true social ordering. Participation is also looked on as a threat, for this could readily be confused with the demands of liberalistic license and destroy the organic unity of society in which each person has his or her God-given function to perform. In the context of Leo's understanding of the untutored multitude, there could be little or no room for participation.

In general, Leo rightly recognized some of the problems of liberalism and individualism. However, his only solution was to turn his back totally on all the developments which were then taking place in the modern world. His solution to the problem was a static, hierarchically structured, authoritarian, and paternalistic view of society. At the very least, Leo lacked the prophetic charism to sort out the good from the bad in the newer developments which were taking place in the nineteenth century and to find a place for the legitimate demands of liberty, equality and participation.[18] The picture emerges of a static and hierarchically structured society governed by the law of God and the natural law under the protection and guidance of the ruler who directs all to the common good and protects his subjects from physical and moral harm.

This explanation of Leo's approach shows the tremendous gulf which exists between his understanding of anthropology and that proposed by Pope Paul VI in *Octogesima Adveniens*. However, one can trace some of the major lines of the developments which occurred from Leo XIII to Paul VI.

Even in Leo XIII there are some aspects pointing in a different direction, but they are found mostly in his 1891 encyclical *Rerum Novarum* on the rights of the worker. In his political writings Leo especially argues against a totalitarian democracy with its emphasis on majority rule and its lack of respect for divine and natural law, but he always upheld the basic rights of individual human beings, which might be abused because of the totalitarian democracy. In *Rerum Novarum* he stresses even more the rights of the individual worker and his approach is less authoritarian and paternalistic. In *Rerum Novarum* against the danger of socialism Leo recalls that the human being is prior to the state and has natural rights which do not depend on the state.[19] The right to private property is based on our nature as rational and provident beings. Every individual has the right to marry. Marriage is older than the state and has its rights and duties independently of the state.[20] The state has an obligation to intervene to protect the rights of the workers, for public authority must step in when a particular class suffers or is threatened with harm which in no other way can be met or avoided.[21] Moreover, workers themselves have the right to organize into unions and associations to promote their own rights and interests.[22] Here appears the basis for participation in the shaping of one's own destiny.

In *Rerum Novarum* Leo repeats his teaching on inequality. The condition of things inherent in human affairs must be borne with. These conditions include natural differences of the most important kinds— differences in capacities, skills, health and strength. Unequal fortune is a necessary result of unequal conditions.[23] However, Leo appears to admit a basic equality of all to have their rights recognized and protected by the state. In fact the poor and badly off have a claim to special consideration.[24] As one would expect, Leo upholds the rights of the individual against socialism. In tension with his other emphases Leo's writings show differing degrees of recognition of some freedom, equality and even of incipient participation as anthropological concerns.

Pope Pius XI (1922–1939) remains in continuity with his predecessor Leo XIII. Liberalism lies at the root of the problems of the modern world. The principal cause of the disturbed conditions in which we live is that the power of law and respect for authority have been considerably weakened ever since people came to deny that the origin of law and of authority was in God the creator and ruler of the world. Liberalism has even fathered socialism and bolshevism. Pius XI insists on the importance of natural law and a hierarchical ordering of society based on it. In *Quadragesimo Anno* on the fortieth anniversary of Leo's encyclical *Rerum Novarum,* Pius XI continues the discussion of justice and the economic order, insisting on the dignity and rights of the individual and also on the social nature of human beings. Here again the two extreme approaches of individualism and socialism are rejected on the basis of an anthropology which recognizes the dignity and rights of the individual as well as the social aspects of the human person.[25]

However, contact with different forms of totalitarianism brought to the fore an emphasis on the defense of the rights, dignity and freedom of the individual. (There has been much discussion in the last few decades about the relationship of the Catholic Church to fascism, nazism and communism. Without entering into the debate, it is safe to generalize that the Catholic Church was much more fearful of the left and showed itself more willing to compromise with the right.) Pius XI defends the transcendental character of the human person against materialistic and atheistic communism. Communism is condemned for stripping human beings of their liberty and for robbing the human person of dignity.[26] Now the Church becomes the protector of human freedom and dignity. In *Non Abbiamo Bisogno,* Pius XI even defends the freedom of conscience with the recognition that he is speaking about the true freedom of conscience and not the license which refuses to recognize the laws of God.[27]

The development continues in the pontificate of Pope Pius XII (1939–1958). The historical context of the struggle against totalitarianism remains, but the significant role of Christian Democratic parties in Europe adds an important new dimension. In his Christmas radio message in 1944, Pope Pius XII insisted on the dignity of human beings and on a system of government that will be more in accord with the dignity and freedom of the citizenry. This emphasis on the dignity and freedom of the human being also calls for greater participation and active involvement of all. The human being is not the object of social life or an inert element in it, but rather is the subject, foundation and end of social life.[28]

In the light of these historical circumstances and of a theoretical insistence on the centrality of the dignity of the human person, Pius proposed an understanding of the state remarkably different from that of Leo XIII. As John Courtney Murray lucidly points out Pius XII abandoned Leo XIII's ethical concept of the society-state and accepted a juridical or limited constitutional state. For Leo there is no distinction between society and the state, for the state is hierarchically ordered with the rulers having the function of guarding and protecting the illiterate masses in every aspect of life. By emphasizing the dignity, freedom and responsibility of the individual person, Pius XII clearly accepts a limited view of the state which sees it as only a part of society with a function of defending the rights of human beings and of promoting the freedom of the people. The state has a limited juridical role and does not act as the parent who guides the entire lives of his or her children. No longer is the state understood in terms of the relationship between *principes* and the un-tutored multitudes. The rulers are representatives of the people, and the people are responsible citizens.[29]

Despite these significant changes in the importance of the dignity of the person and the recognition of limited constitutional government, Guzzetti still detects an air of the aristocratic about Pius XII's ap-proach.[30] Also on the matter of inequalities in society Pius advances over Leo, but still insists that natural inequalities of education, of earthly goods and of social position are not obstacles to brotherhood and com-munity provided they are not arbitrary and are in accord with justice and charity.[31]

The short pontificate of John XXIII (1958–1963) with its convo-cation of the Second Vatican Council had a great impact on Roman Ca-tholicism. In the area of social ethics John in his two encyclicals, *Mater et Magistra* and *Pacem in Terris*, defends human dignity in the midst of the ever increasing social relationships and interdependencies which characterize our modern world. *Pacem in Terris* gives the most detailed statement in the papal social tradition of human rights based on the dig-nity of the person, but also adds the corresponding duties thereby avoid-ing the danger of individualism. The dignity of the human person requires that every individual enjoy the right to act freely and responsi-bly. The dignity, freedom and equality of the human person are high-lighted and defended, but many of the assumptions of an older liberalistic individualism are not accepted.[32]

There is one fascinating development even within John's own writ-ings. The papal social tradition consistently emphasized that life in so-ciety must be based on truth, justice and love. John XXIII repeated the importance of this triad in *Mater et Magistra* in 1961.[33] However, in 1963 in *Pacem in Terris* a fourth element was added: a political society is well ordered, beneficial and in keeping with human dignity if it is grounded on truth, justice, love and freedom.[34] Even in John there was only a later recognition of the fundamental importance of freedom along-side truth, justice and love.

From the first encyclical of Leo XIII on the question of economic ethics there was some recognition for participation and responsibility, especially in terms of the workers' right to form organizations and unions to promote their own interests. John XXIII recognizes there is an innate need of human nature calling for human beings engaged in productive activity to have an opportunity to assume responsibility and to perfect themselves by their efforts. Participation of workers in medium size and larger enterprises calls for some type of partnership.[35]

Two documents of the Second Vatican Council are most significant for our purposes—the Declaration on Religious Freedom and the Pastoral Constitution on the Church in the Modern World. It was only at the Second Vatican Council that the Roman Catholic Church accepted the concept of religious liberty—a concept which was anathema to Leo XIII. However, the council is careful to show that its acceptance does not stem from the tenets of an older liberalism and indifferentism. Religious liberty is not the right to worship God as one pleases, but rather the right to immunity from external coercion forcing one to act in a way opposed to one's conscience or preventing one from acting in accord with one's conscience. The basis for religious liberty is stated very distinctly in the opening paragraph—the dignity of the human person which has been impressing itself more and more deeply on the conscience of contemporary people and a corresponding recognition of a constitutional government whose powers are limited. A limited government embraces only a small part of the life of people in society, and religion exists beyond the pale of the role of civil government.[36] The council brings out all the implications of a limited constitutional government which in principle had been accepted by Pius XII. The Roman Catholic Church thus became a defender of religious liberty even though in the nineteenth century Pope Leo XIII stood as the most determined opponent of religious liberty.

The dignity of the human person serves as the cornerstone of the Pastoral Constitution on the Church in the Modern World—*Gaudium et Spes*. The first chapter of the theoretical Part One of the document begins with the dignity of the human person and its meaning and importance. Authentic freedom as opposed to license is championed by the conciliar document. In earlier documents there was a great insistence on the moral law as the antidote to any tendency to license. Now the emphasis is on conscience—the most secret core and sanctuary of the human person where one hears the call of God's voice. The shift from the role of law which is traditionally called the objective norm of morality to conscience which is called the subjective norm of human action is most significant in showing the move to the subject and to the person. Of course the document stresses the need for a correct conscience, but the impression is given that truth is found in the innermost depths of one's existence.[37]

Gaudium et Spes gives much more importance to equality than some of the earlier documents. Inequalities are still recognized, but now the existence of inequalities appears in subordinate clauses with the main emphasis being on equality. For example: "True, all men are not alike from the point of view of varying physical power and the diversity of intellectual and moral resources. Nevertheless, with respect to the fundamental rights of the person, every type of discrimination, whether social or cultural, whether based on sex, race, color, social condition, language or religion, is to be overcome and eradicated as contrary to God's intent."[38] "Moreover, although rightful differences exist between men, the equal dignity of persons demands that a more humane and just condition of life be brought about. For excessive economic and social differences between the members of the one human family or population groups cause scandal, and militate against social justice, equity, the dignity of the human person as well as social and international peace."[39]

There is also a call for responsibility and participation. The will to play one's role in common endeavors should be encouraged. The largest possible number of citizens should participate in public affairs with genuine freedom.[40] A greater share in education and culture is required for all to exercise responsibility and participation. The active participation of all in running the economic enterprise should be promoted.[41] The juridical and political structure should afford all citizens the chance to participate freely and actively in establishing the constitutional basis of a political community, governing the state, determining the scope and purposes of different institutions and choosing leaders.[42]

In the light of this line of development, the teaching of Pope Paul VI in *Octogesima Adveniens* on the eightieth anniversary of *Rerum Novarum* does not come as a total surprise: "Two aspirations persistently make themselves felt in these new contexts, and they grow stronger to the extent that people become better informed and better educated: the aspiration to equality and the aspiration to participation, two forms of man's dignity and freedom."[43] Such an anthropology stressing freedom, equality and participation should have significant methodological consequences for Christian social ethics.

Historical Consciousness

Before considering the methodological consequences of this new anthropology, historical consciousness, which affects both anthropology and methodology, should be considered. Historical consciousness, which is very pronounced in *Octogesima Adveniens* but clearly absent from the documents of Leo XIII, gives great significance to historical conditions, growth, change and development and has often been contrasted with a classicist approach. In the area of methodology, the classicist approach emphasizes the eternal, the universal, the unchanging and often employs a deductive methodology. The historically conscious approach emphasizes the particular, the individual, the contingent and the historical and often employs a more inductive methodology.[44]

The importance of historical consciousness becomes very evident in the deliberations of the Second Vatican Council on religious freedom. Pope Leo XIII had condemned religious liberty. Perhaps the most pressing question facing the fathers of Vatican II was how to reconcile Leo's condemnation with the acceptance of religious liberty less than a century later. John Courtney Murray in his writings on religious liberty provided a solution. One has to interpret Leo in the light of the circumstances of his own day. Leo was struggling against a continental liberalism with its denial of any place for God in society and its acceptance of an omnicompetent state with no recognition whatsoever of the divine law or of natural law. In reaction to this approach Leo called for the union of Church and state as the way of rightfully recognizing and protecting the role and function of the Church. However, the constitutional understanding of the separation of Church and state was not based on a continental liberalism but on a notion of a constitutional government which claimed only a limited role for itself in the life of society. The constitutional understanding did not deny a role or a place for religion in society; the role and function of religion existed beyond the pale of the limited scope and function of the state. Murray's historically conscious hermeneutic distinguished the polemical-historical aspect of Leo's teaching from the doctrinal aspect. There has been no change in the doctrinal. The recognition of historical consciousness provided the key to the problem of development and change in the Church's teaching.[45] Murray made a remarkable contribution by his historical hermeneutic. In retrospect it is both easy and necessary to criticize Murray's theory as too benevolent.

One should admit some error in the Church's teaching in the nineteenth century and even some doctrinal discontinuity and evolution in the teaching on religious liberty.

The acceptance of historical consciousness in our understanding of anthropology also has important methodological ramifications in the papal social teaching. The earlier teachings were deductive, stressing immutable eternal principles of natural law. However, a more inductive approach began to appear in the 1960s. The encyclical *Pacem in Terris* is divided into four major parts: order among people, relations between individuals and public authority within a single state, relations between states, relations of people in political communities with the world community. Each part concludes with a section on the signs of the times— the distinctive characteristics of the contemporary age.[46] There was much debate about the term "signs of the times" at the Second Vatican Council. Early drafts and versions of the Constitution on the Church in the Modern World gave great importance to the term. In the final version "signs of the times" was used sparingly because some Council fathers did not want to use a term whose biblical meaning was quite different— the eschatological signs of the last days.[47] However, in the second part of the Pastoral Constitution which treats five problems of special urgency in the contemporary world each consideration begins with an empirical description of the contemporary reality even though the terminology "signs of the times" is not employed. Such an approach gives greater emphasis to the contemporary historical situation and does not begin with a universal viewpoint and deduce an understanding applicable to all cultures and times.

Methodological Consequences

The anthropology of the papal social teaching by the time of *Octogesima Adveniens* in 1971 stresses freedom, equality, participation and historical mindedness. The methodological consequences of such an anthropology are quite significant and show a remarkable change from the methodology employed in the earlier documents. The earlier approach highlighted the universal, all-embracing character of the teaching. In the economic realm there appeared especially with Pius XI in 1931 a plan for the reconstruction of the social order in accord with what was called a theory of moderate solidarism. Pope Pius XI was much more negative about the existing abuses and injustices of the social order than was Leo XIII. Undoubtedly the problem of the depression influenced Pius's negative judgment about the existing social order and the call for a more radical reconstruction of society according to a solidaristic model based in general on the guild system with its intermediary institutions bringing together both workers and owners. The Pope continued to condemn laissez-faire capitalism and the opposite extreme of socialism. In place of these two systems, Pius XI proposed a third way which would eliminate the bad features of extreme individualism and extreme socialism while giving due importance to the personal and social nature of the individual person. This third way, although somewhat vague in its development and detail, was thought to be a universally applicable plan.[48]

Pius XII continued in the same line as his predecessor with emphasis on reconstruction and not merely on reform. Professional organizations and labor unions are provisional and transitory forms; the ultimate purpose is the bringing together and cooperation of employees and employers in order to provide together for the general welfare and the needs of the whole community. Pope Pius XII also distinguished his reconstruction plan from mere co-management or participation of workers in management. Pope Pius XII originally continued in the footsteps of his predecessor, proposing a universally applicable plan of reconstruction deduced from the principles of the natural law and corresponding in significant ways to the guild system of the middle ages. However, after 1952 Pius rarely mentioned such a plan of reconstruction.[49] In *Mater et Magistra* Pope John XXIII merely referred to Pius XI's orderly reorganization of society with smaller professional and economic groups existing in their own right and not prescribed by public authority.[50] In John's encyclicals, in the conciliar documents and in Paul's teaching there was no further development of Pius XI's plan for social reconstruction.

Reasons for the abandonment of a plan of social reconstruction applicable throughout the world can be found in the later documents themselves. These documents recognize the complexity of the social problem and historical and cultural differences which make it difficult for a universal plan to be carried out in all different areas. *Mater et Magistra* emphasized the complexity of the present scene, the multiplication of social relationships, and many new developments in the field of science, technology and economics as well as developments in the social and political fields.[51] The social questions involve more than the rights and duties of labor and capital. In *Populorum Progressio* Pope Paul VI early in his encyclical stated that today the principal fact that all must recognize is that the social question has become world-wide.[52] The complexity of the question increases enormously when one brings into consideration the entire world and the relationship between and among countries, especially poor nations and rich nations. The approach of the Pastoral Constitution on the Church in the Modern World by beginning with the signs of the times also called for doing away with a deductive methodology resulting in an eternal, immutable plan of God for the world.

At the same time as Pius XI and Pius XII were talking about a program of reconstruction according to solidaristic principles of organization, the term "social doctrine" was used by these popes to refer to the official body of Church teaching consisting of the principles of the economic order derived from the natural law and the plan of reconstruction based on them. Pius XI distinguished this social doctrine from social and economic sciences. The social doctrine contains the immutable truths taught by the popes, whereas social science is the area for research and scholarly enterprise. Precisely the authoritative nature of the doctrine distinguishes it from the empirical social sciences of economics or sociology.[53] Such an approach was called for by some Catholic sociologists who claimed that the major of their argument was supplied by authoritative Church teaching, the minor came from their scientific research; and from these one drew the conclusion.[54] Pope Pius XII frequently speaks about Catholic social doctrine. According to Pius XII the earlier papal teaching became the source of Catholic social doctrine providing the children of the Church with directives and means for a social reconstruction rich in fruit.[55] Social doctrine is the authoritative teaching proclaimed by the hierarchical magisterium, deduced from the eternal principles of the natural law, and distinguished from the contribution of the empirical sciences.

Both the term "social doctrine of the Church" and the reality expressed by it, namely, a papal plan or ideology of social reconstruction, gradually disappear from official Church documents after Pope Pius XII. Later references are to the social teaching of the gospel or the social teaching of the Church. Gone is the vision of the universal plan deductively derived from natural law and proposed authoritatively by the Church magisterium to be applied in all parts of the world. No longer

will there be such a separation between ethically deduced moral principles and the economic and social analysis of the situation. Rather one
now begins with the signs of the times and with an analysis of the contemporary situation and not with some abstract principle divorced from
historical reality.[56]

Octogesima Adveniens with an anthropology insisting on personal
freedom, equality, participation and historical consciousness employs a
methodology quite at variance with that employed in the early papal documents. Early in the document Pope Paul VI recognizes the wide diversity of situations in which Christians live throughout the world. In the
face of such diversity it is difficult to utter a unified message or to put
forward a solution which has universal validity. The Christian communities themselves must analyze with objectivity their own situation and
shed on it the light of the gospel and the principles of the teaching of the
Church. It is up to the Christian communities with the help of the Spirit
in communion with the bishops and in dialogue with other Christians and
people of good will to discern the options and commitments necessary
to bring about the urgently needed social and political changes.[57] Rather
than a universal plan based on natural law, Pope Paul VI recalls the importance and significance of utopias. Utopias appeal to the imagination
of responsible people to perceive in the present situation the disregarded
possibilities within it and to provide direction toward a fresh future. Such
an approach sustains social dynamism by the confidence that it gives to
the inventive powers of the human mind and heart. "At the heart of the
world there dwells the mystery of man discovering himself to be God's
son in the course of a historical and psychological process in which con-
straint and freedom as well as the weight of sin and the breath of the
Spirit alternate and struggle for the upper hand."[58]

The methodological changes are quite significant. There is no universal plan applicable to all situations, but rather Christians discern what
to do in the midst of the situation in which they find themselves. What
to do is not determined by a deductive reasoning process based on the
eternal and immutable natural law. Rather, a careful and objective scrutiny of the present reality in the light of the gospel and of the teaching
of the Church is central to the discernment process. Commitments and
options are discerned in the situation itself. The approach is dynamic
rather than static. The appeal to utopias, imagination and the mystery of

the human person at the heart of the world all testify to a less rationalistic discernment process. There is also a call for the individual in the Church to be self-critical, thereby recognizing the dangers that might come from one's own presuppositions.

Octogesima Adveniens concludes with a call to action.[59] All along the Church's social teaching has called for action, but the call is now more urgent and more central to the very notion of the social mission of the Church. The importance of responsibility and the urgent need to change structures call for the active involvement of all. Once again emphasis is on the concrete and the need to take concrete action despite the fact that there can be a plurality of strategic options for Christians.

Both the anthropology and the methodology employed in *Octogesima Adveniens* call for a different understanding of the role of persons in the Church itself and in the social mission of the Church. An older approach, especially associated with the concept of Catholic Action proposed by Pope Pius XI and Pope Pius XII, saw the function of the laity to carry out and put into practice the principles which were taught by the hierarchical magisterium. Now that there no longer exists a clear-cut dichotomy between the deduced principles and the concrete commitments and options, so too there no longer can exist this total dichotomy between the role of hierarchical magisterium and role of the laity in the Church. As is evident even in this document, the whole Church must discern what options are to be taken in the light of an analysis of the signs of the times and in the light of the gospel even though there remains a distinctive role for the hierarchical magisterium. No longer are the laity the people who receive the principles and the instruction from the hierarchy and then put these plans into practice. All in the Church have a role in discerning and in executing.[60]

Contemporary Catholic social ethics mirrors and at times even goes beyond the approach and methodology employed in *Octogesima Adveniens*. David Hollenbach has recently employed a similar methodology in his attempt to revise and retrieve the Catholic human rights tradition.[61] Political and liberation theology shows some of the same tendencies but even goes beyond the methodological approach of *Octogesima Adveniens*. Critical reason insists on the importance of action. Praxis becomes primary in many of these approaches, and theology becomes reflection on praxis. For many liberation theologians true theology can only grow out of praxis.[62] At the very least, the methodology of Catholic social ethics is thus greatly changed from the time of Leo XIII especially in the light of changing anthropological understandings.

II
Social Aspects of Anthropology

Another important aspect of anthropology concerns the social nature of human beings. Catholic social ethics has consistently recognized the social nature of human beings. As a result Catholic social ethics looks upon the state as a natural society, for human beings are called by nature to live in political society. In some Christian ethics the origin of the state is grounded on human sinfulness. The power and coercion of the state are necessary to prevent sinful human beings from destroying one another.[63] Pope Leo XIII follows in the Catholic tradition by his insistence that the state is a natural society. Human beings with their inequality and differences come together to achieve what the individuals as such are not able to accomplish. Leo's understanding of political society as an organism and an organic whole with individuals carrying out different functions shows that the state is based on human nature and does not exist merely on the basis of a contract made by discrete individuals.[64]

The papal social teaching in the last century has recognized both the legitimate rights of the individual and the social nature of human beings. The Catholic approach to the economic problem traditionally has condemned the two extremes of individualistic capitalism and collectivistic socialism. Throughout its history Catholic social ethics has tried to uphold both the personal and the social aspects of anthropology. However, there have been varying nuances in the approach over the years. This section of the essay will now consider two significant questions in which there has been a development in giving more importance to the social aspects of anthropology—private property and socialism.

Private Property

Pope Leo XIII recognized the misery and wretchedness pressing so urgently upon the majority of the working class because of the hard-heartedness of employers and the greed of unchecked competition. To remedy these ills the socialists do away with private property. However, Leo's solution is the opposite. Everyone has a right to private property. The dignity of the individual will be protected if one is able to have one's own property and thus make oneself secure against the vicissitudes of the industrial order. Private property protects and promotes the security of the individual and of the family. By investing wages in property and in land the worker has the hope and the possibility of increasing personal resources and of bettering one's condition in life.

However, the most important and fundamental fact for Leo is that private property is a demand of the natural law. The human being is distinguished from animals precisely through rational nature because of which one has the right to possess things in a permanent and stable way to provide for the future through private property. By virtue of labor and work the human being makes one's own that portion of nature's field which he or she cultivates. The principle of private ownership is necessarily in accord with human nature and is conducive in the most unmistakable manner to the peace and tranquility of human existence. The right to private property of the individual is strengthened in the light of human social and domestic obligations, for it provides security for the entire family. The first and most fundamental principle to alleviate the impoverished conditions of the masses is the inviolability of private property.[65]

There are a number of interesting facets about Leo's defense of private property as the solution to the misery of the working masses. First, Leo's solution indicates the rural and preindustrial perspective with which he approached the problem. Private property for Leo is usually the land and one's right to the fruits of the labor which has been expended in cultivating the land. If one possesses one's own land, then one can provide food and basic necessities for one's family no matter what the vicissitudes of the industrial order. Human dignity is preserved and human needs will be met if the workers can own and work their own plot of land. This solution obviously fits better in an earlier time and in a more agrarian situation. Its practicality as a reasonable solution in the industrial era of the late nineteenth century is open to serious question.

Second, Leo does not deal realistically with the most significant aspect of private property existing at that time—the abuse of private property by the rich at the expense of the poor. The failure to recognize this fact in the very first part of the encyclical and to deal with it realistically marks a definite lacuna in Leo's approach. The real problem of the day concerns especially the ownership of the goods of production, since abuses on the part of those who own the goods of production contributed greatly to the economic woes of the worker. Leo reminds the rich of their obligation to share with the poor, but such a reminder does not go to the heart of the problem.

Third, and somewhat connected with the two previous observations, Leo justifies private property only on the basis of labor. No other titles are mentioned by Leo in *Rerum Novarum* to justify ownership. The single title of labor again shows the rural vision which Leo brought to the question and does not take into consideration the many problems of abuse through inheritance and other ways of acquiring private property. In *Quod Apostolici Muneris* Leo held that inheritance was a valid means of acquiring wealth but did not justify this title.[66] Leo's discussion of the titles to private ownership is very incomplete and again fails to deal with the real abuses and problems of the times.

Fourth, Leo's teaching on private property disagrees with that proposed by Thomas Aquinas. Thomas Aquinas discusses the question of private property in two articles.[67] First he responds affirmatively to the question whether the possession of external things is natural to human beings. God created all reality and ordained that the lower creation serve the higher. Dominion over external things is natural to humans because as a rational creature made in the image and likeness of God the human being is called to use external goods to achieve his or her end. But then in a second question Thomas discusses the right to possess something as one's own with the power of procuring and disposing of it. Human beings have the right to private ownership which involves the procuring and disposing of external goods. This right is necessary for human life for three reasons: 1) Individuals are more solicitous about procuring things that belong to themselves alone and are not owned in common. 2) A more orderly and less confusing existence will result from private property. 3) A more peaceful state of existence ensues when everyone is content with one's own things. However, with regard to the use of private property human beings are to use external goods as though they were common and not proper because these goods should serve the needs of all.

Thomas Aquinas's teaching on private property differs from Leo's on a number of significant points. Thomas clearly distinguishes between a generic dominion that belongs to all human beings to use external things and the specific type of dominion in the system of private property. In Leo's discussion in the beginning of *Rerum Novarum* this distinction seems to be almost entirely lacking.[68] In fact, the argument based on rational human nature, which Thomas uses to prove the generic dominion of all people over the goods of creation, is employed by Leo to argue for the rights of private property in the strict sense. Thomas's arguments for the right to private property in the strict sense are not really based on human nature as such; but, rather, the three arguments given are all grounded in the existence of human sinfulness. If it were not for human sinfulness, there would be no need for private property in the strict sense. Elsewhere, Thomas maintains that in the state of innocence there would be no need for the strict right of private property.[69] Thomas makes the right to private property in the strict sense instrumental and sees it in the light of the more general right of all human beings to the use of external goods. Likewise, he bases his argument for private property in the strict sense primarily on human sinfulness and not on human nature as such.

Later on in his encyclical, Leo does recognize the social aspect of property and the fact that the use of private property is to be common in accord with Aquinas's teaching. From this communal use of property he derives the duty of charity, not of justice except in extreme cases, to give one's superfluous goods to the poor. Leo's differences with Aquinas's teaching on private property seem to come primarily from what was introduced into the scholastic tradition by Taparelli d'Azeglio in the nineteenth century.[70]

It is interesting to note that John A. Ryan, the major figure in Catholic social ethics in the United States in the first half of the twentieth century, proposed an instrumental understanding of the right to private property understood in the strict sense. Ryan's argument makes explicit some of Thomas's presuppositions and clarifies the whole meaning of an instrumental understanding of private property. For Ryan, who considers the question primarily in terms of the ownership of land, the first thing to be said about the goods of creation is that they exist to serve the needs of all human beings. Ryan accepts private ownership in the strict sense as what he calls a natural right of the third class. A right of the first class has as its object that which is an intrinsic good such as the right to life. A right of the second class has as its object that which is directly necessary for the individual, such as the right to marry. A right of the third class has as its object not what is directly necessary for the individual but what is indirectly necessary for the individual because it is necessary as a social institution providing for the general welfare. Private ownership in the strict sense provides better for the general social welfare than any other institutional arrangement about the distribution of property. This necessity is proved empirically and inductively. If socialism or some other system would better serve the general welfare, it should be adopted.[71] Ryan's position with its clear and careful relativization of the right to private property in the strict sense would find an echo in the later papal social teaching.

In *Quadragesimo Anno* Pius XI gave more stress to the social function of property. He notes the right to private property exists not only so that individuals may provide for themselves and their families but also so that the goods of creation which are destined by the creator for the entire family of humankind may serve their God-given purpose.[72] However, precisely how private property accomplishes this purpose is not developed. In addition, Pope Pius XI neatly covers one of Leo's lacunae in *Rerum Novarum* by asserting that ownership is acquired both by labor and by occupancy of something not owned by anyone, as the tradition of all ages as well as the teaching of his predecessor Pope Leo clearly states.[73] No footnote or reference is made to where Leo makes that statement about occupancy.

There was some evolution in the teaching of Pius XII and later in John XXIII. John recognized the realities of the modern industrial society and the importance of professional skills, education and social insurance and security as ways of protecting the dignity of the individual worker. However, he hastens to add that despite all these modern developments the right of private property including that pertaining to goods devoted to productive enterprises is permanently valid.[74] It appears there is still a tendency to give absolute rather than relative or instrumental value to the right of private property understood in the strict sense.[75]

Gaudium et Spes and *Populorum Progressio* made more clear the distinction between the generic right of dominion which belongs to all human beings and the right to private property in the strict sense. *Gaudium et Spes* begins with the recognition that the goods of creation exist to serve the needs of all. Each of us has a right to a share of earthly goods sufficient for oneself and one's family. Whatever forms of ownership might be, attention must always be paid to the universal purpose for which created goods exist.[76] After affirming the principle of the universal destiny of the goods of creation, *Populorum Progressio* maintains that all other rights including that of private property and free commerce are to be subordinated to this principle.[77] Here we have the same teaching as that proposed earlier by John A. Ryan. All must admit that in the course of one hundred years the official Catholic teaching has relativized the right to private property in the strict sense and called attention to the need to judge all property institutions in accord with the universal destiny of the goods of creation to serve the needs of all.

Socialism

There has also been a change in the attitude of the papal teaching to socialism. Pope Leo XIII in the first year of his pontificate issued the encyclical *Quod Apostolici Muneris* which pointed out the errors of "that sect of men who, under various and almost barbarous names, are called socialists, communists or nihilists."[78] These people deny the supernatural, the plan of God, God's law and the role of the Church. They assert the basic equality of all human beings and deny that respect is due to majesty and obedience to law. They support a revolutionary doctrine, oppose the indissolubility of marriage and deny the natural law right of private property. In *Rerum Novarum* in 1891, Pope Leo XIII returned in a somewhat systematic way to a discussion of socialism and considered especially its denial of the right of private property which is against the law of God and of human nature. However, Leo overemphasized the strength of socialism and its force as a worldwide conspiracy. Also he failed to recognize the moderate strands of socialism which were then existing in many parts of the world.[79]

Pope Pius XI in 1931 in *Quadragesimo Anno* recognized the differences existing between a more violent socialism called communism and a more moderate form of socialism which rejects violence and modifies to some degree, if it does not reject entirely, the class struggle and the abolition of private ownership. Obviously communism with its unrelenting class warfare and absolute extermination of private ownership stands condemned. But what about moderate socialism which has tempered and modified its positions? Has it ceased to be contradictory to the Christian religion? ''Whether considered as a doctrine, or an historical fact, or a movement, Socialism, if it remains truly Socialism, even after it has yielded to truth and justice on the points which we have mentioned cannot be reconciled with the teachings of the Catholic Church because its concept of society itself is utterly foreign to Christian truth.''[80] Socialism like all errors contains some truths, but its theory of human society is irreconcilable with true Christianity.[81] However, in his portrayal of moderate socialism he wrongly seems to characterize such socialism as sacrificing the higher goods of human beings to the most efficient way of producing external goods.[82] In the 1930's Pope Pius XI concentrated most of his attacks on communism, as seen in his later encyclical *Divini Redemptoris* of March 19, 1937.

In other parts of the Catholic world there was even a greater recognition of the changes in moderate socialism. The British hierarchy made it clear that the Labor Party in Britain was not condemned for Catholics.[83] In the United States John A. Ryan, while acknowledging the teaching and practical conclusion of Pius XI, pointed out there were only two questionable planks in the 1932 political platform of the Socialist Party and even these could be interpreted in conformity with Catholic principles.[84]

In the aftermath of the Second World War, the rise of communism led to the cold war in which the Roman Catholic Church stood squarely against communism. Roman Catholicism underwent persecution in communist countries in Eastern Europe. However, a thaw began with the pontificate of Pope John XXIII in 1959 under whose reign there emerged what was often called ''the opening to the left.'' In *Pacem In Terris,* without directly referring to communism, John pointed out the need to distinguish between false philosophical teachings on the nature, origin and destiny of human beings in the universe and the historical movements which were originally based on these teachings. The historical movements are subject to change and evolving historical circumstances. In addition these movements contain some elements that are positive and deserving of approval. Work in common might be possible to achieve economic, social, political and cultural ends. Great prudence however is required in these common enterprises. ''It can happen, then, that meetings for the attainment of some practical end, which formerly were deemed inopportune or unproductive, might now or in the future be considered opportune and useful."[85]

Pope Paul VI in *Octogesima Adveniens* built on, made explicit, and carried further the distinction between philosophical teaching and historical movements proposed by John XXIII. Both a liberal and a socialist ideology exist, but there are also historical movements. There are different kinds of expressions of socialism—a generous aspiration and seeking for a more just society; historical movements with a political organization and aim, and an ideology which claims to give a complete and self-sufficient picture of human beings. In Marxism there are also various levels of expression: 1) Marxism as the practice of class struggle; 2) the collective union of political and economic power under the direction of a single party; 3) a socialist ideology based on an historical materialism; 4) a rigorous scientific method of examining social and political realities. While recognizing all these different levels of expression, it would be illusory to forget the link which binds them together. The document then describes the liberal ideology with its erroneous affirmation of the autonomy of the individual.[86]

In the midst of these encounters with the various ideologies, the Christian must discern what is to be done. "Going beyond every system, without however failing to commit himself concretely to serving his brothers, he will assert, in the very midst of his options, the specific character of the Christian contribution for a positive transformation of society."[87] This presentation is remarkable in many ways. Both the liberal and Marxist ideology as complete and self-sufficient positions on human nature and destiny are rejected. However, with due prudence and discretion one could opt for a Marxist analysis of social reality provided that one recognizes the danger of its connection with Marxist ideology. As mentioned in the first part of this study the Church's teaching is not proposed as a third approach. There is no mention of the social doctrine of the Church but rather only the principles which help one to discern the concrete options that are to be taken. The option of a Marxist sociological tool is open to the Christian provided that one recognizes the danger and does not become imprisoned in an ideology. This marks the greatest openness in a papal statement to the Marxist position.

The development in the understanding of Marxism and socialism in the papal documents did not take place in an historical vacuum. In the 1960's discussions between Christians and Marxists began. Once Christian theology gave greater importance to eschatology and the relationship between the Kingdom of God and this world, there was ample room for dialogue with Marxists about improving the lot and condition of human beings in their earthly existence. Christian theologians also recognized that the Marxist's critique of religion as the opiate of the people called for a response. Political theology as a fundamental theology examining the context of revelation called for a deprivatization of theology and a greater emphasis on the political and social dimension of human existence and of theology. On the practical side especially in Latin America some Catholics struggling for social change found themselves working hand in hand with Marxists for particular social goals. The 1979 meeting of the Latin American Bishops Conference at Puebla has revealed some of the tensions connected with liberation theology and Marxism in South America. Groups of Christians for Socialism began forming in Latin America in the 1970's. But with the return of more repressive regimes these groups have often been scattered. However, in Europe there are small but apparently significant groups of Christians for Socialism.[88]

Meanwhile, changes also occured in Marxism. The differences between Russian and Chinese Marxism became evident, as did differences between Moscow and the Eastern European countries. In theory some Marxists called for a humanistic Marxism which gives more importance to the person and also recognizes the importance of the participation of the person in deciding one's future. Euro-Communism also flourished for a while but now seems to have become less important. In these contexts both in theory and in practice some Christians have been trying to discern how they could cooperate with Marxists and even share some of their approaches, especially in terms of a sociological analysis of the ills of society.[89] However, many Catholics still remain opposed to any socialist option.

This study has attempted to trace significant developments in the anthropology present in Catholic social ethics. Significant changes have occurred in the personal aspects of anthropology culminating in an emphasis on freedom, equality, participation and historical mindedness. At the same time the social aspects of anthropology have been stressed as illustrated in the changing attitudes towards private property and socialism. In a sense the perennial challenge of social ethics is to do justice to both the personal and the social aspects of anthropology. However, this challenge now exists in a new context. Christian social ethics building on the present developments must strive to respond to that demand of recognizing the social aspects of human existence and at the same time highlighting the freedom, equality, and participation of all within an historically conscious perspective.

Notes

1. For the best commentary available in English, see Jean-Yves Calvez and Jacques Perrin, *The Church and Social Justice: The Social Teaching of the Popes from Leo XIII to Pius XII, 1878–1958* (Chicago: Henry Regnery Co., 1961), also Jean-Yves Calvez, *The Social Thought of John XXIII* (Chicago: Henry Regnery Co., 1964).

2. John F. Cronin, "Forty Years Later: Reflections and Reminiscences," *American Ecclesiastical Review* 164 (1971), 310–318. For Cronin's major contribution in the field, see John F. Cronin, *Social Principles and Economic Life,* revised ed. (Milwaukee: Bruce Publishing Co., 1964).

3. The most significant contribution to an understanding of development in the papal teaching on religious liberty was made by John Courtney Murray. For a summary of his approach, see John Courtney Murray, *The Problem of Religious Freedom* (Westminster, Md.: Newman Press, 1965). This small volume originally appeared as a long article in *Theological Studies 25* (1964), 503–575.

4. For the best study of development in the papal teaching on economic questions before the Second Vatican Council, see Richard L. Camp, *The Papal Ideology of Social Reform: A Study in Historical Development, 1878–1967* (Leiden: E. J. Brill, 1969). For other helpful studies showing development in Catholic social ethics, see Marie Dominique Chenu, *La dottrina sociale della Chiesa: origine e sviluppo, 1891–1971* (Brescia: Editrice Queriniana, 1977); David Hollenbach, *Claims in Conflict: Retrieving and Renewing the Catholic Human Rights Tradition* (New York: Paulist Press, 1979).

5. One very significant aspect of anthropology which will not be discussed here concerns the relationship between anthropology and eschatology and Christology. Before the Second Vatican Council Catholic social teaching accepted a distinction and at times almost a dichotomy between the natural and the supernatural. Grace, gospel and the Kingdom of God had little or nothing to do with life in the world. Contemporary Catholic social ethics strives to overcome that dichotomy as illustrated in liberation theology. The emphasis now rests on

the one history in which God is offering freedom from sin and from all the other forms of oppression in the political, social and economic orders. In the light of this understanding one can readily see that the social mission of the Church is a constitutive dimension of the preaching of the gospel and of the Church's mission for the redemption of the human race as was pointed out in *Justice in the World* (n. 6), the document released by the Second General Assembly of the Synod of Bishops, November 30, 1971. For my discussion of this most significant development in Catholic social teaching, see my "Dialogue with Social Ethics: Roman Catholic Social Ethics—Past, Present and Future," in *Catholic Moral Theology in Dialogue*, paperback ed. (Notre Dame, Indiana: University of Notre Dame Press, 1976), pp. 111–149.

6. To facilitate a further study of the papal and Church documents, references will be given to readily available English translations. For the documents from the time of Pope John, see *The Gospel of Peace and Justice: Catholic Social Teaching Since Pope John*, ed. Joseph Gremillion (Maryknoll, New York: Orbis Books, 1976). References will include the page number in Gremillion as well as the paragraph numbers of the documents which generally are the official paragraph numbers found in the original and in all authorized translations. Thus the present reference is: *Octogesima Adveniens*, n. 22; Gremillion, p. 496. Another readily available compendium of Catholic Church teachings on social ethics is *Renewing the Face of the Earth: Catholic Documents on Peace, Justice and Liberation*, ed. David J. O'Brien and Thomas A. Shannon (Garden City, New York: Doubleday Image Books, 1977).

7. References to the encyclicals of Pope Leo XIII will be to *The Church Speaks to the Modern World: The Social Teachings of Leo XIII*, ed. Etienne Gilson (Garden City, New York: Doubleday Image Books, 1954). Thus the present reference is: *Libertas Praestantissimum*, n. 23; Gilson, p. 72.

8. *Libertas Praestantissimum*, nn. 19–37; Gilson, pp. 70–79. See also *Immortale Dei*, nn. 31–42; Gilson, pp. 174–180.

9. *Quod Apostolici Muneris*, especially nn. 5, 6; Gilson, pp. 192, 193.

10. *Humanum Genus*, n. 26; Gilson, p. 130.

11. *Rerum Novarum*, nn. 18, 19; Gilson, pp. 214, 215.

12. Murray, *The Problem of Religious Freedom*, pp. 55, 56.

13. *Libertas Praestantissimum*, n. 23; Gilson, p. 72.

14. *Immortale Dei*, n. 5; Gilson, p. 163.

15. *Immortale Dei*, n. 31; Gilson, pp. 174, 175.

16. Murray, *The Problem of Religious Freedom*, pp. 55–57.

17. *Libertas Praestantissimum*, n. 15; Gilson, pp. 66, 67.

18. For similar judgment on Leo's approach to liberty, see Fr. Refoulé, "L'Église et les libertés de Léon XIII à Jean XXIII," in *Le Supplément*, n. 125 (mai 1978), 243–259.

19. *Rerum Novarum*, n. 7, Gilson, pp. 208, 209.

20. *Rerum Novarum*, nn. 6–12; Gilson, pp. 208–211.

21. *Rerum Novarum*, n. 36; Gilson, pp. 224, 225.

22. *Rerum Novarum*, nn. 49–51; Gilson, pp. 231–233.

23. *Rerum Novarum*, n. 17; Gilson, pp. 213, 214.

24. *Rerum Novarum*, n. 37; Gilson, pp. 225, 226. Here I disagree with Camp who on page 32 seems to deny in Leo a basic equality of all before the law.

25. References to the encyclicals of Pope Pius XI will be to *The Church and the Reconstruction of the Modern World: The Social Encyclicals of Pope Pius XI*, ed. Terence P. McLaughlin (Garden City, New York: Doubleday Image Books, 1957). McLaughlin, "Introduction," pp. 6–15.

26. *Divini Redemptoris*, n. 10; McLaughlin, pp. 369, 370.

27. For a further explanation of this change in the light of opposition to totalitarianism especially from the left, see G. B. Guzzetti, "L'impegno politico dei cattolici nel magistero pontificio dell'ultimo secolo con particolare riguardo all'ultimo ventennio," *La Scuola Cattolica* 194 (1976), 192–210.

28. Radio message, December 24, 1944; *Acta Apostolicae Sedis* 37 (1945), 11–12; 22.

29. Murray, *The Problem of Religious Freedom*, pp. 59–65.

30. Guzzetti, *La Scuola Cattolica* 194 (1976), 202.

31. Radio message, December 24, 1944; *Acta Apostolicae Sedis* 37 (1945), 14.

32. *Pacem in Terris*, nn. 8–34; Gremillion, pp. 203–208. See David Hollenbach, *Claims in Conflict*, pp. 62–69.

33. *Mater et Magistra*, n. 212; Gremillion, p. 188.

34. *Pacem in Terris*, n. 35; Gremillion, p. 208.

35. *Mater et Magistra*, nn. 82–103; Gremillion, pp. 161–165.

36. *Dignitatis Humanae*, nn. 1, 2; Gremillion, pp. 337–339.

37. *Gaudium et Spes*, nn. 12–22; Gremillion, pp. 252–261.

38. *Gaudium et Spes*, n. 29; Gremillion, p. 266.

39. *Ibid.*

40. *Gaudium et Spes*, n. 31; Gremillion, p. 267.

41. *Gaudium et Spes*, n. 68; Gremillion, pp. 304, 305.

42. *Gaudium et Spes*, n. 75; Gremillion, pp. 310–312.

43. *Octogesima Adveniens*, n. 22, Gremillion, p. 496.

44. Bernard Lonergan, "A Transition from a Classicist World View to Historical Mindedness," in *Law for Liberty: The Role of Law in the Church Today*, ed. James E. Biechler (Baltimore: Helicon Press, 1967), pp. 126–133.

45. John Courtney Murray, "Vers une intelligence du développement de la doctrine de l'Église sur la liberté religieuse," in *Vatican II: La Liberté Reli-*

gieuse (Paris: Les Éditions du Cerf, 1967), pp. 11–147; Murray, "Religious Liberty and the Development of Doctrine," *The Catholic World* 204 (February 1967), 277–283.

46. *Pacem in Terris,* nn. 39–45; 75–79; 126–129; 142–145; Gremillion, pp. 209–210; 217–218; 227–228; 231–232.

47. Charles Moeller, "Preface and Introductory Statement," in *Commentary on the Documents of Vatican II, V: Pastoral Constitution on the Church in the Modern World,* ed. Herbert Vorgrimler (New York: Herder and Herder, 1969), p. 94.

48. *Quadragesimo Anno,* nn. 76–149; McLaughlin, pp. 246–274.

49. Camp, *The Papal Ideology of Social Reform,* pp. 128–135.

50. *Mater et Magistra,* n. 37; Gremillion, p. 150.

51. *Mater et Magistra,* nn. 46–60; Gremillion, pp. 152–156.

52. *Populorum Progressio,* n. 3; Gremillion, p. 388.

53. *Quadragesimo Anno,* nn. 17–22; McLaughlin, pp. 224, 225.

54. Paul Hanly Furfey, *Fire on the Earth* (New York: Macmillan, 1936), p. 8.

55. Calvez and Perrin, *The Church and Social Justice,* p. 3.

56. Bartolomeo Sorge, "E superato il concetto tradizionale di dottrina sociale della Chiesa?" *La Civiltà Cattolica* 119 (1968), I, 423–436. However, I disagree with the assignment of roles which Sorge gives to the hierarchical magisterium and the laity. See also Sorge, "L'apporto dottrinale della lettera apostolica 'Octogesima Adveniens,' " *La Civiltà Cattolica* 122 (1971), 417–428.

57. *Octogesima Adveniens,* n. 4; Gremillion, p. 487.

58. *Octogesima Adveniens,* n. 37; Gremillion, p. 502.

59. *Octogesima Adveniens,* nn. 48–52; Gremillion, pp. 509–511.

60. The understanding of eschatology mentioned in footnote 5, which tends to overcome the dichotomy between the supernatural and the natural and the Church and the world, also influences the position taken here. For a refutation of a distinction of planes approach in the social mission of the Church, see Gustavo Gutierrez, *A Theology of Liberation* (Maryknoll, New York: Orbis Press, 1973), pp. 53–58. For an approach which still tends to distinguish too much between the teaching role of the hierarchy and the executing role of the laity, see the articles of Sorge mentioned in footnote 56.

61. David Hollenbach, *Claims in Conflict.*

62. Gutierrez, *A Theology of Liberation;* Juan Luis Segundo, *The Liberation of Theology* (Maryknoll, New York: Orbis Books, 1976).

63. For an authoritative study, see Heinrich A. Rommen, *The State in Catholic Thought* (St. Louis: B. Herder, 1945).

64. Gilson, pp. 11–15.

65. *Rerum Novarum,* nn. 5–15; Gilson, pp. 207–213.

66. *Quod Apostolici Muneris,* n. 1; Gilson, p. 190.

67. Thomas Aquinas, *Summa Theologiae,* IIa IIae, q. 66, aa. 1 and 2.

68. For an interpretation which sees Leo in greater continuity with Aquinas, see Calvez and Perrin, *The Church and Social Justice,* pp. 259–268.

69. *Summa Theologiae,* Ia, q. 98, a. 1 ad 3.

70. Léon de Sousberghe, "Propriété, 'de droit naturel.' Thèse néoscholastique et tradition scholastique," *Nouvelle Revue Théologique* 72 (1950), 582–596. See also Camp, *The Papal Ideology of Social Reform,* pp. 55, 56.

71. John A. Ryan, *Distributive Justice* (New York: Macmillan, 1916), pp. 56–60; Reginald G. Bender, "The Doctrine of Private Property in the Writings of Monsignor John A. Ryan" (S.T.D. dissertation, The Catholic University of America, 1973).

72. *Quadragesimo Anno,* n. 45; McLaughlin, p. 234.

73. *Quadragesimo Anno,* n. 52; McLaughlin, p. 237.

74. *Mater et Magistra,* nn. 104–109; *Pacem in Terris,* n. 21; Gremillion, pp. 165, 166; 205.

75. Here and in the following paragraphs I am basically following the analysis of J. Diez-Alegria, "La lettura del magistero pontificio in materia sociale alla luce del suo sviluppo storico," in *Magistero et Morale: Atti del 3° congresso nazionale dei moralisti* (Bologna: Edizioni Dehoniane, 1970), pp. 211–256. For an analysis which disagrees with some of Diez-Algeria's conclusions especially his denial of the contemporary validity of an approach based on common use and private possession, but which agrees with the material proposed here, see Angelo Marchesi, "Il pensiero di S. Tommaso d'Aquino e delle encliclice sociali dei papa sul tema della proprietà privata in una recente analisi di P. Diez-Alegria," *Rivista di Filosofia Neo-Scholastica,* 62 (1970), 334–344.

76. *Gaudium et Spes,* n. 69; Gremillion, p. 305. For an in-depth analysis of the teaching of *Gaudium et Spes* on the distribution of the goods of creation, see E. Lio, *Morale e beni terreni; la destinazione universale dei beni terreni nella Gaudium et Spes* (Rome: Città Nuova, 1976).

77. *Populorum Progressio,* n. 22; Gremillion, p. 394.

78. *Quod Apostolici Muneris,* n. 1; Gilson, p. 189.

79. Camp, *The Papal Ideology of Social Reform,* pp. 56, 57.

80. *Quadragesimo Anno,* n. 117; McLaughlin, p. 260.

81. *Quadragesimo Anno,* n. 120; McLaughlin, p. 261.

82. *Quadragesimo Anno,* n. 119; McLaughlin, p. 260.

83. Peter Coman, "English Catholics and the Social Order," *Ampleforth Journal* 81 (1976), 47–57.

84. John A. Ryan, *A Better Economic Order* (New York: Harper and Brothers, 1935), pp. 133, 134.

85. *Pacem in Terris,* nn. 159, 160; Gremillion, pp. 235, 236.

86. *Octogesima Adveniens*, nn. 26–35; Gremillion, pp. 498–501.

87. *Octogesima Adveniens*, n. 36; Gremillion, p. 501.

88. Peter Hebblethwaite, *The Christian-Marxist Dialogue: Beginnings, Present Status and Beyond* (New York: Paulist Press, 1977).

89. For an attempt to show that Christianity is compatible with a humanistic socialist option, see Gregory Baum, *The Social Imperative* (New York: Paulist Press, 1979), especially pp. 184–202.

Laborem Exercens and
Social Morality

Richard A. McCormick, S.J.

This article originally appeared in *Theological Studies*, 1982.

May 15, 1981 was the 90th anniversary of the encyclical *Rerum novarum*. This same year was also the 50th anniversary of *Quadragesimo anno*, the 20th of *Mater et magistra*, and the 10th of *Octogesima adveniens*. Not surprisingly, these anniversaries were not overlooked. On Sept. 15 Pope John Paul II belatedly issued his long encyclical *Laborem exercens* to commemorate the occasion.[1]

This encyclical, clearly in substance the work of the pontiff himself,[2] is in my judgment an outstanding piece of work. The early journalistic reception given it was extremely interesting. A few samples will set the tone. The irrepressible Malachi Martin sees it as the "most amazing papal document since Alexander VI sat down in the early 1500's and . . . calmly disposed of one quarter of the globe."[3] Both the right and the left "recoiled" from the encyclical because "it contained stark rejections of both their positions." Martin feels that "with one stroke John Paul . . . has severed the economic chain that has shackled Christendom to capitalism." Francisco Forte, a professor of economics, and historian Valerio Castronovo view the encyclical as a bit old hat ("una sorta di rerum vecchiarum").[4]

Quite the contrary, argued sociologist Pier Luigi Zampetti. "The real novelty of the encyclical escaped for the most part both supporters and critics of *Laborem exercens*."[5] He sees this novelty in the papal concept of work which can "modify the structure of capitalism." Michael Novak sees here a "text more philosophical and more experiential than any in this ninety-year tradition."[6] It "radiates with new and unusual angles of light." Arthur Jones asserts that "it further thrusts Church teaching as a weapon into the hands of those struggling for economic justice here and globally."[7] Peter Hebblethwaite regards it "more like a position paper for discussion than an authoritative statement."[8] The Holy Father is attempting to "breathe some new life into Catholic social teaching."

Harley Shaiken (Massachusetts Institute of Technology) argues that in the United States the Pope "would be viewed as among the more radical leaders," because "the teachings that are being stressed in the encyclical would require a profound change to implement."[9] Michel Schooyans believes that the encyclical "is without doubt the most important document ever devoted to the social teaching of the Church by a sovereign pontiff."[9a] Bartolomeo Sorge, S.J., editor of *Civiltà cattolica,* proposes that the encyclical, distancing itself from both collectivism and capitalism, "is an invitation to elaborate together a new model for living together."[10] Flaminio Piccoli praises the document for its positive tone, "not lamentations and condemnations" but cogent proposals for social justice.[11] *Il Tempo* notes that while the reactions in Italy contain pros and cons, in Poland there was "broad and enthusiastic agreement."[12]

Bryan Hehir calls attention to the gradual development of Catholic social thought from national problems to international ones, and finally in *Laborem exercens* to transnational problems.[13] Nicholas von Hoffman underlines the difference in world view between John Paul II's encyclical and the economism of the Reagan administration, or, as he puts it, "between the Christian way and the American way, between social justice and the social models purveyed by Ron Reagan and Al Haig."[14] He says that "if the pope be inspired from on high, then it would appear that the late doggedly and dedicatedly liberal Hubert Humphrey sitteth at the right hand of the Creator with full permission to beam down the liberal agenda."

It will be some time, of course, before serious studies of the encyclical appear. But already the editors of *Civiltà cattolica* have some helpful remarks.[15] They note that *Laborem exercens* has a different methodology than *Populorum progressio* and *Octogesima adveniens.* John Paul II wanted to treat a single theme in depth,[16] whereas Paul VI's documents ranged over a whole host of social problems. Thus John Paul II underscores the point that "human work is a key, probably the essential key, to the whole social question." In approaching work, the Pope wants to provide an overall vision. Thus the positive tone of the encyclical.

The editors see as absolutely fundamental the principle that work is for man, not man for work. The encyclical is constructed on this foundation. Furthermore, the novelty of the Pope's approach is that he rigorously remains on the ethical-religious plane, and this provides him with "exceptional clarity and freedom of judgment." But it also means fewer of the concrete pastoral judgments found in *Mater et magistra* and *Octogesima adveniens*. Far from being a step backwards—as some commentators stated—this simply indicates John Paul II's different purpose and method. He wanted, the editors assert, to offer a "gospel of work" (the Pope's words), a kind of profound meditation. He leaves to us the choices to be made "to safeguard the personalistic character of work, to overcome the mentality of economism and materialism, to change unjust economic structures."

Laborem exercens deserves careful reading and discussion. Rather than detailing and commenting further on its substantial content, I want to offer three remarks stimulated by this encyclical's style and content. First, the encyclical seems to represent a different type of teaching, one describable perhaps in terms of enlightenment and understanding rather than prescriptions and prohibitions. It is as if John Paul II is inviting us to share an ongoing philosophical meditation with him. This has not always been the style of so-called "authoritative teaching," and especially so in the areas of what might be called domestic morality. In this latter area, concrete prescriptions and proscriptions have played a central role.[17]

Second, the enlightenment occurs by identifying, analyzing, and constantly returning to certain basic and general notions. In the case of *Laborem exercens* there are two key notions. (1) Work is for the person (unfortunately, the rendering is constantly "man" in the English version), not the person for work. Hence the evil dimension of any system that reduces the person to a mere instrument. Work should bring about growth and a sense of accomplishment in the human person. It is, therefore, not primarily what is done but the person doing it (work in the subjective sense) that is primary. (2) The priority of labor over capital. Capital is for labor, not vice versa. Thus the error of an economism that considers labor only according to its economic purpose. Both capitalism and socialism are critiqued by these principles. John Paul II returns over and over again to these two principles, examines them from several points of view, and traces everything he subsequently says to these bases. This means that he provides an element of unity and simplicity in what could otherwise collapse into a confusion of details and of unrelated particulars.[18]

Finally, such a procedure leaves room for specification by other disciplines and for disagreement about applications and tactics. The Pope is providing a prophetic vision, a way of construing the world theologically, rather than providing a series of concrete answers. The *National Catholic Reporter* referred to it as "philosophy and ground rules from which Catholics and others can begin forays in search for new answers."[19] That strikes me as an excellent direction for the magisterium to take, and for several reasons. For one, it is much more likely to persuade, and it is precisely persuasive analysis that commands assent in moral matters.[20] For another, it properly recognizes the competence and responsibility of others in the development and implementation of the Church's social teaching. Responsibility is to be underlined here. There is a gap between formulated social teaching and its practical implementation. That gap reflects the socially dormant conscience, and this notwithstanding Vatican II's statement: "Let everyone consider it his sacred obligation to count social necessities among the primary duties of modern man."[21]

If there are aspects of this encyclical that may provoke critical comment, I suspect that they may organize around four points. First, the treatment of management in *Laborem exercens* seems inconsistent, because in the papal categories it is a form of labor, yet a part of capital. Management and its dynamics and philosophy have a powerful, even dominating influence in contemporary times on work and workers.

Second, the political dimension of organized labor may be viewed by some as treated too uniquely with a view to the Polish situation. The Pope sees political activity as creating the danger that unions will "lose contact with their specific role, which is to secure the just rights of workers." In many Western democracies union political activity is precisely the means of securing these rights.

Third, there appears to be some ambiguity about the role of women. Should they aspire to some role other than wife and mother? It is clear in the encyclical that they should receive equal pay, should not be discriminated against, etc. But is their very presence in the labor force a reluctant concession on the part of John Paul II?

Finally, there is the very composition of the encyclical. It seems clear that *Laborem exercens* is substantially the work of the Pope himself. But is that really appropriate? Philip Land, S.J., at a conference on the encyclical, suggested that ''the day of a pope writing encyclicals by himself ought to be over. People in this room ought to be helping writing encyclicals.''[22] At the same conference George Higgins, surely one of the nation's most expert persons in this area, stated that ''there ought to be a more collegial way of writing these documents.''

The Land-Higgins statements—which in no way derogate from the timeliness and power of *Laborem exercens*—bring to mind a very remarkable article that many have missed. Though it appeared in 1971, it is still highly pertinent. It is Oswald von Nell-Breuning's account of his authorship of *Quadragesimo anno*.[23] Wlodimir Ledochowski, then the General of the Society of Jesus, was entrusted with the preparation of this commemorative encyclical. He in turn assigned the task to Nell-Breuning. ''In strict secrecy. . . . Neither my local superior nor my provincial knew what work I had to do for the General.'' Nell-Breuning could consult no one and ''was left wholly on my own.'' At the end of this absorbing article Nell-Breuning remarks: ''When I think back on it today, it seems to me that such a procedure, that allowed the whole bearing of an official document to be determined by a consultant . . . without any countercheck worth mentioning, seems frighteningly irresponsible.'' He finds it distressing that ''even today [1971], apparently, if the occasion arose, they would proceed in a manner similar to that for *Quadragesimo anno*.'' His final paragraph reads:

> Today people expect that announcements of the highest Church authorities—on questions in which the profane sciences also have a voice—be on just as high a level as that of scientific statements of the most qualified international bodies. This presumes that an international group of recognized specialists in the sciences participate in the elaboration and assume the technical scientific responsibility for such new statements.

Nell-Breuning's words point to the continuing interesting literature on the magisterium.[24] Just a single article will be noted here in passing.[25] Since everyone has a dream these days (e.g., Cardinal Hume at the Synod of 1980), Karl Rahner presents his. He is present at a meeting in 1985 where the pope is addressing leading representatives of the Christian churches from all over the world. The pope is attempting to put papal teaching authority in a more understandable context to still non-Catholic fears and misgivings. Rahner's pope has several interesting observations. One is that since the pope is, in his ex-cathedra decisions, defining the faith of the Church, "the pope must necessarily have recourse to the sense of the faith of the whole Church." An explicit recourse to the episcopate is "absolutely morally necessary," and a "moral obligation." An analogous "moral obligation" would seem to be the case in the situation of practical moral matters.

But what is of more interest is the statement of Rahner's pope on noninfallible teaching. He states: "Even the second Vatican Council did not speak clearly enough about such authentic but reformable Roman doctrinal decisions." The pope then adds: "Roman procedure after the council left something to be desired by way of straightforward clarity and modesty."

It is a well-known fact that Rahner refuses to believe that no. 25 of *Lumen gentium* is the last word on authentic noninfallible papal pronouncements. The matter is mentioned here for the record, so to speak. There are still theologians whose theology has no room for dissent. This overlooks the fact observed by Rahner's pope: "The ordinary magisterium of the pope in authentic doctrinal decisions at least in the past and up to very recent times was often involved in error and, on the other hand, Rome was accustomed to put forward and insist on such decisions as if there could be no doubt about their ultimate correctness and as if any further discussion of them was unbecoming for a Catholic theologian."

In the course of *Laborem exercens* John Paul II makes note of "a principle that has always been taught by the Church" (scil., the priority of labor over capital; no. 12). He also states that his reflections are "in organic connection with the whole tradition" of early social teaching. When one hears the phrase "the social teaching of the Church," the impression left is one of a coherent body of unified teaching. In an extremely interesting study, John Coleman, S.J., shows convincingly that this is not the case.[26] For instance, Leo XIII viewed private property as "an almost metaphysical right." This is in sharp contrast with *Mater et magistra* and *Populorum progressio,* where such a right is not absolute, and to John Paul II's noted phrase about "a social mortgage" on all property.

Similarly, subsequent tradition would not follow Pius XI when he asserted (*Quadragesimo anno*) that "no one can be at the same time a sincere Catholic and a true socialist." Indeed, more to the point there is Pius X's distorted interpretation of *Rerum novarum,* in which he asserted that the authority of capital over labor is as essential to the social organism as the authority of the Church, government, or family. John Paul II would certainly frown over that tenet. Then there is the heavy philosophical emphasis prior to Vatican II, but after that council "explicitly theological thought strongly informs the papal teaching." Coleman sees this as "a massive sea change," his only point being that history will not bear out the contention that in social teaching there is an unbroken coherent unity untouched by the waves of time.

To discover these waves of time or the historical context of encyclicals, we must attend to a whole variety of factors: the mind of the principal author (e.g., Nell-Breuning for *Quadragesimo anno*), the movements and disputed questions to which the pope was responding, the other writings of the papacy, etc.

Coleman's article deserves careful thought. Undoubtedly there will be some who will see in such historical exegesis a systematic undermining of the authority of papal statements. After all, the argument would run, what does it matter that Nell-Breuning wrote *Quadragesimo anno*? The pope "made it his own." *That* is what counts. I have heard this response many times before. An answer might be: "Of course it counts. But for what?" Certainly it does not purge the document of its limited perspectives and human ingredients. If one thinks so, then that person is attributing in a quite magical way a more unearthly, unhistorical character and authority to papal composition than we do to the composition of the Gospels. The recognition of limited, imperfect, even inconsistent elements in these magisterial documents should detract no more from their abiding value than do similar elements from the inspired word.

In a long and thorough article Charles Curran amply documents the thesis of Coleman.[27] He shows that from Leo XIII to the present there have been important anthropological shifts, both personal and social, that ground Catholic social ethics. At the personal level, these changes have culminated in our contemporary emphasis on freedom, equality, participation, and historical consciousness. The methodological consequences of this are considerable. For instance, Curran sees in the early documents the formation of a social doctrine drawn out of a deductive reasoning process based on the immutable natural law applicable to all nations. Over the decades the approach has shifted to an "objective scrutiny of the present reality in the light of the gospel and of the teaching of the Church," a much more dynamic discernment process.

As examples of the social aspects of a shifting anthropology, Curran adduces private property and socialism. From the rather hardened attitude of Leo XIII, a certain relativizing characterizes magisterial statements on both these aspects. For instance, the right of private property is now seen as subordinate to the universal destiny of the goods of creation. Similarly now "with due prudence and discretion one could opt for a Marxist analysis of social reality provided that one recognizes the danger of its connection with Marxist ideology." Why? Because *Octogesima adveniens* acknowledges that there are various levels of expression in Marxism, even though it would be illusory to forget the link that binds them together.[28]

Curran's study is a fine synthetic overview of an important and still developing papal literature.

Before the publication of *Laborem exercens,* the editors of *Civiltà cattolica* published a study that makes many of the points noted by Curran and Coleman.[29] They note that in a sense *Rerum novarum* is a document that has to be "written on an ongoing basis" ("deve continuare ad essere scritta"). It is a kind of dynamic presence in all the social encyclicals that followed it. This dynamic presence and the real novelty of *Rerum novarum* is found not in its conclusions, many of which are dated, but in the fact that for the first time the Church's social concerns were given a systematic philosophical and theological justification. Thus its continuing relevance consists in the method in which it approached social problems.

However, that encyclical must be continually reworked, because the social teaching of the Church developed in stages. *Rerum novarum* represents the first stage. It was dominated by "Christian philosophy" and a "rigidly deductive" method, as Curran noted above. This had two shortcomings. First, it left no room for the relevance of the sciences (political science, sociology, economics). Second, and a consequence, doctrinal elaboration was seen as an exclusively hierarchical task, lay persons being merely "faithful executors."

The second stage covers the pontificates of Pius XI and Pius XII and might be called the stage of "social doctrine." Indeed, *Quadragesimo anno* used this term for the first time. It referred to an organic corpus of universal principles still rigidly deduced from social ethics and constituted a kind of third way between liberalism and socialism. However, there is greater emphasis on the historical moment and applications of principles to practice, hence the beginnings of a re-evaluation of the place of lay persons in the process. Pius XI distinguished "unchanged and unchangeable doctrine" from social action, this latter being the competence of lay persons.

The third stage began with John XXIII. John moved from the deductive to the inductive method, his point of departure being the "historical moment," to be viewed in light of the gospel. This led to a complete reevaluation of the place of lay persons vis-à-vis social teaching, a re-evaluation completed by Vatican II. Lay persons do not simply apply the Church's social teaching; they must share in its very construction.

The novelty of this third stage is clear in the fact that the social teaching of the Church no longer refers to an immutable corpus of doctrine. Even the term "social doctrine" has fallen into disuse and is reserved for the period from Leo XIII to John XXIII. It is also clear in the new emphasis on the responsibility of the Christian community in the elaboration and application of the Church's social teaching, an emphasis most completely stated at Puebla (no. 473).

This extremely interesting and very realistic analytic chronicle suggests a question: Has such a development occurred in the area of the Church's approach to familial and sexual morality? The answer is rather clearly no. Perhaps the question were better worded as follows: Should not such a development occur in the approach to these other questions? If a clearly deductive method, one that left little room to the sciences and lay experience, prevailed in the elaboration of social teaching, it is reasonable to think that the same thing occurred in familial and sexual morality. And if this method has evolved and changed during the pontificates of John XXIII, Paul VI, and John Paul II, as the editors of *Civiltà cattolica* correctly note, it is reasonable to think that the same thing ought to happen in all areas of Church teaching. Yet two things seem clear about the Church's teaching on sexual and familial morality. First, earlier popes are invariably cited for their conclusions, not simply their systematic method. Second, the sciences and lay experience remain marginal factors in the continuing reflection of the Church on familial and sexual matters, as noted above.

Adverting to some of the changes mentioned by Curran and Coleman, Oswald von Nell-Breuning, S.J., asks if the Church's social teaching has not lost its identity.[30] Not surprisingly, his answer is a firm no. But one must distinguish between the changeless principles and their concrete application. These latter are conditioned by historical times and changes, and the perspectives of those living in such times. This happens even in our times. Thus, even Vatican II views the "Church in the Modern World" within a pronounced European-American (developed) perspective. For our social teaching to be freed from this narrowing of perspectives, we need the voice of the Third World bishops.

Nell-Breuning reviews the social teaching of the Church to highlight the distinction between abiding principles and time-conditioned and no longer valid applications. For instance, he cites two encyclicals of Leo XIII (*Diuturum* [1881] and *Immortale* [1885]). Leo correctly recognized the basically different duties of church and state—and this assertion is timeless and unchanging. Here he breaks with the Middle Ages. However, he remained within the confines of *his* time and context. Leo grew up in a Catholic country and was familiar only with Catholic countries. Therefore for him the state is the political unity of a people united in the Catholic faith. Out of these perspectives he developed much of his teaching on the relation of church and state. But because these perspectives are time-conditioned, the normative conclusions he draws from them do not pertain to changeless principles. When this distinction is properly made and carefully applied, we will see that the Church's social teaching is a system of "open statements," what Nell-Breuning calls a "constant learning process."

He concludes the essay by insisting that most magisterial statements are not the best formulations of the matter, and that that which does get expressed is not an exhaustive account of objective reality, but merely a piece of it. Nell-Breuning's essay further confirms Wright's distinction between faithfulness to the magisterium and magisterial fundamentalism.

The distinction between abiding principles and time-conditioned application is also at work implicitly in Andrew Greeley's essay.[31] Greeley argues that Catholics have forgotten the fundamental social theory of *Quadragesimo anno* and "replaced it with a slightly baptized form of vulgar Marxism." The dominant social wisdom is concerned about the conflict between self and society. The individual strives for freedom; society strives to constrain this. Greeley sees this as a false picture of the relationship. There is an informal, intimate network of relationships that integrate self and society.

The common themes suggested by *Quadragesimo anno* are solidarity, decentralization, smallness, co-operation, respect for pre-existing networks of workers, families, and neighbors. This is the unique and still radical critique mounted by *Quadragesimo anno* in the face of both capitalism and Marxism. But Greeley despairs of its having any effects because "no one is even remotely aware" anymore of this Catholic heritage. Greeley seems to be suggesting that *Quadragesimo anno* is a relic because we never really did grasp its abiding substance.

An excellent article by David Hollenbach, S.J., represents a kind of contemporary footnote to *Laborem exercens*.[32] It points out that human rights are the central norms of social morality proposed by the Church. These rights, based on the dignity of the human person, concern essential *needs*, basic *freedoms*, and *relationships* with others. These needs, freedoms, and relationships are equally and integrally normative in the Church's approach.

However, the papal supposition that these values should be simultaneous and equally important is rejected by both the right and the left. Both Marxist socialists and authoritarian capitalists endorse a restriction of freedom for the alleviation of poverty. Both ideologies regard the Catholic "third way" approach (clearly that of John Paul II in *Laborem exercens*) as naive and moralistic in its failure to recognize genuine conflicts and the need for hard and nasty choices.

In his response to this criticism, Hollenbach distinguishes three distinct but related levels of analysis. (1) The foundational level (based on the dignity of the human person an an *imago Dei*). There is little disagreement at this level. (2) The level of social contexts most conducive to the realization of these fundamental values. (3) The level of analysis that proposes explanations of what causes the realization or destruction of these values. The sharpest and most heated disagreements occur at the second and third level.

For instance, one reading of the context and cause for the denial of human dignity sees imperialist capitalist governments and multinational corporations as the key driving force. Another reading would emphasize the deprivation of human rights as the context and cause. These models of interpretation can gradually get identified with the fundamental value of human dignity itself. When they do, they become ideologies that easily spawn blinding and misdirected passion.

Hollenbach argues that the Church is particularly, and rightly, sensitive to the dangers of identifying a model of social context and causality with the basic value of human dignity itself. She has a long memory about the injustices associated with both authoritarian regimes and liberal capitalism. Furthermore, living as she does in a variety of cultures and economic regimes, the Church is properly sensitive to their differences. Finally, her mission is particularly concerned with the fundamental values. These three considerations keep her alert to the dangers of competing ideologies and lead her to emphasize "the provision of *both* bread *and* freedom" as the appropriate goals of political economy.

As I read John Paul II's *Laborem exercens,* it is discussing above all Hollenbach's foundational level and from that level providing food for thought for the levels of context and causality. It constitutes a critique of any absolutizing at this second and third level.

Notes

1. John Paul II, "On Human Work," *Origins* 11 (1981) 225–44.

2. This becomes clear when we read Card. Casaroli, "La célébration de l'anniversaire de 'Rerum novarum,' " *Documentation catholique* 78 (1981) 626–30.

3. *The Prince George's Journal,* Oct. 9, 1981.

4. *L'Espresso,* Sept. 25, 1981.

5. *Gente,* Oct. 2, 1981.

6. *National Review,* Oct. 16, 1981, 1210.

7. *National Catholic Reporter,* Sept. 25, 1981.

8. Ibid.

9. Ibid.

9a. *La libre belgique,* Sept. 23, 1981.

10. *Oggi,* Sept. 30, 1981.

11. *Il popolo,* Sept. 16, 1981.

12. *Il tempo,* Sept. 17, 1981.

13. Bryan Hehir, "A New Era of Social Teaching," *Commonweal* 108 (1981) 585.

14. *New Republic,* no. 3486, Nov. 4, 1981.

15. "Scoprire i nuove significati del lavoro umano: L'enciclica sociale di Giovanni Paolo II," *Civiltà cattolica* 132, no. 3151 (1981) 3–14.

16. This is also noted by Oswald von Nell-Breuning, "Menschliche Arbeit," *Orientierung* 45 (1981) 195. Nell-Breuning calls attention to the fact that Leo XIII and subsequent popes, never having been workers, spoke of the subject "from above." John Paul II was a worker and could speak to the subject from his own experience.

17. Cf. Kenneth R. Overberg, *An Inconsistent Ethic? Teachings of the American Catholic Bishops* (Lanham, Md.: University Press of America, 1980).

18. There is an interesting detail in the encyclical that is suggestive. When speaking of emigration (no. 23) John Paul II refers to it as "in some aspects an evil." But it is, as he writes, "a necessary evil." He continues: "Everything should be done . . . to prevent this *material* [emphasis mine] evil from causing greater moral harm." This reflects the distinction between moral and nonmoral evil. That John Paul II is utterly familiar with this language is clear from Andrzej Szostek's *Normy i Wyjatki* (Lublin: Katolicki Universytet Lubelski, 1980), for which dissertation the then Cardinal Wojtyla was a reader.

19. *National Catholic Reporter,* Sept. 25, 1981, 10.

20. As James Burtchaell, C.S.C., notes of a bishop who encounters things that grieve him in the Catholic press: "Better to exercise what authority one does have by becoming a more persuasive (and hence more authoritative) shepherd by becoming a more cogent teacher" ("The Catholic Press and Church Authority," *Origins* 11 [1981] 304–8, at 305). In this respect I recommend highly a little gem of an essay by Quentin de la Bedoyere ("Christian Disobedience," *Tablet* 235 [1981] 518–19). He notes: "What is required at the spiritual level . . . is for the Church consciously to become the leader in the development of moral autonomy. . . . To her surprise she will, I believe, discover that her influence will become greater rather than less, and this influence will be effective not only among her own members but in a society which is looking for moral leadership." He asserts that the way the Church has exercised her authority in the past (and the way it still does exercise it) has "produced Catholics who have

either been conformists or have broken away dramatically from the moral order.''

21. *Gaudium et spes*, no. 30.

22. *Washington Post*, Oct. 24, 1981, C10.

23. Oswald von Nell-Breuning, S.J., ''Quadragesimo anno,'' *Stimmen der Zeit* 187 (1971) 289–96.

24. B.C. Butler, ''Ordinary Teaching,'' *Clergy Review* 66 (1981) 3–8; Pierre Grelot, ''L'Eglise et l'enseignement de la morale,'' *Esprit et vie* 91 (1981) 465–76, 481–89; Karl Lehmann, ''Lehramt und Theologie,'' *Internationale katholische Zeitschrift* 10 (1981) 331–38; Joseph A. Komonchak, ''Research and the Church: A Theologian's View,'' *Living Light* 18 (1981) 112–20; M. Seckler, ''Eine Wende im lehramtlichen Theologie-Verständnis?'' *Theologische Quartalschrift* 161 (1981) 131–33; Ludiger Oeing-Hanhoff, ''Ist das kirchliche Lehramt für den Bereich des Sittlichen zuständig?'' *Theologische Quartalschrift* 161 (1981) 56–66.

25. Karl Rahner, ''Dream of the Church,'' *Tablet* 180 (1981) 52–55. Cf. also *Concern for the Church* (New York: Crossroad, 1981) 133–42.

26. John Coleman, S.J., ''Development of Church Social Teaching,'' *Origins* 11 (1981) 33–41. For a comparison of the social teaching of Leo XIII and John Paul II, cf. Ph.-I. André-Vincent, ''Pour le centenaire de 'Rerum novarum,' '' *Esprit et vie* 91 (1981) 509–11.

27. Charles E. Curran, ''The Changing Anthropological Bases of Catholic Social Teaching,'' *Thomist* 45 (1981) 284–318.

28. For critiques of Marxist analysis, cf. Pedro Arrupe, S.J., ''Marxist Analysis by Christians,'' *Catholic Mind* 74, no. 1355 (1981) 58–64; Quentin Lauer, S.J., ''Christians and 'Marxist Analysis,' '' *Ateismo e dialogo* 16 (1981) 43–47.

29. ''Dalla 'Rerum novarum' ad oggi,'' *Civiltà cattolica* 132 (1981) 345–57.

30. Oswald von Nell-Breuning, S.J., ''Hat die katholische Soziallehre ihre Identität verloren?'' *Internationale katholische Zeitschrift* 10 (1981) 107–21.

31. Andrew Greeley, ''Quadragesimo anno after Fifty Years,'' *America* 145 (1981) 46–49.

32. David Hollenbach, S.J., ''Both Bread and Freedom: The Interconnection of Economic and Political Rights in Recent Catholic Social Thought,'' forthcoming in the bimonthly *Freedom at Issue* (Freedom House).

John Paul II's Encyclical on Labor

Gregory Baum

This article originally appeared in *The Ecumenist*, 1981.

In his new encyclical *Laborem exercens,* John Paul II, the Pope from Poland, argues that the key for the understanding and the overcoming of the present world crisis is human labor. It is the economic system everywhere that is the principal cause of the oppressions, the tensions, the conflicts, the poverty and the misery of the world. In the West the Pope recognizes that despite the many reforms of capitalism and despite a period of extraordinary prosperity, the system has become ruled by giant corporations, many of them transnational, that organize the world in accordance with their own economic interests. Ever wider sectors of the population are being excluded from access to the wealth produced. In the East, the governments in control of the means of production constitute highly centralized, all-powerful organizations that manage production and distribution in accordance with their political purposes and hence neglect the care of their own people. John Paul II agrees with his predecessors that an economic crisis is both a structural and a moral failure. Is it possible to find an analysis of the present situation that applies equally to the West and to the East? Is it possible to recommend principles of thought and action that fit both situations? The Pope thinks so. He offers to the Church his own, original reflections. His teaching raises Catholic social doctrine to a new height: it remains in continuity with the traditional doctrine but rereads it in the light of new and original insights.

The Pope believes that the key to the social question is always "labor". Human labor is the key for understanding man's historical vocation and man's social projects. Through labor people create their world, their social world, and in doing so they in some sense create themselves. The reader recognizes that the Pope's position is the result of an extended, critical and creative dialogue with Marxism. The Pope establishes the principle of "the priority of labor over capital" which, when observed, steers society toward justice and peace. The violation of this principle leads to injustice and economic crisis.

THE PRIORITY OF LABOR

In this discussion of *Laborem exercens* I will confine myself to the explanation of this principle, even though the encyclical has many other things to say in regard to social justice.

By labor the encyclical refers to all human activity that builds society: this includes industrial labor but also the work of farmers, clerical employees, teachers, social workers, scientists, managers, those who exercise responsibility in government and homemakers who look after the well-being of the family. Work makes humans different from animals. Work enables people to create their world, and in making this world they themselves are being transformed. Through work they may suffer damage or become more authentically human. Human work is the primary factor in the creation of history. This is obviously a Marxist perspective, yet John Paul II goes beyond Marx by widening the notion of labor beyond economic production and by showing that working together people are in need of symbols that unite and direct them and of a spirituality that harnesses their interiority for the great task.

The encyclical distinguishes between the objective and the subjective dimension of work. The *objective* dimension refers to the objects produced by work, i.e., the portion of nature or the world transformed by human labor—and this signifies anything from material goods to the social reality itself. The *subjective* dimension of labor refers to man's personal involvement in work. Work is an essential form of human self-expression, work actualizes human beings, work transforms them. While it often damages their subjectivity, it is meant to unfold their powers and possibilities. The encyclical argues that the subjective dimension of work has priority over the objective one. While the products of labor, including the organization of society, are important, what is even more important is personal engagement, personal transformation, the actualization of the working persons. The dignity and worth of workers are not derived from the object they produce, but from their subjectivity, from their engagement and self-actualization. This is a thoroughly egalitarian principle in keeping with ancient Christian wisdom. This priority of the subjective is not derived from Marxism; it is biblical and humanist. It is not at odds with Marx's thought, for he saw himself as an heir of the humanist tradition, yet he paid little attention to subjectivity.

This priority of the subjective has many important social consequences. The Pope insists that man always remains the subject of work. However complex and sophisticated the technological tools, they can never be the subject of work. Man alone is the responsible author and cause. The industrial machinery itself is the result of human labor. When technological tools are assembled to produce new products, it is again people who do the assembling. And when machines mass produce and when computers provide new information, it is people who control them, supervise them, repair them, utilize them for their purposes. Even the massive, ultra-modern means of production—John Paul II often refers to them as the giant "workbench" at which people labor—remain simply the instrumental cause; man alone is the efficient cause. As subject man retains the priority in the work process.

The encyclical applies this reasoning to gain a better understanding of capital. Capital refers to the productive tools or industrial machinery and to the resources used in production. Capital, the Pope argues, is simply the accumulation of labor. For the industrial machinery has been made by workers—it is their work—and even the natural resources, while being a portion of nature and hence ultimately a gift of the Creator, are made available to production through the human labor of the extractive industries. Capital is not an independent reality, with an essence of its own, which could be contrasted or even opposed to labor. Capital itself is labor and the result of labor. In this the Pope follows Marx's thought, almost his very words. For Marx, capital was "congealed labor". Where the Pope differs from Marx here is simply in his wider understanding of human labor, including, for instance, the managerial skills. Because capital is essentially labor it must serve labor. The separation between capital and labor, in fact the opposition between capital and labor, which we find in the liberal economists of the eighteenth century, was a terrible theoretical mistake grounded in the wicked practice of the early industrialists who exluded laborers from participating in the fruits of their work and organized their capital in opposition to labor.

What does the Pope mean by the expression that "capital must

serve labor"? First, capital must serve the people laboring in the particular industry, it must serve their joint endeavor, and finally because of
the interconnectedness of all work in modern society, capital must serve
the whole of the working society. This is what the Pope means by the
priority of labor over capital. Whenever this order is violated, whenever
capital is no longer made to serve labor, the economic system will generate injustices, exclude certain sections of the population from the
wealth produced by them, create hardships among the great majority and
thus destabilize society, preparing its own downfall. The priority of labor
over capital is used by the Pope to offer a critical analysis of Western
capitalism and Eastern collectivism.

The Pope defends, as the Church has always done, the right to the
private ownership of means of production. At the same time, this right
must be qualified. While ownership may indeed be in the hands of individuals, its use must be social; capital must serve the common good.
To this traditional formulation of Catholic teaching, the Pope now adds
that private ownership of capital can only be justified if its use serves
labor. The free market system unrestricted by government legislation
and political counterweights—the Pope speaks here of "rigid capitalism"—is at odds with the right order of things, because it inverts the
essential priority of labor over capital. The Pope recognizes that in most
Western countries, the free market system has been modified. Governments, thanks to the pressure of organized labor and other social forces,
involve themselves in varying degrees in industrial and agricultural policies, promote certain industries, and discourage others, and claim that
they want to steer the free enterprise system, possibly with the help of
publicly owned companies, to serve the common good, that is to say,
the laboring society. Still, capital continues to dominate labor, more especially through the transnationals. The Pope argues convincingly that
the nationalization of industries by itself does not necessarily protect the
priority of labor over capital. For the men in authority, i.e., the government offices which plan and manage the national industries, may indeed
exercise their task to make capital serve labor, but they may also plan
and manage the economy to serve their own political purposes. This in
fact is the situation in the socialist countries of the East.

In the perspective of the encyclical, the ownership question is not
the crucial one. What counts is whether or not capital can be made to
serve labor. It is significant that the Pope usually refers to the economic

system of the Eastern European countries as "collectivism". He does not want to concede to them that they are truly socialist. He argues that whenever the priority of labor over capital is reversed, then the system, under whatever name it may present itself, must actually be called "capitalist". The allusion is here quite clear. Because of the subjugation of workers in the Soviet bloc countries, their economic system based on the public ownership of the means of production is in fact a form of state capitalism.

It is easy to see that the encyclical will play an important role in Poland where its teaching supports the workers of Solidarity, wrestling with government and communist party, in the name of socialism correctly understood. The encyclical also confirms the social program of the Nicaraguan revolution, which preserves a mixed economy, including private and public ownership; the revolutionary government, including its Catholic members, believe that they will be able to steer the use of capital to serve the people as a whole and hence to serve labor. In the Western capitalist countries the encyclical has on the whole been greeted with silence. However, Catholics who have followed the recent shift to the left in Church teaching and have therefore acquired socialist sympathies are delighted with the encyclical and understand it as a confirmation of the direction in which they have moved.

SOCIAL STRATEGY

Pope John Paul II argues that the reason for the crisis of unemployment, inflation, insecurity and growing poverty is the violation of the priority of labor over capital, both in the Western and Eastern societies. How can these violations be overcome? The Pope proposes changes in the economic system on two levels. First and foremost he demands that in an ever increasing measure workers participate in the policy-making of their industries. Governments by themselves cannot assure for long the priority of labor over capital. Those who labor must involve themselves in the upholding and defense of this principle. If the decision-making powers regarding industry and agriculture are concentrated in the hands of the government, then the wealth of society may, for a while, be made to serve the workers and their ongoing work, but the enormous power thus placed into the government's hands, unchecked by institutional counterweights, inevitably prepares the great abuse, the domination of workers, the violation of labor's priority over capital. The Pope argues for economic pluralism. He reasons that people want to work for themselves and for others; they want to take part in the work process as sharers in responsibility and as those who enjoy the fruit of their work. Workers must in some way become co-owners of the "workbench" at which they labor. In this connection the Pope praises the various attempts in Eastern and Western societies of introducing some form of workers' co-determination, such as joint ownership, the shareholding of labor, and participation in policy-making. The workers themselves must become the guardians of the priority of labor over capital.

Second, however, the principle of decentralization just mentioned must be accompanied by a principle of centralization. Because of the interconnectedness of the industries in one country and in fact in the entire world, it has become increasingly necessary to have a plan, a rational plan, for the production of goods, for the use of resources, for the appropriate training of workers, and for the availability of employment. The Pope's views are here directly opposed to those of President Reagan. To make convincing the idea of the planned economy, especially in regard to employment, the encyclical introduces a distinction between the "direct" and "indirect" employer of labor. The direct employer is the person or group of persons who actually hire workers and make a contract with them. The indirect employer refers to the various historical factors that enter into the making of the contract between workers and direct employers. The indirect employer thus includes labor legislation, conditions of production, availability of markets, training provided in schools, and so forth, all factors ultimately linked to society as a whole and in particular to the government. It is an illusion to think that the problem of unemployment can be solved through the initiative of enterprising industrialists ready to hire laborers; the whole of society, as indirect employer, must become involved. To overcome the present crisis of unemployment, profound structural changes are required. Government agencies, possibly aided by international agreements, mediated by bureaus of the United Nations, will have to engage in long-range planning for full employment. God has given us enough resources, the Pope holds; the shortages and the scarcity we experience at present are due to our own inadequate stewardship.

The decentralizing trend of the worker-run industries must be balanced by the planning activity of the government. The cooperation and the tension between these two guarantee an interplay of forces and protect society from the bureaucratic centralism characteristic of Eastern European collectivist economies. Yugoslavia has an economic system which, however imperfect it may still be, does correspond to the prescriptions of *Laborem exercens*. The social-democratic parties of Western Europe, the euro-communist party of Italy, and the New Democratic Party of Canada still emphasize the socialist idea of central planning without paying much attention to the socialist principle of co-ownership and co-determination. What the Pope presents as the solution to the present crisis comes very close to an approach called self-governing socialism promoted by groups in Western and Eastern society.

We note that the Pope follows the Marxist perspective in understanding society and history very largely in terms of human labor. However, he transcends Marxism at a number of crucial points. He emphasizes that man always remains the subject of work, that the subjective dimension of work overrides in importance the objective dimension, that labor, i.e., working people (and this includes practically all citizens), has priority over capital. This emphasis allows the Pope to assign a dignity and importance to the human person that is not found in Marxism. It also allows him to demystify a number of Marxist concepts such as "class struggle" and "the laws of history" and resolve them into people acting together because they recognize that class solidarity or other forms of group solidarity are the only way in which they can struggle for social justice. The Pope enters into a Marxist perspective, and by applying certain Marxist insights and some Christian ones at the points where Marxism is weak, he explodes Marxism, or better he transcends Marxism from within—but not in the direction of political theories popular in capitalist countries. He offers the Church a philosophy of praxis, in which people as workers (and this includes practically the whole of society) are the author and subject of history through a collective struggle for justice, in which God is graciously present to them.

One word about the third world. Since the oppressed in the underdeveloped societies are not simply the workers, but the masses of people excluded from production and almost totally dispossessed, it becomes necessary to reinterpret the theory of labor. The encyclical argues that the dispossessed are meant to become workers, that they are destined to participate in society, and hence that they are at least potentially included in the demand that labor have priority over capital. Again transcending Marxism, the Pope borrows a concept from liberation theology and the Latin American Bishops' Conference. He speaks of "the poor". It is through these poor that God will act; it is through their discovery that only in solidarity will they be able to struggle against oppression, overcome present injustice and build a more human society. The Church not only demands solidarity of the poor and with the poor, the Church itself, in fidelity to the Lord Jesus Christ, must identify itself in solidarity with the poor. Only through such a struggle for justice can these poor enter responsibly into their history and become the subject of their own collective existence. Again, the Pope transcends Marxism here, for this entry into history is not caused by the unfolding of an historical law following an inner necessity, but it is the people themselves, freely discovering who they are and what their oppression is, freely organizing in the name of justice and engaging in struggle, who are the driving force of their liberation. The good news addressed to them is that present to their freedom and their solidarity is the gracious God revealed in Jesus Christ. What the encyclical does not say in this context, a point strongly made by many liberation theologians, is that God's grace is operative in people's struggles for justice, even when they fail, even when people are humiliated, tortured and murdered, for they will live in the risen Christ.

Laborem Exercens:
Toward a New Solidarity

Bartolomeo Sorge

This article originally appeared in *Theology Digest*, 1984.

To assess the contributions made by Pope John Paul II's *Laborem exercens,* we must see the encyclical as [i] maintaining continuity with preceding papal statements and [ii] breaking new ground.

POINT OF ARRIVAL

Laborem exercens [LE] lies along the trajectory of evolving papal thought on the "social question" and contributes the conviction that "human labor is a key, and probably the essential key, to the whole social question."

The "Social Question"

As early as 1891, Leo XIII (*Rerum novarum*) focused his discussion of the social question on the working class. Pius XI's *Quadragesimo anno* expanded the horizon from the working class to the whole *nation:* with the Great Depression, labor was seen to be a pivotal point for the whole of social and economic life. John XXIII's *Mater et magistra* [MM] and Paul VI's *Octogesima adveniens* advert to the "new proletariat": today's "poor"—in a world of abundance!—must include the disadvantaged and handicapped, chemical dependents, old people abandoned to themselves and, in the Third World, entire peoples and nations.

Labor is seen as integral to world peace and development, to the international equilibrium between industrialized nations and the Third World.

These jointly expanding horizons of "social question" and "labor" provides the context for *LE*: the social question transcends economic development and international equilibrium and involves the *human* meaning of work. If the social question is to be solved by making "human life more human," "the key of human labor acquires a basic and decisive importance."

Awareness of Mission

Having a mission to the world, the church must make its contribution to the social question. What should that be?

Reacting against classical Liberalism and Marxism, the church first tried to set up a "counter" ideology—Leo XIII's "Christian philosophy" and Pius XI's "Christian society" as a "third way" between the extremes of capitalism and socialism. The labor question became a chapter in social ethics, and the answers lay in deducing conclusions from natural-law first principles, there being no need for historical analyses and no standing accorded sciences like sociology and economics.

With John XXIII, Vatican II and Paul VI, however, we now realize that the Christian answer to the social question is not to propose "alternatives" (thus reducing the Christian to the ideological) but to go beyond ideology and, in the Gospel and the genuinely ethical, to find the truly *human*.

This mature ecclesiology influences *LE*. The encyclical confronts the social question from a religious and ethical optic so as to find common ground for believer and non-believer, Western democracies and socialist regimes, "developed" countries and Third World—*LE* essays resonance in all sincerely seeking the meaning of human life and labor.

Lay "Mediation"

In the 19th century, labor issues were viewed as moral questions reserved to magisterial competency, and the laity as passive executors of hierarchical decrees. Nonetheless, Leo XIII saw that the laity must mediate between ethics and economics (politics), faith and history.

With John XXIII, Vatican II and Paul VI, full recognition is accorded the necessary role of lay mediation. Social questions (even with an ethical dimension), says *MM*, are of diverse origin—historical, political, economic. Hence a new methodology is needed: [a] observe, [b] judge, [c] act. Starting with the "signs of the times" [a], we interpret these in the light of Scripture and tradition (magisterium) [b] and so establish not only ethical orientations for action but—thanks to professional, lay mediation—social, economic and political options as well [c]. In a word, lay mediation is a decisive moment both in applying and in elaborating the church's social teaching.

As a magisterial-hierarchical document, *LE* keeps to the religious and ethical and does not get into historical, sociological and scientific analyses. For this reason, some think the encyclical a retreat into past centuries. But the Pope believes that discerning the signs of the times, authoring scientific analyses, and deciding on options belong to the Christian community.

POINT OF DEPARTURE

If the key to an increasingly complex social question is human work, then it must first be freed from ideological readings and restored to its "authentically human meaning." Hence *LE*'s "gospel" of work: "the value of human work lies not in the type of work done but in the fact that the one doing it is a person." This "basic principle"—work must be viewed not objectively (man for work) but subjectively (work for man)—inspires the entire encyclical.

An Act Done by God's Image

Only if work is consciously experienced as an activity of the person can we affirm our identity as person and our call to being-person. Work both transforms nature and realizes our humanness.

Early capitalism's error was subverting this order; Marxist collectivism and current socialisms and neo-capitalism merely repeat this basic error of regarding workers as instrument and not in their true dignity as subject and author of work. As free, responsible agent (whatever the occupation) the worker may never be reduced to mere means—neither for the work itself, "capital," property or scientific research.

A Creative Act

Since human work creates wealth and goods, it establishes man's priority over the world. As the person comes before work, so work comes before the means of production and the resultant goods. For the same reason that the person may not be subordinated to work, human work may not be subordinated to capital. Capital is born of human labor and bears its stamp. Like any economic materialism, both capitalism and collectivism commit the error of setting production over work. Capital and the logic of production thus become an anonymous subject independent of man and work.

Since human work is creative, it comes before property. Since work gives title to property, this means of production may not be set in conflict with work nor possessed for its own sake: the only just title to *any* means of production is to serve work and to guarantee that goods are equitably distributed and that all have the right of access to such means. Since work is meant to produce and develop wealth and not destroy it, there follows the duty of obeying the norms of reasonableness and austerity in using natural resources and of giving priority to the quality of work by ordering economic development to the moral (and spiritual) needs of human existence.

An Act of Solidarity

Work is signed by its power to unite; herein lies its strength to build community—"community" includes workers themselves, those who dispose of means of production and those who work for society's material and spiritual advance.

From the beginning of the industrial revolution, this potential for solidarity was first expressed in "working class" unions—morally just reactions against exploiting and degrading the human agent of work. Despite advances, injustices remain and grow worse—because, in part, workers' solidarity was grounded in ideology and not in work's authentic, human meaning. While not infringing on lay competency to determine concrete structures for promoting a new solidarity, the Pope affirms the legitimacy of labor unions, of socializing some means of production, and of workers' co-ownership and co-participation in managing business enterprises.

An Act of the Human Spirit

Whether blue-collar or white-collar, work is an act of the whole person. The Pope's "gospel" of work here reaches its apex. Work achieves its full meaning only when it takes on the value it has in God's eyes as part of the work of salvation. For this reason the church's judgments may not be restricted to the moral or the human, but must encompass the value work has to bring us closer to our Creator and Redeemer, to share his saving plan for man and world, to deepen intimacy with Christ.

Far from alienating or distracting from the arduous task of transforming the world, work's religious dimension teaches workers that their labor contributes to the work of creation. This fuller meaning lets us see work's inevitable sweat and fatigue as collaboration with Christ (Worker par-excellence), as working humanity's liberation. The Pope invites the worker (believer and non-believer) to view work with Christ's own love and respect.

Faced by the past century's injustices that cried for vengeance, industrial workers came to discover both their shared misery and the strength of united action. As "indispensable components of social life" and "expressions of the struggle for social justice," labor unions, says the Pope, must open themselves to the common good. With this orientation, they will show that workers are not alone or isolated, will express a common solidarity in defending the rights that derive from work, will be the vehicle for active participation in humanizing work. Labor unions present an opportunity for a wider solidarity of *all* who work and can overcome corporate and class egoism, preventing the union from being chained to party interests and accepting responsibility for the unemployed and for those whose work conditions are difficult—women, migrants, share croppers, the handicapped. Since work grounds and gives meaning to existence, this new solidarity can be something fully human, "a solidarity without frontiers."

Societal complexity and inter-dependence, concludes *LE*, have rendered secondary the direct provider of work and made primary the indirect provider (institutions, collective bargaining). In his Geneva address (June, 1982) the Pope evokes the primacy of "a common good that is not limited to a more or less satisfactory compromise between interested claims or is based on purely economic concerns." New ethical choices are imperative if a new worldwide awareness is to be formed, a new solidarity based on the true meaning of human work. Such would be not a "solidarity-against" but a constructive "solidarity-for."

A solidarity that finds its origin and strength in the nature of human work—in the primacy of the human person over things—will know how to create avenues of dialog and collaboration, to become a step toward resolving opposition while not destroying the opponent.

John Paul II: Continuity and Change in the Social Teaching of the Church

J. Bryan Hehir

This article originally appeared in *Co-Creation and Capitalism*, 1983.

My purpose is to analyze dimensions of continuity and change in John Paul II's contribution to Catholic social teaching. The analysis will consist first, of a sketch of the social teaching he inherited; second, of an examination of general issues of substance and style which shape the Pope's impact on the received tradition; and third, of a discussion of specific issues where lines of continuity and change can be identified.

CATHOLIC SOCIAL TEACHING: LEO XIII-PAUL VI

John Paul II declares at the outset of *Laborem Exercens* that his reflections are intended "to be in organic connection" with the twentieth-century tradition of Catholic social teaching. The phrase "social teaching" has become a technical term in Catholic theology, referring to the body of papal, conciliar and synodal teaching which extends from Pope Leo XIII, who died in 1903, to John Paul II.[1] In order to give the phrase its proper specificity it is necessary to distinguish Catholic social teaching from the social implications of Catholic faith. There has always been a social dimension of Christian faith; the detailed history of the social consequences of Christianity is found in Ernst Troeltsch's *Social Teach-*

ing of the Christian Church. Christianity, with Catholicism in a specific way, has been a social institution of significant proportion.

The phrase social teaching, however, refers to the twentieth century effort to provide a systematic, normative theory relating the social vision of the faith to the concrete conditions of the twentieth-century. John Paul II refers to and draws upon this normative doctrine even as he reshapes and extends it in *Laborem Exercens.* To assess his contribution it is necessary to have a sense of the historical development and analytical categories of the social teaching. In Part One of the latest encyclical he notes the fact of development in the social teaching, distinguishing the "labor question" from the global perspective which one finds in the post-World War II period. It is possible to be more specific and distinguish three stages of growth in the social teaching between 1891 and 1978. Each period is marked by a "sign of the times" to which the social teaching responds.

For the first period, the question is the Industrial Revolution; the relevant texts span the period from Leo XIII's *Rerum Novarum* (1891) to Pius XII's *Pentecost Address* (1941). In these documents the unit of analysis is the nation and the theme is economic justice in nations undergoing industrialization. The topics addressed included: 1) the role of the state in the economy; 2) the right of laborers to organize; 3) the conditions of work in factories; and 4) proposals for diversifying ownership of productive property. The ideas and issues of this first stage of the social teaching persist to the present and find new expression in the work of John Paul II, but the outbreak of World War II and the post-war developments, politically, economically and socially produced a new set of issues which required change and development in the social teaching.

The question of the second period is the interdependence of the post-war world. The reality of interdependence as it is found in the social teaching has multiple causes: the emergence of over 100 new states in thirty years; the increasing interpenetration of economies among the industrialized nations (Western Europe, the United States and Japan), and the impact of these societies on the developing world; the fact of material interdependence highlighted by trade, financial and raw materials exchange between the North and South; the recognition of transnational problems (population, energy, environment), and the rise of transnational actors (private or governmental). The social teaching notes the increasing material interdependence of all the international system and focuses on the challenge of shaping moral interdependence which will yield both institutions and ideas equal to the challenge of a new age. In this second period the unit of analysis in papal teaching is no longer the nation but the international system. The topics addressed include:

> 1) the need for a political authority beyond the nation-state, one capable of addressing the needs of the "international common good;" 2) the protection and promotion of human rights in a world of nation-states; 3) a critique of prevailing patterns and institutions of international economic exchange because of their impact on developing countries; 4) an emphasis (since John XXIII) on agricultural development, the need for land reform, the imperative of a food security system which addresses the problem of hunger and malnutrition; 5) a critique of superpower policies which subordinate the needs and self-determination of small states to larger geopolitical designs.

The third stage of development is found in Paul VI's 1971 apostolic letter, *Octogesima Adveniens,* which addresses the "new social questions" of post-industrial society. This document is perhaps the most creative yet least known of the social teachings. It recapitulates the two previous periods and also opens new issues for discussion. The "new social questions" which Paul VI identifies are issues arising in the societies which first underwent the Industrial Revolution and now are highly urbanized, pluralistic and secular, penetrated by mass communication and continually changed by revolutionary technologies. In this complex setting Paul VI probes issues like the role of women, the task of education, and the existing but inadequate modes of political and social organization seeking to direct these societies. While the stress in the letter is on these issues, the international themes are revisited, including a series of questions on Christian-Marxist dialogue and the political vocation of Christians. The role of utopian vision in Christian social thought and the place of the local church in the social ministry are mentioned but left for further study and discussion.

While this historical explanation of the social teaching allows us to trace major themes, it does not provide a complete framework to assess the contribution of John Paul II. A different method of analysis, focusing on the structural categories of the social teaching provides a second means of understanding the legacy inherited by John Paul II. Structurally, it is possible to distinguish two major themes which have shaped the papal and conciliar social teaching in the last two centuries. The two themes coalesced and were stated with a new tenor and orientation at Vatican II. The two pervasive questions of the nineteenth and twentieth centuries have been the "church-state" controversy and the "church-society" issues. In an authoritative commentary on the social thought of Vatican II, John Courtney Murray writes:

> The first point here is the new conception of the problematic. Its terms are not now, as they were for Leo XIII, the Catholic Church and human society in Europe. The terms are wider—religion in its full ecumenical sense and human society throughout the wide world. The second point is that, again in continuity with Leo XIII, the Council situated the narrow issue of Church and state within the context of its own widened problematic. Thus it effected a further transformation of the state of the narrower question. And in consequence it opened the way to a development of doctrine on the matter.[2]

John Paul II indicates in *Redemptor Hominis, Laborem Exercens* and his *Address at the United Nations* that he will be a key contributor to the development of doctrine. He inherits the church-state/church-society questions as they have been formulated by Vatican II. Behind the conciliar texts are two broad arguments, which comprise the social teaching. The church-state argument is rooted in the nineteenth-century Catholic response to the democratic revolutions. This argument extends from Gregory XVI, through Pius IX and Leo XIII to Pius XII and John XXIII.[3] The dynamic of the argument illustrates a slow but progressive assimilation by the church of key tenets regarding "the democratic freedoms" and the "human rights" language which supports them. Leo XIII is a pivotal figure in opening Catholicism to dialogue with the constitutional state, but he was not able himself, conceptually or historically, to formulate an affirmative response. This task was left to Pius XII, who significantly enhanced the human rights content of the social teaching, and John XXIII whose *Pacem in Terris* joins themes of the natural law and natural rights traditions in his statement of a Catholic case for a society based on justice, love, truth and freedom. This line of development culminates in the church-state teaching of *Dignitatis Humanae* at Vatican II. The issues in the church-state argument have been political and juridical in character; they have been principally concerned with how the institution of the church relates to the institution of the state and how both are called to the service of the human person. This argument has been principally a western phenomenon, with its roots in Europe, its terms drawn from the clash of the organic natural law ethic and the contractual liberal philosophy, and its dynamic one in which the church has significantly been a learner, a useful critic but eventually an advocate of the position which seeks to limit state power by the instrument of law for the purpose of protecting the freedom and dignity of the person.

The church-society argument has had different themes and a wider scope than the church-state question. It is the church-society discussion which runs through the social encyclicals. The themes are not political but socio-economic; the emphasis is less institutional and more on the presence of the church as a teacher, a community and a leaven in the society. The key figures in this argument have been Leo XIII, Pius XI, John XXIII and Paul VI. The conciliar text which states the church-society issue and which constitutes a major development in the argument is *Gaudium et Spes*.

This distinction between the "political" tradition and the "socio-economic" tradition is identifiable in the social teaching but it is not an absolute dichotomy. The relationship between the church-state and church-society themes is a structured relationship. The first is the inner core of the second; the limited, institutional definition of how the church relates to the political process of a country often sets the general tone for the wider activity of the church in society. This does not mean that the church takes its direction for social ministry from the state, but that different forms of the state provide different challenges for the church. To function in a secular democracy is one question; to face an authoritarian military junta is a very different task; and to relate to a theocratic regime presents other questions.

Post-Vatican commentators have noted the shift in Catholic teaching which today gives the church-society question primacy of place, seeing the church-state issues as subordinate to the larger issue of the church's total witness in society. *Laborem Exercens* fits into the church-society argument; it draws upon earlier stages of this tradition (e.g. *Rerum Novarum*), it expands Catholic teaching on key issues (e.g. workers' rights) and it generally does not address structural political questions in detail. John Paul II, however, has addressed the church-state side of the argument in other writings, particularly on the issue of religious liberty. In his political writings he shows a keen sense of the importance of the state, of a theory of the state and of the need for a church-state theology.

In the following two sections, I will comment on the influence of John Paul II on both dimensions of the social teaching, showing how he relates the two and what his contribution is to each.

JOHN PAUL II: SUBSTANCE, STYLE AND SOCIAL TEACHING

Prior to examining specific issues in the social thought of John Paul II, this section will concentrate on general characteristics of his teaching. Specifically, the proposition being argued here is that John Paul II's impact on Catholic social teaching is a mix of what he says, how he says it and what he does. The proposition implies, therefore, that he shapes the social tradition as both a teacher and an actor, as a moralist and a statesman. In examining these three modes of influence, I shall relate each to an issue affecting the development of Catholic social teaching today.

The first issue which opens the way for a contribution by the present Pope is the post-conciliar state of Catholic social teaching. In 1966 Fr. Murray described the state of the question:

> The simple conclusion here is that the two conciliar documents, *Dignitatis Humanae* and *Gaudium et Spes,* have made a joint contribution toward the renewal of traditional doctrine with regard to the ancient issue of church and state. . . . The relevant principles have been stated with a new purity, which was made possible by the new perspectives in which the whole issue was viewed. . . . This doctrinal work was inspired by the maxim of Leo XIII, "Vetera novis augere et perficere". A work of systematization remains to be done under the same inspiration.[4]

Principal among the systematic tasks to be achieved is a work of *integration* of the social teaching with other constitutive dimensions of the faith. The need for integration is precisely the product of the multiple developments which have marked the social teaching from Pius XII through Paul VI. The conceptual advances made in this period have decisively shaped the tradition. The developments have been in moral argument (e.g. the precision given to human rights claims in *Pacem In Terris*) and in ecclesiological understanding (e.g. the significant advances in *Gaudium et Spes* and *Justitia In Mundo*). The developments have been diverse and rapid; a work of integration is required if this understanding of the significance of the social dimension of the faith is to be made available to the whole Church.

From the beginning of his pontificate John Paul II has cast his social teaching in a systematic framework which can be used to relate the social teaching to the core of Catholic faith. The framework is most clearly evident in the *Puebla Address* and in *Redemptor Hominis,* but aspects of it appear throughout the papal writings including *Laborem Exercens.* The framework is rooted, as much of John Paul II's theology is, in *Gaudium et Spes,* but he pushes the conciliar teaching forward.

The framework has four interrelated categories: anthropology, christology, ecclesiology and social ethics. There is an inner logic among the categories, each one building on the previous one. At the heart of John Paul's social thought is a statement of (theological) anthropology: the "complete truth about the human being constitutes the foundation of the Church's social teaching and the basis also of true liberation. In the light of this truth, man is not a being subjected to economic or political processes; these processes are instead directed to man and are subjected to him."[5] The person has long been the center of Catholic social thought and John Paul II's stress on the theme places him squarely in the line of Pius XII's *Christmas Addresses,* John XXIII's *Pacem In Terris* and the conciliar texts *Dignitatis Humanae* and *Gaudium et Spes.* But John Paul is not simply repeating previous teaching; he uses both his developed philosophical skills and his experience of struggle with an authoritarian regime (precisely over the question of whether the church or the state would own the person's allegiance) to sharpen and deepen Catholic teaching on the dignity of the person. In his extraordinary intellectual biography of John Paul II, Professor George H. Williams observes: "In the perspective of generations of Christian scholarship it will come to be noted that the evolving papal stress on the dignity of man received its most notable and swift expansion in the prepapal and papal pronouncements of Pope John Paul II."[6]

An example of how the Pope puts his distinctive stamp on the theme of human dignity is his personalist treatment of work in *Laborem Exercens*. Catholic teaching has never been satisfied with an explanation of the meaning of work in purely instrumental terms; the human investment in work always was the reason behind the social encyclical's insistence on a just wage. But *Laborem Exercens*, drawing upon both biblical and philosophical themes, invests the process of work with new meaning and purpose: "Work is a good thing for man—a good thing for his humanity—because through work man not only transforms nature, adapting it to his own needs, but he also achieves fulfillment as a human being and indeed in a sense becomes 'more a human being.' "[7]

The Pope's tendency to relate biblical and philosophical themes is a topic addressed below, but it must be cited here as a characteristic of his framework for social teaching, particularly in the way he moves from anthropology to christology. Here again he shows himself to be, in the words of Father Henri de Lubac, "a man of *Gaudium et Spes*."[8] One of the striking characteristics of the conciliar pastoral constitution is its christological stress. Each of the first four chapters closes with a resounding christological summation of the theme being analyzed.[9] In this respect the treatment of the human person in its chapter one is notably different from that of *Pacem In Terris* only two years earlier. John XXIII's defense of the person was elegantly cast in the philosophical terms of natural law; *Gaudium et Spes* roots human dignity in theological soil. John Paul II is decisively on the side of the conciliar text because he believes that only in the person of Christ is the true potential of human dignity perceived. Williams summarizes the case: "In a word, he has been saying that Christ is not only a revelation *of God* and his salvific will for all mankind through the church but also a revelation *of man*, of what man was intended to be at creation and is by reason of the Incarnation of the Son of God and by reason of the Crucifixion, Resurrection and Ascension of the God-Man Jesus Christ."[10]

The logic of the Pope's argument moves from anthropology and christology to ecclesiology. Here again, the contribution of John Paul II may be primarily to relate in explicit terms dimensions of the social teaching which have been developing in parallel fashion but require systematic integration. The social teaching as found in the social encyclicals always had a strong grounding in human dignity but a noticeably weak ecclesiology. *Pacem In Terris* is eloquent about human dignity and human rights and is prophetic about specific social issues, but it is silent about ecclesiology. This gap leaves the social ministry in a precarious position, devoid of legitimation in terms of a definition of the church's essential ministry. The decisive contribution of *Gaudium et Spes* was to provide the social ministry with a sound ecclesiological basis; this development has been solidified in the 1971 and 1974 synodal documents, *Justitia In Mundo* and *Evangelii Nuntiandi*. John Paul II uniquely enhances this theme both by his use of the conciliar text and by his personal reflections on the linkage of ecclesiology and anthropology. Relying on paragraph 76 in *Gaudium et Spes* (i.e. the church is called to be ''a sign and a safeguard of the transcendence of the human person''), John Paul II makes the striking affirmation that ''man is the primary route that the church must travel in fulfilling her mission: He is the primary and fundamental way for the church, the way traced out by Christ himself, the way that leads invariably through the mystery of the incarnation and the redemption.[11]''

The consequence of John Paul's teaching on anthropology and ecclesiology is that it ties together in creative fashion the social tradition's emphasis on the person and a definition of the church's pastoral ministry which places the person—with all his/her needs—at the center of the church's work. The defense of human dignity and the protection of human rights are not simply significant humanistic and moral truths, they are today for the Catholic Church an ecclesiological imperative. From this imperative flows the need for a social ethic—the fourth element in John Paul's framework; the function of a social ethic is to specify the challenges confronting the church in defense of human dignity.

The second contribution of John Paul II to the social teaching requires less specific commentary but it should be noted. It is not *what* he is saying but *how* he speaks on social issues. There has been in Catholic social ethics a growing discussion of *how* the church should cast its social message.[12] The terms of the debate are set by *Pacem In Terris* and *Gaudium et Spes*. As noted above, John XXIII's encyclical epitomized the ''classical'' Catholic social ethic, a strong philosophical statement, rooted in a religious vision but expressed in terms accessible to all people of goodwill. The conciliar text is dramatically different (only two years later) with its pervasive theological themes of christology and ecclesiology and its extensive use of biblical imagery. There are assets in each of these traditions, the philosophical and the theological, and the post-con-

ciliar debate in social ethics has sought to adjudicate the cost/benefit relationship for each style. The issues at stake, of course, are much larger
than terminology; *how* the church speaks to a social question is due in
part to its conception of who the audience is, how the church conceives
its social function and what style of analysis is judged to be most adequate in assessing complex social issues.

These questions cannot be adjudicated here; the more modest point
is to define the question and to locate John Paul's teaching in light of it.
A noted authority on the Pope's writings has said: "The core of John
Paul the Second is undoubtedly philosophical. In his pastoral writings,
addresses and sermons, as well as in his pronouncements concerning the
Church's politics, the premises of his thought refer, in the last analysis,
directly to properly philosophical views."[13] In light of this commentary
it is surprising to examine the Pope's social thought, since it is decidedly
on the *Gaudium et Spes* side of the debate in social ethics. Both of the
Pope's encyclicals, *Redemptor Hominis* and *Dives in Misericordia* are
strongly biblical-theological documents and his general framework, discussed above, continually leads him from philosophy to theology. There
are exceptions such as his *U.N. Address,* which faithfully reflected the
argument of *Pacem In Terris.* Undoubtedly the Pope's own commitment
to philosophical reflection will assure a strong philosophical grounding
to the social teaching, but his style thus far enhances the strain in contemporary Catholic thought which stresses a biblical and theological ex-
plicitness in the Church's social message. The ultimate direction of the
larger debate will be affected by many voices, but the Pope's orientation
thus far is significant if not determinative.

The third general impact of John Paul II on Catholic social teaching
is related to his actions as Pope. The office of the papacy is always a
unique forum in world affairs; now a fascinating personality with an activist conception of his ministry fills the office. Commentators as different in their perspective as George Will and Tad Szulc both agree that
John Paul II is the most significant single figure on the world stage.[14] It
is too simple to adopt a rubric that we should watch what the Pope does
rather than what he says, but it would be an inadequate interpretation
which ignored the nature and consequences of his major initiatives. Assessing the relationship of word and deed in John Paul requires an essay
in itself; a proven intellectual, wedded to a belief in the power of the
word, he is also an actor with a sensitive appreciation of the power of

gestures—political and personal. The analysis here will be limited to a comment on his style of leadership and then a set of examples intended to highlight the consequences of his actions.

There is always a risk in using secular political analogies to probe ecclesial questions, but I will run the risk and argue that papal style today is significantly Gaullist. A strong leader with a well-honed conceptual design; a decisive style which is prone to act and let others react; a tendency to appeal directly to his constituency (i.e. the church or, at times, world public opinion) over the heads of organized elites; a remarkable self-possession and a capacity to move mass opinion by word and deed; all are found in John Paul II. The long-term impact of this style of leadership, on both church and state, cannot be assessed as yet, but many of the Pope's most celebrated actions have influenced the social ministry. Two forms of action are of interest.

First, John Paul's willingness to be specific about controverted, complex questions. Most of the social teaching, including his own, is understandably cast in general terms, leaving specific application to others in church and society. Several of John Paul's public positions complement his general teaching. Examples include his support for the SALT II treaties expressed not only in one of his weekly addresses in Rome but also in his reference to them while in Washington just as the Senate was about to consider the treaties; his support for the Camp David agreements, a particularly difficult choice given the Holy See's position on the Middle East; and his decision to send members of the Pontifical Academy of Science to heads of state in the United States, the Soviet Union, France, and Great Britain to warn about the escalating nuclear arms race. All of these actions, while nuanced and carefully shaped, were understood in very concrete terms.

Second, while on pilgrimage to various countries the Pope has been willing to match cautionary statements about the Church's political involvement with specific comments about social injustice. The two preeminent cases have been his statement in Oaxaca, Mexico, about the justification, under specified circumstances, to resort to expropriation of property; and his direct comment to President Marcos of the Philippines that claims about state security are not justifications for "subjugating to the state the human being and his or her dignity and rights."[15]

These general characteristics of John Paul's social style set the background for examining specific issues. Issues come and go, and are always limited and often local in their significance, but the horizon of the Pope's words and deeds serves to give larger meaning to his specific teaching on concrete cases and questions.

CONTINUITY AND CHANGE: ISSUES AND EXAMPLES

The issues selected for examination are drawn from the categories used in Part One of this paper: church-state, church-society and one specific international question.

The Church and Politics: The classical church-state issue is how the church as an institution relates to the political order. It is a perennial question which has produced a wide spectrum of responses from the Roman Empire through twentieth-century democracy.[16] Surprisingly the issue has not received much sustained attention in the church-society literature. John Coleman's masterful review of the encyclical tradition notes the reticence to speak directly about the church and politics.[17]

John Paul II has not been reluctant to address the question and his statements have stressed the non-political nature of the church's ministry. The texts abound from his Puebla Address in 1979 through his remarks to the Jesuit Provincials in Rome in 1982.[18] The strength and frequency of these cautionary statements have inevitably raised the question whether the Pope's cautious church-state views are designed to restrict the church's witness on the church-society issues of justice, peace and human rights.

To assess the content and consequences of John Paul's church-state teaching it is necessary to place it in the context of the framework established by Vatican II. One way to interpret the conciliar theology is to say the church has become less political but correspondingly more active in its social witness. The church is less political in that it seeks no special status or privileged position in the political order. The thrust of the Council's document *Dignitatis Humanae* was to say that the one demand the church makes of the political process is the freedom to fulfill its ministry.[19] The church seeks *freedom from* interference; it does not *ask for* special status. In this sense the church is less tied to any existing government. John Paul's statements reinforce this sense of distance from the state.

Freedom, however, is not an end in itself, but a pre-condition for the church to fulfill its social witness. The controlling text for interpreting this witness is *Gaudium et Spes,* paragraphs 40–42; one cannot make sense of John Paul's social teaching apart from these passages.[20] In a terse compact fashion they set forth the parameters of the church's social witness:

1) the church has no specifically political mandate or ministry;
2) the church is a religious community whose ultimate goal is to contribute to the building of the Kingdom of God;
3) the Kingdom, however, grows in history—mysteriously but actually;
4) hence, as the church pursues its religious objective it has four consequences: protecting the dignity of the person, promoting human rights, fostering the unity of the human family and informing human activity with meaning.

These four consequences are not narrowly defined political goals, but they cannot be pursued apart from the political process. The church contributes to the realization of these four objectives in its own distinctive mode of action, but the consequences of a religious ministry directed toward these ends will be felt in the political process. Both John Paul's social teaching and his personal witness stress the importance of these goals—human dignity, justice, rights and peace—for the church's life today. In the same speeches in which he cautions priests not to play specifically political roles, he also urges them to include the protection and promotion of human rights in their ministry.[21]

In summary, the conciliar legacy of a less political but more socially engaged church is sustained in John Paul's social teaching. To be precise, he does oppose specific forms of church engagement in the political process—notably the participation of institutionally representative figures in elective office; but there is no basis for using these specific limits to say that John Paul II is eroding or constraining the church's social witness.

A final point which is relevant to this balance of the political and the social is the Pope's strong sense of the distinction of roles and functions in the church. For the social ministry this has meant a strong stress on the vocation of the laity in the socio-political arena. This is hardly a new theme, but it has received renewed attention from a Pope cautious about church-state matters but activist in his sense of the social relevance of Christian faith. Two points are significant about this stress on the lay vocation.

First, anyone acquainted with the church's social ministry, theoretically or practically, recognizes the need for this emphasis. Particularly in the United States we have been less than successful in the postconciliar period in providing the laity proper scope in the social ministry. Second, the shift which did occur at Vatican II was not designed to lessen the lay role, but it did describe the priestly and religious life in a manner allowing for more direct involvement in the social ministry. It is questionable, therefore, whether the model of distinct roles used in the time of Pius XI and Pius XII can today be reinstituted. That model proposed a ''first-order'' direct role for the laity in the socio-political realm and a ''second-order'' role of education for the church professionals. The present visible, active role which the bishops play on social questions goes beyond a ''second-order'' function, and this makes it less likely that the old distinction will hold.

These broad comments on the church and politics have to be concretized in different cultures and political systems, some of which require very flexible interpretation of these principles. The central point is to see that John Paul's teaching stands in continuity with the conciliar framework; he may seek to restrain certain specific forms of political engagement, but he has not directed his teaching to a withdrawal of the church from the social witness advocated in post-conciliar Catholicism.

Human Rights: The principal way in which John Paul II addresses the social questions is through human rights categories. His use of this theme continues a pattern rooted in Pius XII and expanded by John XXIII and Paul VI. In itself this is a noteworthy theme in the social teaching, since papal thought in the nineteenth and early twentieth centuries was cautious about human rights language. The reason was well-known; it is a standard commentary to distinguish the eighteenth century natural rights tradition from the older natural law philosophy. The contribution of Pius XII and particularly John XXIII has been to incorporate aspects of the natural rights tradition within the natural law framework.

John Paul's use of human rights is notable in two ways. First, his frequent appeals for human rights on his pilgrimages not only allows him to speak to a variety of specific issues, but it also reinforces the human rights ministry of the local church. This was visibly the case in his address to sugarworkers in the Philippines and to laborers in Brazil.[22] It was uniquely the case, of course, in his visit to Poland.

Second, John Paul II not only applies the human rights teaching of his predecessors, he is also developing his own distinctive interpretation of human rights. His *Address to the United Nations* gave the broadest interpretation yet accorded to human rights in Catholic social teaching. He developed an interpretation of the international system based on human rights, going so far as to link the roots of war with human rights violations. Some would question whether the category of human rights can bear the weight the Pope places on it, but he may push our understanding beyond convenient interpretations of the theme.

His conceptual contribution to the human rights argument also moves in the direction of seeking a unified interpretation of different kinds of rights. The U.N. distinctions of political-civil and social-cultural-economic rights reflect a broader divergence rooted in distinct philosophical and political systems. The Pope's U.N. address sought to cut across this divide on the basis that both material and spiritual values are essential to human dignity and must be provided for in any political system.

The human rights theme raises a final question on which John Paul's views are less well known. The 1971 synod of bishops raised the question of the role of social justice and human rights categories within the Church. This proposal to use the concepts traditionally applied to society in an assessment of ecclesial life and structures is still in its rudimentary stages in Catholic social teaching. There is an intellectual question here of determining how to make the transition from secular structures to analogous but not necessarily identical structures within the church. As yet John Paul has not addressed himself explicitly to this theme in spite of its connection with the broader human rights ministry with which he is so solidly identified.

War and Peace: Among the international issues in Catholic social teaching none has been more carefully assessed than the war and peace question. The extensive analysis of the morality of war from the biblical period through Pius XII faces a qualitatively new challenge in the nuclear age. Like his predecessors, John Paul II has felt compelled to confront the nuclear question, but in his own way.

In his analysis of the nuclear arms race, the Pope has cast his argument in terms of the relationship of technology, ethics and politics.

The theme is a central one in his thought, one he uses to address medical-moral questions as well as international relations. In his first encyclical, the *Redeemer of Man (Redemptor Hominis)*, and in his recent address at Hiroshima he used the prism of technology and ethics to analyze the meaning of the arms race. John Paul II's analysis involves two steps. First, the nuclear arms race is depicted as the most visible example of a larger question: how modern technology can move beyond both moral and political guidance thus submitting the human person to an impersonal power. The technological dynamic of the arms race fits this pattern—new improvements in weaponry are always one step ahead of the most recent attempts to control them.

Second, this technological dynamic means that the challenge for the human community is to reestablish the primacy of ethics and politics over technology. In his address to scientists and intellectuals at Hiroshima, John Paul II stated his basic theme:

In the past, it was possible to destroy a village, a town, a region, even a country. Now it is the whole planet that has come under threat. This fact should finally compel everyone to face a basic moral consideration: From now on, it is only through a conscious choice and through a deliberate policy that humanity can survive.[23]

The realm of moral choice on this issue lies ultimately, although not exclusively, in the political process. Scientists, journalists, educators and religious leaders prepare the atmosphere of choice, even shape the categories for choosing, but effective action on the arms race requires decisive political action. At the United Nations and at the White House in 1979, John Paul II acknowledged this and called for political measures to control and reverse the spiral of the arms race.

Four of the last five popes (with the exception of John Paul I) have made distinctive contributions to the social teaching. This paper points to the factors which guarantee that John Paul II will forcefully shape this tradition. He is a man of the tradition but knows that a living tradition must grow and develop. Development will be the product of many forces not simply papal teaching, but John Paul's voice will be a catalyst to other efforts.

Notes

1. For a summary of the teaching, see Joseph Gremillion, *The Gospel of Peace and Justice: Catholic Social Teaching Since John XXIII* (N.Y.: Orbis Books, 1976); John Coleman, "Development of Church Social Teaching," *ORIGINS*, 11 (June 4, 1981) p. 34ff.

2. J. C. Murray, "Church and State at Vatican II," *Theological Studies* 27 (1966) p. 585.

3. J. C. Murray, "The Problem of Religious Freedom," *Theological Studies* 25 (1966) p. 503–575.

4. Murray, "Church and State," p. 606.

5. John Paul II, Puebla Address, *ORIGINS*, 8 (Feb. 8, 1979) p. 535.

6. George H. Williams, *The Mind of John Paul II: Origins of His Thought and Action* (N.Y.: Seabury Press 1981) p. 264.

7. John Paul II, On Human Work, *ORIGINS*, 11 (Sept. 24, 1981) Para. 9.

8. I am indebted to one of Fr. Henri de Lubac's students for this reference.

9. Vatican II, *Gaudium et Spes*, cf. Para. 22, 32, 39, 45.

10. Williams, p. 265.

11. John Paul II, *Redemptor Hominis*, Para. 14.

12. Cf. D. Hollenbach, et al, "John C. Murray's Unfinished Agenda," *Theological Studies* 40 (1979) p. 700–715.

13. A-T. Tymieniecka, "The Origins of the Philosophy of John Paul II," *Proceedings of the American Catholic Philosophical Association*, 53 (1979) p. 16.

14. T. Szulc, "Politics and the Polish Pope," *New Republic* (Oct. 28, 1978) p. 19ff.

15. John Paul II, "The Pope's Address to President Ferdinand Marcos," *ORIGINS*, 10 (Feb. 26, 1981) p. 591.

16. Cf. Murray, "The Problem of Religious Freedom."

17. Coleman, "Development of Catholic Social Teaching," p. 39.

18. Cf. Puebla Address; Pope to the Brazilian Bishops; Address to Filipino Men Religious, *ORIGINS*, 1979–1982.

19. Cf. Murray, "Church and State at Vatican II," p. 587.

20. Ibid., p. 582.

21. Address to Filipino Men Religious, *ORIGINS*, 10 (Feb. 26, 1981).

22. Address to Rural Peasants at Oaxaca, *ORIGINS*, 8 (Feb. 8, 1979).

23. Address at Hiroshima, *ORIGINS*, 9 (Oct. 11, 1979) p. 266.

The Popes and Politics: Shifting Patterns in Catholic Social Doctrine

Peter Hebblethwaite

This article originally appeared in *Religion and America,* 1983.

Pope John Paul II, on September 14, 1981, published his third encyclical letter, *Laborem exercens.* This title was translated as *In the Exercise of Work,* which is about as uneuphonious and unilluminating as the Latin. The purpose of the encyclical, according to its author, was "to highlight—perhaps more than has been done before—the fact that human work is *a key,* probably *the essential key,* to the whole social question, if we really try to see that question from the point of view of man's good" (3).[1] The "social question": it is a long time since anyone had used this nineteenth century expression. "Human work": it is a long time since anyone had dared to address the Church and "all men of good will" on a topic of such vast generality. Many Anglo-Saxons are skeptical about the philosophical or theological discussion on work, and are more sympathetic to the down-to-earth approach of Bertrand Russell: "Work is of two kinds: first, altering the position of matter on or near the earth's surface relatively to other such matter; second, telling other people to do so."[2]

John Paul's encyclical, however, is not just a lofty philosophical disquisition; it also contains some practical proposals. It weaves a path between capitalism and communism in suggesting that the way ahead lies in joint ownership of the means of work; sharing by the workers in the management or profits of businesses, or so-called shareholding by labor; and so on (14). There are also sharp condemnations of transnational and multinational companies that allegedly "fix the highest price for their products, while trying at the same time to fix the lowest possible price for raw materials'' (17). John Paul declares that unemployment "is in all cases an evil and, when it reaches a certain level, can become a real social disaster" (18). These are presented as moral rather than political judgments. But unless they are meaningless statements, designed merely to soothe the conscience of the utterer without changing the situation, they are political through and through. If I come to believe, for example, that unemployment in the United States or Britain has reached the level at which it is "a real social disaster," especially for the young who have never known what it is to work, I am in duty bound to oppose the monetarist policies that have contributed to it.

But my purpose is not to discuss this most recent encyclical in any detail. My interest in the encyclical is that it puts itself forward as an instance of "the Church's social teaching" (3), which has more usually been called "Catholic social doctrine" (henceforth CSD). Moreover, it is explicitly presented as in continuity with the "great social encyclicals" of the past, starting with Leo XIII's *Rerum Novarum* of May 15, 1891, which it commemorates. Seen against that background, the originality—or lack of originality—of John Paul's latest encyclical will appear more clearly.

For some years there has been an animated debate on CSD. The English-speaking world has paid little attention to it because most of the discussion has taken place in France, with an occasional contribution from Latin America. The argument was about whether CSD was dead or alive, and if dead, what should replace it. But what may seem like a futile academic quarrel in fact raised some far-reaching questions about how Christians should relate to the world, and the world of politics in particular. Some account of this debate will also enable us to see that John Paul, in trying to breathe new life into CSD, is taking a very firm stand against some recent trends in the Church. He is taking sides.

As representative of the "CSD-is-finished" school, we can take the veteran French Dominican, Marie-Dominique Chenu, who in 1979 published a short book called, significantly, *La "Doctrine Sociale" de l'Eglise comme Idéologie*.[3] By placing *doctrine sociale* in quotes, Chenu is suggesting that it is a figment; by calling it an ideology, he is saying why it is unacceptable. Chenu's position has been utterly rejected by Fr. Roger Heckel, S.J., who at the time was Secretary of the International Justice and Peace Commission in Rome,[4] the pontifical body responsible for issues of social justice and international relations. In a series of pamphlets published by the Commission, Heckel notes the frequency of the term "social doctrine" in the speeches of John Paul, and defends its use.

In practice, CSD starts with Leo XIII's *Rerum Novarum* in 1891. I say in practice, because (as we shall see) John Paul and Heckel are extremely reluctant to speak in this way, since it would involve the admission that the Church had *no* social doctrine until 1891. Thus the attempt is made to put together a tradition based on the book of Genesis ("Subdue the earth"), the fact that Jesus was a carpenter and worked with his hands, and the remarks of some ancient Church Fathers to the effect that the poor are the real treasure of the Church. This attempt to found a tradition leaves large tracts of time uncovered; it is difficult to imagine what sort of CSD could come from the Borgia popes or indeed any pope who was saddled with ruling the Papal States. In any case, one can perfectly well admit that some kind of social *thinking* has gone on in the Church, but that it was scattered and sporadic; it would become social *doctrine* only if it were more systematic and complete. This point relates to the main discussion in the following way: If there has always been a CSD, it is less likely to have died in the 1960s. If, on the other hand, it actually came into existence in 1891, it will be time-bound, bear the marks of its age, and perhaps be doomed.

Thus—more cautiously this time—it may be said that CSD in the modern sense, as a more systematic pontifical exercise, began in 1891. What is not in dispute is that it caused a sensation at the time, for *Rerum Novarum* was the first pontifical document to pay any attention to the consequences of the industrial revolution. "Gradually," Leo noted, "the workers, isolated and defenseless, are handed over to the mercy of inhuman masses and made the victims of frenzied competition." Nearly fifty years after the *Communist Manifesto*, the Church was trying to recover lost ground.

Leo's justification for tackling what was known at that time as "the social question" (the very language used ninety years later by Pope John Paul) was that "no effective solution to it could be found without recourse to religion and the Church" (8). The Church was not interfering in politics when it made pronouncements on these matters, because politics itself was a moral activity, directed towards the realization of the common good. Not to speak would be a dereliction of duty.

On this one may make three comments. Leo could only come to the defense of the workers because his predecessor, Pius IX, had lost the Papal States in 1870. Though Leo felt resentful about this loss, and still hoped that something would be restored, he also realized that it was a liberation for the papacy that could become the "conscience of the world" or (to use a much later expression) the voice of those who have no voice. Second, to make use of the term "common good" was a splendid move. Not only did it carry a reminiscence of Aquinas (whose study Leo also revived), but it provided as well a middle terrain in which the difficult question could be eluded: Which, when the crunch comes, has primacy—the papacy, now reduced to a spiritual power, or the Italian state, now the acting temporal power? Third, the kind of CSD put forward by Leo had a condescending and paternalistic note that would prove difficult to get rid of. The poor are the object of the discourse; they are not seen as agents in their own transformation. Most dangerous of all, CSD comes actually to mean, "what *popes* have to say on social questions."[5]

Forty years later, Pius XI published *Quadragesimo Anno*, the title indicating continuity. He agreed that the world had changed in the intervening period. The financial crash of the late twenties had alarmed everyone, and was seen by Marxists as presaging the final end of capitalism. The Bolshevik Revolution had introduced a new and menacing factor into international affairs. But while noting these changes, Pius continued the line of Leo XIII. CSD is envisaged as a set of principles, enunciated by the Church (actually the pope), that if acted upon, could transform the world. Unfortunately, these principles had not been heeded, and consequently the world was in a mess. The approach to problems was moralistic and individualistic. There was no examination of the structuralist, built-in causes of modern problems. There was no attempt to interpret contemporary movements in the light of their Christian potential. Socialism was rejected out of hand.

The result was that Catholics had to hive off into movements of their own. Catholic Action, which organized groups by categories, was seen as the best way to implement CSD. This meant forming separate Catholic labor unions wherever this was possible. On this, Chenu comments: "To divide the labor movement in order to evangelize it was to make an error about the Gospel. For the real task was not to create a separate

Catholic workers' group but to bring the Church to birth within the workers' movement as it actually existed."[6]

CSD as conceived in the 1930s lectured the world from the outside. It stated abstract, intemporal principles that ignored the diversity of situations. It was nostalgic for a vanishing rural and peasant world. It ignored the fact of class conflict, which it tried to gloss over with the concept of *interclassissmo*—the harmonious collaboration of all social classes—which brought comfort only to dictators like Franco in Spain and Salazar in Portugal, both of whom claimed to be implementing CSD.

The difficulty of CSD was this: it could fly so high in the stratosphere of principles that, from above, the whole landscape was flattened out and no details could be perceived; or—more rarely—it could hew so close to the ground that its particular statement was too localized to be applicable elsewhere. The problem, to put it another way, was how to relate Christian faith to ongoing history.

The change began with Pope John XXIII, who succeeded Pius XII in October 1958. Despite his seventy-six years, there was freshness and vigor in the way he set about his pontificate. He had a keener sense of history than any other pope of this century. "History will be our guide," he told the Second Vatican Council, which will always be associated with his name. He inaugurated a new approach (it was of course a rediscovery) to social problems that depended on a new methodology. He began to speak of the need to discern "the signs of the times." In Luke's Gospel, Jesus says to the Pharisees and Sadducees, after quoting proverbs about weather-forecasting, "You know how to read the face of the sky, but you cannot read the signs of the times" (Luke 12:54–56). The parallels to this text (cf. Matthew 11:3–5; 12:28; and 16:3) suggest that "the times" refers to the new messianic age, and that "the signs" are the miracles worked by Jesus. Pope John used this text and gave it an accommodated meaning, not always to the satisfaction of the exegetes. In *Humanae Salutis,* the apostolic constitution by which he convoked the Second Vatican Council, he writes of the immense new tasks facing the Church, the tragic period of history the world had just come through, and the need to bring the Church and the world together, so that "the vivifying and perennial energies of the Gospel" should be brought to bear on the temporal ordering of the world.

But how was this to be achieved? Pope John went on: "Indeed we make ours the recommendation of Jesus that one should know how to discern 'the signs of the times,' and we seem to see now, in the midst of so much darkness, a *few indications which augur well* for the fate of the Church and humanity."[7] (*italics added*)

The indications that augur well remain rather vague. One gets a better idea of what was in his mind from *Pacem in Terris,* his final encyclical, which was, in effect, his last will and testament. (It also has the distinction of being the only papal encyclical that has been set to music: by Olivier Messaien.) Each of the four sections into which it is divided concludes with a review of contemporary developments. For example, the section headed *Order between Persons* notes that "workers refuse to be treated as if they were irrational objects," that "women will not tolerate being treated as mere material instruments," and that the nations emerging from colonialism have found a new sense of dignity. So far, so banal, it might be thought.

But if these trends, or tendencies, however difficult to pin down, are not merely regarded as a Good Thing but can actually be related to the Gospel, an important shift has occurred. No longer does CSD simply parachute down principles from a great height. Instead, it takes the hopes and aspirations that people really have and reads in them a message from the Holy Spirit. The Spirit is at work in the men and women and movements of our age. This is not a matter of blessing every contemporary fad or fashion. But it does mean starting from what is happening (the "world will provide the agenda for the churches" was the way the World Council of Churches would say the same thing later). It means a new humility before the data. It means listening carefully to what is being said, and then discerning (i.e., seeing in difficult circumstances) the hand of the Lord. The consequences of this shift of emphasis were considerable. They affected the work of the Second Vatican Council and the subsequent postconciliar history of the Church. The main consequences as they relate to CSD are:

1. The first was the simple principle that one should look before pronouncing. A credible empirical starting-point is needed. If men of God are unconvincing in their account of this world, they are unlikely to carry conviction when they speak of the invisible world. The more accurate the preliminary description, and the more it leads people to say, "Yes, that's the way it is," the more

its subsequent teaching will carry authority. But it will be the authority of competence, and not merely of hierarchy.

2. Who is charged with this task of discerning the Spirit? As *Gaudium et Spes,* the document of Vatican II closest to the aspiration of John, put it: "With the help of the Holy Spirit, it is the task of the entire people of God, especially pastors and theologians, to hear, distinguish and interpret the many voices of our age, and to judge them in the light of the divine word" (44).

3. It follows, further, that the Spirit, far from being held captive within the boundaries of the Church, can be found in the most surprising places. *Gaudium et Spes,* for example, speaking of the concern for human rights and where the impulse to defend them comes from, says, "God's Spirit, who with a marvellous providence directs the unfolding of time and renews the face of the earth, is present to this development. The ferment of the Gospel arouses in men's hearts a demand for dignity that cannot be stifled" (26).[8]

4. The "ferment of the Gospel": this phrase was not lightly chosen. It refers to the way the Gospel can shatter conventional and comfortable ways of thinking and acting. It further implies that this ferment, once released upon the world through the preaching of the Church, can perfectly well break loose from its ecclesiastical moorings and invade what we think of as secular society. Yet even when this happens, there will still be a real relationship between the aspiration toward human dignity and the Holy Spirit. The whole concept of "anonymous Christians" starts from this truth.[9] The Spirit "without" speaks to the Spirit "within."

5. Thus the whole relationship of Church and world changes. The Church is not "over against" the world: such a view leads to the reduction of the Church to a sect that fundamentally rejects the world and is content merely to snatch a few brands from the world's fire. Nor was the Church seen as a fortress besieged by a fundamentally hostile world. It was a people, a people on the march toward the realization of the Kingdom of God, its eventual true home, but which meanwhile shared for good or ill in everyday human problems. This was why *Pacem in Terris* could be addressed, for the first time ever, to "all men of good will."

It was not at that time a platitude; it was a breakthrough. For John's teaching was no longer based on the authority or the claims of the Church; it was based on the Church's *experience*, and appealed to the aspirations of ordinary people and the tissue of hopes and basic solidarities that make up human history.

6. This was the deeper meaning—now largely forgotten—of the magnificent opening chord of *Gaudium et Spes:* "The joys and the hopes, the griefs and the anxieties of the men of this age, especially those who are poor or in any way afflicted, these too are the joys and the hopes, the griefs and anxieties of the followers of Christ" (1). The Kingdom, or better, the Reign of God, that horizon toward which Christians consciously move, was to be discovered in solidarity with others, not in separation from them. Normally it would be unnecessary to congratulate a human grouping on discovering that it belonged to the human race; but in the case of the Roman Catholic Church, which, especially with its CSD, had talked *at* people rather than *with* them, it was an important shift of attitude.

7. Finally, this opening statement of *Gaudium et Spes* also contained a hint—not fully worked out in the rest of the document, but pregnant with the future—that the poor were to be privileged in the Church. This was a return to the evangelical source: "The Spirit of the Lord is upon me because he has anointed me; he has sent me to announce good news to the poor" (Luke 4:18)—Jesus quoting Isaiah.

The same evangelical spirit was reflected in Pope Paul VI's social encyclical, *Populorum Progressio* (1967). Its express aim was "to throw the light of *the Gospel* on the social questions of our age" (2). It avoided any use of the term "social doctrine." Its main theme was the interdependence of all the peoples of spaceship Earth. It was a prophetic document in that it was ahead of most conventional wisdom of the 1960s. It anticipated that the North-South conflict would turn out to be more important than that between East and West. No doubt that was why *The Wall Street Journal* dismissed it as "souped-up Marxism."

Meanwhile, local churches had begun to work out for themselves the implications of the stand taken by Pope John and the Council. The "signs of the times" could not be discerned universally: they had to be studied on the local level. The Latin American bishops (CELAM), meeting at Medellin, Colombia, in 1968, interpreted "salvation" for their peoples as liberation from social, political, and economic oppression. This was the starting point of "the theology of liberation" that proliferated during the next decade. It involved a more sympathetic, though not uncritical, approach to Marxism (with the emphasis on the young, humanistic Marx); sometimes the *anawim,* or poor, of the Gospels were identified with the oppressed proletariat; and there was a firm insistence that orthodoxy (thinking right) needed to be filled out by orthopraxy (living out what one thought, or being consistent). CSD as traditionally understood was abandoned, and frequently derided, as well.

Although Paul VI did not show any contempt for CSD, he abandoned it on the grounds that it was unworkable. In his letter to Cardinal Maurice Roy,[10] published in 1971 on the occasion of the eightieth anniversary of *Rerum Novarum,* he wrote, "In view of the varied situations in the world, it is difficult to give one teaching to cover them all or to offer a solution which has universal value" (4). But that had been precisely the claim of CSD. It was now abandoned, and Paul VI even added that the pretension to a universal message was neither his intention nor his mission.

But this did not mean that the Church had nothing to say on these social issues. The task that Paul VI felt incompetent to fulfill was entrusted to Christian communities throughout the world, who had the duty of scrutinizing "the signs of the times" in their own situation. No one else could do this on their behalf. This was not a feeble abdication on the part of Paul VI: it was, rather, a recognition of the change in the method sketched above. Solutions could not be handed down from on high: that was the illusion of CSD. Rather, they could only be discovered through patient work, in which the human sciences would play a part, in collaboration with others involved in the same field.

The Justice and Peace Commission, set up by Paul VI in 1967, was an organizational expression of the same principle. Though it had a central office in Rome, its strength lay in the national branches, who saw it as their task to "sensibilize" Catholics to local problems. It did this patchily, with more or less success, and with more or less support from the local hierarchy. "Justice and Peace" became, in effect, the Catholic euphemism for politics in the 1970s. No one ever indulged in "politics" (still regarded as a somewhat tainted occupation); they strove for justice and peace. One of the most significant pointers to the changed attitudes was a statement by the 1971 Synod of Bishops, which had on its agenda the admittedly vast topic of "justice in the world," that said, "The struggle for justice is a *constitutive* dimension of the preaching of the Gospel." (*italics added*) In other words, it is not an optional extra, not something you think about when you have preached the Gospel; it is, rather, the way to preach the Gospel in the world of today. The Society of Jesus made this text the basis for a rethinking of its entire work at its 32nd General Congregation in 1975.[11]

At this point one might be tempted to conclude that CSD was finished. All that remained was to write its epitaph, which Chenu did in his book. For him, it is a museum piece, the social equivalent of that "deism which neutralized the Gospel and which was the ideology of the bourgeoisie in the nineteenth century." He means that Leo XIII, while claiming to present some kind of intemporal Catholic social doctrine, was in fact merely reflecting the current bourgeois ideology toward the end of the nineteenth century, a charge difficult to deny. Leo's denunciation of socialism and assertion of the right to private property were just what the bourgeoisie wanted to hear in 1891. But, as Chenu concludes, "faith is not an ideology":[12] that is, it is not an unconscious way of legitimating my unexamined prejudices. There could be no more devastating way of undermining CSD.

CSD is dead, apparently, but it will not lie down. John Paul II has deliberately set about the task of rehabilitating it. He has done so knowing perfectly well that the term "social doctrine" has its critics. But that stimulates him even more. He is not someone who ducks a challenge. He told the Latin American bishops, assembled at Puebla in 1979 for a follow-up meeting to Medellin, that the social doctrine of the Church must be studied and applied, "even though some people seek to sow doubts and lack of confidence in it" (III, 7). Quite clearly, he does not accept these criticisms.

On the other hand, he is not doing battle for a mere word. This can be seen in the way he sometimes puts social doctrine in quotation marks and uses, more commonly, a whole arsenal of semiequivalent expressions: social morality; social thought of the Church; social and humanitarian teaching; doctrine, or directives, of the encyclicals; doctrinal inheritance; social teaching of the apostolic see, or social doctrine of the popes.[13]

This multiplication of semiequivalent terms can be seen as an attempt to assert that the Church, the popes, and the Gospel—the three terms are not in fact interchangeable—have always had something to say on social questions. The tradition did not begin with Leo XIII. The most striking affirmation of this supposed continuity is to be found in the apostolic constitution[14] *Catechesi Tradendae.* After noting that catechesis must include "the search for a society with greater solidarity and fraternity, the fight for justice and the building of peace," John Paul goes on:

> Besides, it is not to be thought that this dimension of catechesis is altogether new. As early as the patristic age, St. Ambrose and St. John Chrysostom—to quote only them—gave prominence to the social consequences of the demands made by the Gospels. Close to our own time, the catechism of Saint Pius X explicitly listed oppressing the poor and depriving workmen of their just wages among the sins that cry out to God for vengeance. Since *Rerum Novarum,* especially, social concern has been actively present in the catechetical teaching of the Popes and the Bishops (29).

Potted history is always dangerous, and "disingenuous" would be a mild term to describe this summary of twenty centuries of history. The leap from Ambrose and John Chrysostom to Saint Pius X is enough to make one suspicious. And the latter's paternalistic concern for the workers should be set alongside the outrageous statement made in his 1906 encyclical *Vehementer:* "As for the multitude, it has no right other than to be led and, as a faithful flock, to follow its pastors."[15] The claim to a continuous tradition is extremely dubious.

This does not deter John Paul. *Catechesi Tradendae* is not presented as an original work, but as a synthetic response to the 1977 Synod that was devoted to catechetics. Thus his desire to revivify CSD appears as a request put at the Synod: "Many Synod Fathers rightly insisted that the rich heritage of the Church's social teaching should, in appropriate forms, find a place in the general catechetical education of the faithful" (29). One of them was Cardinal Karol Wojtyla. He was thus in perfect agreement as pope with what he had said as cardinal.

But in his interpretation of the 1977 Synod, a crucial position taken by an earlier Synod (1971) is implicitly abandoned. In 1971, when the

Synod was allowed to write its own texts, it stated that "the struggle for justice is a constitutive dimension of the preaching of the Gospel." "Constitutive" was the key word, for it meant that not to struggle for justice was to be unfaithful to the Gospel. It was a blow aimed at separated spirituality or escapist mysticism. The 1977 Synod, as presented by John Paul, says, rather, that this struggle is *another* dimension of catechesis, necessary no doubt, but one that is tacked on at the end after other, more essential elements have been dealt with. It appears as an afterthought. It is certainly no longer seen as "constitutive" of the preaching of the Gospel.

John Paul clearly believes that CSD has a future. On the other hand, his use of the term is circumspect. Roger Heckel points out that "social doctrine" has been talked about in two principal contexts: Latin America and Poland. CSD was mentioned during the visits to Mexico and Brazil, and has recurred in many of the *ad limina* visits of Latin American bishops to the Vatican. As for Poland, the first visit home in June 1979 provided an opportunity to develop his thoughts on CSD for the benefit of Edward Gierek, still at that time Secretary of the Polish Communist party, and the Polish bishops, who were doubtless more familiar with these ideas.

It is legitimate to ask why Latin America and Poland provide the "right" context. The answer will not be quite the same in each case. "Social doctrine" was used in Latin America because CSD has been much criticized there for its abstractness. In fact, in the sixties and seventies it had been very largely abandoned and replaced by various versions of "the theology of liberation." The failure of the "decade of development" led to a radicalization of political oppositions, with the growth of military governments on the one hand and revolutionary or guerrilla movements on the other. The middle way between capitalism and communism, which CSD was commonly supposed to represent, had chalked up no successes in Latin America, and was now squeezed out altogether.

But John Paul *needed* CSD in Latin America; it provided the ground on which he could stand to criticize the theology of liberation. It would be hard to criticize it without either offering something to put in its place or retreating from political commitment altogether. There can be no doubt that John Paul was highly critical of liberation theology. A whole section of his Puebla speech to the assembled bishops of Latin America is devoted to "a correct Christian idea of liberation" (III, 6)—the implication being that there are incorrect ideas in the air. John Paul's concept of liberation, however, rejects the primacy of politics that has so often been asserted in Latin America, and replaces it with "the primacy of the spiritual." He speaks of a liberation "that in the framework of the Church's proper mission is not reduced to the simple and narrow economic, political, social or cultural dimension, and is not sacrificed to the demands of any strategy, practice or short-term solutions." There was a populist appeal in his suggestion that "the humble and simple faithful, as by an evangelical instinct, spontaneously sense when the Gospel is served in the Church and when it is emptied of its content and is stifled with other interests" (III, 6).

But the assertion of the primacy of the spiritual does not mean an abstention from the world of politics. CSD fills the vacuum. At this point, something very odd happens. John Paul seeks to answer the objection that social doctrine had confined itself to the abstract and therefore irrelevant statement of principles. "This social doctrine," he explains, "involves . . . both principles for action and also norms for judgment and guidelines for action." Social doctrine, in other words, is "cashed" in "praxis." The oddity is that this observation is backed up by a reference to *Octogesima Adveniens* (4), which says nothing of the kind, and is precisely the passage in which Paul VI abandoned the ambition of propounding a social doctrine for the whole Church, and entrusted the task of "discerning" particular situations to the local Christian communities.

John Paul's use of social doctrine in the context of Poland is more easily understood, and provides a key to his attitudes more generally. In the Belevedere Palace on June 2, 1979, beneath the chandeliers and the television lights, John Paul was in a unique situation. He had just listened to Edward Gierek extol the splendors of "thirty-five years of socialism." John Paul pointedly ignored this, spoke instead of the tradition of more than a thousand years of Christianity, congratulated Gierek on rebuilding the Royal Castle in Warsaw "as a symbol of Polish sovereignty," and multiplied quotations from his predecessor Paul VI on the theme of disarmament and better relations between nations. "In these words," he added, "the doctrine of the Church is expressed, which always supports authentic progress and the peaceful development of humanity." He then denounced "all forms of political, economic or cultural colonialism which are in contradiction with the basic demands of international order.'' Few Poles watching this on television did not think of the Soviet Union at this point. The ground for Solidarity was being prepared. And once again the social doctrine of the Church provided the base from which to attack, deftly, but nonetheless clearly, the reigning Marxist doctrines. It was criticized in the name of the common good.

Political activity, John Paul told the Polish bishops at Czestochowa on June 5, 1979, is defined by its concern for the good of man, and therefore is of its very nature an ethical activity. Then he spoke of the ''so-called social doctrine of the Church'':

> It is here that the deepest roots are to be found of the so-called social doctrine of the Church which, particularly in our period, beginning at the end of the nineteenth century, has been enormously enriched by all contemporary problems. This does not mean that it emerged suddenly in the last two centuries: it existed in fact from the beginning as a consequence of the Gospel and of the Christian vision of man in his relations with other men, especially in community and social life.

Like the passage in *Catechesi Tradendae* quoted above, this attempt to broaden the basis of CSD delivers the concept from too narrow an interpretation. At the same time, however, the use of ''so-called'' indicates a certain hesitation. In using the term, John Paul does not mean, or does not simply mean, a return to the teaching found in the social encyclicals of Leo XIII and Pius XI. By admitting that ''new problems have arisen,'' he is conceding that new solutions have to be sought.

Despite his philosophical background, John Paul is not a systematic thinker. He strikes out in one direction after another as occasions present themselves, journeys suggest, or his speech-writers propose. The result is that despite the immense number of words already uttered during his pontificate, and the enforced leisure imposed by the bullets of Mehemet Ali Agca, it is still difficult to perceive the precise direction in which he is moving. The revival of CSD does not mean a return to Pius XI. But there are signs that it involves a critique of some aspects of the approach of Pope John and the Council. Here are three examples of the difficulties that remain, even after one has used the quasi-magical term CSD.

The first symptom of change is that the phrase ''signs of the times,'' whose importance we have seen, has almost completely disappeared from the papal vocabulary. Thus the preliminary empirical grip on social and political realities is bypassed. Yet the term has been used, but in contexts that distort its meaning. Addressing sisters in Washington on October 7, 1979, John Paul said: "As daughters of the Church . . . you are called to a generous and loving adherence to the authentic *magisterium* [teaching authority] of the Church, which is a solid guarantee of the fruitfulness of all your apostolates and an indispensable condition for the proper interpretation of 'the signs of the times.' " A similar warning was issued in his address to Indonesian bishops on June 7, 1980.[16] But the relevant text of *Gaudium et Spes* makes no mention of the *magisterium* of the Church. It simply says: "To carry out its task, the Church has always had the duty of scrutinizing the signs of the times and interpreting them in the light of the Gospel" (4). That is a task for the *whole* Church. To reduce it to a function of the central authority is to bowdlerize the text and domesticate the doctrine. It makes the local churches once more dependent on the center, it deprives them of initiative, and it suggests that the study of local situations can be replaced by judgments emanating effortlessly from the *magisterium*. This is the most "reactionary" statement uttered by John Paul. But since everyone knows it is unworkable, perhaps it does not matter.

More serious was a speech in Turin on April 13, 1980. It was his first real encounter with the world of work. Turin, headquarters of the Fiat car industry, now in recession, was also the city where the drive toward Italian unity began in the nineteenth century. But John Paul made no mention of the *Risorgimento* or of Camillo Cavour, its main architect. No Italian pope could have gone to Turin without reconciling himself to the democratic history of his country. But the Polish pope has another image of Italy, the land of countless shrines to the Madonna. In his map, Turin represented the Holy Shroud and St. John Bosco. And from this vantage point he denounced the two intellectual forces that have shaped the modern world—liberalism and Marxism:

> There is on the one hand the rationalist, scientistic, enlightenment approach of the secular so-called "liberalism" of the Western nations, which carried with it the radical denial of Christianity; and on the other hand the ideology and praxis of atheistic Marxism whose materialistic consequences are taken

to their most extreme consequences in various forms of contemporary terrorism.

As a matter of fact, the last phrase was toned down, at the last moment, to avert the suggestion—offensive and misplaced in Turin—of a link between Marxism and terrorism. The result was that the condemnation of "so-called 'liberalism'" seemed even harsher than the condemnation of Marxism. It seems that John Paul was not seeking dialogue or an overlap with secular systems. The evenhanded criticism of East and West may give the impression of independence from power blocs, but it can also suggest a plague-on-both-your-houses lack of serious commitment. Are there not some criteria for preferring one system rather than the other? Once the Church is placed outside the melee, as in the Turin speech, there is no longer any need to answer that question. Mother Church knows best—though she cannot in fact point to any instance of the realized Kingdom on earth. But she knows that the others are wrong.

No one could claim that the People's Republic of the Congo is a vivid realization of the Kingdom of God. It calls itself a Marxist state, but even so has diplomatic relations with the Holy See. Having gone to Kinshasha in Zaire, John Paul could not have omitted to cross the Zaire River and visit the People's Republic of the Congo. He duly did. On May 6, 1980, he addressed the President, Denis Sassou-Ngnesso, and developed the theory of Church and state as two not quite coincident societies:

The Church is a spiritual institution, even if it also has a social expression; it lies beyond temporal "fatherlands" [*patries*] as the community of believers. The state is an expression of the sovereign self-determination of peoples and nations, and is its ordinary realization in the social sphere; from it derives its moral authority. To become aware of this difference of nature will permit one to avoid confusion and to go forward in clarity.

The two realms having been thus distinguished, the way was open for an appeal for religious liberty, which is, said the pope, "at the heart of the respect for all freedoms and all the inalienable rights of the person." In exchange for religious liberty, the Church would offer "loyal collaboration."

But, one might ask, are there no further questions to be asked of the president of Congo-Brazzaville other than that he should respect religious liberty (of Catholics)? It may be fundamental, but it is not the only human right that needed to be asserted. At the end of his long life, Pope John had concluded that "today, more than ever, we must be concerned to serve man as such and not just Catholics, and to defend the rights of everyone and not just of the Catholic Church."[17] That vision is lost sight of when "loyal collaboration" (with no further questions asked) is offered in exchange for religious liberty.

*　　*　　*

The reintroduction of social doctrine does not of itself indicate a return to the teachings of Leo XIII and Pius XI (though they are honored as pioneers). It contains a reference to the Gospel that they, in their concern for natural law, tended to omit. But it reveals a deep suspicion for the theology of liberation and for the new signs-of-the-times method that set it in motion, and involves also the conviction, or the presumption, that something of universal validity can actually be said. To test whether this is true, I want to take two examples from *Laborem Exercens*, the encyclical of John Paul with which we began. Though his approach is austerely philosophical (based on the axiom of "the primacy of labor over capital"), he does reach some extremely precise conclusions. Two in particular have aroused surprise.

The less emotional example had best be taken first. There is a section on labor unions that, come what may, will inevitably be read in the light of the experience of Solidarity in Poland. Like Leo XIII ninety years ago, John Paul defends the "right of free association." But that is the basis of Solidarity's *very existence* as an autonomous and free union in a country that previously had only unions that were the "conveyor belt" of party decisions. What are unions for? John Paul's answer is that "their task is to defend the existential interests of the workers in all sectors where their rights are concerned" (20). That positive implies a negative, and it duly comes. Unions should be concerned with "struggle" only insofar as it is motivated by a quest for justice. They are not a reflection of class divisions or an instrument of the class war. They are not out to eliminate their opponents. And they should not "play politics, in the sense this is usually understood."

John Paul's welfare concept of unions leads him to conclude that "unions do not have the character of political parties struggling for power; they should not be subjected to the decision of political parties or have too close links with them" (20). As a piece of pragmatic advice for Solidarity, this is eminently sensible. Given that the Polish government cannot renounce "the leading role of the communist party" without committing suicide, it is wise for Solidarity to "stay out of party politics." There is no room for party politics in Poland. This interpretation is confirmed by the fact that within two days of the encyclical, the Polish bishops published a statement quoting this passage and urging Solidarity "to return to the negotiating table." There can be no doubt that John Paul's view of the purpose and role of unions is relevant to the Polish situation.

The question is whether it is equally relevant anywhere else. Transfer this judgment to other countries, and it becomes immediately problematical. The British Labor Party, for example, is locked in with the unions constitutionally, and other Western socialist parties have the same system. This may be a bad thing, and a perfectly sensible case can be made for saying that unions should be independent of political parties and vice-versa. What is difficult to swallow is that this should be presented as a major tenet of Catholic social doctrine. This, unfortunately, is characteristic of the whole approach of CSD, even in its updated form. Where it is vague, it can be blamed for its vagueness; but where it is precise, it can be blamed for its precision.

My second example concerns women. Catholic feminists, already outraged by his use of the generic "man" for human being and his refusal even to consider the possibility of women entering the ministry, will be inclined to dismiss John Paul altogether when they read that

> it will redound to the credit of society to make it possible for a mother—without inhibiting her freedom, without psychological or practical discrimination, and without penalizing her as compared with other women—to devote herself to taking care of her children and educating them in accordance with their needs, which vary with age. Having to abandon these tasks in order to take up paid work outside the home is wrong from the point of view of the good of the family when it con-

tradicts or hinders these primary goals of the mission of a mother (19).

If we try to understand this position—as contrasted with attacking or defending it—the first thing to notice is that he is not speaking of the role of the *woman* but of the role of a *mother*. That is an important distinction: a woman does not have to be a wife and a mother, but if she is, certain consequences follow. But perhaps the most important point about this passage is that what John Paul is objecting to is not that women should work outside the home, but that they should be *forced* to work outside the home, that they should have no option. And what he is objecting to is precisely what happens in Poland, where women are expected to work and merely add their work in the factory or wherever to their domestic work. Two recent Polish films by women directors, J. Kamienska's *Working Women* and K. Kwinta's *The White Women*, confirm this. According to David Robinson, they are both "terrible indictments of working conditions that seem to belong to the last century."[18] If in other countries it can be a liberation for a woman to go out to work, in Poland it is more likely to be an added burden. Therefore, to say that women should not be forced to work serves their cause.

Thus on two major points John Paul's contribution to CSD springs from his Polish experience and speaks eloquently to that experience. But it is difficult to apply elsewhere. His statements cannot be generalized— or only after so many modifications that they become valueless. I believe that Paul VI was right when he said, "In view of the varied situations in the world, it is difficult to give one teaching to cover them all or to offer a solution which has universal value" (*Octogesima Adveniens,* 4). But John Paul regards such an attitude as defeatist and fainthearted. That is why he needs a revived CSD as a form of universal teaching on social questions. He is unwilling to relinquish this task to the local churches. But unless the present revival of CSD becomes a stimulus to local discussion of social morality, and not regarded merely as a substitute for it, it will go the sad way of its predecessors.

Notes

1. Papal encyclicals and texts of Councils are usually set out in numbered sections. That is how they will be referred to here.

2. *In Praise of Idleness* (London: Allen & Unwin, 1935).

3. Editions du Cerf.

4. Fr. Heckel has since been made Archbishop of Strasbourg, France.

5. A course in "Catholic Social Doctrine" used to be given at Plater College in Oxford. It consisted exclusively of a commentary on papal social encyclicals.

6. Chenu, *La "Doctrine Sociale" de l'Eglise comme Idéologie,* p. 22.

7. Walter Abbott, *The Documents of Vatican II* (America Press, 1966), p. 703.

8. I have modified the Abbott translation here because the Latin puts it positively: *Spiritus Dei . . . huic evolutioni adest.* Abbott has "was not absent," which is more grudging than "is present."

9. For a treatment of this point, compare my *The Status of "Anonymous Christians"* in *The Heythrop Journal,* January 1977, pp. 47–55.

10. Quite obviously, this text was designed as an encyclical: it has the sweep and the scope of an encyclical. But at the last minute it was turned into a letter to Cardinal Maurice Roy, Archbishop of Quebec, and President of the Pontifical Commission for Justice and Peace. Only a pedant would conclude that it therefore had less authority.

11. The Jesuits are important not only because of their size—despite losses they still number above twenty-six thousand—but because of their influence on other religious congregations, especially the women's congregations, which treat Jesuit documents as though addressed to themselves. This is one of the reasons for the misunderstanding between Pope John Paul II and Fr. Pedro Arrupe, Superior General of the Jesuits.

12. Chenu, *La "Doctrine Sociale,"* pp. 90, 96.

13. Cf. Roger Heckel, *The Social Doctrine of John Paul II,* Justice and Peace Commission, p. 25.

14. Though lower in status than an encyclical, an apostolic constitution is still an important document. This one is presented as the papal response to the Synod of 1977. But in 1977 Cardinal Karol Wojtyla was a member of the Synod. Elected pope in October 1978, he thus became the recipient of his own advice.

15. Chenu, *La "Doctrine Sociale,"* p. 30.

16. Fearing that the expatriate missionaries were likely to be expelled at

any time, the Indonesian Bishops had been advocating the ordination of married men.

17. Diary for May 24, 1963, in *Giovanni XXIII, Profezia nella Fedeltà*, Angelina and Giuseppe Alberigo (eds.) (Brescia: 1978), p. 494.

18. *The Times,* London, September 17, 1981.

PART THREE:
EVALUATIONS AND PERSPECTIVES

Methodological Differences:
The Holy See and the
World Council of Churches

Thomas Sieger Derr

This article originally appeared in *Barriers to Ecumenism*, 1983.

Ways of Doing Ethics

The methodological difference most often mentioned is the Roman Catholic preference for relating positions on social questions to the tradition of natural-law ethics, and the World Council's predilection for discovering the divine revelation in the freshness and uniqueness of each event. Of course, these standard, rounded generalizations have their faults. The place of natural law is challenged within Catholic circles, and the World Council's large Orthodox component does not come bearing the so-called Protestant tradition of an ethic of the contextual divine word. Nevertheless, stereotypes do not usually come into being without referring to some large truth, and such is the case here.

The World Council has been called more an organism than an organization, something that has grown in response to stimuli, exercising a ministry of need. It is a ministry which, to quote the constitution of its Churches' Commission on International Affairs (CCIA), "necessitates engagement in immediate and concrete issues as well as the formulation of general Christian aims and purposes." The emphasis is on specific ways of Christian action in specific situations.[1] The Uppsala committee on the CCIA actually expected methodological agreement with the Roman Catholic Church:

In terms of approach there seem to be strong similarities between their thinking and ours. The approach should be, not so much by formal structures and protocol, as by step-by-step experimentation, and by dealing *ad hoc* with common opportunities as they arise.[2]

But this proved an incorrect assessment of Catholic method.

Statements on social matters from the World Council's Central Committee do indeed seem to rise from a particular incident—say, for example, the Middle East crisis—to a general principle, for example, national territorial integrity, where the enunciation of the principle is clearly influenced by the circumstances that gave rise to it. This gives the unfortunate impression that the World Council is primarily a social action organization that slights the theological component in Christian ethics. This impression is heightened by the news media, which give attention to political statements and activities while slighting the less newsworthy theological work. It is not surprising that critics, including Catholic critics, think of World Council statements as belonging more to the political order than to the moral order—political and economic judgments clothed in the mantle of religious ethics. Because of its penchant for particularity, it makes many more statements than the Vatican, adding to the impression that politics take precedence over theology. The statements it makes, critics acknowledge, may be quite true, justified as political judgments, and yet not be what the Church as *Church* should be doing. It is morally good to be engaged in secular pursuits—St. Thomas would have said as much—but this style blurs the distinction in the Roman Catholic mind between secular judgments and sacred judgments.

The World Council is not insensitive to such criticism, but in its own understanding it means to integrate study and action. This is the action-reflection model of Christian ethics in which action stimulates and guides study as well as vice versa.[3] Certainly the method is not above reproach and has its critics within the World Council as well as without. Even M. M. Thomas, in 1969 when he was chairman of the Central Committee, noted a need for "clearer enunciation of criteria for taking positions and action by the WCC" in international affairs.[4] Yet it is a viable model with a history in Christian ethics, defended as the characteristic biblical method, where theology emerges not systematically but as reflection on concrete situations.[5] The result is not random action, either. It is probably fair to say that there is a touchstone that provides consistency to the World Council's particular and contextual actions, namely, commitment to the poor and oppressed—and no one would deny that *that* test of action is solidly rooted in the New Testament.

For the Roman Catholic tradition the level of abstraction is higher. Statements deal more with general principles, less with the unique features of particular situations. There are, accordingly, fewer statements. They may be called forth by specific situations and sound particular enough—see *Populorum Progressio,* for example. But they start logically, systematically, from principles developed in the long tradition of Catholic social thought. No matter how particular the occasion of a statement, it will be read and judged as applicable to all similar contexts, past, present, and future—e.g., a statement on revolution in Latin America will be heard as applying to eastern Europe. The shorter World Council tradition is freer of the necessity to relate what it does to the teaching of the past and is not bound by its method to be read in the same way in all contexts.

The Catholic tradition, of course, is that of natural law—Thomistic, structural, and rational. The scriptural injunctions that inspire Christian ethics are carefully integrated with the long tradition rather than "heard afresh in the contemporary context." In theory the Church states the principles, and their application is left to others. If the Church attended too zealously to the application, it would be accused of clericalizing politics—a good argument for making more abstract statements. At any rate a fairly clear contrast with the World Council appears, one that could explain many a difference on issues. For example, there was a failure to agree on a joint statement on the Vietnam War because the World Council wanted to mention the American bombing and the Vatican found that issue too specific.

Yet like all contrasts this one can be overdone. In actual practice the Holy See does not always ignore the task of particular application, which it may accomplish, for example, by directing a nuncio to pass on a quiet word. It knows how to prescribe in great detail when it wishes to, for example, the rules for Catholic hospitals. And it generally wants the *right* to intervene specifically, even if it does not do so. In the theory, too, there is room for specificity; for the natural law that lies at the base of Catholic moral teaching is always to be "illuminated and enriched by

divine Revelation,'' which means in practice that ''the teaching authority of the Church is competent to interpret even the natural moral law.''[6]
Also orthodox Thomism is less dominant now, and there is uncertainty
within Catholic thought about the foundations of social ethics. Catholic
priests in other parts of the world have developed their own style of action-reflection ethics.

Within the World Council, on the other hand, for all the critics who
see in traditional Catholic methodology the risk of irrelevance and the
danger of platitudinous statements, there are other elements who never
were hostile to the natural-law tradition and who appreciate the intent of
Catholic procedure. From a practical point of view, also, there are those
who value the symbolic role of the Holy See and its usefulness in blessing the *general* direction of programs, a blessing to which one may make
effective appeal in particular settings. Some take seriously the criticism
that political and theological categories are blurred when worldly causes
are too quickly legitimized by use of the Bible.[7] Even the action-reflection model has been relatively recently articulated; the World Council's
method in the past was a largely unspecified process in which the seeking
of consensus before action played a large role. The current popularity of
the action-reflection method may be partly a way of escaping the western
parliamentary model of voting on resolutions. Instead, it starts with the
action of people without trying first to list agreements and refine distinctions. In short, the World Council's methodology is mixed and of
uncertain etiology, not wedded exclusively to a single style that sets it
forever apart from the Roman Catholic Church, although current differences in practice are readily discernible.

THE EFFECT OF IDEOLOGY

There is a further divisive methodological or procedural issue in the
role of ideology in formulating Christian social judgments. The apostolic
letter *Octogesima Adveniens* of 1971 sharply criticizes ''Marxist ideology,'' ''liberal ideology,'' and ''revolutionary ideologies'' in general,
in part, of course, for reasons of their particular content but also notably
because the social teachings of the church should be flexible and not
''authenticate a given structure or . . . propose a ready-made model'' or
''put forward a solution which has universal validity.''[8] There is a fair

amount of irony here, since many would say that the articulated Catholic natural-law tradition is itself a "given structure" claiming "universal validity." The World Council, on the other hand, should be protected by its flexible contextualism from according universal validity to any ideology, and thus meet the intent of *Octogesima Adveniens*.

Yet of course the issue between the Holy See and the World Council here is precisely that the latter has listened to revolutionary ideology, and sympathized much with those Christians, including Catholics, who have found in Marxism a powerful tool on the side of the poor and oppressed. For them it is a commitment whose ethical passion is its Christian justification, quite apart from its economic and political analysis. The Church ought not necessarily to take ideological sides, but it must recognize the positive uses of ideology for justice and acknowledge the ideological component already present in Christian thinking. A non-Christian ideology cannot be accepted as a secular faith, but may often be welcomed as a weapon for social change.[9]

If the role of ideology is ambivalent for the World Council, it is positively threatening to the Holy See. Fearing the impact of Marxism in Italy and the defection of militant priests in Latin America, the Vatican views such an ideological commitment as a challenge to the transcendence and ultimacy of Christian teaching, and hence incompatible with it. Catholic documents, particularly the speeches of Pope John Paul II as he travels to various Third World countries, reflect this fear. A commitment to the liberation of the poor and the defense of their rights is put reasonably strongly, but drawn solely from the gospel to the exclusion of any contribution from "ideological systems," i.e., Marxism.[10] The specific content of Marxist ideology is attacked, sometimes directly, more often in oblique references to "certain ideologies." It is condemned for "its atheistic materialism, its dialectic of violence, the way it absorbs individual freedom in the collectivity, at the same time denying all transcendence to man . . . ," for its doctrine of class war, and of course for its oppression of religion. It is wrong to think we can accept Marxism on one level and reject it on others, for all are bound together and end in a "totalitarian and violent society."[11]

SALVATION AND LIBERATION

In this insistence on a strict separation between Christian faith and any aspect of a historical ideology, we meet that dimension of Catholic thought often called, whether in praise or blame, "otherworldly," and contrasted with the "this-worldly" activism of the World Council. This distinction is such an old cliché that one advances it with some hesitation, and yet there is something to it after all. Roman Catholicism has been traditionally reluctant to identify salvation with any intramundane liberation. Salvation is not historically immanent, does not deal with the material situation, but is beyond all temporal hopes. The kingdom of God is reached by faith and membership in the Church, not "by the mere changing of structures and social and political involvement." It should not be interpreted "as being present wherever there is a certain type of involvement and activity for justice." The Church's commitment to the needs of the disinherited notwithstanding, "it is wrong to state that political, economic, and social liberation coincides with salvation in Jesus Christ." "This idea of Christ as a political figure does not tally with the Church's catechesis." "[Christ's] mission was not in the social, economic, or political order. Likewise Christ did not give the Church a mission which is social, economic, or political, but rather a religious one."[12]

This conception of the Church as separated from the temporal order is reflected in John Paul's repeated insistence that priests and nuns be a caste apart—"signs and instruments of the invisible world," living among human beings but not *of* this world. Their vocation is unique, possessed of a singular charism, and should not be touched by secularizing currents. In particular, its uniqueness should be made visible to the world by a distinctive religious garb, "an evident sign of complete consecration to the ideals of the kingdom of heaven, . . . a sign of definitive detachment from merely human and earthly interests." The Church apart, served by the caste apart, aspires to no temporal power or privilege, nor does it oppose civil authority. (It may thus justly claim freedom from the state's restrictions, a useful consequence of this otherworldly conception of the Church and a point obviously on Rome's mind.) John Paul claims that the direction he has charted is not a reversal of or recoil from the so-called openness of the Church to the world set in motion by the Second Vatican Council, especially the council's talk of the common priesthood of the laity. But to many observers it appears to be just such a turning back to otherworldliness, a conception in which many of this pope's themes—insistence on discipline and loyalty to the pontiff, movement to restrain dissent, emphasis on clerical celibacy as permanent (like the permanence of marriage, he says), restrictions on the laicization of those who wish to leave the priesthood, prohibition of non-Catholic Christians from the Eucharist, and limits on the forms for mixed marriages—all combine with the general themes of separation of the Church from the world to form a consistent picture.[13]

Given its insistence on the sharp distinction between Church and world, the Holy See would be bound to be suspicious of "liberation theology," quite apart from its Marxist component. There are even echoes here of the old dispute over the relation of the kingdom of God to history, over the extent to which the transcendence of the kingdom relativizes historical accomplishments and perhaps drains them of their urgency. The Vatican may fear that the World Council is making the old error of liberal theology, which is to think of worldly betterment as a prelude to the coming kingdom.

Again, the contrast should not be overdrawn. There are many Catholics now who think in terms of the humanization of this world more than of the perfect other realm that is the soul's destiny. The bishops' synods have been quite direct about declaring that Christian love implies an "absolute demand for justice," and that we must therefore "dedicate ourselves to the liberation of man even in his present existence in this world." Paul VI, who spoke clearly enough of salvation as "transcendent and eschatological," that is, as distinct from material and other temporal needs, nevertheless insisted that this salvation be related to both personal and social life, and include a concern for peace, justice, development, and liberation. Even the current pope, guardedly and with studied ambiguity, will occasionally allow the theological legitimacy of the term "liberation" to include a concern for justice; and he can say that even though "earthly progress must be carefully distinguished from the growth of Christ's kingdom," human advance in this world "even now is able to give some kind of foreshadowing of the new age," and thus "is of vital concern to the Kingdom of God."[14]

Nor is liberal theology regnant within the World Council, where participation in movements for social change is seen as a direct response to the love of Christ, not a precursor of utopia. The World Council may and does make a point of condemning otherworldliness and proclaiming its Christian obligation to be involved in struggles for political and economic liberation, an involvement that manifests the presence of the kingdom among us. But it is as ready as the Holy See to criticize structures and systems as false gods, and equally willing to remind the faithful (though not so often!) that liberation from sin and evil has also a private and eternal dimension. Moreover, the Orthodox tradition, also of course very much a part of the World Council, speaks of the spiritual transformation of humanity rather than of the direct confrontation of structures as the route to salvation—a viewpoint different from either Catholic or most Protestant traditions, and further complicating any effort to describe a neat contrast between the World Council and the Holy See.[15]

PASTORAL AND PROPHETIC STYLES

Another old typology that is often applied is that of the "priest"— the Catholic approach—against the "prophet"—the World Council's *modus operandi*. The priest has a pastoral function and is responsible for all his people. The Vatican accordingly avoids visible acts whose impact is uncertain and prefers the classic methods of quiet diplomacy. The idea, says John Paul II, is not to "brand and condemn individuals and peoples, but to help change people's behavior and attitudes." So there may be a private letter from the pope to the archbishop of a troubled country, or a private representation of the papal nuncio to the government. The nuncio may be successful in securing the release of political prisoners by such representation, where a public condemnation from the Vatican might serve only to stiffen the defiant resolve of the denounced government. Later, if need be, the Holy See may speak publicly.[16]

This approach involves the Vatican in dealing with the world's powers on particular issues, in spite of its *public* declaration that on social matters it speaks only on general principles. Such a method, priestly and diplomatic, is inherently conservative, disturbing the status quo as little as possible to accomplish its immediate ends. The aim is to humanize the given order.

The prophetic style of the World Council, on the other hand, tends to be less attached to established orders. It is not a church with essentially pastoral functions, but a movement of change, willing to make mistakes as the necessary cost of keeping its dynamism. It *exists* to engage in demonstrative acts, to seize opportunities, to make public pronouncements on specific topics, lest by silence it appear to show unconcern. Its condemnations and denunciations are characteristically given to the press. Its tone, like that of its biblical prophetic models, is forceful and often blunt, eschewing the nuanced voice that the Holy See prizes. Its style alone would be an irritant to Rome, even where there was no substantial disagreement on the issue at hand.

Mutual criticism is inevitable. To the Vatican the World Council's frequent rush to the press looks irresponsible, unreflective, and ineffectual. It is like an unsecured cannonball crashing about the deck of the good ship *Oikoumene*. In its emphasis on the prophet's function it forgets that the Church has a pastoral responsibility to care for *all* of its people. When World Council members, like the Moscow patriarchate or German Lutherans, criticize its actions as too specifically political, the protest is understood in Rome. The Vatican also fears the infectious effect the World Council's actions may have on Catholic radicals, so much so that at one point General Secretary Eugene Blake felt the need to reassure Pope Paul, lest the Holy See recoil from the WCC, that the tension between radicals and conservatives was common to almost all churches and was not only a Roman Catholic problem.[17]

The Vatican, by contrast, has in its own eyes the virtue of ministry to *all* peoples, with their varied and even conflicting needs. Its caution is the reflex of accountability. One of the many merits of its style is that it recognizes the limits of church power. It does what can be done, without squandering the Vatican's credibility in hopeless crusades. The papal office still has symbolic power, but that could erode if it were committed too often to lost causes. Better to encourage lay people, their consciences enlightened by the Church's teaching, to act in specific areas of their competence. The Vatican is even reluctant to see local churches or dioceses act politically, even though, or more likely because, their image is often interventionist. John Paul's speeches regularly argue against direct political participation by the clergy; notice, for example, his removal of Father Robert Drinan from the United States Congress, a move consistent with his general policy of sharpening the demarcation between Church and world. The social and political arena should be left to the laity. Priests and nuns should stick to a purely spiritual role and have "no intention of political interference, nor of participation in the working out of temporal affairs." Justice can only be a secondary concern for priests, whose "main service is that of aiding souls to discover the Father. . . ."[18]

The Vatican's critics suspect that secret diplomacy is not nearly as effective as its apologists claim. The Church does not usually have that kind of power any more. Attempts to exercise it involve the Church with the interest of existing power structures and severely compromise its Christian witness. Worse yet there are darker suspicions that in some countries where the churches have been in conflict with the government on issues of social justice the Vatican's secret diplomacy has in fact abandoned the protesting Christians for the sake of its longer term position in that country. "Recognition" becomes more important than speaking out on human rights. The institution's interests take priority over the care of individuals, who may then have only the choice of submission to evil or martyrdom.

Whether or not this last serious charge has any truth in it, the secretive Vatican style can hardly be popular in the World Council. And when that restraint is imposed on organizations like Justice and Peace and Sodepax, their effective cooperation with the World Council fades away, whatever those who serve them might wish. They are reduced to listening, studying, and making proposals, but not to action with their own programs, lest they affect the prophet's mantle and discomfit their priestly superiors. That reinforces the conviction in Geneva that little prophetic Christian action is likely to come from Rome.

Once again some caveats are in order. The Holy See can speak out when it wants to: Examples that come readily to mind include Uganda under Idi Amin, the rights of Palestinians, religious liberty in Albania, the Argentina-Chile border dispute, condemnation of Franco's execution of terrorists, direct public intervention in Italian politics over divorce and abortion referenda, and criticism of the Israeli bombing of Iraq's nuclear reactor. The record is dotted not only with these specific references but also with some oddly indirect ones that become direct and clear because of the context of the reference, e.g., "that great nation . . . whose extraordinary human richness is famous" for Russia, in a speech defending the right to dissent; or an attack on violence as plain murder in a speech delivered in Ireland; or a reference to human rights in a speech in the Philippines with President Ferdinand E. Marcos present; or references to violations of international law that seemed to the press at least to refer to Iran's seizure of American hostages (John Paul also privately asked Ayatollah Ruhollah Khomeini directly, but in vain, to free them); or another similar reference that seemed to criticize the Soviet Union's invasion of Afghanistan.[19]

For its part the World Council knows the merits of keeping quiet when the occasion warrants. The surprisingly effective mediation in the Sudanese civil war is a case in point; and inevitably there is a lot of silent work that never comes to public documentation, a necessary public modesty. Pastoral, priestly considerations can overrule prophetic ones, and working through regional or national councils of churches may often be more effective than speaking directly in the WCC's own name—and also more comfortable for the member churches, some of which are occasionally uneasy about the World Council's selection of issues and the number of its statements.

Yet despite these caveats the general differences of method between the two are real, the World Council prefering the direct, plain statement, the Holy See the indirect one, crafted with enough oblique wording to allow some face-saving. The reaction to the assassination of Archbishop Oscar Romero of El Salvador is a textbook case of the differences. The pope's telegram of pain called on the people of the country to eschew violence and vengeance, but made no reference to the political context that caused the murder, even though Romero himself had asked President Carter not to send further arms to the Salvadoran government forces. The World Council, on the other hand, in its condemnation of the assassination, made explicit reference to the political struggle, and quoted approvingly a statement from the United States National Council of Churches critical of American arms shipments to El Salvador. Subsequently John Paul condemned the violence of both guerrillas and armed forces, and called for a halt to the influx of arms. But in these, and in similar remarks about Guatemala, he still remains evenhanded and highly generalized, considerably less specific than the World Council, which continues to denounce American aid to the regime. The pope is even less specific than the United States Catholic Conference, which also openly opposes the Reagan administration on arms shipments.[20]

The Polish martial law crisis has put a considerable strain on the traditional Vatican style. One can almost watch John Paul struggling to keep his public remarks on the usual level of abstraction, but gradually yielding to greater and greater specificity, first departing from his prepared texts to voice his exasperation with the Polish and Russian governments in an informal way, then finally coming to direct, explicit, formal criticism of the restraints imposed on the labor union Solidarity and on the Polish people in general—and all the while visibly consulting with the church in Poland as it seeks to deal with the new situation.[21] Whether this development signals a change in Vatican style remains to be seen. But one may guess that it does not, that we have in this instance a pope sorely tried by national loyalties and operating in an atypical manner on this one issue, undoubtedly in the process making the curial staff nervous. In the long run there is more at issue here than the personality of a particular pontiff, and a methodological convergence with the WCC is still unlikely. The different ways of dealing with the world's troubles are built into the two organizations, are characteristic of their nature, and are likely to remain, as they are now, a source of considerable tension and even anger between them.

Notes

1. *Uppsala Report*, p. 493.
2. Ibid., p. 221.
3. See the comments of the structure study committee, *Minutes, Central Committee*, 1971, p. 159, and the mandate of Unit 1 (Faith and Witness), ibid., p. 162; *Minutes, Central Committee*, 1979, p. 16.
4. *Minutes, Central Committee*, 1969, p. 130, a perennial request; see also *Minutes, Central Committee*, 1976, p. 98.
5. And so Thomas defended it at Nairobi, *Nairobi Report*, p. 237.
6. *Humanae Vitae* 4.
7. For example, see *Minutes, Central Committee*, 1979, p. 17, mixed reactions to the "Just, Participatory, and Sustainable Society" study.
8. *Octogesima Adveniens* 4, 25, 26, 27, 28, 31, 35, 42, 45, 49, 50.
9. *Minutes, Central Committee*, 1972, pp. 46–47, 169–73; *Minutes, Central Committee*, 1974, pp. 31–32; *Nairobi Report*, pp. 81–82.
10. E.g., John Paul II, address to the Third General Assembly of Latin American bishops at Puebla, Mexico, 28 January 1979, III 2, 3; John Paul II,

address to nuns in Mexico City, 27 January 1979, *Origins* 8:547; *Catechesi Tradendae* 52.

11. *Octogesima Adveniens* 26, 32–34; Paul VI, address to diplomats accredited to the Holy See, *Origins* 7:501–2; John Paul II, address to the Organization of American States, Washington, 6 October 1979, *Origins* 9:304; John Paul II, address to students at the University of Kinshasa, 4 May 1980, *Origins* 10:26; John Paul II, speech to diplomats at Nairobi, 6 May 1980, ibid., p. 31; John Paul II, address at St. Denis, Paris, 31 May 1980, ibid., p. 58; John Paul II to German and Italian scholars, Rome, 12 November 1981, *Origins* 11:379; John Paul II, World Day of Peace message, 21 December 1981, ibid., p. 474.

12. *Evangelii Nuntiandi* 27, 28; John Paul II, address at Puebla, 28 January 1979, 14, 8, III 2, 3, 6 (in part quoting John Paul I and *Evangelii Nuntiandi*); *Redemptor Hominis* 13; John Paul II, homily in Nairobi, 7 May 1980, *Origins* 10:27; John Paul II in Rio de Janeiro, 2 July 1980, ibid., p. 124.

13. John Paul II, letter to all priests, 9 April 1979, *Origins* 8:696–704; John Paul II, address to Polish government officials, 2 June 1979, *Origins* 9:53; John Paul II, speech at the Shrine of the Immaculate Conception, Washington, 7 October 1979, ibid., pp. 284, 286 (the speech that drew the immediate and shocking public rejoinder from Sr. Theresa Kane of the Leadership Conference of Women Religious, calling for women's ordination); John Paul II, homily to members of the International Union of Superiors General, 14 November 1979, ibid., p. 410; John Paul II, speech to Zairean priests, 4 May 1980, *Origins* 10:11; John Paul II, speech to Brazilian bishops, Fortaleza, 10 July 1980, ibid., p. 136; John Paul II, address at ordination of priests, Rio de Janeiro, 2 July 1980, ibid., pp. 142–44; letter to dioceses and religious communities from the Vatican Congregation for the Doctrine of the Faith, 1980, ibid., pp. 335–36; John Paul II to Filipino priests, Manila, 17 February 1981, ibid., p. 589; John Paul II, radio message from Manila to Asian peoples, 21 February 1981, ibid., pp. 612–13; John Paul II, message to Chinese Christians, from Manila, 18 February 1981, ibid., p. 614.

14. "Justice in the World" (1971 synod of bishops), in Gremillion, ed., pp. 520–21; "Evangelization of the Modern World" (1974 Synod of Bishops), ibid., p. 597; *Evangelii Nuntiandi* 27–35; John Paul II in a general audience, 21 February 1979, *Origins* 8:600–601; *Laborem Exercens* 27, quoting *Gaudium et Spes* in part.

15. *Nairobi Report,* pp. 45, 63, 136, 233–35, 238–39; *Minutes, Central Committee,* 1979, pp. 16, 42–43; *Ecumenical Review* 30:278–80; *Ecumenical Review* 32:385.

16. John Paul II, World Day of Peace Message, 18 December 1979, *Origins* 9:459. Cf. his defense of these methods in his annual address to cardinals and curia, 22 December 1980, *Origins* 10:490–94.

17. *Minutes, Central Committee,* 1969, p. 142.

18. John Paul II, speech in Sistine Chapel, 17 October 1978, *Origins* 8:293; John Paul II, address to diplomats accredited to the Holy See, 20 October 1978, ibid., pp. 310–11; John Paul II, address to nuns in Mexico City, 27 January 1979, ibid., p. 547; John Paul II, address to priests, Mexico City, 27 January 1979, ibid., pp. 548–49; John Paul II, address to priests, Kinshasa, Zaire, 4 May 1980, *Origins* 10:11; John Paul II, homily in Nairobi, 7 May 1980, ibid., p. 27; John Paul II, address to Brazilian bishops, Fortaleza, 10 July 1980, ibid., p. 135; John Paul II, address at ordination of priests, Rio de Janeiro, 2 July 1980, ibid., pp. 142–44. Cf. directive from the Vatican Congregation for Religious and Secular Institutes, January 1981, ibid., p. 535; "Justice in the World," Gremillion, ed., p. 521; John Paul II, address to Nigerian priests and seminarians, Enugu, 13 February 1982, *Origins* 11:593; John Paul II, address to Jesuits, Rome, 27 February 1982, ibid., p. 627; statement from the Vatican's Clergy Congregation, confirmed by the pope, 8 March 1982, ibid., pp. 645, 647. Some directives against priests in politics may be aimed at local situations and catch others in other countries who are not the primary targets. The policy is, nevertheless, meant to be for the whole Church, universally applied.

19. Paul VI, World Day of Peace Message, January 1978, *Origins* 7:457; Paul VI, speech at Castelgondolfo, 16 July 1978, *Origins* 8:143–44; John Paul I, ibid., p. 272; John Paul II, address to the United Nations General Assembly, 2 October 1979, *Origins* 9:261; John Paul II, speech at Drogheda, Ireland, 29 September 1979, ibid., pp. 272–75; John Paul II, address to youth at Galway, Ireland, 30 September 1979, ibid., p. 276; John Paul II, speech to cardinals, 22 December 1979, ibid., p. 500; John Paul II, address to diplomats accredited to the Holy See, 14 January 1980, ibid., p. 571; John Paul II, speech to diplomats, Nairobi, 6 May 1980, *Origins* 10:31; John Paul II, speech to Philippine people, 17 February 1981, ibid., p. 591; John Paul II, public remarks on the Italian abortion referendum, *Origins* 11:2; statement of the Vatican delegate, Msgr. Mario Peressin, to the International Atomic Energy Agency, Vienna, 22 September 1981, ibid., p. 266.

20. Telegram of John Paul II, *Origins* 9:669; WCC message from Philip Potter, general secretary, 28 March 1980, *Ecumenical Review* 32:324; WCC Central Committee, 1980, in ibid., p. 431; Executive Committee, February 1981, in *Ecumenical Review* 33:189; John Paul II, remarks in Rome, 28 February 1982, *Origins* 11:615, 617; John Paul II, remarks in Rome, 7 March 1982, ibid., p. 630.

21. John Paul II, *Origins* 11:246; John Paul II, ibid., p. 518; John Paul II, address to diplomats accredited to the Vatican, 16 January 1982, ibid., pp. 561–62.

The Problem of
Poverty and the Poor
in Catholic Social Teaching:
A Marxist Perspective

József Lukács

This article originally appeared in *Concilium*, v. 104.

Misery and poverty are an ineradicable human condition neither for Marxists nor for Christians. Christianity appeared in an age when this was already discernible on a world-historical level, but when the actual social prerequisites for the eradication of poverty were not available. Marxism, on the other hand, entered history in an age when the objective premises for a solution were already conceived and when conscientization about this situation, and at the same time the theoretical critique and practical opposition to the social structures which ensured the continued symbiosis of poverty producing riches and riches maintaining poverty, had become practicable.

In spite of unrelenting theoretical differences the possibilities of perceptibly stronger collaboration between Christians and Communists in many countries are favoured by, among other factors, the fact that both are permeated by a sense of responsibility for the future of our human world. The principle 'nil humanum a me alienum puto' was the motto of the same Karl Marx who together with Engels wrote in the *Communist Manifesto* about that future, and said that the old form of civil society with its classes and class antagonisms was being replaced by a form of association in which the free development of each is the condition for the free development of all. Admittedly the authors of the pastoral constitution on the Church in the modern world at Vatican II were motivated quite differently when they conceived the preamble of that important document, and remarked especially that there was nothing truly human that did not find an echo in the hearts of Christ's disciples; they set this affirmation in a context in which this human content was especially associated with the fate of the poor and repressed of all kinds.

It is clear that we are faced with a parallel set of problems leading to unavoidable dialogue.

I

It is impossible to agree with historians who declare that in the ancient East, but especially in the world of the Greek *polis,* the question of the relationship between riches and poverty and the causes of their existence, had not been raised in value terms. Yet in many books of the Old Testament we meet with an insistence not only on a religious but a social transformation which was similarly present, with, that is, the same intensity, in the Greek world only in exceptional cases. The punishment of the rich and powerful is just as strongly desired and treated as an imminent event in the human world as the liberation of the poor and oppressed.

The apocalyptic radicalism of the early Church tried to introduce this consideration into religion in the imagery of the last judgment. Engels, in his study of the early history of Christianity, said that the Book of Revelation showed that Christianity was originally also the religion of the poor and those without the law, and of the nations subjugated or routed by Rome; this opinion can hardly be refuted. Christianity, according to Engels, proclaimed an imminent liberation from the bonds of serfdom and need, and offered the feeling of being involved in a struggle with an entire world and being able to come out victorious. Accordingly there was no question as yet of a religion of love, and there was no mention of loving our enemies. John openly rejoices in revenge taken on the persecutors of the Christians.

The provisional halt to the crisis of the Roman Empire and the failure of the Jewish revolt show that radicalism was to fade. The Christian community was at a crossroads: either it was faced with certain destruction, or it had—if not to approve—certainly to acknowledge existing social conditions, certainly at first in practice and later also in theory. The

Gospels and the Pauline letters show that Christianity certainly retained the Stoic notion of equality but changed it into equality in God—in guilt and redemption. Here riches are primarily an obstacle in the way of salvation, opposed to poverty which may be imbued with evil but essentially (that is, both as lack of worldly goods and as consciousness of our human weakness) represents a more definite readiness and possibility of grace.

But it would be wrong not to acknowledge that Christianity posited the idea of equality as a goal, as equality of the faithful within a Church. In Alfred Weber's apposite words the Church became the 'anti-form' of a social structure based on riches and poverty: it became in fact a kind of 'anti-polis' after the dissolution of the *polis,* where at least the *religious* equality of the minority of the redeemed could be realized.

In a world where no real social alternative could be discerned to the simultaneous existence of poverty and riches, the Church had only two possibilities: either it could turn its back on the 'evil' world, or it had to open up completely to the world, including the ruling classes; in that way a mission became possible and legal, and the idea of a Church active in the world yet retaining its supernatural commission could be grounded both theologically and Christologically. This meant, however, a definite break with important aspects of the ideological world of early Christianity.

After quarrels and deviations, the Church took the second way, which of course meant that soon, in economics, politics and culture, it used the means and methods of the ruling classes to increase its influence. The 'catholic' notion of universality became 'Roman'. It became a community which, in addition to a feudal character, displayed several characteristics of the Roman Empire.

The judgment on poverty in the New Testament, however, was clearly contrary to the practice of the age, and always supported the protest of plebians and burghers against medieval attempts at an integrated Christian tradition. There is a continuous chain of criticism of the Church which identifies itself with the world of the poor, from the Pataria through the Cathars and Waldensians right up to Joachism; it is always strengthened by hope of a change of things as they were. The other direction of criticism was represented by the religious orders; these were for the most part mendicant orders which accepted the existing framework, but within it, through ascetic emphases in personal life, expressed their inward commitment to the Saviour who identified with the cause of the poor, and to the poor themselves.

II

According to Max Weber, Protestantism made asceticism 'this-worldly', by removing its connection with the orders. The rich Church was banished, but only to set against it the riches of the bourgeois individual which relied on thrift, the judicious application of capital, and soon the exploitation of the industrial proletariat. The Church was separated from the state and faith was partitioned off from public activity; the only consequence of this was, however, that instead of the *caritas* of medieval institutions, doing good became an *individual* moral duty, replacing bodies working to alleviate misery and suffering.

Of course the bourgeois Reformation included the protest of its plebeian opponents who—if we are to go by the example of Thomas Münzer, the Anabaptist commune in Münster or the Levellers—would not acknowledge the justice of a democratism organized by and along church lines, the emphasis on a subjective instead of a decreed dogmatic faith, or the rôle of divine providence in salvation.

But this egalitarianism went against the profit-principle of capitalist production. It is hardly by chance that in almost all *developed* capitalist countries, the bourgeois-Protestant form of Christianity became the dominant religious expression of the permanence and self-assurance of the bourgeois order of civil society.

It was not by chance on the other hand that Catholicism, which after the Council of Trent opposed not only the Reformation but the main bourgeois aspirations, retained its power in the semi-feudal countries of central and southern Europe. In that way it was able to preserve, together with the hierarchical structure of the Church, its specific material means for the production of capital.

As a very apt judgment of J. Levada's puts it, bourgeois evolution absorbed the Christian notion of equality, and was able to do so because in the constitution of the bourgeois rights of man, a formal, abstract equality was the actual realization of the two modes of equality before the law and the equality of the market. In the nineteenth and twentieth centuries, social struggles have been and are being conducted in which *class equality* itself and the interconnection of poverty and riches are called in question. It is probably not accidental that in the statements on social problems made by the leading (i.e. most retrograde) church circles there was hardly any mention of the poverty problem until at the end of the nineteenth century the socialist working-class movement went beyond mere economic demands to state its historic aims.

The encyclical *Rerum novarum* and subsequent social encyclicals are fruits on the one hand of the new socio-political situation of the Catholic Church, and on the other of the advancing crisis of bourgeois society and spreading secularization which brought about a lack of interest in religion and the growing atheism of the have-nots, the 'poor'. Perhaps it is not too fanciful to say that the great social changes that took place in and as a result of the October revolution had to happen, for the second Vatican Council to be stirred into declaring that the problem of poverty was not only a conciliar problem but more precisely *the* question itself, when it said that the scandal should be removed of a few nations whose citizens are the majority of those rejoicing in the name Christian, whereas others do not have enough to live on and suffer from hunger, sickness and misery of all kinds. For the first time in human history— the Council declared—the nations were convinced that the advantages of civilization could and must be shared by all mankind.

The diagnosis is accurate, though some points are arguable.

The Church seems to be faced with a double task. On the one hand it is supposed to create the Church of the poor, *ad intra;* on the other, it must contribute, *ad extra,* to the removal of the scandal of poverty. It is obvious too that the Church can hardly encourage the removal of poverty without losing its economic privileges.

The real problem is what solution the Catholic Church is putting forward.

III

To answer this particular question adequately we need a lot of time. A powerful multinational organization like the Catholic Church has to take into consideration extremely diverse social presuppositions in the modern world, which means that its top bodies can only issue somewhat abstract directives.

Expositions of the poverty-riches antagonism are by no means missing from literature of Christian inspiration. In *Capital* Marx quotes the Venetian monk Ortes, who, he says, was one of the great economists of the eighteenth century, and who said that an abundance of goods always meant a lack of them for others. Ortes had discovered the core of the problem, and although the same question was put the other way around in some encyclicals, inasmuch as the simultaneous existence of poverty and riches, and of labour and capital, was derived from natural law, the constitution of Vatican II addresses with sympathy all those who wish to get rid of these shocking contrasts.

The problem of poverty and riches (that is, the way in which goods are distributed) indicates something else: distribution is a mere result of the mode of *production* which produces riches and poverty at the same time. A true critique of impoverishment is criticism of the conditions which produce impoverishment: criticism of the mechanisms which reproduce 'excess' as well as the needy, and freeze this state of things.

Christian social teaching stresses continually that *actio caritativa* should be converted into organized social action, into *actio socialis,* and severely condemns the greed-for-profit of liberal capitalism and the exploitation which springs from it. No small number of theological works warn against any sanctioning of material poverty; the Church approves of a social policy which supports economically disadvantaged individuals and nations.

Up to a point, the promotion of socio-political institutions (the support of those unable to work, invalids, the sick, widows, orphans and the aged, and so on), that is, the protection of social stability, also works to the advantage of modern monopoly capitalism. In most countries big firms try energetically to put the greater part of the burden on the shoulders of the workers themselves. That shows the class content of this form of social policy: the mere emphasis on the imperative demand for justice and love (*iustitia* and *caritas*) does not mean that any view has been expressed of contradictory social interpretations of those commandments.

One of the main sources of impoverishment until recently was unemployment—both in the developed capitalist and in the developing countries. And unemployment is something that cannot be compensated by a system of unemployment benefit or social security, however well it functions. This kind of poverty, which is obviously extremely destructive not only economically but socially, morally and socio-psychologically, is not only a result of the monopoly-capitalist mode of production but its existential condition. As Marx says, in periods of stagnation and medium prosperity this reserve army weighs on the active work force and controls its demands during periods of over-production. Attempts to remove the weight of unemployment collide at a certain point with the interests of the social order itself. The question of how ownership might favour the eradication of poverty is still open.

On the international scene, the eastern European countries, including my own country, are usually counted among the developed nations or, more precisely, the medium developed nations. However, such statistical comparisons often ignore that these countries (including Czechoslovakia and the German Democratic Republic) were among the poor countries before their transition to socialism (not without reason was Hungary known as a nation of three million beggars, and tuberculosis called 'morbus hungaricus'), and that their rise to the status of developed nation, the struggle against poverty, the complete absence of unemployment, the provision of social security, and the far from perfect yet guaranteed rise in the standard of living, are inseparable from the socialist solution to the problem of property. Therefore these countries are models of development which are worth consideration by all interested in the fight against poverty, precisely because of the extremely negative initial conditions.

Gaudium et spes acknowledges the fact that the fundamental law of human perfection, and therefore of world transformation, is the new commandment of love. But the principle of justice determines the way in which conditions are formed and perceived, including the conditions of the ownership of property. 'Therefore men must not only treat the external things that they possess duly as their personal property, but must see them as common property in the sense that those things can be of use not to them alone but to others too. In addition, all men have the right to a share of the goods of the earth which is adequate for them and their families. That was the opinion of the fathers and teachers of the Church who say that it is our duty to support the poor and not only from our surplus. Anyone, however, who finds himself in extreme need has the right to acquire what is necessary for himself from the riches of others' (*Gaudium et spes*).

What counts as excess depends on the age, the social level and individual claims and needs. Apparently the constitution thinks it is justifiable to take as is necessary from others' property only in a state of necessity. But surely mankind is in such a condition when two out of three people are needy, hungry or starving.

Conciliar constitutions and subsequent papal pronouncements do not *in principle* exclude the expropriation of goods in certain cases. Nevertheless, they still see private property as the most essential material prerequisite for the self-realization of the individual, and as the main spur to tasks and duties, and therefore as a characteristic of civic freedom.

Private property should be held in accordance with the common good. The encyclical *Populorum progressio* of Paul VI emphasizes that the right to private property is not unconditional and unrestricted for anyone, and that in certain circumstances the expropriation of the means of production could be a necessary course.

This was not the first time that an emphasis was put on the social aspect of private property in Catholic social teaching. But a statement of the possibilities of expropriation is certainly something new: an acknowledgment of the signs of the times. But the question is difficult to pursue beyond the stage of theory; what are the limits within which private property still helps the individual to be more fully himself?

Of course, for Marxists the possession of consumer goods to satisfy individual needs is the *conditio sine qua non* of self-realization. Personal property is however not the same as *private* property; its nature is to contradict the monopolist character of private property which excludes the property of others; it is not identical with the private ownership of the *means of production*. In this regard we have to ask if property is justified when it is obtained by the work of others, and not by one's own labour; when, that is, it is a means of exploitation. Does it guarantee the development of the personality in circumstances in which big, impersonal monopolies control the major sector of the capitalist economy; where, under pressure of circumstances, the individual forfeits not only his economic basis but the possibility of personal development?

The encyclical *Populorum progressio* warns in such cases against any action which might harm basic human rights and freedoms, and would seem in so doing to attribute to socialist collectivism and the planned economy a social effect that is much more attributable to the system of private property; to the system, that is, that restricts the individual excessively, and allows initiatives which, as the practice of several countries shows, limit rather than support freedom.

However complicated and difficult it is to teach men in association to take responsible and meaningful charge of the expropriated means of production and social potential, and to develop them in accordance with human needs, this is the only way in which we can find a solution.

IV

But the Christian criterion of poverty is not restricted to a stringency of material goods. Even the pastoral constitution requires the Christian to conduct himself privately and socially according to the Sermon on the Mount, but especially in the spirit of the blessedness of poverty. As Lercaro said at the Council, the Church has first to recognize that it is culturally poor.

Of course there are several interpretations of the *content* of the evangelical notion of poverty, of poverty in the Spirit. For nonbelievers, however, the common, rational core of these interpretations is that it would be wrong to ignore the questions of the standard of living and mass consumption, and to limit poverty to the possession of material goods.

Congar sees the meaning of poverty as its stimulus to encounter with God, although he adds that in a certain sense the love of God can be fully realized only in love of our neighbour. Both Congar and Metz examine the meaning of poverty (especially the meaning of poverty in the Spirit) in terms of Jesus's example, and both see the profound meaning of poverty as descent to the condition of the lowest, and taking uncomplainingly on oneself all the consequences of guilt, poverty and slavery, suffering and death by crucifixion, and even descent into hell, without any desire for revenge. This poverty is also an inborn characteristic of human existence: 'Every true human encounter occurs in the spirit of poverty'; in these encounters we surrender a thousand other possibilities—whereas we preserve and express our own possibilities—, we acknowledge our finiteness, until finally our destiny is fulfilled in death: 'Spiritual poverty is fulfilled in obedient endurance of this profound impotence in which one no longer possesses anything but sacrifice itself, and even that only in the experience of complete loss of power'.[1]

The authentic content of spiritual poverty is, in this perspective, awareness of our finiteness, restriction and death. A Marxist feels it incumbent upon him to remark that Christian theology presents certain far from supra-historical characteristics, which were also apparent in Christ's life, as an essential and unavoidable aspect of human destiny in this world. The death of the individual is admittedly an unavoidable necessity, yet it remains the death of the *human being,* who *acts* in full consciousness of it. Even religious belief in an infinite soul is not an expression of profound human impotence in regard to death; it includes at least just as much longing and compulsion to surmount that barrier. Impotence is not an attribute of our human existence; on the contrary, it is work, sensuous and objective activity, which continually reshapes nature, the human condition, and the human countenance; and it is in work that man appears a social being—*zoön politikon.*

Spiritual poverty, the feeling of impotence and of essential limitation are for the Marxist historical circumstances in which the *results* of human behaviour rule man as alien powers, but circumstances which can be overcome with means provided by that very development.[2]

Some Catholic theologians see this essential restriction as a starting-point (determined by original sin),[3] and see the love testified to by Christ as realizable *only within the limits of these circumstances.* The real question of the age is: Is not the Christian bound by the commandment of love to depart theoretically and in practice from circumstances which render impossible the extension of the dimensions of human solidarity: that is, of love?[4]

Though we agree with Catholics that poverty is not only a question of economic circumstances but so to speak *also of human behaviour,* and as such to be treated as social relations, we do not look on this poverty-conditioned behaviour as ineluctable fate. Marxism, as the vanguard of the revolutionary advance of the proletariat, strives to elevate the *proletariat as such* with the means offered by an alienated world—for we have no others—in a long historical process; it struggles not against the finiteness of the human individual, but against the consciousness of his *essential* restriction, *alienation* itself. Put another way, this kind of 'poverty' is not only eliminated by socialism, but realized at a higher level, inasmuch as it is countered not by the ideal of the infinity of material goods, but—on the basis of the satisfaction of material and cultural needs—the *riches of the human individual.*

'Such is the old view', writes Marx in the *Grundrisse,* 'by which man in a restricted national, religious and political mold, also appears constantly as the aim of production. This notion appears to have the advantage over the modern world where production seems to be the aim of man and riches the aim of production. But in fact, once we forget its limited bourgeois form, what is riches but that universality of needs, capabilities, satisfactions, productive forces and so on, of individuals, produced in the process of universal exchange? The full development of human control of the natural forces, both of Nature and of his own nature? The absolute realization of his creative abilities, without any presupposition other than previous historical developments, which make this totality of development, of, that is, the development of all human powers as such, measured by no *given* yardstick, an end in itself? Where he does not reproduce himself in one aspect but in his totality? Where he does not seek to remain anything that has come to be, but is in the absolute movement of becoming . . .?'[5]

Christianity was a protest against the restricted self-satisfaction of the ancient world, and can also protest against the stultification of the bourgeois world. It does *not* see the true goal of man as the possession of goods, as riches. But if Christians want to avoid extending poverty—even unwittingly—by extolling it and thus allowing it an alibi, then they must—*ceterum censeo*—investigate the actual social conditions which at this point in time encourage the development of the riches of the personality.

'In this way we all support world peace . . .' 'All men and all nations have to act in awareness of their responsibility', says *Populorum progressio.* Marxists are prepared, as they testify in the final declarations of the conferences of Communist Parties in Karlovy Vary (Karlsbad), Moscow and (East) Berlin, to advance together with those of different views along the road of discussion and resolution of problems which the forces which desire the progress of the nations could not solve (or could solve only with difficulty) without one another's aid.

Marxists and Christians who advance along that road cannot demand that one or the other should surrender their understanding of the world. But they are entitled to expect of one another that their conduct should be orientated to the interests of those millions of human beings who are denied a proper standard of living and free human development. That is also true of dialogue on poverty.

Translated by J. Maxwell

Notes

1. J.-B. Metz, *Armut im Geiste* (Munich, 1962).
2. Cf. Marx, *Economic and Philosophical Manuscripts of 1844.*
3. I am well aware that this viewpoint is much discussed at present, as was shown in discussion of the Council.
4. Dom Helder Camara's statement in this regard (quoted by Oriana Fallaci) is noteworthy: 'We clergy are responsible for the fatalism always shown by the poor in the resignation with which they acknowledged their poverty and the backwardness of the underdeveloped nations. Here Marxists show their perception in seeing religion as an alienated and alienating force, as—in other words—the opium of the people.'
5. Marx, 'Grundrisse der Kritik der politischen Ökonomie' (draft) in: Karl Marx and Friedrich Engels, *Werke,* vol. 46, pp. 378–88.

From Catholic "Social Doctrine" to the "Kingdom of Christ on Earth"

James V. Schall

This article originally appeared in *Communio*, 1976.

> Venerable brothers and beloved sons, beginning with that marvellous letter of Leo, we have thus far considered with you the varied and serious issues which pertain to the social conditions of our times. From them, we have drawn norms and teachings, upon which we especially exhort you not merely to meditate deeply, but also to do what you can to put them into effect. If each one of you does his best courageously, it will necessarily help in no small measure to establish the Kingdom of Christ on earth. . . . And this we shall someday leave to go to that heavenly beatitude, for which we were made by God, and which we ask for with most ardent prayers.
>
> John XXIII, *Mater et Magistra,* #261

The notion that a specifically Catholic "social doctrine" contains a definite set of principles, practices, and policies, situated somewhere between Marxism and classical liberalism, was at one time rather widely accepted and even acted upon.[1] Both a nineteenth and a twentieth century version of this assumption existed. The nineteenth century—which lasted from the French Revolution to World War I—concentrated upon the political question of the forms of government, the nature and origin of civil power. Among Catholics, moreover, there was a liberal and a conservative approach to this issue. Indeed, it might be argued that the nineteenth century largely witnessed the defeat of the conservative view so that the popular institutions of the democratic state—even though on the continent of Europe these were espoused mainly by freemasons, deists, anti-clericals, and agnostics—were gradually recognized, from the time the future Leo XIII was nuncio in Belgium to Lammenais to the German Center Party, to be the best guarantee for religious objectives in the modern world.

To be sure, it took perhaps another half century or so, until the Christmas Message of 1944 of Pius XII and *Pacem in Terris* of John XXIII, for this understanding of democracy to be accepted as the best form of government as such. This involved, of course, a rediscovery of the more abiding values of the conservative tradition, usually through the instrumentality of the Anglo-Saxon mentality, along with an exhaustion of the secular ideologies of the nineteenth century.[2] Thus, while not denying the older Christian belief that Christianity was indifferent to all political forms of government as such provided only that they recognized some minimal human rights and religious freedoms, there nevertheless came to be, as best exemplified in *Pacem in Terris* and *Gaudium et Spes,* a kind of Christian descriptive response to the classical problem of the best form of government and the good life. In its central lines, this Christian reflection always clearly maintained that the best form of government for men in this world was not likewise the answer to the ultimate happiness of men as such.

The twentieth century was more a concentration on social and economic problems so that the political question of the forms and institutions of the "modern state," whose theoretical foundation went back to Machiavelli's declaration of its absolute autonomy, became subordinate to the success of modern economy and technology in improving the lot of the poor and the working class. The intervening totalitarian experience during the 1920's and 1930's (*Mit Brennender Sorge, Divini Redemptoris, Non Abbiamo Bisogno*) became the prime agency in effecting a reconciliation between the modern state and religious values since it became clear, for a time at least, that the modern state had to accept some limits to its own omnicompetence. But more and more, the major issue seemed to lie not so much in political theory but in economic performance. Soon it was realized that legal democratic forms did not necessarily guarantee public well-being or even liberty. This realization began to dawn on the world after 1929; it became self-evident after World War II.

For this reason, *Rerum Novarum* (1891), although it came some fifty years after the Communist Manifesto, has, nevertheless, always been looked upon by Catholics as a prophetic, forward-looking document, whereas Leo's politically oriented encyclicals were soon forgotten or at least ignored. Thus, the modern national state, for all its theoretical difficulties, came to be regarded by Catholics not only as a vehicle of political progress within which specifically religious rights were allowed to be exercised but also as the primary instrumentality for achieving a sufficient level of well-being now seen as necessary for the common man to practice virtue and decency—an idea Leo already had found in Aquinas. The "condition of the working class" with its evocation of Christianity's ancient concern for the poor and the weak came to be seen as the major public religious-civil problem of modern times. In fact, the decline of religious practice was often reduced to precisely this neglect of economic welfare. Undoubtedly what the evolution of this problem in the twentieth century has proved is that the political-economic level of this problem cannot be solved by the value-free social sciences upon which the century started but must itself look again to religious and ethical values. [3]

The passage from Leo XIII to *Quadragesimo Anno* to *Mater et Magistra* and *Populorum Progressio* is fascinating and consists in an ever-growing realization of the greater dimensions of the problem, from the structure of the national-state to a world political-economic order that could assist in providing well-being and dignity for all men during their earthly sojourn. The very breadth of this newer approach forced a definite confrontation with the problem of diverse religions and cultures. The question of the "unity of mankind" became much more problematic and profound than when first treated in Pius XII's first encyclical in 1939. The ethical-religious-philosophical basis upon which this whole theory was built and argued came to be that of the dignity and value of the human person which was felt, at least up until the controversy over population, to be a foundation upon which all men could agree. [4] From this point of view, Catholic social thought has undoubtedly tended to downplay the national-state in recent years in search of some kind of larger authority which, at the same time, could be seen as political, rational, and effective. [5]

The lack of such authority, moreover, has created not a little tension both because its lack is one of the major causes of ideology which substitutes for real human development and because the national state is forced to assume responsibilities which it is incapable of assuming. *Octogesima Adveniens* (1971) is without doubt a milestone in Catholic thinking since it questions so severely many of its own previous solutions—its perceptive critique of labor unions is a case in point—and the ideological and utopistic proposals for the betterment of mankind. In retrospect, too, it is interesting to note the abiding refusal of Catholic social thought to entertain balance of power theories or imperial-paternal notions in place of a valid, operative world government and economy guaranteeing both political participation and economic adequacy if not abundance. In this connection, the address of Paul VI to the United Nations (4 October 1965) remains something of a monumental classic.

Up until the time of John XXIII, it was more or less accepted that Christians had a specific program which, in contrast to other Marxist, liberal, fascist, conservative, or nationalistic solutions, could best succeed in achieving this eventual end of large-scale well-being and civil peace which yet respected the cultural diversity of mankind. Christians, it could not be denied, had been stung by Marx's quotable aphorism—religion is the opium of the people—and wished to prove that they could do a better job in the world than anyone else—or at least as good a one. Especially before Pius XII and World War II, this Christian contribution was generally conceived to be operative within the national state. More recently, however, especially in Europe and Latin America, it has become rather a commonplace to hold that there is no longer nor can there any longer be such a thing as definitive Catholic "social doctrine," but only a "pluralism" of choices among which Christians—now considering themselves after the famous decree of Vatican II to be free and mature in their consciences to vote and act responsibly in the modern democratic state, so brilliantly delineated in *Pacem in Terris*—are quite at liberty to choose the political and economic line they think best seems to serve their particular situations in a humanly fitting manner. This often entails, furthermore, as in the case of the Italian divorce referendum (May, 1974), a freedom to vote against the explicit advice of the local hierarchy, even against the advice of the papacy.[6] Perhaps the attitude of the French hierarchy during the late presidential campaign is even more significant, for it refused to give any official advice even when it was quite possible for a socialist-communist government to win the election.[7]

In practice, then, this change of attitude means that Catholics are no longer adhering to Christian Democratic type parties or Christian labor unions—the two responses in the public order to the nineteenth and twentieth century problems—but are themselves joining in large numbers the socialist and Marxist parties and unions or attempting to reinterpret the Christian oriented organizations in this direction.[8] The reflection of Jean-Marie Domenach in this regard is instructive:

> The great part of practicing Catholics voted regularly for the right. Then in 1972, only 65% of them voted for a majority which was more or less of the right. But now there is an ever more surprising figure: in 1973, 64% of the priests under forty said that they voted for the left. When one listens to the preaching of young priests, or when one participates in a conference of bishops, one has the impression that the principal themes of the left—social justice, pacifism, the emancipation of the oppressed and the colonized—have impregnated a good part of the clergy.[9]

What is of especial interest here from an historical and theoretical point of view, however, is undoubtedly the ease with which this new found freedom of political and economic choice votes straight "left" in European terms. The beginnings, at least, of a new conformism are definitely present.

Almost paradoxically, this seems to revert to problems of the identification of politics and religion which the modern age set out to separate. Domenach is also most perceptive here:

> But "the option for socialism" has made great progress among Catholic associations without this socialism being particularly well-defined. And we can ask if many French Catholics, after having vested a part of their religious convictions in the constitutional order, are not now simply transferring it into a more or less anarchic socialist one. . . .
>
> The separation of church and state is an enormous progress. But its effects risk being diminished if clericalism (uti-

lizing the spiritual for temporal ends) and episcopalism (utilizing both the temporal and the spiritual ends) do not do other than change camps. From this point of view, one notes that a manifesto published by *Temoignage Chrétien* believed it could justify a vote for Mitterand with the "adhesion to Christ" and "evangelical exigencies." Thus, Christians devoted to the left risk repeating the error of Christians devoted to the right—namely, to deduce a politics from their religious faith.[10]

Anyone familiar with the literature will unhesitantly recognize that this is not merely a new gallicanism or a new Boussuet deducing politics from Scripture—though it is at least that—but an effort to identify a religion with a secular movement so that the mystical and ethical overtones which have become so prevelant in recent years are believed to find their natural home in the revolution which takes as its essential point of departure not grace or revelation but the improvement of mankind's earthly lot.[11]

Perhaps the best way to underscore the historical meaning of so many Christians today seeking a kingdom of God in some earthly movement designed to bring all men to what is known as "liberation" is to return for a moment to the difficulties Christians had with the nineteenth century secular state. Luigi Sturzo, writing in the late 1930's in the context of nationalist fascism, noted:

The historic significance of the conquest of freedom of conscience, worship, assembly, speech and press, paled when the laic state rid itself of the remains of absolutism and confessionalism, which had reappeared with the Restoration. It was not long before the positions were reversed; in all the varied and chaotic experience of the new state a kind of 'laic confessionalism' was making its reappearance, in as much as the state, in order to defend itself against its adversaries, old and new, denied them the liberties on which it itself was founded. . . . Instead of a confession of faith in God and in the Church, there was a kind of confession of faith in the laic state. As little by little this was extending its sway over individual activities, with control and monopoly in culture and education, and sub-

sequently in economic and political life, liberties were restricted or falsified or suppressed. This reversal of positions
has reached its climax today with what is known as the totalitarian state.

The Church, which towards the end of the XVIII century
and the beginning of the XIX century, had been against the
introduction of political liberties, in the following period of
veiled or open separation and strife was compelled by events
to demand these liberties for herself, in place of the old liberties that had been absorbed, if she would carry on her religious activity. But liberties are coherent or they cannot exist;
if they were denied to the Church as the adversary of the state,
they would be soon denied to all who were considered as adversaries of the state . . . till they became the monopoly of the
government and its factions.[12]

In this light, it becomes quite clear that the main intellectual task of
Christians in confrontation with the modern state was precisely to so re-
found its practices and values that they no longer rested upon absolutist
ideas. This is the meaning of *Pacem in Terris, Dignitatis Humanae,* and
Gaudium et Spes.

Sturzo went on, reflecting especially on the Portugal, Spain, and
Austria of his time, to warn of a danger which seems to be taking in a
much different environment today. "Every totalitarianism bases itself on
certain mystical elements (race, class, empire, nationality, and the like);
there could be nothing more dangerous than a totalitarianism basing itself
on Catholicism, or uniting Catholicism with its own profound my-
thus."[13] This was written at a time when the primary cause of totalitarianism was considered to be the nation-state. What seems to be different
in recent years is that the effort to solve the problems of poverty and
suppression exists on a world scale. Meantime we are diligently in search
of an ideology to overcome the moral vacuum found in the very theoretical structure of the modern social sciences and the modern national
state. For many today, this means that Catholicism can become this new
ideology to overcome the failure of the economic and technological sciences to create a world fit for all men when they undoubtedly have the
capacity to do so. Perhaps the most widely known effort to make this

transition is Giulio Girardi's *Cristianesimo, Liberazione Umana, Lotta di Classe*.[14]

The intellectual origin of this effort in modern times is, in many ways, Henri de Saint-Simon. This chaotic, prophetic man—who stood behind Suez and l'Ecole Polytechnique—was the first to see that modern technological development required a religious foundation. His "New Christianity," moreover, not only was designed to supply the ethical direction which progress decidedly needed but also was a Christianity reformulated in precisely this-worldly though Christian terms.

> In New Christianity all morality will be derived directly from the principle that "men should treat each other as brothers." This principle, which belongs to primitive Christianity, will undergo a transfiguration by which it will be proclaimed as the aim of all religious activity. This principle, regenerated, will be proclaimed as follows: religion should guide the community towards the great aim of improving as quickly as possible the condition of the poorest class.[15]

When Christianity is so redefined to include as its very essence the direct alleviation of the poor, when salvation history is so reinterpreted to identify class struggle and revolutionary change as the very essence, locus, and meaning of the divine such that religion's authenticity is to be found only where the political and economic establishment of this new Kingdom is taking place, of course, we have a faith quite different from that appearing in the long history of Christianity and that emphasized as the basis of the social thought of the modern Church.[16]

The effort to reinterpret Christianity today in such a fashion that it can lay claim to the ethical and moral vacuum found both in science and revolution is certainly the most momentous spiritual struggle of our time.[17] Writing of the beginning of the Middle Ages, Christopher Dawson reflected, "The Christian mystery . . . was essentially the mystery of eternal life. It was not concerned with the life of nature or with culture as a part of the order of nature, but with the redemption and regeneration of humanity by the Incarnation of the Divine Word."[18] Traditionally, this has been understood to mean that the essential origin and purpose of Christianity lies beyond this life, that men are essentially wayfarers and homeless. The indifference of Christianity to specific forms of government, even its acceptance of the lot of the poor in someone like Francis of Assisi, was a consequence not of political or economic theory but of the belief that a transcendant life of God was the destiny of all men no matter what their earthly lot might have been. Saints and sinners were to be found in every economic and political condition such that what made their lot before God was something resulting from their freedom in whatever condition they found themselves. Indeed, in many ways the poor were believed to have rather an advantage over the rich in this regard.

The major task of Christian social thought today remains its ability to encourage men to do what they can do, especially for the poor and the weak and this on a world scale, while at the same time constantly reminding men that the world is a passing thing and that religion is not and cannot be identified with any political or economic movement, or to put it differently, religion has a right and duty to be present to men under whatever social or economic conditions they find themselves in. In this sense, religion can never wait for the revolution since that would be betraying one generation to another. It seems more than ironic that cultures long influenced by Catholicism are the ones most in need of this clarification. The tendency to identify this world with the next seems, in a way, to bear out the thesis of R. H. Tawney:

> Tawney believed, and it remains a debatable belief, that revolutions and basic reforms occur not because of gross inefficiencies or gross deprivations. They arise rather when remedial action has already been put in train by people who have lost confidence in the moral justification of their power and who respond to a parallel loss of confidence among the population at large.[19]

This probably explains why so much Christian revolutionary theology is seen in terms of changing Church structures to conform to what is considered a necessary historical exigency.[20] Yet on a broader scale, there is a desperate search for meaning in personal life and in the public order. It is precisely the exhaustion of Marxism and liberalism—the two doctrines contrasted in practically every social document since Leo XIII as somehow containing part of the truth—that provides religion the opportunity to suggest an evident value—the alleviation of the poor—as the definition of religion itself. From this, it is but a short step to elevate politics into a theology (or vice versa, depending on one's taste) and economics into a mysticism.

In retrospect, however, what has been remarkable about the public social doctrine or thought of the Church has been its ability to see the extent Christian life can and does influence not only personal but civil lives of people. In this context, *Quadragesimo Anno* was perhaps more significant than we are wont to realize precisely because it did suggest that economic and political structures were basic to enabling men to lead fully human lives. Yet there is always a level of this thought not found in other civil tracts of our time, a judgment of the world as well as a love for it which seems ever pragmatic, ever based upon the real persons who do exist and concerning whose care and activities all economics, politics, nations, and ideologies are evaluated.

Does Catholic social thought, then, have a future? Has it said all that it can say? It seems clear that men will confront problems fifty, a hundred, a thousand years from now that will be as different from today as those issues of fifty, a hundred, a thousand years in the past. In a way, it seems presumptuous to suggest that we have said all we can say either as men or as Christians, even though we may well be entering a period of cultural and even intellectual stagnation because of the loss of confidence that has suddenly gripped our civilization. But the basic twofold task found in all social thought will undoubtedly remain—the need to remind men of their ultimate destiny which is a gift of God not the result of a political evolution solely conditioned by ourselves, the need to remind the powers that be, powers that we are in the Pauline sense to obey, of the values inherent in the human persons that do exist in the world. Undoubtedly with the growth of biological-technological control over man, his reproductive, aging, and psychic processes, this effort to protect man will become ever more central. The perennial problems of the poor and liberty remain as does the religious level of man that lies beyond the public order of this world no matter what shape it may take. It is a worthwhile task, indeed a necessary one, for Christianity to become an active force within historical movements. The distinction of John XXIII between ideological statement and its historical incarnation was a positive, far-seeing one. There is no question that it is legitimate to plunge into the heart of modern socialism or Marxism of whatever variety in the hope of adding to it precisely those values of civil liberty, freedom of belief and information, recognition of creativity and variety that are so often lacking to them. The appearance of Alexander Solzhenitsyn in the West is surely a major sign of the growing spiritual exhaustion within the established Marxist movements.[21]

Solzhenitsyn too is probably indicative of the next kind of social statement that Christians will undoubtedly have to make—namely, on the relation of nature, development, technology, animals, and the human person. Pius XII, in his last Christmas messages, was very much concerned with the overemphasis of technology in modern society. Indeed, this problem was long a theme of existentialists like Gabriel Marcel as well as of the romantic and conservative traditions. The energy-pollution controversy has entered into the very heart of the position already taken on development and the care for the poor in recent papal pronouncements. That the ecology movement is often seen as a movement against the world's poor and weak cannot be denied. And there is considerable justice to this opinion. The relation of man, God, nature, and technology has a long tradition going back to Genesis and Aristotle. As this issue has been developing over recent years, we seem to be witnessing a rapprochement between Marxism and Christianity analogous to the rapprochement between Christianity and the liberal state heralded in the last century by Bismarck's decision to combat nascent socialism by dropping the Kulturkampf policies.

It is popular, indeed almost obligatory in many circles, to see *Humanae Vitae* as simply an error in this context. However, as this issue evolves, it becomes ever clearer that the newer nature mystique that is rapidly taking hold in the West is, in many ways, an attack upon the very possibility of further human development on a world scale and a re-emergence of values subordinating man to nature, views long forgotten in the West.[22] Marxism and Christianity are closer together from this angle than ever before. This is why the Solzhenitsyn letter—with its proposal for a restricted-local-national ambitus—is seen by Third World representatives as an attack on their future. This problem cannot be left unresolved at an official level so that we should expect some document "On Nature" in the not too distant future.

But are the pluralists right? Is it worth the effort for some religious organ to make such observations any longer? Why do not liberty and maturity decide? The question is subtle. The Augustinian tradition about the sinfulness and weakness of all men and movements must be still kept in mind in our time. How easy it is to slip from making religion a politics whose sole justification is to help the poor to a religion that has little to do with the real world—a problem that arose in modern theory with Marsilius of Padua's effort to limit religion to the absolutely spiritual—can, perhaps, be seen from the following lines of Malachi Martin:

> One thing is clear and certain: Paul is presiding over an inner and, barring miracles, an inevitable decadence. Inner, because there exists no longer that cohesion among people, priest, bishop, cardinal and pope built on absolutely accepted dogma and affecting the daily life, personal decisions and intimate thoughts of millions. Inevitable, because the structure is out of kilter with the fashion of mind, the bent of will and the social development rife among the nations that once fitted snugly into the 1,000 year-old cohesion of the ecclesiastical Church. That was a juridical Church, all its efforts went precisely to foment a juridical structure. But, originally, all structure and discipline were meant to subserve only the spirit.[23]

Historically, of course, Marsilius limited the Church's powers to the spirit in order to leave the world wholly to the civil powers. Here we discover the spirit also used to free religion from its own structures, a question which, of course, suggests that Christ did not found a "Church" but a spirituality. Martin goes on:

> For, in the Roman view, the power of moral authority and of the spirit derives from Jesus and not from sociopolitical structures. This power requires another human environment of which only the merest beginnings are found today in the fragmented reality of human beings—mechanized, tormented, rebellious and searching as they are, but wonderfully charged with excitement. Never before, as far as one can judge from history, has there been such a leavening of all men and women, a melting of all man-made barriers so that the divine can manifest itself and the Castle vision, can become a shared thing among all men and women and children.
>
> Foreseeably, throughout the world, they will be utterly indistinguishable one from the other, no longer divided by par-

ticularisms and prejudices. For such an environment, it was proclaimed in Rome long ago, Jesus came. And the only situation promising further life for that vision of the human Castle is this: humans everywhere heightening their awareness of the spirit as distinct from the body; wearying of all psychological substitutes for inner morality; impatient with dead heroes, transitory wonderworkers, indeed with any leader who is merely clay as they themselves are; and insistent that their humanness be guaranteed by some force and power that does not share the mortality and the weakness of human things.[24]

Such may be noble ideals, of course, but they are not Christianity. *Verbum caro factum est*—the spirit is in the body, in the whole person, not somehow distinct from it. All inner morality must have external effect. And what guarantees our humanness in the public world is moral force derived from Jesus through social and political structures. The Marxist and Christian traditions are right in this. The rule of pure spirit is invariably the rule of tyranny. And we cannot escape our weakness. The mortality and fragility of all things human is precisely the glory of Christianity. Our guarantee is not that we will find some way to escape from the kind of beings we are.

The voice of the organized Church will be heard in different ways and in different contexts as time passes. What is not clear is how we can dispense with it in favor of some brooding "spirit." The history of modern social thought is remarkable mainly in its almost uncanny feeling for what helps and what ultimately hurts the existing human person. "For the Christian faith," René Coste wrote, "human history is at the same time a work of God and work of men. God directs it sovereignly and accomplishes his design of salvation even across the errors and crimes of men, but he fully respects their liberty so that it is good for man to assume his proper destiny."[25] This manifestation of what the Christian Church holds about man's personhood is now more than ever to be heard "in liberty." The Roman Church undoubtedly needs a further statement of the meaning of liberty within its own structures to parallel the Council document and the notions of John XXIII on the civil order. Probably it is already true, as the spirit of the papal social documents since John clearly indicates, that the mode of discourse is now more pastoral, more patient, more reflective, more suggestive than the juridical formulae in which they appeared before. Yet, the "pluralism of options" cannot mean that all things are equally helpful to human dignity in this world or in the *next*—to which John always referred us. We should be blind and naive to believe that all programs and plans presented for man for building a world and an action are equally good and wise.

"Christ did not establish his Church as an institution of social criticism. Were he to have done this, he certainly would also have provided a way unconditionally to perform such a task, without which it could not fulfill its mission. The Church is commissioned to teach and to admonish. . . ."[26] When we are taught or admonished, it is enough. There is no secular arm to religion. A religion that is also a worldly order is precisely what we must avoid in our efforts to make the world a fitting home for men who are merely passing through it, as an older tradition used to put it. But liberty is liberty. The plurality of options means no less than at least the possibility of Christians creating a world totalitarianism in the name of the poor or of drifting into nature worship or mystical irrelevance. Mysticism itself, of course, is not irrelevant but stands at the very apex of civilization. But it is not a politics or a substitute for it. The organized Church cannot prevent any of these choices from happening. This should be clear. Teachings and admonitions are only that. This is why the level of sin and evil must always be a part of any adequate religious and political theory, for men must also know what to do when they fail. In the central line of Christian social thought, the *here* has a basic place but ever subordinated to the *hereafter*. Both are of this social thought. Indeed, it seems that precisely because both are stressed and related that such a social thought can be called specifically Christian.

In conclusion, it seems fitting to cite E.E.Y. Hales' remark about John XXIII: "Innocent III, Pius IX, Pius XII, and John XXIII were all at one in their belief that the ultimate authority in human affairs rested by right with the Vicar of Christ. The difference consisted in Pope John's attitude, not shared by his predecessors, that it was best for the Church to leave politics alone."[27] A decade later, this observation seems almost conservative. The radical position is that the Church should reenter politics for the welfare of men. Almost the only certain thing that can be said about the validity of a responsible, official line of social thought in Christianity is that without admonition or teaching, Christians will too easily end up saying things little different from what is said by others.

That Christians have, in fact, believed that they did have something else to say about man's relation to life and death seems to be the essential astonishment of this long tradition. From social doctrine to the Kingdom of God on earth is, no doubt, a long journey. Yet, as Nell-Breuning has remarked, the introductory lines of *Immortale Dei* (1885) remain the essential ones that have not changed and according to which all institutions are judged for the good of the person: "The Catholic Church, that imperishable handiwork of our all-merciful Creator, has for her immediate and natural purpose the saving of souls and securing our happiness in heaven. Yet in regard to things temporal, she is the source of benefits as manifold and as great as if the chief end of her existence were to ensure the prospering of an earthly state." And while this seems rather unpleasantly triumphant today, it remains the great criterion and priority by which the presence of this faith is seen and manifested—first that there is an eternal life that surpasses all worldly kingdoms, second, that the worldly kingdoms are of dignity and importance because they are concerned with the growth and well-being of all men, beginning with the least. What is perhaps new in the world of today in this connection is not the need to find a place for value and even mysticism in the public order, but rather to decide what value and mysticism men will choose. Catholics and Christian social thought have long suspected that not all choices are equally neutral if the human person is really the basis of all social, political, and cultural life of men in the world.

Notes

1. Cf. John F. Cronin, "Forty Years Later: Reflections and Reminiscences," *The American Ecclesiastical Review* (May, 1971), 310–18; Oswald von Nell-Breuning, "Quadragesimo Anno," *Stimmen der Zeit* (May, 1971), 289–96. For more complete discussions of the history of Catholic social thought, cf. Richard L. Camp, *The Papal Ideology of Social Reform* (Leiden: E. J. Brill, 1969); Melvin J. Williams, *Catholic Social Thought* (New York: Ronald Press, 1950); P. Bigo, *La Doctrine Sociale de l'Eglise* (Paris: Presses Universitaires de France, 1966); J. Calvez and J. Perrin, *L'Eglise et Sociéte Economique* (Paris:

Aubier, 1966); G. van Gestel, *La Doctrine Sociale de l'Eglise* (Brussels, 1963); J. Villain, *L'Enseignement Sociale de l'Eglise* (Paris: Spes, 1963); B. Masse, *The Church and Social Progress* (Milwaukee: Bruce, 1966); Georges Jarlot, *Doctrine Pontificale et Histoire* (Rome: Gregoriana, 1964).

2. Cf. E.E.Y. Hales, *The Catholic Church in the Modern World* (New York: Image, 1960).

3. This theme is more and more to be found in books dealing with economic and political modernization. Cf. Denis Goulet, *The Cruel Choice* (New York: Atheneum, 1971); David Apter, *The Politics of Modernization* (Chicago: University of Chicago Press, 1965); Lucian W. Pye, *Aspects of Political Development* (Boston: Little, Brown, and Company, 1966).

4. The theoretical significance of much of the population controversy centers directly about the meaning of the inviolability of the human person. This has been too little recognized. Cf. the author's *Human Dignity and Human Numbers* (New York: Alba House, 1971).

5. Cf. Oswald von Nell-Breuning, "Weltverantwortung der Wirtschaft oder 'Unser tägliches Brot gib uns heute'," *Die Politik und Das Heil,* ed. by R. Hörl (Mainz: Grünwald, 1968), pp. 38–42; *La Conscience chrétienne et les Nationalismes,* Semaine des Intellectuels Catholiques, Novembre 5–11, 1958 (Paris: Pierre Horay, 1959); J. T. Delos, *Essai sur l'ordre politique national et international* (Paris: Dalloz, 1974); John La Farge, "The Catholic Church and World Order," *World Order: Its Intellectual and Cultural Foundations,* ed. by F. E. Johnson (New York: Harper, 1943), pp. 117–23; A. de Soras, *Morale internationale* (Paris: Fayard, 1961).

6. "Un Comunicato della CEI (Conferenza Episcopale Italiana) sui Risultati del Referendum," *Osservatore Romano,* May 15, 1974; L. Bedeschi, "Dal Concilio al Referendum," *Paese Sera,* Rome, May 15, 1974; L. Furno, "Perché Hanno Votato No Due Milioni di Cattolici?" La Stampa, Turin, May 26, 1974.

7. For a general survey of varying positions in the French church, cf. "Der französische Katholizismus auf der Suche nach einer neuen Plattform," *Herder Korrespondenz,* February, 1974, pp. 67–70.

8. Cf. B. Sorge, "Il Moviemento dei 'Cristiani per il Socialismo'," *La Civiltà Cattolica,* April 24, 1974, pp. 111–30; M. Cuminetti, "I Cristiani nell'Italia, '73," *IDOC Internazionale,* January 31, 1974, pp. 38–40.

9. "Separazione fra Stato e Chiesa," *Corriere della Sera,* Milan, May 24, 1974.

10. *Ibid.* Perhaps another logical consequence of such an approach of politicizing religion can be seen in the following report of Paul Hoffman: "In one of the most radical statements published so far, more than 500 Catholics meeting in Oporto, the country's second city, urged all the bishops to resign. The Oporto

declaration accused the church hierarchy of having remained silent about the oppression, police tortures and colonial wars under the former regime." ("Portuguese Clergy Attacked for Supporting Dictators," *Herald-Tribune*, Paris, June 4, 1974).

11. ". . . La teologia nuova nasce, invece, dall'impegno rivoluzionario; la prassi liberatrice degli oppressi deviene l'unico autentico luogo teologico, il criterio di una rilettura completementa nuova della Parola di Dio, della tradizione, della fede. La fede, dunque, non è prima né al di sopra della cultura umana della storia; ma è ad esse immanente, ad esse si accompagna" (Sorge, *op. cit.*, p. 128).

". . . The Church will be able to cope with the consciousness of the Third World only to the extent that it can disengage itself from its present outmoded institutional settings and adopts the shape of what many have called a 'prophetic community,' judging itself and history in terms of an eschatological promise and hope. It can also be expected that nothing better than an intimate contact with the world of the poor and the powerless will enable it to achieve this necessary transmutation" (J. da Veiga Coutinho, "The Church and the Third World," *Jesuit Missions*, Newsletter #14, December, 1968 [also in *Cross Currents*, Fall, 1968]).

12. *Church and State*, Vol. II (Notre Dame: University of Notre Dame Press, 1962), pp. 526–27.

13. *Ibid.*, p. 544.

14. Assisi: Cittadella Editrice, 1972.

15. "New Christianity," *Social Organization, the Science of Man and Other Writings*, ed. by F. Markham (New York: Harper Torchbooks, 1964), p. 87.

16. Cf. the exchange between the French bishops and a group of radical Christians on these issues—an exchange which is perhaps a model of the changing relations between hierarchy and critics. "Cristiani nella Rivoluzione per l'Avvenire del Mundo," *IDOC Internazionale*, January 15, 1974, (Assemblea Internazionale di Lione, November 12–18, 1973), pp. 9–15.

Cf. also Oswald von Nell-Breuning, "Die Kirche—Institution der Sozialkritik?" *Stimmen der Zeit*, March, 1974, pp. 201–03.

17. Cf. #105, "Options politiques de l'église," *Lumière & Vie*, November-December, 1971.

18. *Religion and the Rise of Western Culture* (New York: Image, 1957), p. 42.

19. "A Socialism Based on Christianity," *The Times Literary Supplement*, April 28, 1972, p. 463.

20. Cf. J. Guichard, "Options politiques et structures idéologiques dans l'église," *Lumière & Vie, ibid.*, pp. 73–93.

21. A. Solzhenitsyn, "Letter to the Soviet Leaders," *The Sunday Times,* March 3, 1974.

22. "Es besteht jedoch die Gefahr, dass die biologisch und ökologisch verstanden Natur zu alleinigen Norm erhoben wird. In diesem Fall bekommt die 'neue Ethik' naturalistische Züge; sie hält as für ihre Pflicht, im Namen eines allmächtigen Naturgesetzes die radikale und totale Einordnung des Menschen in den Naturzusammenhang zu fordern. Der frei sich entfaltende Mensch erscheint dann als Störenfried, der notfalls mit Gewalt dem Naturgesetz unterworfen werden muss. Wenn es darum geht, zu überleben, ist politische Zimperlichkeit nicht am Platze. Vor allem in der Frage der Übervölkerung wird die inhumane Kehrseite dieser 'neuen Ethik' sichtbar. Die pauschale Feststellung, 'dass es zu viele Menschen auf der Erde gibt', zeugt nicht gerade von besonderem Respekt vor der Würde des Menschen. Für manche scheint Ökologie zu einer Ersatzreligion zu werden: der um seine Geschöpfe besorgte Vatergott wird ersetzt durch die 'Mutter Erde', die uns nährt" (Friedrich Hartl, "Umweltkrise und Naturrecht," *Herder Korrespondenz,* March, 1974, p. 125).

23. "The New Castle: Rome," *Intellectual Digest,* January, 1974, p. 54.

24. *Ibid.*

25. *Evangile et Politique* (Paris: Aubier, 1968), p. 272. This is one of the better discussions of the various ways in which politics, economics, and religion are related in Christianity. Cf. also O. Cullmann, *Jésus et les révolutionnaires de son temps* (Neuchatel: Delachaux & Niestlé, 1970); F. Perroux, *Le pain et la parole* (Paris: Cerf, 1969).

26. von Nell-Breuning, "Die Kirche . . . ," p. 202.

27. E.E.Y. Hales, *Pope John and His Revolution* (New York: Image, 1965), p. 220. Perhaps the best survey of this counter-trend to reinvigorate politics with religion is Frederick C. Turner's *Catholicism and Political Development in Latin America* (Chapel Hill: University of North Carolina Press, 1971).

The Bias Against Democratic Capitalism

Michael Novak

This article originally appeared in *The Spirit of Democratic Capitalism*, 1982.

"Any serious Christian," Paul Tillich once said, "must be a socialist."[1] In the history of the last two hundred years, the favored ecclesiastical word for democratic capitalism has been "liberalism." This word is almost always used pejoratively in the papal documents—not only in "The Syllabus of Errors" of Pope Pius IX in 1864, but also in the encyclicals of subsequent popes. In 1980, the superior general of the Jesuits, Father Pedro Arrupe, S.J., wrote: ". . . the type of social analysis used in the liberal world today implies an individualistic and materialistic vision of life that is destructive of Christian values and attitudes."[2]

The traditional accusations against democratic capitalism fall into two categories: those against democracy and those against capitalism. Over the years, the former have fallen away. The churches have learned to cherish democracy and religious liberty, but resistance to capitalism remains. The generic and fundamental accusations against capitalism are that it is individualistic, materialist, and anarchic. At times, it is also suggested that capitalism fosters inequality (although comparisons are seldom undertaken with respect to inequality under other historical systems).

There are some excellent summaries of church teachings in this area.[3] Instead of repeating them, it may be more useful to exhibit the sort of mental horizon, the complex of images and sensibility, which a devout Christian is likely to encounter in the church teachings on economics. There are many misunderstandings.

The first known use of the word "individualism" occurs in an essay by the French writer Joseph de Maistre in 1820.[4] De Maistre used the word in an expression of disdain "for this deep and frightening division of minds, this infinite fragmentation of all doctrines, *political protestantism* carried to the most absolute individualism."[5] In 1829, the prominent French Catholic writer Lamennais assaulted "individualism" as a doctrine which nourishes "power without obedience" and "law without duty." He added: "The same doctrine which produces anarchy among minds produces in addition an irremediable political anarchy, and overturns the basis of human society." Both de Maistre and Lamennais influenced the course of nineteenth-century Catholic liberalism. Both were French, surely among the most individualist of peoples. And both respected social traditions and inarticulate social connections as did British Whigs like Edmund Burke. They were disturbed by the anti-clerical, anti-religious revolutionary secularism of France.

From the nineteenth-century Vatican, democratic capitalism seemed far away and heretical. In the nineteenth century, the social structure of Catholic Italy, Spain, and Austro-Hungary was still feudal, monarchical, and mercantilist. In 1864, the at first liberal pope, Pius IX (whose reign lasted 32 years, 1846–78), embittered by his experiences with Italian anti-clerical republicans, condemned nearly every thesis of a liberal society root and branch in his famous "Syllabus of Errors."[6] In 1891, Leo XIII at last addressed the large social questions racking the first modern societies in a letter addressed to the entire world, "On the Condition of Labor." He was the first architect of what came to be thought of as the Catholic "middle way."[7] He roundly condemned socialism, even in its milder forms. He upheld the notion of the limited state and the critical role of private property as the protector of liberty.[8] But he was soundly critical not only of certain practices of capitalism but of some of its philosophical bases, especially its individualism and its radical dependence on the free market.

The Catholic bishops of the United States played an important role in persuading Leo XIII to defend the rights of labor.[9] In 1891, Catholics in the U.S. numbered about 9 million in a population of 65 million. Many laymen, priests, and bishops were active in the labor movement. In a sense, the strong social traditions of Catholics and Jews led both communities in the United States to early and strong support for labor. American Protestants, with their strong traditions of individualism, long found it more natural to oppose unionization. Even the "Social Gospel" movement among American Protestants had to struggle mightily to bring authoritative religious support to the cause of the unions.[10]

Forty years after *Rerum Novarum,* in 1931, Pius XI (pope 1922–39) advanced the thought of Leo XIII in a new letter, "On the Reconstruction of the Social Order." Pius XI, not quite as hostile to liberalism as Pius IX had been, nonetheless described individualism and collectivism as "twin evils." Because of the Catholic tradition favoring limited government and private property, his treatment of the twin evils was not symmetrical. He described "Christian socialism" as a contradiction in terms, and held, "No one can be at the same time a sincere Catholic and a true socialist." He did not symmetrically condemn capitalism. But he did blast the "tottering tenets of liberalism" and "the evil of individualism."[11]

> Just as the unity of human society cannot be built upon "class" conflict, so the proper ordering of economic affairs cannot be left to the free play of rugged competition. From this source, as from a polluted spring, have proceeded all the errors of the "individualistic" school. This school, forgetful or ignorant of the social and moral aspects of economic activities, regarded these as completely free and immune from any intervention by public authority, for they would have in the market place and in unregulated competition a principle of self-direction more suitable for guiding them than any created intellect which might intervene. Free competition, however, though justified and quite useful within certain limits, cannot be an adequate controlling principle in economic affairs. This has been abundantly proved by the consequences that have followed from the free rein given to these dangerous individualistic ideals.[12]

The pope observed fairly that the horrible "pauperism" of the days of Leo XIII is "less prevalent today. The condition of the workingmen has indeed been improved and rendered more equitable in many respects, particularly in the larger and more developed States, where the laboring class can no longer be said to be universally in misery and want."[13] But how did this happen? The pope showed no inclination to inquire.

Next, Pius XI made a grave charge against "capital":

Capital, however, was long able to appropriate to itself excessive advantages. It claimed all the products and profits and left
to the laborer the barest minimum necessary to repair his
strength and to ensure the continuation of his class. For by an
inexorable economic law, it was held, all accumulation of
riches must fall to the share of the wealthy, while the workingman must remain perpetually in indigence or reduced to the
minimum needed for existence.[14]

It is not at all clear who "claimed" this. No serious thinker in the democratic capitalist tradition is directly confronted.

Closer to our own time, Pope Paul VI wrote in *Octogesima Adveniens* in 1971:

The liberal ideology . . . asserts itself in the name of economic
efficiency, for the defense of the individual against the increasingly overwhelming hold of organizations, and as a reaction
against the totalitarian tendencies of political powers. Certainly personal initiative must be maintained and developed.
But do not Christians who take this path tend to idealize liberalism . . . while easily forgetting that at the very root of philosophical liberalism is an erroneous affirmation of the
autonomy of the individual in his activity, his motivation and
the exercise of his liberty.[15]

Pope John Paul II, in his encyclical *Laborem Exercens* (1981) for
the ninetieth anniversary of *Rerum Novarum*, went beyond these early
texts in four ways. He clearly distinguished "early nineteenth-century
capitalism" from recent capitalism ("rigid capitalism" from modern).
He drew from broad experience the lesson that the socialist collectivi-
zation of property takes from one class to give power to a new class. He
identified as "labor" many sources of creativity—the work of inventors,
intellectual workers, management experts and the like—which go far beyond blue-collar workers. Under "labor," he included all those who
contribute to production, even entrepreneurs and managers, discoverers
of new processes and inventors of new techniques. Finally, he empha-

sized the creativity of modern work by drawing on the theological symbols of the Creator and his creation. These are giant steps toward the tradition of John Locke, Adam Smith, and later democratic capitalism. In his capsule history of early-nineteenth-century capitalism, however, Pope John Paul II may have intended only to provide an illustration. As illustration, his material works; as history, it appears to be as deficient as the views of his predecessors have been.

All the popes, it is true, have respected some of the fundamental principles of democratic capitalism. All have favored the limited state (in keeping with the liberal tradition) and the indispensable role of private property. They have resisted, however, both "individualism" and the "so-called liberalism of the Manchester School," in part confusing these with the anti-clerical, anti-religious republicanism of Italy, France, and Mexico, and in part simply by misunderstanding Anglo-Saxon cultures. Their resistance to democratic capitalism has not been due to illusions about socialism. On the contrary, they were from the beginning alert not only to the latter's materialism and atheism but to its utopianism and its potential for state tyranny.

In a sense, by standing outside the historical stream of democratic capitalism, the popes were able to make some legitimate criticisms of abuses and errors within it, and to support many proposals for humane reforms eventually adopted by it. Yet, simultaneously, the remnants both of the medieval world and state mercantilism were crumbling all around them. Resisting socialism and standing outside democratic capitalism, Catholic social teaching laid claim to a certain neutrality—but gradually came to seem suspended in air. Catholic thought began to deal with every sort of regime, traditional and modern, even while its talk of a Catholic "middle way" seemed empty, since there are, in fact, no existing examples of that middle way. Catholic social teaching has, therefore, occupied a sort of utopian ground—literally, no-place. It came to seem uncharacteristically abstract, otherworldly, deracinated. Popes and scholars might make astute and valuable comments from time to time, but the platform on which they stood no longer seemed connected to real experience.

For this reason, perhaps, the programs of the 1940s and the 1950s in which Catholic thinkers had invested so much hope for "the reconstruction of the social order"—Catholic Action, the Young Christian Workers, the Christian Democratic parties—achieved some notable successes but lacked the force of an alternative ideal. To be anti-communist and anti-socialist, and only halfheartedly committed to democratic capitalism, is to represent not a "middle way" but a halfway house. Such movements collapsed of their own lack of a serious ideal.

After the Second Vatican Council, first under "good Pope John" (Pope John XXIII) and then under Pope Paul VI, this vacuum in Catholic social thought began to be filled from two directions. First, in Western Europe, chiefly in Germany, the new "political theology" began to move in a socialist direction.[16] Socialism cherishes images of community, unitary authority, and integrated life which are closer to those of traditional feudal society than to those of democratic capitalism. The new political theology practiced by Johannes Metz and others has turned away from the Enlightenment and embraced the philosophy of praxis (understood in the tradition of Marxism rather than in that of the American pragmatists).[17] It has shown contempt for bourgeois society, favored a "Christian-Marxist" dialogue, and taken an almost medieval delight in the supposed rediscovery of an "age of limits." This new political theology provides a novel form of socialism in Europe. More recently, in Latin America and in the formerly French, Belgian, and Portuguese colonies of Africa and Asia, another form of socialism has arisen under the title "liberation theology."

Following Vatican II, a special Vatican Commission on Peace and Justice was established, and peace and justice commissions were opened in many dioceses around the world. These commissions freed many priests and sisters from traditional pastoral duties so that they might engage in social action. It was natural for them, in many situations, to ally themselves with an adversarial spirit. Increasingly, these groups appear to have taken on an anti-capitalist and, at times, anti-democratic ideology. Employing the language of "standing with the poor and the oppressed," they easily fall into the language of class struggle. Beginning as reformers, they often find the language of their socialist peers captivating. If they become concerned about world hunger, they seldom blame shortages of foodstuffs on the failures of socialist agriculture; they are more likely to blame "multinational conglomerates." Many such activists deny that they are Marxists or even socialists, but one seldom hears them employing the ideas or the methods of democratic capitalism. Instead, they frequently denounce democratic capitalist societies as selfish, sick, greedy, materialist, individualist, etc. They seem to assume the correctness of their views; the quality of their intellectual arguments suffers from lack of self-criticism.

Perhaps their fatal flaw lies in the omission of the symbol "liberty." Peace and justice there may be even under authoritarian societies. The innermost secret of democratic capitalism is liberty. A Vatican Commission on Peace, Liberty, and Justice would sound a universal clarion.

But more than symbols are at stake. The intellectual model for peace and justice offered by Catholic social teaching is at present closer to a mild form of socialism than to democratic capitalism. It has little to say about markets and incentives, the ethics of production, and the habits, disciplines, and organization necessary for the creation of wealth. It seems to take the production of wealth for granted (as if wealth were as limited and static as in medieval times) and preoccupies itself with appeals for redistribution. The discoveries of modern economics seem to have affected it hardly at all. There are virtually no signs in it of sustained theological reflection upon democratic capitalism. There are many signs in it of conformity to the conventional thinking of socialists in Europe and the Third World. Some interpreters argue that socialism is the emerging wave of the future in Catholic social teaching.[18] A new confluence between secular and ecclesiastical authoritarianism under socialism may seem to some attractive.

One of the themes emergent in this new social teaching is that "development is the new name for peace." Empirically, however, it does not seem to be true that a developing country necessarily commits itself to peace; some are armed to the teeth. Among the nations, socialist models of development—of which since World War II there have been scores—seem woefully gray, economically dependent, and politically oppressive. The social teachings of the Catholic church at present do not seem to be rooted in sound empirical and theoretical reflection upon such outcomes, although Pope John Paul II has begun to make a difference. His reflections on creativity also show promise. Any economic system whatever, if it is not to stagnate, must produce more than it invests. It must yield capital accumulation. Profit is, therefore, a condition of development; without it, there are only losses or stagnation. The church seems poised, at last, to think about the creative causes of wealth.

One would think that Catholic theologians, in particular, would be more modest in speaking of development. The record of wholly Catholic countries in the history of economic and social development is not entirely laudable. (The same is true, alas, of their record in establishing democracies.) Is it possible that there are some intellectual *lacunae* in Catholic teachings on political economy? Are there some insights missing?

Such reflections as these have led me, over the years, to believe that just as the Catholic tradition has something to teach America, so also American democratic capitalism has some new things to add to the Catholic tradition. The Catholic church has heretofore learned from the intellect of Greece and Rome, Germany and France. Why not also from America?

Notes

1. "Once, following a lecture to students, Paul Tillich was asked whether he still supported socialism. The eminent theologian's answer came quickly: 'That is the only possible economic system from the Christian point of view.' This exchange took place in 1957." J. Philip Wogaman, *The Great Economic Debate* (Philadelphia: Westminster Press, 1977), p. 133.

2. Pedro Arrupe, S.J., "Marxist Analysis by Christians," *Origins* 10 (April 16, 1981): 693.

3. See, for example, Franz H. Mueller, "The Church and the Social Question," in *The Challenge of Mater et Magistra,* eds. Joseph N. Moody and Justus George Lawler (New York: Herder & Herder, 1963), pp. 13–153.

4. See Steven Lukes, "Types of Individualism," in *Dictionary of the History of Ideas,* 4 vols. (New York: Charles Scribner's Sons, 1973), II: 594–604.

5. Ibid., p. 594 (emphasis added). Ibid., also, for Lamennais.

6. See E. E. Y. Hales, *Pio Nono* (Garden City, N.Y.: Doubleday-Image, 1962), pp. 266–73.

7. See E. E. Y. Hales, *The Catholic Church in the Modern World* (Garden City, N.Y.: Doubleday-Image, 1960), chap. 16.

8. "We have seen that this great labor question cannot be solved except by assuming as a principle that private ownership must be held sacred and inviolable. The law, therefore, should favor ownership, and its policy should be

to induce as many people as possible to become owners.'' Again: ''The *Socialists,* working on the poor man's envy of the rich, endeavor to destroy private property, and maintain that individual possessions should become the common property of all, to be administered by the State or by municipal bodies. . . . But their proposals are so clearly futile for all practical purposes, that if they were carried out the working man himself would be among the first to suffer. Moreover, they are emphatically unjust, because they would rob the lawful possessor, bring the State into a sphere that is not its own, and cause complete confusion in the community.'' Pope Leo XIII, *Rerum Novarum,* para. 35, 3; see *Seven Great Encyclicals* (Glen Rock, N.J.: Paulist Press, 1965), pp. 22, 2.

9. See John Tracy Ellis, *American Catholicism* (Chicago: University of Chicago Press, 1956), p. 105–06.

10. See Reinhold Niebuhr, ''Walter Rauschenbusch in Historical Perspective,'' in *Faith and Politics* (New York: George Braziller, 1968), pp. 33–45 (an essay written in 1957).

11. Pope Pius XI, *Quadragesimo Anno,* para. 120, 27, 78; see *Encyclicals,* pp. 158, 131, 147.

12. Ibid., para. 88; see *Encyclicals,* pp. 149–50.

13. Ibid., para. 59; see *Encyclicals,* p. 142.

14. Ibid., para. 54; see *Encyclicals,* p. 140.

15. Pope Paul VI, *Octogesima Adveniens,* para. 35, in *The Gospel of Peace and Justice,* ed. Joseph Gremillion (Maryknoll, N.Y.: Orbis Books, 1976), p. 501.

16. See Dorothee Soelle, *Political Theology* (Philadelphia: Fortress Press, 1974). In the *Concilium* series, published in New York by Herder & Herder and Seabury Press, see the following collections of essays, primarily by Europeans: *The Mystical and Political Dimension of the Christian Faith* (1974), *Christianity and Socialism* (1977), *Christianity and the Bourgeoisie* (1979), and *Christian Ethics and Economics: The North–South Conflict* (1980).

17. Metz uses the Marxist rather than the Anglo-American sense of *praxis,* most notably in *Faith in History and Society: Toward a Practical Fundamental Theology* (New York: Seabury Press, 1980); see esp. chap. 4.

18. Bishop Dom Helder Camara of Recife, Brazil ''has called for a synthesis of Marxism and Christianity like the synthesis St. Thomas Aquinas achieved between Aristotle and Christianity in the Middle Ages.'' See McGovern, *Marxism: An American Christian Perspective,* p. 2. In a similar regard, Jacques Maritain once wrote, ''. . . to do with Hegel what St. Thomas did with Aristotle, would involve . . . making over Hegel from head to toe. Just let them try it, they will break their teeth.'' *The Peasant of the Garonne* (New York: Macmillan, 1969), p. 169.

Economic Systems, Middle Way Theories, and Third World Realities

Denis Goulet

This article originally appeared in *Co-Creation and Capitalism*, 1983.

A new challenge now comes to Christians from John Paul II's encyclical *On Human Work:* They are enjoined to create a middle-way between two opposing ideologies of human labor—capitalism and Marxist collectivism. Middle- or "third way" economic experiments have a past history, however, which is now briefly reviewed.

MIDDLE WAYS: A VIEW FROM HISTORY

On Human Work, like earlier papal encyclicals, denounces "the various trends of materialistic and economistic thought."[18] Because capitalism and socialism alike are criticized by popes, Catholic social thinkers have long yearned for "middle ways" which, so they hope, avoid the worst abuses of each system. They reject Marxist collectivism because it treats human persons as mere producers and capitalism because, notwithstanding noble rhetoric about individual liberties and political rights, it reduces workers to being mere "factors of production" ruled by impersonal economic laws. John Paul II reaffirms the traditional principle that:

> the basis for determining the value of human work is not primarily the kind of work being done, but the fact that the one who is doing it is a person. The sources of the dignity of work

are to be sought primarily in the subjective dimension, not in the objective one.[19]

Papal condemnations of communism *in principle* on grounds that it is an inherently atheistic and materialistic system have been rendered obsolete, however, by philosophical breakthroughs achieved in Marxist-Christian dialogues. Serious communist philosophers now concede that "religious alienation" is dissociable from economic and social alienation.[20] Christians, in turn, especially in Latin America, experience no difficulty in calling themselves Marxists without falling into contradiction.[21] In 1963 Pope John XXIII distinguished between error and those who err in good faith.[22] In the encyclical John Paul II differentiates genuine from unsatisfactory socialization.[23] Christian socialists draw encouragement from papal overtures such as these.

The popes never condemn capitalism *on principle,* but denounce its abuses *in practice,* thus leaving unanswered the question whether capitalism's practical abuses are separable from its organizing principle of economic activity, competitive profit-seeking.[24] Critical interrogation by many Christians into the Gospel's application to economic ideologies has led them to conclude that middle-way models could ally capitalism's dynamic efficiency to socialism's compassionate regard for society's weak members. The enduring Christian dream is to find an economic system which is both efficient and just, and to inspire managers to be both hard-headed and gentle-hearted.[25]

The late Emmanuel Mounier articulated a communitarian personalist philosophy to steer a middle course between capitalism's atomistic competitiveness and communism's depersonalizing collectivism. Mounier wants not collectivities but communities or free associations of persons choosing to ratify their destinies as social beings. According to Mounier, true personhood requires community because, in its absence, persons cannot fully realize themselves. Therefore, economic and political life must be designed to foster this dual, interrelated growth. Liberal economics cannot be allowed to impose impersonal "laws" which subordinate persons to the process of production. Similarly, the Marxist "laws" of history are rejected because they condemn societies to be the playthings of ineluctable class struggle. The personalist believes that relations of production no less than the means of production can be organized in humane fashion.

Mounier died in 1950, but already in 1941 another French Christian movement had been founded. This was "Economy and Humanism," whose basic premise states that all societal arrangements—economic, political, and institutional—are subordinated to achieving the comprehensive good of the human person.[26] Like Mounier, "Economy and Humanism" condemned all reductionism and defined the societal task as the construction of a political economy which promotes a humanistic order and fosters civilizations of solidarity.

Manifestly, middle-way theories are nothing new in Christian circles and John Paul II's letter *On Human Work* brings no fresh elements to theoretical reflection on third ways. The Pope's letter is to be read as a fervent re-affirmation of the principle that no economic system or ideology is moral if it dehumanizes those who work in it. Problems arise because no successful strategy for making middle-way policies work has ever been devised.

In short, operational experiments are the key. Accordingly, it is instructive to review a few efforts launched under the banner of middle-way theories.

A. *Yugoslavia*

Yugoslavia under Tito had good reasons for not tying its economic destiny too closely to the Soviet Union. With economic dependence came intolerable levels of political and ideological subordination. And the centralized Soviet pattern of economic decision-making was largely inapplicable to Yugoslavia's regionally diverse groups: Serbians, Croatians, Montenegrins. More autonomy had to be left to decentralized economic units if conflicting political loyalties were to be retained by Yugoslavia's central authorities. In its search for a practical incentive system to make decentralization work, Yugoslavia resorted to worker-management within industry.

This essay is not the proper venue to describe or evaluate Yugoslavia's experiments in worker-management.[27] Its purposes are adequately served by noting that middle-way strategies, like those they supplant, produce only relatively satisfying results. The very relativity of these results is a salutary reminder that "middle ways" are not panaceas.

Yugoslavia is not the only country, however, to have experimented with alternative approaches to socialism; several African nations have sought to frame indigenous models of "African" socialism.

B. African Socialism

Underlying the quest of African nations for their own brand of socialism is a two-fold aspiration. The *political* objective is to assert relative independence of the two super-powers, each epitomizing a dominant ideological system. The *cultural* goal is to tread a road to development which respects their past history and cultural heritage. Such ambitions can vary modally, however. Thus Julius Nyerere preaches "ujamma" or "familyhood" for Tanzania, whereas Leopold Senghor discourses on "negritude" as the basis of a distinctive identity and a unique "socialist" model for Senegal. Both leaders reject Marxism's one-dimensional emphasis on production and capitalism's atomistic competitiveness. Senghor does not want Africans to be mere consumers of civilization, because he believes they have their own contribution to make to the universal civilization in gestation. And Nyerere adds that, for him, "socialism" means subordinating individual goals to the needs of society, particularly those of its weakest members.[28]

Amilcar Cabral, theorist and military leader of Guinea-Bissau's independence struggle, likewise sought a development model suited to his country's specific conditions. Although he borrowed elements of social organization, ideology, and political practice from East and West, he urged Guinea-Bissau to create its own model in accord with past traditions and new conditions.[29]

These three African leaders all reject the central values held by the West's two main ideologies, capitalism and centralized socialism. Both systems undermine the traditional basis for solidarity, a value which accounts for the survival of African cultural identity through centuries of slavery and colonialism. If class conflict is taken as the law of life in society, solidarity becomes meaningless. Solidarity is likewise rendered meaningless if each person in society seeks only individual gains from collective efforts to produce and govern. This is why indigenous African socialists stand on a middle ground between individualism and impersonal collectivism.

In Africa as in Yugoslavia, however, practical results have been only relatively successful. Middle-ways are not panaceas and, on balance, their economic, political, and cultural performance record is not significantly better than that of societies following standard capitalist or socialist prescriptions. One must not suppose, however, that only socialism breeds hybrid systems: capitalism likewise generates alternative forms.

C. Neo-Capitalism

Capitalism and socialism are generic labels which subsume, under their respective banners, various specific forms of social organization. Japanese capitalism displays its uniqueness, for example, through tenured lifetime work contracts, the practice of farming out work to artisanal family units, and fidelity to traditional seniority systems in promoting managers. Here we have a hybrid form of capitalism standing midway between U.S.-style reward systems and traditional Japanese work hierarchies. Indeed much of what in Asian countries is called "capitalism" constitutes a mixed system in which standard capitalist patterns merge with pre-capitalist institutional forms and values. This is most visibly the case in the continent's "successful" capitalist economies—Korea, Taiwan, Singapore, and Hong Kong.

Syncretistic patterns assumed by capitalism in another Asian country, Saudi Arabia, are especially interesting. Saudi rulers faced the challenge of preserving a feudal political order while harnessing the dynamic entrepreneurship of American capitalism to economic activities. That political order still rests on a strong and generalized adherence to Islamic beliefs and morality. Consequently, value tensions between capitalistic profit-seeking and Islamic norms for justice had to be harmonized through the creation of novel institutions and practices. The most intriguing of these is the Islamic bank, explicitly designed to circumvent the Koran's strict ban on usury, the charging of interest on monies loaned. Under modern financial conditions money is not some inert treasure to be preserved, but a dynamic asset for creating new wealth. Saudi Arabia's Islamic banks solve their moral dilemma by accepting deposits and making loans without charging interest to lenders and borrowers, although they do levy a service charge. A "shared risk" system allows banks to receive a percentage of profits realized by borrowers once their own investments bear fruit. In turn, Islamic banks distribute a "share" of their monetary receipts to their own depositors. Cynics may charge that funds circulating among borrowers, banks, and lenders are no different from "interest" or what the Koran would call "usury." Nevertheless, Saudis go to great lengths and expense to institute separate accounting, management and loan negotiation mechanisms to assure that "interest" is not paid. Saudis have devised an effective "middle way" between standard capitalist practices and traditional Islamic lending norms, which did not make use of mediating institutions such as banks.[30]

In many other Third World countries, "mixed" approaches to planning and economic management likewise characterize daily practice. To illustrate, capitalists hold that the recruitment and promotion of personnel should be based on merit, which is assessed by a combination of certified credentials and performance tests. In countless Third World countries, however, the nomination of people to posts is dictated by nepotism; traditional allegiances to family, kin, or ethnic community outweigh considerations of merit. Defenders of this practice point out that, notwithstanding rhetoric about the merit principle, matters may not work so differently in countries like the United States, where "old boy" networks of school alumni or social club members may play the functionally equivalent role exercised by nepotism elsewhere. The net effect in both cases is to circumvent the strict merit system.

D. Chile

No "third way" experiment is more illuminating than that conducted by Chile under Presidents Eduardo Frei and Salvador Allende between 1964 and 1973. Frei, leader of Chile's Christian Democrat Party, admired Konrad Adenauer and Alcide de Gasperi as creative practitioners of a "third way," more socially compassionate than capitalism yet free of Marxist totalitarianism. European and Latin American Christian Democracies alike drew their ideological nourishment from the social encyclicals, a specialized *corpus* of papal writings which defends several normative principles. These are:

(1) private ownership of productive assets is a natural right;
(2) this right is not absolute but relative, and its specific institu-

tional modalities vary with circumstances and are always subordinated to the "common good" of society;

(3) this "common good" places an obligation on the state to assure
sustenance to all its citizens at a level consonant with their spiritual dignity as persons. In a word, social justice is distributive
as well as commutative;

(4) the salary system is not intrinsically exploitive;

(5) class conflict is not the inherent law of social history but a pernicious error which prevents labor and capital from joining efforts to pursue the common good;

(6) the so-called "laws of economics" must be subject to the demands of the spiritual vocation of all human beings; and

(7) the value of persons must not be judged solely, or primarily,
on the basis of their contribution to economic production.

Christian Democratic parties translated this humanistic vision into
a political platform which was simultaneously anti-communist and reformist. On the one hand, the platform censured communism as intrinsically evil because it is atheistic and totalitarian. On the other, it
condemned capitalism, not in principle but in its concrete practice, because it valued competitive success more highly than providing essential
goods to all members of society. Because history offered numerous examples of countries which were both capitalistic and democratic, Christian Democrats assumed that political welfare decisions could attenuate
evils attendant upon capitalism. This politics could accomplish by distributing economic, political, and organizational powers over multiple
institutions, each serving as a check upon the other.

Thanks to the towering stature and political shrewdness of Adenauer and de Gasperi, aided by post-war conditions and the visible presence of a communist enemy, European Christian Democrats achieved
great prestige in the two decades following World War II. Latin American Christian Democrats gladly rode the coattails of that prestige. Indeed, in the late 1950's and early 1960's, they had not yet been
disillusioned by revelations of widespread corruption, anti-reformist
conservatism, and cynical perpetuation in power which, in later years,
tarnished the guilded image of German and Italian Christian Democracy.
Adenauer and de Gasperi were tough but noble and incorrupt politicians.
Unfortunately, however, their party later became a seedbed of mediocre

and cynical office-holders. More importantly, objective social conditions in Latin American countries differed radically from those found in Europe.

Unlike Germany and Italy, Latin American countries were peopled by vast majorities of poor; their economies were still in transition away from the production of primary commodities for export to manufacturing; their labor unions were relatively powerless at the bargaining table; their political institutions were not pluralistic or democratic; and their press had no tradition of free and critical public education. Latin American Christian Democrats saw government's role to be promoting structural reform, not merely balancing competing interest within a framework presumed to be equitable in its foundations. Chile's first generation of Christian Democrats denounced capitalism as exploitative and repudiated communism as dictatorial and materialistic. They proposed a reformist "third way" which would blend socialism's thirst after justice with liberal democracy's regard for freedom. Of course power must be decentralized: economic power could not be vested in the same institutions as political power, and free associations must be permitted so that individuals might have collective negotiating strength to keep the state from becoming omnipotent. Some nationalization of basic industries was advocated, but the universal seizure of productive assets by the state was ruled out. Similarly, reforms in land tenure, tax structures, administrative, educational and fiscal systems were urged; but these reforms had to be approved by voters and legislators, not imposed by an omnipotent party allegedly acting in the name of proletarian masses.[31] Frei was elected in 1964 on such a reform program. Over the next six years, notwithstanding Frei's probity, political skills, and Chile's general high level of political sophistication, his "third way" failed. Why? The reasons had nothing to do with the party's noble principles or with Frei's personal qualities: they were structural. As I have written elsewhere:

> Frei had won his mandate because enough people who wanted far-reaching change had thought they could get it from him, and simultaneously enough conservative voters who feared "the worst" (socialism and Allende) thought it was safer to accept partial change under Frei, who was quite solidly committed to parliamentary democracy and free enterprise, than to

risk losing everything should a more radical candidate win.
Hence Frei's seemingly noble experiment failed because, despite the appearances, it was essentially a program of pallia-
tives. Furthermore, he could not bring himself to overstep the
ideological limits of his own Christian Deomocrat model of
development.[32]

I cannot here retrace in detail the reasons for the model's failure.
But fail it did, as witnessed by the defection of Frei's leading Christian
Democrat ideologue, Jacques Chonchol, to Allende's camp and by the
election of Allende in 1970 by the same electorate which had feared to
vote in a socialist president in 1964. Experiments in Christian Democracy in Venezuela—under Rafael Caldera (1969–1974) and Herrera
Campins (1979 to the present) have further confirmed the limitations of
Christian Democracy as a formula for developmental reform. Precisely
because it is a hybrid "third way" standing midway between capitalism
and socialism, the Christian Democrat political platform wins the un-
qualified allegiance of almost no one. Conservatives tolerate it as the
lesser of two evils, a means of avoiding what they deem to be a
"greater" evil, namely, socialist reform. Meanwhile, progressive reformers endorse it but timidly, viewing it as the best that is realistically
obtainable, given the strength of opposition forces hostile to more fundamental reform. In almost literal terms, the "third way" is everybody's
bastard, the object of disavowed paternity from all quarters, a political
orphan with few ardent supporters anywhere. Christian Democrat governments in developing countries face a disturbing choice: either push
ahead with reforms consistent with their principles, thereby risking losing their conservative or moderate supporters, or compromise with capitalistic or semi-feudal vested interests in the name of preserving
"democracy," thereby alienating their reformist supporters.

A painful lesson emerges here: namely, that those who would have
the best of both political worlds risk getting the worst of each. As the
Pakistani economist Mahbub ul Haq writes:

And here we come to the second of the disastrous decisions—
the choice of the mixed economy. In most cases, such a choice
has combined the worst, not the best, features of capitalism
and socialism. It has often prevented the developing countries

from adopting honest-to-goodness economic incentives and using the free functioning of the price system to achieve efficiency in a capitalistic framework, if not equity. In reality, there have been too many inefficient administrative controls and price distortions. At the same time, the choice of the mixed economy has prevented these societies from pursuing their goals in a truly socialistic framework, since mixed economy institutions have often been more capitalistic than not. The end result, therefore, has often been that they have fallen between two stools, combining weak economic incentives with bureaucratic socialism. Neither the ends of growth nor equity are served by such confusion in social and political objectives within the framework of a mixed economy.[33]

Haq explains that political constraints which dictate the choice of a mixed system prevent leaders from implementing policy measure capable of generating success on either front. Echoing Martin Luther's "If you must sin, sin boldly", Haq concludes:

that the days of the mixed economy are numbered. The developing countries will have to become either more frankly capitalistic or more genuinely socialist. The capitalistic alternative is workable only in those situations where the society is willing to accept income inequalities over a long period of time without exploding or where extremely high growth rates (10 to 15 percent) can be financed with a generous inflow of resources from Western friends. Otherwise, the only alternative is a genuinely socialist system, based on a different ideology and a different pattern of society. But this does not mean bureaucratic socialism; it means a major change in the political balance of power within these societies and drastic economic and social reforms. Whether the developing countries can manage such a change without violent revolution is a critical question of our time.[34]

In the real world impoverished masses are rarely "willing to accept income inequalities over a long period of time without exploding;" these inequalities are imposed upon them.[35] Even achieving high growth rates financed with "a generous inflow of resources from Western friends" does not guarantee social peace. A critical reading of Brazil's economic miracle[36] undermines Haq's optimism. Moreover, if the alternative is a socialist system which can be obtained only through violent revolution, can one be optimistic? If we are to believe Robert Heilbroner's dismal *Inquiry Into the Human Prospect*,[37] not at all! Waging a violent revolution does not guarantee that either sound development or less human suffering will ensue. Kampuchea's destiny under Pol Pot's fanatics invites us to sober skepticism here.[38]

Where, then, are we left standing in the wake of these reflections on the past history of "third ways?" If we stand anywhere at all it is on a thin, and perhaps shrinking, sliver of intellectual and political space.

The history of "third ways" warns us against any naive, ahistorical exegesis of Pope John Paul II's exhortations on the subject. Most searches for "third way" paradigms in recent years take the form of a quest for alternative development strategies. A brief look at the dynamics of this quest sheds light on the policy implications of new societal models.

ALTERNATIVE DEVELOPMENT STRATEGIES

Growing numbers of strategists reject conventional development models.[39] With few exceptions growth policies have not led to material well-being and jobs for the masses, or greater social and political freedom. Even where high aggregate growth has been achieved, distribution of benefits has been grossly inequitable,[40] and sacrifices imposed on populations in the form of economic hardship, political coercion, and violations of personal rights have often been excessive.[41]

After three decades of "rational" resource planning within nations and international resource transfers, the gaps between rich and poor countries, regions, and social classes have widened.[42] Wealth has been highly concentrated in cities at the expense of the countryside. Michael Lipton correctly denounces the built-in urban bias to development efforts in most parts of the world.[43]

Third World industrialization has bred more, not less, dependency. Hopes nurtured by earlier strategists that "self-sustaining" economic growth would follow once a certain income threshold was reached, have proven illusory.[44] A dependency sequence is in operation, with new technological, managerial and market servitudes replacing vulnerabilities founded on the shortage of capital or skilled people. Financial interdependencies, in turn, have grown so complex that one is hard pressed to know who has greater leverage: banks lending to uncreditworthy clients or nations which, like Zaire and Poland, borrow beyond their means.[45] Very few countries, capitalist or socialist, have combined economic growth with distributional equity, minimal protection of human rights, and respect for political liberties. This is why strategists search for other than traditional ways of gaining development.

Alternative developers stress three components: meeting BHN's, promoting self-reliance, and minimizing cultural damage.[46] Notwithstanding the optimistic rhetoric surrounding most discussions of alternative development strategies, serious political obstacles stand in the way of their implementation. As a result, the values underlying the alternative model play only a modest role in shaping planning priorities and resource allocations. More importantly, few countries have formulated successful "strategies for the transition" away from distorted development toward comprehensive human well-being. Although hopeful initiatives abound at the level of local projects or programs, these cannot be extrapolated to the level of national strategies. In short, "third way" strategies are more easily praised than practiced, more readily designed than implemented. And, truth to tell, few countries have seriously tried to implement true alternatives to capitalism or socialism. Most national experiments are more accurately characterized as variants of capitalism or socialism than as genuine alternative pathways to development.

Measures taken by one non-governmental grass-roots movement in Sri Lanka, however, provide a helpful lesson. I refer to the Sarvodaya Shramadana Movement,[47] whose leaders state that the goals of development must be borrowed neither from countries already "developed" nor from pre-existing theories, but drawn from a critical assessment of latent dynamisms found in traditional values and institutions. A.T. Ariyaratne, Sarvodaya's founder, considers that "a poor country like Sri Lanka would have gone 99% down the road to development if development goals were properly defined and understood by the people."[48]

In its first decade (1958–1968) Sarvodaya centered its efforts on the total personality awakening of participants in volunteer work camps performing tasks useful to their community. A second phase aimed at the total awakening of villages. Yet, as Ariyaratne explains:

> the awakening of a village community is closely linked up with the national environment of which the villages are an integral part. Therefore, as the number of village communities participating in Sarvodaya activities increased, concepts of national development as relevant to village people's traditions, experience and aspirations also developed among them. Thus *Deshodaya or the awakening of the nation also became a Sarvodaya ideal.*
>
> In the present day world no community or nation can pursue a path to development without influencing and being influenced by what is happening in other countries . . . as the Movement took national proportions it also had to develop its own concepts on world development. In other words *Vishvodaya or the awakening of the world* community as a whole became a fourth ideal to strive for by the adherents of the Movement.
>
> Thus the Sarvodaya Movement in Sri Lanka works towards the integrated ideal of the development of Man and Society as persons, families, village and urban groups, nations and one world community.[49]

Sarvodaya draws its answer to the central question "Awakening to what?" from classical doctrines of Theravada Buddhism which counsels a middle way between all extremes: indulgence and abnegation, absorption in the world or total flight from it, atomistic salvation or collective deliverance. In Theravada Buddhism each person is summoned to awaken fully to the nature of reality's inter-related evils—suffering, death, old age and impermanence. These evils have a common underlying cause, namely, the stubborn persistence in individuals of craving, that immoderate desire which renders them acquisitive, exploitative and violent. All satisfactions born of desire are ephemeral, however, and doomed to corruption. What is worse, they addict one to further desires which are themselves condemned to futile repetition in a Karmic cycle of endless births, deaths, rebirths, and new deaths. The key to human deliverance, therefore, lies in breaking out of this vicious circle of interconnected evils, thereby putting an end to the radical *cause* of human suffering. Hope rests on Buddha's achievement, twenty-five centuries ago, of enlightenment as to the meaning of life, nature, and history. Buddha was no god but a mere mortal, distinguished from others only by his successful attainment of supreme enlightenment. After reaching full understanding, however, Buddha did not withdraw to blissful *Nibbana,* the serene and total absence of suffering and craving, but remained instead in this perishable flesh to teach others the way, the *eightfold path* to deliverance.

For Theravada Buddhism, the goal of historical existence for all individuals is to progress toward full enlightenment. Social conditions should favor such progress. This is why Sarvodaya relativizes all "goods" held out by capitalist or socialist conceptions of development, refusing to treat them as absolutes. It also relativizes the manner in which they must be sought: Benefits must not be pursued violently, in a mode which alienates men and women in craving after illusory satisfactions, in ways which exclude participation of the masses in favor of political despots.

Ariyaratne insists that:

> Development should start from the grass-roots, from the village up. People should fully participate in planning for development and in the implementation of such plans. The technological knowledge prevailing at the people's level and the available local resources should be used initially. Progressively and appropriately it could be upgraded with advanced knowledge. National development plans should be based, not partially but totally on this broad-based people's participation. It should first strive to satisfy the basic needs of the people and not artificially created wants that are a blind imitation from materialistic cultures . . . The ideal of Sri Lanka being a "Dharma Dveepa" (Land of Righteousness) and "Chanyagara" (Land of Plenty) is always foremost in the minds of the Sarvodaya workers.[50]

Sarvodaya treats *all modern visions of development instrumentally.* The conventional goals of modernity—material well-being, technological efficiency, and institutional modernity—are tested to see if they foster what Sarvodaya calls genuine development, namely, the full awakening of the human personality in all its dimensions. This approach is the antithesis of most others, in which strategists uncritically assume that the proper goals of development are the three facets of modernity just outlined. Modernists treat traditional values *instrumentally,* as mere aids or obstacles to be manipulated in moving toward goals copied from societies deemed to be already "developed." In truth, however, no country is satisfactorily "developed" if we concede that true development is the

> full realization of human capabilities: men and women become
> makers of their own histories, personal and societal. They free
> themselves from every servitude imposed by nature or by op-
> pressive systems, they achieve wisdom in their mastery over
> nature and over their own wants, they create new webs of sol-
> idarity based not on domination but on reciprocity among
> themselves, they achieve a rich symbiosis between contem-
> plation and transforming action, between efficiency and free
> expression. This total concept of development can perhaps
> best be expressed as the 'human ascent'—the ascent of all men
> in their integral humanity, including the economic, biological,
> psychological, social, cultural, ideological, spiritual, mysti-
> cal, and transcendental dimensions.[51]

"Advanced" societies are poor models for "backward" nations to follow because what they call development is distorted development, or what Preiswerk calls mal-development.[52]

My earlier remarks on the failure of "third way" models in developing nations are germane to the formulation of social policy in "developed" countries as well. The reason is that conventional development paradigms are bad for the Third World *not only* because they are exported to an uncongenial social terrain, *but also* because, even in their societies of origin, they institutionalize selfishness over community, material achievement over cultural creation, and intellectual aggression over wisdom.

I am not pleading here for technological backwardness, cultural stagnation, or economic passivity. There is no merit in adopting a museum or mausoleum outlook on traditional cultures. Change must certainly come to these cultures, but the vital question is: change on whose terms? Something is wrong if traditional societies can gain access to modernity only by committing value suicide.[53] The wiser course is to view traditional wisdoms as harboring latent dynamisms capable of giving birth to new indigenous forms of modernity.

In my view, "third way" alternatives to capitalist and socialist development models should be based on development from tradition.[54] My contention is that valid "middle ways" can only be created out of social experimentation by a community of need living out new kinds of development in harmony with its own values. Third ways cannot be deduced from theoretical paradigms lying equidistant from capitalist and socialist models. This very conclusion, however, calls for additional comment.

DICHOTOMOUS FRAMEWORKS ARE TOO NARROW

Capitalism and collectivism, modernity's two dominant paradigms, share several alienating anti-developmental value assumptions. Both equate the fullness of good with the abundance of goods. Yet Erich Fromm warns that "*affluent alienation . . .* can be as dehumanizing as *impoverished alienation.*"[55] Moreover, if we flee the romantic dreamworld of ideologues, and examine the historical incarnations of capitalism and socialism, we observe that both are cruelly ethnocentric in their dealings with indigenous cultures. Capitalist and socialist regimes throughout the globe behave as steamrollers, arrogating to themselves the mandate to promote their own favored model of modernity. This is the pattern displayed by China in crushing Tibetan culture; it is the pattern displayed by agribusinessmen running roughshod over Indian communities in Mexico. Capitalist and socialist modernists share a narrow, one-dimensional approach to defining national identity, to the exclusion of pluri-dimensional views. Reductionist policies of assimilation preside over social policy in the United States, the Soviet Union, China and countless African nations. Nevertheless, the Mexican anthropologist Rodolfo Stavenhagen considers that "Mexico as a nation will enrich itself with the cultural contribution made by all and each one of the ethnic groups within its borders. And authentic national culture is the mosaic of the ethnic and regional cultures of the country."[56]

Assimilationist policies, as I have noted elsewhere, almost always fail. The reason is that:

> Dominated culture groups, in fact, resent efforts made to ab-
> sorb them into some dominant pattern. Even when assimila-
> tion seems to succeed, it is tantamount to the supreme cultural
> insult, like telling a people that they are not worthy to function
> as a community in the twentieth century. Not surprisingly,
> therefore, it results in intolerable coercion and exploitation, as
> in the annihilation of Indians in Brazil, along nineteenth cen-
> tury U.S. policy lines, ethnic bloodbaths in Burundi, and so
> on. Consequently, in most cases, assimilation is to be rejected
> on both political and ethical grounds.[57]

Assimilation strategies are the offspring of a simplistic vision of social integration. Many "third way" social strategies likewise fail because of policymakers' infatuation with another simplistic image, in this
case, dyadic formulations of ideological options. The infatuation with
dyadic "either-or" formulas carries over into the formulation of "third
ways". But perhaps it is best not to define Vision Number 3 in terms of
Visions Number 1 and 2. Perhaps the best alternatives should be designed not as functions, even as reactive functions, of what they repu-
diate.

To illustrate why a wider gamut of social policy models should replace dichotomies, we may ask if dyadic formulations explain revolutions in Latin America. In their recent study of the Mexican Revolution,
Hodges and Gandy reject the classical Marxist dichotomy which declared apodictically that the only political options for Latin America lay
between Mexico's populist revolution and Cuba's socialist one. Brazil,
they argue, has wrought a third kind of revolution which Marxists could
not account for, namely, a political revolution that was, nevertheless,
ideologically and economically reactionary. Although the Brazilian gen-
erals, they explain, "have brutally suppressed the leftwing parties striving for socialism, objectively they have also transferred political power
from a class of property owners to the military sector of the new bureaucratic class. Contrary to conventional Marxism, a bureaucratic political revolution may take a military repressive form."[58] Military
forces, even when their ideology and economic program are reactionary,

can be vectors of a political revolution. In Brazil, Hodges and Gandy continue,

> a military-bureaucratic class seized the government and pushed the bourgeoisie aside. This was a politically revolutionary act. But the bureaucracy reacted economically by opening the door to American capital. This—as well as its repression of nationalist and socialist tendencies and its physical eliminations of much of the Brazilian left—meant that it played a counter-revolutionary role.[59]

These authors reject still another Marxist dichotomy, that postulated by Trotsky to outline the roads bureaucracies may take after a revolutionary seizure of power. The bureaucracy, Trotsky asserted,

> can govern either by converting itself into an instrument of foreign capital and shackling the proletariat with the chains of a police dictatorship or by maneuvering with the proletariat and making concessions, thus enjoying the possibility of a certain independence with respect to foreign capitalists.[60]

But Trotsky, Gandy and Hodges tell us, overlooked "a third possibility. The bureaucracy may balance the interests of foreign capital against those of the working class in order to develop the weak local bourgeoisie. This is what really happened in Mexico."[61]

My point is that dichotomous frameworks are too narrow to cover all possibilities. The important correlative point states that "third way" models conceived in function of the initial dichotomy also fail to exhaust the range of alternative possibilities. This is surely the case in experimental development strategies; the Sri Lankan example given suggests that "third ways" should situate themselves elsewhere than on some middle ground between capitalism and socialism. Instead, genuine "third ways" need to emerge from the experimental practice of communities testing out the latent dynamisms present in their own traditions. The claim that third ways should *not* be conceptualized with reference to pre-existing dual frameworks is confirmed in Richard Critchfield's recent book, *Villages*. Critchfield writes:

The West was offering peasant villages just two basic ways to modernize: one capitalist, the other communist. The choice presented was industrialization-urbanization, or Marxist-Leninist revolution followed by a state-run, state-owned society. Both, I believe, have failed the villager—the first because capitalism has not been able to supply enough jobs and incomes in the Third World cities. This has to be hedged a bit because eight countries in east Asia—South Korea, Taiwan, Hong Kong, Singapore, Thailand, Burma, the Philippines and Malaysia—during the late 1970s achieved something near to or above the 7 percent annual economic growth rate that doubles real GNP in a decade. (Brazil and Mexico made rapid strides in manufacturing too.) But their combined populations are but a fifth of the Indian subcontinent's and Indonesia's together. Communism's failure is denial to villagers of privately owned land and hence sufficient incentives; it goes against basic human nature. Historians, I hope, will someday look back and say that Marxism-Leninism began to burn itself out, at least in Asia, the day Chou En-lai or whoever it was placed his first order for Dr. Borlaug's seeds. This victory was not won on the battlefields of Indochina, but that's part of it; who could wish Cambodia's fate on his own country? We may have won in Vietnam after all.

What Toynbee did not foresee, because technology did not advance enough to make this possible until the 1960s, was that the West would come up with a third way to modernize: the rapid transfer of farm science, made possible by new discoveries in tropical plant genetics, to bring about the kind of agricultural revolution on which its own wealth and industrial power was orginally based. . . .

If the Green Revolution had not come along precisely when it did, I think it quite possible that Toynbee's prophecy would be a lot closer to fulfillment.[62]

Whether or not one accepts Critchfield's reading of the transition to modernity, he is correct, I think, in holding that dyadic conceptions of social evolution do not exhaust available alternatives.

CONCLUSION

Readers of John Paul II's encyclical do well to recall this as they search for "third ways." Ideologues of every stripe are displeased by this document. A recent *FORTUNE* magazine piece complains that "Judging from the general tenor of *Laborem Exercens,* the Church remains wedded to socialist economics and is increasingly a sucker for Third World anti-imperialist rhetoric."[63] Liberation theologians, on the other hand, "wish he would give a little on his ideas about the person and about freedom, since these, they say, may have to be bent somewhat in order to achieve a just society."[64] Richard Neuhaus defends John Paul because,

> As leader of a universal community, the pope cannot overtly take sides in the many-faceted conflicts between East and West, between capitalism and socialism. In his public announcements, John Paul appears to criticize evenhandedly atheistic totalitarianism and capitalism consumerism.[65]

Ours is not the first generation of Christians tempted to design societies according to Gospel lights. The existence of medieval Christendom as an imperial polity gives the lie to Chesterton's barb that "Christianity has not been tried and found wanting, but found difficult and left untried." In fact Christendom proved to be a quite viable form of social organization for several centuries. It broke down, however, because it could not guide societies through the passage from post-feudal commercialism to industrial capitalism. More significantly, as the recent history of Christian Democracy in Germany, Italy, Chile, and Venezuela suggests, that particular variety of Christian "third ways" holds out little promise to contemporary societies.

Does this mean that Christian values cannot inspire new paradigms of social construction as we enter the post-industrial age? Perhaps not, but successful paradigms will not resemble the aborted "third ways" of the 1960's.

Although facile readings of the encyclical are ruled out, many valuable themes highlighted in the document can inspire innovative social policy. Both capitalism and socialism, the Pope notes, fail to treat human beings as *subjects* of work, seeing them merely as *objects* in a production cycle. John Paul II invites manager and workers to a lofty vision of shared responsibility for promoting human welfare in society. He insists on the right of weak and disabled workers to a dignified livelihood, even though the spirit of the age favors a utilitarian calculus which ignores their intrinsic value as persons. John Paul II calls for change in the world's economic structures to assure equitable development for all. He condemns statist patterns of "socialization" of productive property as spurious. Finally, he demands that Christianity reject all forms of materialism and economicism.

In reading this letter on the dignity of human labor, one is reminded of Sarvodaya's conception of "right livelihood." In opposition to most development experts, Sarvodaya judges that a paid job is not a basic human need, but merely one possible means of providing a right livelihood. The essential value and basic need is a right livelihood. As Sarvodaya's founder explains it,

> Lord Buddha in His Noble Eight-fold Path leading to perfect enlightenment has included Right Livelihood as its fifth factor. In one of His discourses Lord Buddha mentions the four characteristics of a right approach to economic action, namely, (i) diligence in efficient productive activity, (ii) preservation of what is produced and conservation of nature, (iii) the right social milieu in which one should work, and (iv) a balanced approach to consumption.[66]

This normative view of labor embraces several broad human values:

(i)   the joy of personality awakening through constructive and creative labour,
(ii) harmonious social integration by working as a member of a group and
(iii) satisfaction of the needs of life through productive work. In this economic philosophy there is an in-built motivation for self-aggrandizement that activates both the employee and the employer. Instead of productive work debasing their human relationships, they are lifted up to higher human levels and relationships. There is no alienation of the human being from his essential self or his work.[67]

Marx cursed capitalism because it alienates human beings from their deeper selves and the very fruits of their work. And popes have condemned Marxism because, they argue, it violates the true vocation of human beings to be co-creators of a humane world. John Paul II's encyclical *On Human Work* is the latest in a line of heartfelt pleas issued by socially conscious Christian leaders NOT to treat workers as mere workers. He adds his voice even to those whom he condemns when he insists that "it is through man's labor that . . . human dignity, brotherhood and freedom must flourish on earth."[68]

Notes

1–17. These notes have been omitted in this edition.

18. Pope John Paul II, *On Human Work* (Washington, D.C.: U.S. Catholic Conference, 1981), p. 15.

19. *Ibid.,* p. 14.

20. See, e.g., Paul Oestreicher (editor), *The Christian Marxist Dialogue* (New York: The Macmillan Company, 1969); Adam Schaff, *A Philosophy of Man* (London: Lawrence and Wishart, 1963); Leszek Kolakowski, *Toward a Marxist Humanism, Essays on the Left Today* (New York: Grove Press, 1968); special issue of *Tri Quarterly,* "A Leszek Kolakowski Reader," No. 22 (Fall, 1971); Ernst Bloch, *Man on His Own, Essays in the Philosophy of Religion (New York: Herder and Herder, 1970); Ernst Fischer, Art Against Ideology* (London: Allen Lane, Penguin Press, 1969); Jan Lochman, *Encountering Marx: Bonds and Barriers Between Christians and Marxists* (Philadelphia, PA: Fortress, 1977); and, Lochman, *Reconciliation and Liberation: Challenging a One-Dimensional View of Salvation* (Philadelphia, PA: Fortress, 1980).

21. John Eagleson (editor), *Christians and Socialism, Documentation of the Christians for Socialism Movement in Latin America* (Maryknoll, NY: Orbis Books, 1975).

22. Pope John XXIII, *Pacem in Terris,* April 11, 1963, paragraph #158. Reproduced in Joseph Gremillion, *The Gospel of Peace and Justice: Catholic Social Teaching Since Pope John* (Maryknoll, NY: Orbis Books, 1976).

23. Pope John Paul II, p. 33.

24. On this see Joseph H. Carens, *Equality, Moral Incentives, and the*

Market (Chicago: University of Chicago Press, 1981); cf. Karl Mannheim, *Freedom, Power and Democratic Planning* (London: Routledge and Kegan Paul Ltd, 1951).

25. Representative Christian efforts to apply the Gospel to capitalist economics include David M. Beckman, *Where Faith and Economics Meet, A Christian Critique* (Minneapolis: Augsburg Publishing House, 1981); Richard K. Taylor, *Economics and the Gospel* (Philadelphia: United Church Press, 1973); and Ronald H. Preston, *Religion and the Persistence of Capitalism* (London: SCM Press Ltd., 1979).

26. L.J. Lebret and R. Moreux, *Manifeste d'Economie et Humanisme* (Marseille: Economie et Humanisme, 1942).

27. Branko Horvat, *The Yugoslav Economic System: The First Labor-Managed Economy in the Making* (M.E. Sharpe, 1976); Jaroslav Vanek, *General Theory of Labor-Managed Market Economies* (Ithaca, NY: Cornell University Press, 1970) and Jaroslav Vanek, *The Labor-Managed Economy: Essays* (Ithaca: Cornell University Press, 1977).

28. Julius Nyerere, *Crusade for Liberation* (New York: Oxford University Press, 1978); Julius Nyerere, *Freedom and Development* (New York: Oxford University Press, 1973); and Julius Nyerere, *Man and Development* (New York: Oxford University Press, 1974). Cf. also William R. Duggan and John R. Civille, *Tanzania and Nyerere: A Study of Ujamma and Nationalism* (Maryknoll, NY: Orbis Books, 1976). See also, Léopold Senghor, *Pour une societé sénégalaise socialiste et démocratique* (Dakar: Nouvelles Editions Africaines, 1976), and *Les Fondements de l'africanité ou Négritude et arabité* (Paris: Presence Africaine, 1967).

29. Amilcar Cabral, *Unity and Struggle, Speeches and Writings of Amilcar Cabral* (New York: Monthly Review Press, 1979); cf. Denis Goulet, *Looking at Guinea-Bissau: A New Nation's Development Strategy* (Washington, D.C.: Overseas Development Council, Occasional Paper No. 9, March 1978), 66 pages.

30. Muhammad Abdul-Rauf, *The Islamic Doctrine of Economics and Contemporary Economic Thought* (Washington, D.C.: American Enterprise Institute for Public Policy Research, 1979). Cf. "How Islamic Finance Works," no author's name given, *Business International,* March 16, 1979, p. 82.

31. For an introduction to Chilean Christian Democratic theory in the 1960's see Jacques Chonchol, *El Desarrollo de America Latina y la Reforma Agraria* (Santiago de Chile: Editorial del Pacifico, S.A., 1964); also, Julio Silva Solar and Jacques Chonchol, *El Desarrollo de la Nueva Sociedad en America Latina* (Santiago de Chile: Editorial Universitaria, S.A., 1965).

32. Denis Goulet, *A New Moral Order, Development Ethics and Liberation Theology* (Maryknoll, NY: Orbis Books, 1974).

33. Mahbub ul Haq, *The Poverty Curtain, Choices for the Third World* (New York: Columbia University Press, 1976), p. 44.

34. *Ibid.*, p. 44–5.

35. For a general treatment of these issues, see Peter L. Berger, *Pyramids of Sacrifice* (New York: Basic Books, 1974). Cf. Charles R. Frank, Jr. and Richard C. Webb (editors), *Income Distribution and Growth in the Less-Developed Countries* (Washington, D.C.: The Brookings Institution, 1977).

36. Cf., e.g., Sylvia Ann Hewlett, *The Cruel Dilemmas of Development: Twentieth Century Brazil* (New York: Basic Books, 1980); cf. Denis Goulet, "Democracy or Dictatorship?" *Commonweal*, Vol. 108, No. 8 (1980), pp. 237–240; and Marcos Freire, *Divida Social—o grande pecado do Brazil* (Brasilia: Senado Federal, 1980).

37. (New York: W.W. Norton and Co., 1974).

38. On the costs attendant upon revolutions, see Barrington Moore, Jr., *Reflections on the Causes of Human Misery* (Boston: Beacon Press, 1970); and his *Social Origins of Dictatorship and Democracy* (Boston: Beacon Press, 1967).

39. See *What Now? Another Development* (Uppsala, Sweden: Dag Hammarskjold Foundation, 1975); Marc Nerfin (editor), *Another Development: Approaches and Strategies* (Uppsala: Dag Hammarskjold Foundation, 1977); International Labour Office, *Employment, Growth and Basic Needs: A One-World Problem* (New York: Praegar, 1977).

40. Hollis Chenery, *et al.*, *Redistribution With Growth* (London: Oxford University Press, 1974); Irma Adelman, "Redistribution Before Growth—A Strategy for Developing Countries," Working Paper 78–14, University of Maryland, Dept. of Economics, 1978.

41. See, *e.g.*, Charles Elliott, *Patterns of Poverty in the Third World* (New York: Praegar, 1975).

42. *U.S. Foreign Policy and the Third World, Agenda 1982*, Roger D. Hansen and contributors for the Overseas Development Council (New York: Praegar, 1982); and *World Development Report 1981* (Washington, D.C.: The World Bank, 1981).

43. Michael Lipton, *Why Poor People Stay Poor, Urban Bias in World Development* (Harvard University Press, 1976).

44. The liberal illusion that "all good things come together"—economic progress, social mobility, political stability, greater democracy—is persuasively refuted in Robert Packenham's *Liberal America and the Third World* (Princeton: Princeton University Press, 1973).

45. For an illuminating treatment of these matters see Anthony Sampson, *The Money Lenders, Bankers and a World of Turmoil* (New York: Viking Press, 1981).

46. On this see Denis Goulet, "Sufficiency for All: The Basic Mandate of Development and Social Economics," *Review of Social Economy,* Vol. 36, No. 3 (December, 1978), pp. 243–261; and Goulet, "An International Support System for Meeting Basic Needs." *The Review of Politics,* Vol. 43. No. 1 (January 1981), pp. 22–42.

47. On Sri Lanka, see Gamani Corea. *The Instability of an Export Economy* (Colombo, Sri Lanka: Marga Institute, 1975): *Welfare and Growth in Sri Lanka* (Colombo: Marga Institute. 1974): and Satchi Ponnambalam. *Dependent Capitalism in Crisis. The Sri Lankan Economy,* 1948–1980 (London: Zed Press. 1981). On Sarvodaya, see Detlef Kantowsky. *Sarvodaya: The Other Development* (New Delhi: Vikas Publishing House, 1980). Cf. Denis Goulet, *Survival With Integrity: Sarvodaya at the Crossroads* (Colombo: Marga Institute, 1981), Goulet, "Development Strategy in Sri Lanka and a People's Alternative," paper prepared for the McGill University Centre for Developing Area Studies Seminar Series, February 15, 1981 and to be published in 1982, and Goulet, "Development as Liberation: Policy Lessons from Case Studies," *World Development,* Vol. 7, No. 6 (June, 1979), pp. 555–566.

48. A.T. Ariyaratne. Address to the Society for International Development. Sri Lanka Chapter, on "Integrating National Development with the Rural Sector," November, 1979 at Bandaranaike Memorial International Conference Hall, Colombo, Sri Lanka, p. 2.

49. A.T. Ariyaratne, *Sarvodaya and Development* (Moratuwa, Sri Lanka: Sarvodaya Press, n.d.), p.1.

50. A.T. Ariyaratne, *Collected Works, Volume I* (Dehiwala, Sri Lanka: Sarvodaya Research Institute, n.d.), p. 134.

51. Denis Goulet, "An Ethical Model for the Study of Values," *Harvard Educational Review,* Vol. 41. No. 2 (May, 1971), pp. 205–227.

52. Roy Preiswerk, *Mal-Développement, Suisse Monde* (Geneva: Le Centre Europe-Tiers Monde (CETIM), 1975).

53. On this see, Denis Goulet, "In Defense of Cultural Rights: Technology, Tradition and Conflicting Models of Rationality." *Human Rights Quarterly,* Vol. 3. No. 4 (1981), pp. 1–18.

54. Denis Goulet, "I Valori Tradizionali e il Loro Ruolo Vitale Nello Sviluppo," in Roberto Gritti and Eleonora Barbieri Masini (editors), *Società e Futuro,* (Roma: Città Nuova Editrice, 1981), pp. 189–204. Cf. special issue of *Development, Seeds of Change, Village Through Global Order* (1981: 3/4), entitled "Culture, The Forgotten Dimension."

55. Erich Fromm, "Introduction", in *Socialist Humanism,* ed. Erich Fromm (New York: Doubleday, 1966), p. ix. Italics Fromm's. Cf. Georges Perec, *Les Choses* (Paris: Julliard, 1965).

56. Rodolfo Stavenhagen, *Problemas Etnicos Y Capesinos, Ensayos* (Mexico: Instituto Nacional Indigenista, 1979), p. 17. Translation mine.

57. Denis Goulet, "Socialization and Cultural Development," *Interchange,* Vol. 10, No. 3 (1979–80), p. 5.

58. Donald Hodges and Ross Gandy, *Mexico 1910–1976: Reform or Revolution?* (London: Zed Press, 1979), pp. 177–67.

59. *Ibid.,* p. 166.

60. *Ibid.,* p. 167.

61. *Ibid.*

62. Richard Critchfield, *Villages* (New York: Doubleday, Anchor Press, 1981), p. 333.

63. Daniel Seligman, "Unfair to Capitalism," *Fortune* (November, 1981), p. 63.

64. Richard John Neuhaus, "The Mind of the Most Powerful Man in the World," *Worldview,* Vol. 24. No. 9 (September, 1981), p. 13.

65. *Ibid.*

66. A.T. Ariyaratne, *Collected Works, Volume II* (Dehiwala, Sri Lanka: Sarvodaya Research Institute, 1980), p. 71.

67. *Ibid.*

68. Pope John Paul II, *op. cit.,* p. 60.

Global Human Rights:
An Interpretation of
the Contemporary Catholic
Understanding

David Hollenbach, S.J.

This article first appeared in *Human Rights in the Americas*, 1982.

The emergence of human rights as a central concern for contemporary Roman Catholicism is a remarkable historical development. From some points of view it is even an astonishing development. The Catholic church was a vigorous opponent of both the democratic and socialist revolutions which were the chief proponents of the civil and social rights enshrined in twentieth-century human rights declarations.[1] In recent years, however, various groups within the Catholic church have become highly visible on the global horizon as advocates for the full range of human rights.[2] Also, the central institutional organ of the Catholic church, the Holy See, has adopted the cause of human rights as the prime focus of its ethical teaching and pastoral strategy in the domain of international justice and peace. This rapid change in the Catholic church's stance toward global human rights is a crucial fact which must be taken into account in any effort to understand current church theory and practice in the rights field.

The interpretation presented here is just that: an interpretation. The Catholic church is a highly differentiated community composed of subcommunities, divided from each other along regional, cultural, economic, and educational lines. This interpretation attempts to grasp the predominant understanding of human rights in the Catholic church, i.e., the one which is setting the course on which the church as a whole seems presently embarked. Therefore, in addition to providing a descriptive account of the prevailing understanding of human rights in the church, what is said here contains an element of prediction. The uncertainty of such an approach may be counterbalanced by the interest it sparks.

The first part of this chapter argues that the impetus for the rapid development of the Catholic understanding of the church's role in the human rights field came from a major event in the modern history of Catholicism: the Second Vatican Council and the pontificate of Pope John XXIII. Part I tries to show that it was not only the developments in theology which occurred at the Council which brought about this change. Rather, under the leadership of John XXIII, Vatican II was the occasion of a fundamental shift in the church's understanding of its social and institutional place in a pluralistic world. The effort to respond to this newly understood social location caused a rapid development in the church's normative stance on human rights. Part II outlines the content of this development and shows its relationship to the central elements of previous Catholic social thought. It shows how a major and unexpected development was legitimated by appeals to tradition. Finally, Part III makes some suggestions about the contribution which the newly developed Catholic understanding of human rights can make to current discussions. Also, some of the questions about human rights that remain unanswered in Catholic thinking will be highlighted.

I
THE CONTEXT FOR DEVELOPMENT:
A TRANSNATIONAL CHURCH IN A PLURALISTIC WORLD

Perhaps the single most significant statement contained in the collection of decrees, constitutions, and declarations of the Second Vatican Council is the following apparently innocuous sentence from the first article of the Declaration on Religious Freedom: "This sacred Synod intends to develop the doctrine of recent Popes on the inviolable rights of the human person and on the constitutional order of society."[3] In fact, the statement is far from innocuous, for it represents an an acknowledgment on the highest level of church teaching that Catholic doctrine can develop, can change. The importance of this assertion has been noted by the theologian who was chiefly responsible for the drafting of the Declaration: "In no other conciliar document is it so explicitly stated that the intention of the Council is to 'develop' Catholic doctrine."[4]

In its immediate context the statement was a prelude to the unambiguous affirmation of the fundamental right of every person to religious freedom. In earlier Catholic teaching this right had been variously qualified and even denied. It is remarkable enough to find a reversal of the explicit content of church teaching coming from as traditional a body as the worldwide episcopacy of the Catholic church assembled in council. In the context of the overall influence of the Council on the church's life, however, the statement is even more noteworthy. It suggests that the development in question touches the basic structure of the church's understanding of human rights and constitutional order. The fact that the need for such development is acknowledged most directly in the Religious Freedom Declaration provides a clue for interpreting the fundamental shift in the Catholic understanding of rights which occurred at the Council. The reorganization of the normative foundations of the Catholic understanding of human rights was produced by the same social force which precipitated the Declaration on Religious Freedom, namely, the reality of pluralism. At the Council the modern Catholic church for the first time was compelled to come to grips in an official way with the realities of the religious, cultural, social, economic, political, and ideological pluralism of the contemporary world. The most obvious effect of this acknowledgment of pluralism was the Council's movement from the kind of unitary model of church/state relationships which prevailed through almost all of previous church history to a pluralistic model based on the right of all persons to religious liberty.

The new experience of the reality of pluralism, however, was not limited to the religious sphere. The diversity of political and economic systems and the conflicting social ideologies present in contemporary global society were also a central concern. This concern is evident in the Council's Pastoral Constitution on the Church in the Modern World, which says:

> Today, the human race is passing through a new stage in its history. Profound and rapid changes are spreading by degrees around the whole world . . . although the world of today has a very vivid sense of its unity and of how one man depends on another in needful solidarity, it is most grievously torn into op-

posing camps by conflicting forces. For political, social, economic, racial and ideological disputes still continue bitterly.
. . . True, there is a growing exchange of ideas, but the very
words by which key concepts are expressed take on quite different meaning in diverse ideological systems.[5]

In the Council's view, this diversity of political, social, economic, and
ideological systems is a threat to peace and an obstacle to justice. The
depth of disagreement between the fundamental social and ideological
visions prevailing around the globe leads to disagreement about the
meaning of peace itself and justice itself. This basic conflict in interpretations of the central normative foundation of social order was one of the
"signs of the times" which inspired the Council's examination of the
place of the church in the world today.

Had the Council followed the lead of past Catholic tradition in formulating its response to the reality of contemporary pluralism and conflict, it would have proposed a normative model of social structure and
political order chosen on the basis of compatibility with Catholic tradition and faith. Such an approach would have repeated past Catholic solutions to the problem of religious pluralism—the proposal of a single
ideal religious order in which Catholicism would hold a privileged place.
But just as the option of a single normative social-religious system was
rejected as the Catholic ideal in the Declaration on Religious Freedom,
so also conciliar and post-conciliar Catholic teaching has rejected the
ideal of a single, normative model of political and economic order. This
parallelism is also evident in the kind of solution actually proposed for
dealing with pluralism and conflict. In the religious sector the Council
did not abandon Catholic commitment to the truth of the Christian religion. Far from it. Rather, it asserted that a Christian understanding of
the human person, rooted both in the Christian tradition and the tradition
of reason, demands that human dignity be respected through the civil
guarantee of religious freedom. Similarly, the conciliar response to social and ideological pluralism did not take the form of a retreat by the
church from the effort to establish justice and peace in global society.
Rather, it affirmed that there are basic rights in the social, economic,
political, and cultural fields which all systems and all ideologies are
bound to respect. These are the basic rights of the human person, derived
from the fundamental dignity of the person.

In the midst of Vatican II, Pope John XXIII issued his encyclical letter *Pacem in Terris* in which he sought to move the Council toward this new perspective. In his words:

> Any human society, if it is to be well ordered and productive, must lay down as a foundation this principle, namely, that every human being is a person; that is, his nature is endowed with intelligence and free will. Indeed, precisely because he is a person he has rights and obligations flowing directly and simultaneously from his very nature. And as these rights are universal and inviolable so they cannot in any way be surrendered.[6]

Following John XXIII's lead, the Council affirmed the full array of human rights spelled out in *Pacem in Terris* as the norms to which every society is accountable no matter what its political, economic, or ideological system, and to which the international order itself can be held accountable. These rights include both the civil and political rights generally associated with Western democracies and the social and economic rights emphasized in socialist societies. In following John XXIII, the Council did not propose a single model of society or nostalgically seek the elimination of pluralism. It adopted a normative framework for a pluralistic world.

This move amounts to a definitive shift in Catholicism from a social ethic which proposed a concrete model of society as demanded by the natural law to a social ethic in which all social models are held accountable to the standards of human rights. The difference between the two perspectives is the acceptance of social, political, and ideological pluralism as an inescapable fact in the contemporary world. Human rights norms do not lead to the prescription of any single economic, political, or ideological system as the natural law ethic which dominated past Catholic thought has often claimed to do. Rather, basic human rights set limits and establish obligations for all systems and ideologies, leaving the precise form in which these systems will be organized undefined. In making this somewhat more modest claim, conciliar and postconciliar Catholicism has actually increased its capacity to make a critical and creative contribution to the social life of a pluralistic global society.

How did this substantial shift in the foundation of Catholic social thought come about? There were a variety of intellectual and theological currents operating in the church in the two decades immediately preceding the Council which prepared the way for the change. From the viewpoint of social rather than intellectual history, however, an equally important cause can be discerned. As an event in the social history of the church, the Council had an impact on Catholic thought similar to the influence which the founding of the United Nations exerted on the content of secular political thought in general. Both events gathered representatives from all regions of the globe, persons with vastly different cultural backgrounds, from countries with enormously different levels of economic development and wealth, from societies with opposed political and ideological systems. Though the events leading to the creation of the United Nations and those which transpired at the Vatican Council had evidently different purposes, they had a common concern with the problem of the unity of the human community and the task of finding norms and structures for world peace in the face of ideological pluralism and conflict. It is true that Westerners had the largest voice both in the founding of the United Nations and at the Second Vatican Council. But in both assemblies the conflicts between East and West, between Western and non-Western culture, and between rich nations and poor nations were conflicts *internal* to the two assemblies themselves. The need to find consensus on a normative basis for international justice and peace without suppressing the legitimate differences between regions and social systems led both bodies to a human rights focus. The early years of the United Nations saw the first really significant efforts at the elaboration of a fundamental set of internationally accepted standards for a pluralist globe. The Second Vatican Council attempted the same task for a church newly aware of itself as a transnational, transcultural community.

Theologian Karl Rahner has suggested that the most fundamental significance of the Second Vatican Council lies in the qualitative difference between the broad representation of non-European regional subunits of the church which occurred at the Council and the Europocentrism of the history of Catholicism since the days of the Apostle Paul. In Rahner's view the Second Vatican Council marked the beginning of Catholicism as a genuinely worldwide community. At Vatican II, "a world church as such begins to act through the reciprocal influence exerted by all its components."[7] In other words, at the Council the Catholic church became, at least incipiently, a genuinely transnational body rather than a European one with missionary outposts.[8] Though the Council was obviously a Christian assembly, the forms of Christianity represented were culturally diverse and had been shaped by very different economic, political, and ideological contexts. At Vatican II these diverse forms of Christianity were brought into direct contact with each other. It should, therefore, have been almost predictable that a new emphasis on the full range of human rights, both civil/political and social/economic, would develop once the decision had been reached to convoke a Council of the transnational Catholic church.

Since the Second World War nongovernmental organizations, like the International Commission of Jurists and Amnesty International, which are both transnational and also advocates for international justice and peace, have increasingly employed the perspective of human rights as the normative basis for their activities.[9] In a world which is simultaneously pluralistic and interdependent, human rights norms have gained a central place because they attempt to articulate the immunities and entitlements which are due every person "simply by virtue of being a human person, irrespective of his or her social status, cultural accomplishments, moral merits, religious beliefs, class memberships, or contractual relationships."[10] This quality of universality and the status of human rights as "moral claims that human persons can make independently of and prior to their acknowledgment by particular societies"[11] are especially important for groups that aim to contribute to a normative foundation for a pluralist world order and for the elaboration of a transnational ethic.

The impetus for the rapid development of a human rights ethic in the Catholic church came in large part from the non-European regions of the transnational church (from the poor countries of the Third World in the area of social/economic rights and from the United States in the area of civil/political rights, especially the right to religious freedom). The recent systematic elaboration of the normative human rights framework of contemporary Catholicism, however, was initiated principally at the center, namely at the transnational assembly of all the Catholic bishops in Council under the leadership of the chief transnational agent of the church, the Pope. Thus the exigencies of regional and ideological pluralism combined with need for unity at the center to produce a fundamental reorientation in the church's understanding of the appropriate normative foundation for global politics and economy.

All this was only incipient at the Council. But as Rahner insists, the process of developing a transnational perspective and pastoral strategy was definitively begun at the Second Vatican Council. Since the Council the normative framework has been developed in greater detail. The postconciliar period has also seen the development of local, national, regional, and transnational institutional structures within the church for the implementation of the new human rights perspective. This process of implementation has been hesitant, conflictive, and at times self-contradictory. Nevertheless, the understanding of rights which has been developing since the Council in Catholic social thought in response to its newly discovered transnational context is the chief explanation of the new visibility of the church in the human rights struggle. [12]

II
THE NORMATIVE UNDERSTANDING:
AN INTEGRAL THEORY OF RIGHTS

The fact that the Catholic church pursues both its religious mission and its pastoral role in nearly all the regions of the globe has brought it into contact with all the major forms of human rights violations and with the chief ideological interpretations of human rights. In its attempt to formulate an understanding of human rights appropriate to its transnational existence, the church has inevitably had to face the arguments about the central focus of human rights theory which divide the Western democracies from the Eastern socialist bloc. In the liberal tradition of the West the civil and political freedoms of speech, worship, assembly, press, and the juridical guarantees of *habeas corpus* and due process are at the center of human rights thinking. Human rights are rooted in the liberty of the individual person. In Marxist socialism, on the other hand, the rights to work, to minimum levels of nutrition, and to active participation in the process of creating a socialist society are central. These rights are grounded by the conviction that personal freedom is an abstraction unless it is viewed in the economic and social context which conditions it. [13] A similar though not identical polarity characterizes the debate between the industrial powers of the North and the less developed countries of the South. In general, the Northern societies argue for an effort to meet human needs within the context of a social system based on a prior commitment to political and economic liberty. In the countries of the South the emphasis is inverted. Political and economic freedom are regarded as obtainable for the vast majority of the population of these countries only in the context of policies aimed at meeting basic needs for food, clothing, shelter, and minimum education.[14]

These divergent emphases in thinking about human rights have all had an impact on the content of the contemporary Roman Catholic understanding of rights. It is one of the deep biases of the Catholic tradition to respond to basic intellectual and social choices by saying both/and rather than either/or. John XXIII's *Pacem in Terris* includes all the rights emphasized on each side of these East/West and North/South debates. It includes all the rights enumerated in the UN Universal Declaration and its two accompanying Covenants. It affirms the rights to life, bodily integrity, food, clothing, shelter, rest, medical care, and the social services necessary to protect these rights. It includes the rights to freedom of communication (speech, press), to information, and to education. In the area of religious activity it affirms the right to honor God in accord with one's conscience and to practice religion in private and in public. In the area of family life the rights to marry, to procreate, and to the economic and social conditions necessary for the support of family life are all included. Economic rights include the rights to work, to humane working conditions, to a just wage, to appropriate participation in the management of economic enterprises, and to the ownership of private property within limits established by social duties. The rights of assembly and association and the right to organize are also affirmed, as are the rights to freedom of movement and to internal and external migration. Finally, the encyclical asserts the political right to participate in public affairs and the juridical right to constitutional protection of all other rights, including *habeas corpus* and due process.[15]

The appeal of this comprehensive list of human rights is certainly a powerful one, as the enthusiastic reception which *Pacem in Terris* received in many parts of the world testifies. Several questions must be raised about such an all inclusive understanding of rights. The strength of such a universal and integral approach to rights may also be a weakness. In seeking to incorporate the emphases of both East and West, of

North and South, the church's understanding of human rights may be in danger of rising above the actual conflicts of global society which generate human rights violations. It can be asked whether some more recent statements from the Holy See do not show unmistakable signs of using abstract comprehensiveness as a substitute for concrete choice and action in the midst of conflict. For example, Pope Paul VI, after an analysis of capitalism, socialism, liberalism, and Marxism, affirmed that the foundation of Christian engagement in political action "is above and sometimes opposed to the ideologies," and is "beyond every system."[16] At their Third General Conference held in Puebla, Mexico, in 1979, the Latin American episcopate expressed ambivalence about how the commitment of the church to human rights should be related to the major ideologies which currently motivate political action in Latin America.[17]

A response to this problem involves three points. The first concerns the ultimate foundation of the Catholic rights theory. The second deals with the historical background of the theory in modern Catholic thought. And the third addresses once again its relationship to the current context for the protection and violation of human rights in global society.

First, then, the foundational principle of the theory must be distinguished from an abstractly inclusive harmonization of the rights emphasized by the various competing ideologies. The fundamental value which undergirds it is neither simply the liberty of the individual person stressed in the liberal democracies nor simply the social participation and economic well-being stressed in various ways by Marxism and socialism. Rather the theory maintains that respect for freedom, the meeting of basic needs, and participation in community and social relationships are all essential aspects of the human dignity which is the foundation of all rights. The institutional protection of personal freedom is emphasized by liberal democracy. The fulfillment of human needs is stressed by the emerging "basic needs" strategies at the center of the North-South debate. And the restructuring of the social and economic order in a way that allows genuine communal participation in the corporate life of society is the program of socialist thought. Each of these ideologies links its fundamental understanding of human rights with a particular structural obstacle to the realization of human dignity. The contemporary Catholic understanding, however, refuses to tie its notion of human dignity to only one of these three spheres of life in which persons can be either violated or protected by the structure of the social order. As John

XXIII put it, ''The cardinal point of this tendency is that individual men are necessarily the foundation, cause, and end of all social institutions. We are referring to human beings, insofar as they are social by nature, and raised to an order of existence which transcends and subdues nature.''[18] Any political, economic, or social system which is to be morally legitimate must provide respect for these spheres of freedom, need, and relationship. Thus the foundational norm of human dignity does not claim to be an ideological principle of social organization but rather a principle of moral and political legitimacy.

The Catholic tradition offers two warrants for the validity of the foundational principle. The imperative arising from human dignity is based on the indicative of the person's transcendence over the world of things. The ability of persons to think and to choose, their hopes which always outrun the historical moment, and the experienced call to discriminate between good and evil actions—all these indicate that persons are more than things. This warrant for the foundational principle of Catholic rights theory is held to be accessible and plausible apart from the particular doctrines of the Christian faith. The Christian faith does provide, however, a second explicitly Christian warrant for the principle of human dignity. The beliefs that all persons are created in the image of God, that they are redeemed by Jesus Christ, and that they are summoned by God to a destiny beyond history serve both to support and to interpret the fundamental significance of human existence. The theological doctrines both illuminate general human experience and are themselves illuminated by such experience. With this as the basic relationship between theological and philosophical approaches to the norm of human dignity, the Catholic tradition does not hesitate to claim a universal validity for the way it seeks to ground human rights in the dignity of the person rather than in convictions about institutional and structural means for the protection of this dignity.[19]

A full response to the charge that this notion of human dignity is the result of a false abstraction from the realities of social conflict and the need for choice leads to the consideration of a second point. As a norm of political legitimacy the standard of respect for human dignity affirms that political and economic institutions are to serve human persons as free, needy, and relational beings. The primary referent of the term is not abstract and conceptual but concrete and existential: actually existing human beings. At the same time, however, the notion of human dignity is nearly empty of meaning. Unless it is further specified, the notion of human dignity lacks all reference to particular freedom, needs, and relationships. It is for this reason that most ideological systems can appeal to human dignity for moral legitimacy. Therefore, unless the relationship between the transcendental worth of persons and particular human freedoms, needs, and relationships can be specified, the notion of dignity will become an empty notion.[20] The task of determining the concrete political and economic conditions which are in fact required to protect human freedom, meet human needs, and support human relationships is an historical task. The move from the affirmation of the worth of persons to the proposal of *specific* rights which can legitimately be claimed from society is mediated by historical experience and historically accumulated understanding.[21] Historical memory and continuing historical experience are thus the only means by which the notion of dignity gains enough concrete content to support particular rights claims. Therefore every theory of rights which claims human dignity as its foundation necessarily presupposes a tradition of historical memory about the human effects of different kinds of social and political systems in the past. It also presupposes an understanding of the human effects of present patterns of social organization.

Over the past hundred years the Catholic ethical tradition has been self-consciously engaged in a protracted effort to determine more precisely just what conditions *are* necessary if human persons are to be protected in their dignity. During the years of Leo XIII's pontificate, two of these conditions were brought to the fore. The first was the indispensability of minimum economic levels for all, in the form of adequate wages and broad distribution of property. Second, in the political realm it was recognized that the freedom of the majority in a democracy or of the ruling powers in other forms of polity must be limited by their obligation to serve the common good of the whole society. This is the principle of the limited state, a principle which places a check on all forms of totalitarianism by making government accountable for the basic rights and liberties of all citizens. These two principles are respectively the bases of social/economic rights and civil/political rights.

The history of the church's understanding of these principles has followed a circuitous path through the past century. Opposition to anticlerical interpretations of religious liberty led to a limited understanding of the way persons would be protected in their dignity by a constitutional guarantee for civil liberties and political rights. Also resistance to the totalitarianism and irreligion of the Soviet Union led to a narrowed understanding of the potential human benefits of other kinds of socialist models.[22]

Despite the hesitant movement of Catholic understanding of the concrete exigencies of dignity, however, one basic insight was ingrained in the historical memory of the church by its efforts in this area: the conviction that dignity would be violated by any system which denied political freedom in the name of economic rights or which appealed to the primacy of individual liberty as justification for its failure to meet basic human needs. This insight was often expressed in the form of proposals for a "third way" between capitalism and socialism. This middle path was variously elaborated in the social models known as corporatism, solidarism, and Christian democracy. All of these models were based on the assumption that respect for civil and political rights could be combined with protection of social and economic rights in a harmonious, nonconflictual social order. The supposition that this inclusive vision of human dignity could be protected concretely without the continuing presence of social conflict was the chief reason why Catholic concern has often been one step removed from the actual sources of conflict and rights violations. The reluctance to address the reality of conflict often cut the nerve of action which leads to social change. Thus the predominant Catholic disposition to seek resolution of the problem of the pluralism of ideologies and diversity of social systems by direct appeal to social harmony was linked with a reluctance to deal with the realities of power and conflict. This negative side of Catholic human rights thought was, however, directly linked with its experience and memory of the indispensability of both civil/political and social/economic rights.

The shift in appreciation of the reality of ideological and social pluralism which was begun by Vatican II is the focus of the third point to be considered in discussing the charge of abstractness leveled against the current Catholic approach to rights. The transnational and transcultural institutional self-consciousness of the church has reinforced its historic bias against opting for one of the competing ideologies or social models which shape the context in which the church exists. However, the beginning of the legitimation of pluralism which occurred at the Council has freed the church to approach the issue of conflict in a new way. Though this development is still incipient, the post-conciliar church has begun to look for the realization of the fullness of human dignity in the midst of political and economic conflict. Rather than proposing a model of social organization that claims to protect human dignity in every nation or culture, recent statements from Rome have emphasized the ways that the interconnected package of civil/political and social/economic rights is today threatened by a variety of oppressive power configurations. The post-conciliar church's normative statements have increasingly argued that civil/political and social/economic rights are interconnected and that respect for one set of rights is dependent on respect for the other. The historical memory of the church is combining with its present historical experience as a community to produce what amounts to a transnational human rights ideology. The elements of this new ideology are a respect for social pluralism, a conviction that all human rights are interconnected, and a willingness to stand for the rights of those who are simultaneously denied their political and economic rights against those whose disproportionate political and economic power is the cause of this denial.

The basis of this new "human rights ideology" was particularly evident at the 1971 Synod of Bishops, an assembly which, significantly, was a transnational one. The interconnection of all rights was highlighted in the Synod's assertion of the "right to development." This right was defined as "the dynamic interpenetration of all those fundamental human rights upon which the aspirations of individuals and nations are based."[23] It is also evident in the assertion of the right to participation—"a right which is to be applied in the economic and in the social field.[24] Both the "right to development" and the "right to participation" are shorthand ways of affirming the interconnected rights of those deprived of development and excluded from economic and political participation. These two "synthetic" rights are in the best tradition of the Catholic bias to say: *both* political liberty *and* basic human needs. In the light of the other studies of this project, the *both/and* which is lodged in the Catholic historical memory may have new relevance in the context of an interdependent and pluralistic world.

III
IMPLICATIONS: THE RIGHTS OF THE OPPRESSED

Several conclusions about the implications of the contemporary Catholic church's understanding of human rights can be drawn from the generalizations proposed in this essay.[25] If the historical memory and present transnational experience of the Catholic community is in any way accurate, it would seem that the argument between those who say "bread first" and those who say "freedom first" has reached a dead end. And increasingly those without political freedom and access to political power seem to end up without bread. The interconnection of rights has become evident not only in theory but in practice. As J. P. Pronk, Minister for Development Cooperation from the Netherlands put it:

> In Latin America and elsewhere we see in a dramatic way how people set about achieving social justice, how they need to exercise political freedom to do this, and how they are oppressed and become the victims of inhuman tortures. The link between the different categories [of rights] is shown clearly not only in the preambles to treaties but also in the practical exercise of human rights.[26]

The empirical evidence for this interconnection of rights is presented in other papers of this study. But if such an interpretation of the situation is correct, then the charge of "abstractness" and indecisiveness against the inclusive Catholic approach to rights is unfounded. The same can be said about similar charges against the UN Universal Declaration.

Those who would learn from the mistakes of the past, however, should realize that this inclusiveness of Catholic rights theory has hindered the church's capacity for action and frequently fostered a reactionary stance. The condition for translating an inclusive theory of rights into a strategy for action and policy is the recognition that pluralism is inevitably accompanied by conflict. Defense and support of the full range of rights for every person under current patterns of economic and political conflict, therefore, calls for a choice. This choice is one which will orient policy toward preferential concern for the rights of those who have neither bread nor freedom. It means that the rights of the oppressed, those deprived of both political and economic power, should take priority in policy over privileged forms of influence and wealth.

The contemporary Catholic understanding of human rights has just begun to move in this direction. But the leaders of both liberal and authoritarian governments and of capitalist and socialist economies have something to learn from transnational organizations like the Catholic church. It may even be that a community with as long a memory and as pragmatic a style as the Catholic church has something unique to contribute to a global understanding of a new human rights ideology. The potential for such a contribution will become an actuality if and only if the church continues on the course charted at Vatican II.

Notes

1. See Bernard Plongeron, "Anathema or Dialogue? Christian Reactions to Declarations of the Rights of Man in the United States and Europe in the Eighteenth Century," in Alois Muller and Norbert Greinacher, eds., *The Church and the Rights of Man, Concilium,* no. 124 (New York: Seabury, 1979) pp. 39–47; and Arturo Gaete, "Socialism and Communism: History of a Problem-Ridden Condemnation" *LADOC* IV, 1 (September, 1973), pp. 1–16.

2. See, for example: Brian H. Smith, "Church Strategies and Human Rights in Latin America," unpublished Working Paper, Woodstock Theological Center, 1979; Alfred T. Hennelly, Chap. 2 of this volume; Muller and Greinacher, eds., *The Church and the Rights of Man,* pp. 77–121.

3. *Dignitatis Humanae,* no. 1. The translation is that found in Walter Abbott and Joseph Gallagher, eds., *The Documents of Vatican II* (New York: Guild Press/America Press, 1966), p. 677.

4. John Courtney Murray, "Commentary and Notes on the Declaration on Religious Liberty," in Abbott and Gallagher, p. 677, n. 4. See also Murray, "Vers une intelligence du développement de la doctrine de l'Église sur la liberté religieuse," in *Vatican II: La Liberté Religieuse* (Paris: Cerf, 1967), pp. 111–147.

5. *Gaudium et Spes,* no. 4, in Abbott and Gallagher, p. 202–203.

6. *Pacem in Terris,* no. 9. In Joseph Gremillion, ed., *The Gospel of Peace*

and Justice: Catholic Social Teaching since Pope John (Maryknoll, N.Y.: Orbis Books, 1976), p. 203.

7. Karl Rahner, "Towards a Fundamental Interpretation of Vatican II," *Theological Studies* 40 (1979), p. 717.

8. For a fuller discussion of this shift and its implications for the structure, function, and self-understanding of the Catholic church, see Joseph Gremillion, *The Gospel of Peace and Justice* (Maryknoll, N.Y.: Orbis Books, 1976), pp. 57–68; *idem, Harvard Seminar on Muslim Jewish Christian Faith Communities as Transnational Actors for Peace and Justice: Report and Interpretation* (Washington, D.C.: Interreligious Peace Colloquium, 1979, privately circulated), pp. 20–29 and *passim;* and J. Bryan Hehir, "The Roman Catholic Church as Transnational Actor: Amending Vallier," unpublished paper, International Studies Association, Washington, D.C., February 23, 1978.

9. See José Zalaquett, "The Scope of Human Rights: Consensus and Priorities among Practitioners," and John A. Coleman, "The Role of International Non-Governmental Organizations in Promoting Human Rights," unpublished Working Papers, Woodstock Theological Center, October, 1979.

10. John Langan, Chap. 4 of this volume.

11. *Ibid.*

12. See Gremillion, *The Gospel of Peace and Justice,* Section II, "The Church as a Social Actor," pp. 125–132.

13. See John Haughey, "Individualism and Rights in Karl Marx," Chap. 5 of this volume.

14. See Drew Christiansen, "Basic Needs: Criterion for the Legitimacy of Development, Chap. 11 of this volume, and John Weeks and Elizabeth Dore, "Basic Needs in Development Strategies: The Journey of a Concept." Chapter 4, *Human Rights and Basic Needs in the Americas.*

15. *Pacem in Terris,* nos. 9–27. See also Pontifical Commission on Justice and Peace, *The Church and Human Rights* (Vatican City: Vatican Polyglot Press, 1975); and David Hollenbach, *Claims in Conflict: Retrieving and Renewing the Catholic Human Rights Tradition* (New York: Paulist Press, 1979), pp. 62–69, 89–100.

16. Pope Paul VI, *Octogesima Adveniens,* nos. 27, 36, in Gremillion, *The Gospel of Peace and Justice,* pp. 498, 501.

17. For an analysis of this ambivalence, see Gregory Baum, "The Meaning of Ideology," in the Catholic Theological Society of America, *Proceedings of the 34th Annual Convention,* 1979, pp. 174–175.

18. *Mater et Magistra,* no. 219. In Gremillion, *The Gospel of Peace and Justice,* p. 190.

19. For a more detailed discussion of these warrants, see Hollenbach, Chapter 3 of this volume and *Claims in Conflict,* pp. 107–137.

20. For a somewhat similar though not identical argument, see Bruno Schuller, "Die Personwürde des menschen als Beweisgrund in der normativen Ethik," *Theologie und Glaube* 53 (1978), pp. 538–555.

21. See John Courtney Murray, "The Problem of State Religion," *Theological Studies* 12 (1951), p. 170.

22. For an account of this history of modern Catholic reflections on the specific rights essential to the protection of human dignity, see Hollenbach, *Claims in Conflict,* Chapter 2, pp. 41–106.

23. "Justice in the World," no. 15, Gremillion, *The Gospel of Peace and Justice,* p. 516.

24. "Justice in the World," no. 18, in Gremillion, *The Gospel of Peace and Justice,* p. 517.

25. What is said here is argued in somewhat greater detail in Hollenbach, *Claims in Conflict,* Chapter 5, pp. 187–207.

26. J. P. Pronk, "Human Rights and Development Aid," *International Commission of Jurists Review* 18 (June, 1977) pp. 35–36. See also Patricia Weiss Fagen, "The Links Between Human Rights and Basic Needs," *Background* (Center for International Policy) (Spring 1978).

From Rerum Novarum
to Laborem Exercens:
A United States Labor Perspective

Thomas R. Donahue

This article originally appeared in *Rerum Novarum, Laborem Exercens 2000 Symposium,* 1982.

To His Holiness who so graciously and warmly opened this Convocation, to its planners, my fellow participants and observers, I bring greetings from 15 million trade unionists of the United States of America who belong to the American Federation of Labor-Congress of Industrial Organizations (AFL-CIO), our national labor center.

I am particularly delighted to be with you as an officer of that Federation, as a Roman Catholic and as one whose life has been inspired and motivated by the papal encyclicals on the social order.

Much has been written of the development of Catholic social teaching and of the effort to develop a unitary view of that teaching as expressed in the papal social encyclicals.

Father John Coleman, S.J., in a paper delivered in May, 1981, at a convocation commemorating the anniversaries of *Rerum Novarum, Quadragesimo Anno,* and *Mater et Magistra,* stated his view that "the foundation for such a unitary view is the legitimate understanding that social encyclicals form an interconnected social charter and tradition."

> In the sense, [he continued], as the various popes—despite the different historical contexts which I have been stressing—built on one another, so it is legitimate to show the particular Catholic teaching on social issues captured, for example, in key principles and concepts such as human dignity, solidarity, sub-

sidiarity, the right to integral development, participation, the ultimate subordination of economics and politics to human ful-fillment.

As social charters, the encyclicals tended to be read, absorbed and commented on mainly by socially involved Catholics who generally gave them a more progressive inter-pretation than their location in historical context might have warranted. The encyclicals, then, represent in some sense a genuine unified tradition of sane and humane social thought which we both celebrate today and try to bring forward into the future.

. . . they have formed over the past 90 years men and women who have found in them a charter to become concerned about institutional and structural reform, to support organiza-tion for justice, to heed the papal call to respect human dignity and to go to the poor. These men and women and the Catholic movements they have spawned are the best exegesis of the documents.

Ultimately, the future of this tradition will depend less on our ability to parrot its significant terms such as subsidiarity, a just wage, socialization, or to define in precise ways social charity, social justice or the common good, and more on our ability to read the signs of the times in fidelity to the Gospel of human dignity as Leo XIII, Pius XI, Pius XII, John XXIII, Paul VI—with all their historical limitations, biases and fail-ures—tried to do in their times.

John Paul II has given us an excellent reading of the signs of the times in full fidelity to the gospel of human dignity, but more has given us a soaring hymn in praise of that dignity, triumphant over all else.

I would identify myself as one who has been formed by the encyc-licals and who found in them that "charter" to become concerned about reform.

At Manhattan College where I matriculated in the late 1940s, we were introduced to the social encyclicals by the late Brother Cornelius Justin, F.S.C., who made us aware of *Rerum Novarum* and *Quadrage-simo Anno* and the various social action addresses of Pope Pius XII. We gained practical experience with workers' organizations and trade unions, through an activist student organization named in honor of Pope Leo XIII and later through the Association of Catholic Trade Unionists.

I then went to work in the building service industry, became an organizer, later a local union official, then a liaison officer with European trade union organizations, an Assistant Secretary of Labor under President Johnson, a national union vice-president, assistant to the late George Meany, President of the AFL-CIO, and now the secretary-treasurer of that organization. I cite all this solely as one example of the dynamic and inspiring character of the documents we are discussing today.

*   *   *

The American Federation of Labor was formed a decade before Pope Leo XIII issued *Rerum Novarum.*

Indeed, the labor movement in the United States hardly survived its infancy. In those early years, giant American industries such as Carnegie Steel Company and the Pullman Railway Company decided to ignore their workers' just claims, and when those workers went out on strike, the companies stopped at nothing to break those strikes.

But bolstered by the encyclical teachings, great Church leaders such as Cardinal Gibbons and Archbishop Ireland came to the defense of the trade unions, supporting them as free associations seeking justice for their worker members.

In the early part of this century, Archbishop Ireland, in a famous Labor Day address, referred to the days when an economic school of thought "authorized capital to see in the laborer only his output of labor and to purchase that output at the lowest possible price."

Then it was that the operators of the "black fields" of England reduced their miners to the level of beasts of burden and as, even at that level, men seem to cost too much, put women in their stead, and later, for similar reasons, substituted children for women.

How very different is the situation today, [he said]. The change is due to an improved public opinion and an enlarged Christian humanitarianism; but it is due very largely also, and facts could easily be adduced to prove, to the intelligent self-assertiveness of labor itself, and to the new strength coming to it from the aggregation of its scattered units into well-organized societies. Labor unions have a noble mission and are entitled to the sympathy of all intelligent men.

RERUM NOVARUM AND ITS U.S. IMPLICATIONS

The enduring message that Pope Leo XIII conveyed in *Rerum Novarum,* the cornerstone of Catholic social thought was that call for a new order of things, for a new relationship between workers and employers in the new industrial society. With superb Christian charity he pointed out the injustices that had occurred in the development of this new economic order, while reminding men of their common origin and destiny in Almighty God, and their universal brotherhood, despite any class or economic difference.

Protesting against the despotic power of accumulated wealth, he called upon owners of industry to recognize not only the rights of their employees to press their just claims for a share in the wealth they produced, but to recognize as well their natural right to associate in workingmen's associations or unions.

This Encyclical greatly influenced many American Catholic labor leaders and provided new support for them in their opposition to Marxism and its class warfare theories. Indeed, in 1895, Daniel De Leon, a Socialist leader, attempted to form the Socialist Trade and Labor Alliance as a rival to the AFL. This not only failed, but caused a great split in the Socialist movement itself, with Socialist trade unionists rejecting dual unionism and returning to the American Federation of Labor.

But support by Pope Leo XIII and other outstanding religious leaders did little to diminish the opposition of industry to the labor movement.

Professor Carroll Dougherty described the mood of many employers early in this century in his book *Labor Problems in American Industry.* "The more powerful employers," he wrote, "believing that unionism was getting too strong and fearing further encroachment of their control of industry, decided to break off relations, and the years 1902 to the War (World War I) were characterized by increasing anti-unionism."

During this difficult period, the labor movement in the United States found aid and succor in those who were exploring the implications of Leo XIII's Encyclical. Monsignor John A. Ryan, a moralist and economist at Catholic University, published two notable studies on "The Living Wage" and "Distributive Justice." And Monsignor John O'Grady busied himself with the Encyclical's implications as they bore on the government's obligation to care for the disabled and needy citizens beyond their working lives.

The American Bishops on "Social Reconstruction"

All of this activity, participated in by leading Catholic laymen and members of the hierarchy, culminated in the development in 1918 of a document on *Social Reconstruction: A General Review of the Problems and Survey of the Remedies*. The paper, authored by Monsignor John A. Ryan, was presented by Father (later Monsignor) John O'Grady, chairman of the National Catholic Council's Reconstruction and After War Activities Committee, to the Administrative Committee of Bishops. Reviewing and editing the document, the bishops issued it as their own on Lincoln's Birthday, February 12, 1919.

The document was hailed by leading laymen such as Frank Walsh, co-chairman of the National War Labor Board. Walsh saw in the bishops' program proof that the leaders of organized Christianity recognized and acclaimed an identity of interest between "true religion and economic democracy."

John Fitzpatrick, president of the Chicago Federation of Labor, added: "Nothing will do more to strengthen the cause of orderly but fundamental economic reform." "Catholics in organized labor," he noted, "had long denied the Socialist claim that the Catholic Church is on the side of special privilege in the battle between privilege and democracy." Now, he concluded, we are rewarded "with a pronouncement that is undoubtedly the greatest ever put forth by any religious body."

Taking the diametrically opposite position, the president of the National Association of Manufacturers, Stephen C. Mason, protested to Cardinal Gibbons:

It is generally assumed that the Roman Catholic Church of the United States is, and always has been, unalterable in its an-

tagonism to all forms of socialism. It is our belief that a careful
reading of this pamphlet will lead you to the conclusion we
have reached, namely, that it involves what may prove to be
a covert effort to disseminate partisan, pro labor union, socialistic propaganda under the official insignia of the Roman
Catholic Church in America.

Mason's letter did not have its intended effect. In fact, the Church
moved to personalize its teachings and created in 1922 a Catholic Conference on Industrial Problems headed by Dr. David A. McCabe, a professor of economics at Princeton University, with Father Raymond
McGowan, assistant director of the Bishops' Social Action Department,
acting as secretary treasurer.

But the controversy was not to be short-lived. The New York State
Legislature created a Joint Legislative Committee Investigating Sedi-
tious Activities. It filed its first report on April 24, 1929, ten years after
the bishops' program was issued, saying of the bishops' program:

A certain group in the Catholic Church with leanings toward
socialism under the leadership of Rev. Dr. John Ryan, professor at the Catholic University of Washington, issued in January, 1919, a pamphlet called: 'Social Reconstruction: A
General Review of the Problems and Survey of the Remedies.'
Where the socialistic tendency of the committee shows itself
most clearly is what is said under the heading of 'Cooperation
and Co-Partnership.'

Of course, what was called for by the Bishops' program was: (1)
minimum-wage legislation; (2) insurance against unemployment, sickness, invalidity, and old age; (3) a sixteen-year minimum age limit for
working children; (4) the legal enforcement of the right of labor to organize; (5) continuation of the National War Labor Board, for this and
other purposes affecting the relations of employers and employees; (6)
a national employment service; (7) public housing for the working
classes; (8) wartime wages and a long-distance program of increasing
them, not only for the benefit of labor but in order to bring about that
general prosperity which cannot be maintained without a wide distri-

bution of purchasing power among the masses; (9) prevention of excessive profits and incomes through a regulation of rates which allows the owners of public utilities only a fair rate of return on their actual investment, and through progressive taxes on inheritance and income, and excess profits; (10) effective control of monopolies, even by the method of government competition if that should prove necessary; (11) participation of labor in management and a wider distribution of ownership through cooperative enterprises and worker ownership in the stock of corporations; (12) establishment of cooperative stores in order to eliminate unnecessary middlemen, reduce prices to the consumer and train the participants in business methods and in the capacity for cooperation. (It was hardly a prescription for socialism!)

I have gone to considerable length to express my appreciation of the close relationship between the papal statements and actions during this period and the general social progress that has ensued and to point out as well the depth and extent of the calls for social justice which flowed from *Rerum Novarum* and the vehemence of the opposition to those calls. The same extension of calls for action ought to flow from *Laborem Exercens*—and one can only hope that the level of opposition to those calls will be somewhat less strident—though a redefinition of capital and the ringing statements of the primacy of labor will surely excite before they enlighten.

QUADRAGESIMO ANNO—
PART OF THE HERITAGE OF SOCIAL TEACHING ON HUMAN RIGHTS

When Pope Pius XI issued *Quadragesimo Anno,* he continued the great tradition of his predecessor Leo XIII and gave strength to the interpretations of Encyclical teaching by the American bishops. In the next half-dozen years, the United States went through a fairly peaceful social revolution, enacting into law practically all of the points contained in the two Encyclicals and the bishops' program of 1919.

In the last fifty years, many of the Encyclical concepts have found their way into the fabric of non-Communist Western societies. Much, of course, needs to be done, not only in our own nation, where social inequities and social injustices continue to persist, but in an overwhelming sense in what is called the Third World.

The Church, to its credit, is not flinching from this task. Just before I left America I read the statement of Bishop Joseph Sullivan to the U.S. House of Representatives Committee on the Budget on behalf of the Bishops' Conference and the National Conference of Catholic Charities.

> These two institutions bring to your discussions, [he said], two important resources: 1) a rich heritage of social teaching on human rights; and 2) a wide range of direct experiences in providing for the needs of the poor in this country. From this perspective I would like to suggest two points for your consideration: 1) that the impact (on social services) of last year's budget cuts has already been so severe that voluntary agencies have nowhere near the capacity to take up the slack; and 2) that, consistent with the Catholic Church's social teaching, we strongly believe that when other social institutions are unable to do so the government has the responsibility to ensure that the basic needs of all the citizens are met.

The consistency of the Church and the Holy See in these matters is a source of strength to involved Catholic laity. That is why we greeted with joy and gratitude the recent encyclical of His Holiness Pope John Paul II.

LABOREM EXERCENS

Before I treat of *Laborem Exercens,* let me make clear that I have not ignored, nor do I lack appreciation of, the tremendous impact of the other modern encyclicals, but I have confined my remarks to those encyclicals directed to the labor question.

I have no credentials to explore the theology of *Laborem Exercens* nor to offer a scholarly examination of it. Rather, let me concentrate on an examination of its reception in the United States, of the issues it raises (against the background of the current level of development of trade unionism in the U.S.), and of its implications for the future development of the struggle for social justice for workers and its directions.

When it first appeared the Encyclical was hailed in the United States as a major social pronouncement, but the secular press concentrated on two of its subsidiary notes rather than on the major issues raised.

Early attention in my country centered on the discussion of the political activities of unions and of the right of public employees to strike. The former issue obviously was raised in the context of the struggle of *Solidarnosc* with the Polish government, and the latter issue was of great interest because of the Encyclical's publication during our air traffic controller strike.

Only to a lesser extent, and in later analysis, was thoughtful attention given to the principal points of the Encyclical relating to the centrality of man in work, the conflict between capital and labor, the rights of workers and (largely in the Catholic press) to the elements of spirituality in work.

In the Catholic press, the headlines noted "New Encyclical Warns of Evils of Capitalism, Marxism," "Encyclical Offers No Easy Answer to Complex Labor Problems," "New Encyclical Presents Teaching on Work and Ownership," "Papal Labor View Focuses Agenda for U.S. Workers," and "Workers, Not Capital, Key to Moral Order."

All of those lines heralded the publication of what is, for the American labor movement and particularly for Catholics in that labor movement, a document which is a great comfort and a great challenge.

The themes of the dignity of labor and of worker rights, of the need for a just wage, and of the duty of the state to protect the worker's natural right to enter into workingmen's associations, are all carried forward from *Rerum Novarum.*

They were echoed in *Quadragesimo Anno* in its treatment of the unjust claims of capital and labor, the principle of just distribution of wealth and property, and the need for a just wage. Indeed, it was there that we found the first call for workers sharing in some way in the ownership, management or profits of the enterprise.

The same themes, of course, reappeared in that part of *Mater et Magistra,* on the subject of labor, where we found the reaffirmation of the right of workers to organize with the extension to the view that organization of workers is not only desirable but necessary, and where we found, to the great pleasure of trade unionists, praise for labor for having developed "a more responsible attitude toward the greater socio-economic problems of the day." (*Part* II)

In *Mater et Magistra,* we found the statement of the themes later echoed in *Laborem Exercens* that labor must try to reconcile its rights with those of other workers in the community; a repetition (albeit in far more forceful terms) of the instruction that workers should share in ownership as well as management of the enterprise; and the introduction of the concept that traditional collective bargaining should be supplemented by new institutions which will make it possible for workers to exert their influence effectively, beyond the limits of the individual productive units.

Pope John XXIII also clarified that which had been a difficult concept for American Catholic trade unionists—namely, the view of *Rerum Novarum* that the truly appropriate associations of working men were those organized along religious lines. For us in the United States, this was a concept totally outside of our experience. Pope John XXIII, while praising "associations of workers of Christian inspiration" (*ibid.*) gave *equal* praise to work performed with a Christian spirit by other groups and associations of workers.

Mater et Magistra had great importance in the United States and was described by Monsignor George Higgins, then Director of Social Concerns of the United States Catholic Conference, as "positive and constructive in tone." "The Encyclical," he noted, "takes it for granted, almost as self-evident truth, that unions are absolutely indispensable and the scope of their activities should, if anything, be expanded." Monsignor Higgins' comment finds its echo in the use of the word "indispensable" in this latest Encyclical in describing the role of unions in modern society.

While *Mater et Magistra* clearly placed man as a worker at the center of the economic order, and affirmed the view that "the economic order is the creation of the personal initiative of private citizens themselves," (*ibid.*) *Laborem Exercens* goes quite beyond that point when stating the fundamental thought that "human work is *a key,* probably *the essential key,* to the whole social question," (n. 3) and noting that "*the principle of the priority of labor* over capital is a postulate of the order of social morality." (n. 15).

"Indispensable" Unions and the Church as Employer

Monsignor Higgins noted in one article on *Laborem Exercens* that while "previous encyclicals strongly favored the organization of workers into autonomous unions, none had made the point so forcefully as this one. To say, as the earlier documents did, that unions are legitimate or even necessary is one thing, but to say they are indispensable takes the argument one step further."

> Many Americans will gag at this, [he continued], even though the preamble to the basic statute governing labor relations in the United States comes close to saying the same thing . . . [and] powerful forces in the U.S. opposed to unions are prepared to go to almost any length to return to the bad old days of the so-called open shop.
>
> The new Encyclical, [he noted], will probably have little or no influence on people who hold this view, but it will give new hope and encouragement to the labor movement. Eventually, it may be a positive influence on public recognition of the right of workers to organize.
>
> Finally, [he said], it should also help administrators of Catholic hospitals and other Catholic institutions deal constructively with the union question. Some of them have argued that Catholic teaching on unions applies only to workers in industry. However, the Pope says explicitly that workers in all occupations and professions can use them [unions] to ensure their rights.

Indeed, only three months after *Laborem Exercens* appeared, the American Bishops issued a lengthy pastoral letter spelling out a comprehensive position on health care and addressing the need for the government to develop a national policy to provide adequate health care for all. Within that statement, the Bishops also spelled out the moral obligation of Catholic health care facilities to recognize the rights of their workers to organize and to bargain collectively. The statement quoted extensively from *Laborem Exercens* on the right to strike and the limitations on that right and said that the Catholic hospital employer's responsibility to deal justly with their workers on wages, fringe benefits and other matters, "calls for full recognition of the rights of the employees to organize and bargain collectively with the institution through whatever association or organization they choose." Most importantly, in the U.S. context, the letter suggested that workers have the right to select that bargaining representative "without unjust pressures" from their employers or other labor organizations.

The instruction to the managers of Catholic hospitals to avoid "unjust pressures" on workers in their consideration of a bargaining agent is a new one. The Church as employer has great influence with the workers it employs and it has too often in the past used that influence to dissuade workers from choosing union representation. One hopes that managers of all Catholic, and indeed all religious, institutions would adopt the same policies and would observe neutrality when their employees consider union representation. A trade unionist could cite a pattern of past conduct to the contrary in Catholic institutions in which the manager has forgotten his or her special responsibility as a Catholic employer.

THE U.S. LABOR MOVEMENT IN STRUGGLE

To understand fully the new hope and new encouragement which this Encyclical gives to the labor movement in the United States, one must see that movement, as it sees itself,—facing the unrelenting opposition of the nation's employers to every single expression of desire on the part of workers to enjoy the "indispensable" union affiliation of which the Pope speaks.

In our system of labor relations, a union either exists or not at each workplace depending on the majority expression of the workers at that workplace. The union either enjoys "exclusive recognition" as the collective bargaining agent for a defined group of employees or it is not recognized at all.

This fact seems to have encouraged the view of U.S. employers that almost any tactic is permissible in their struggle to convince a majority of their employees that they don't need, or don't want, a union to represent them.

Consequently, our unions struggle every day for recognition, for their right to exist at a particular workplace or in a particular plant, hospital or establishment of whatever kind. The exercise by workers of their right to associate freely with one another is challenged by the employer as if the effort to assert that right could properly be treated as the subject of a contest, of a game. The workers who attempt to form or join a union are arrayed on one side with the employer on the other. The employer's advisers, people who in the U.S. are called "labor-management consultants," mount a campaign of propaganda, pleas for loyalty to the employer, and often, intimidation and coercion. Arrayed on the other side are the union adherents, their professional staff and their campaign—intended to offset the employer's propaganda, to attract new adherents to the union cause and to minimize any intimidation or coercion.

The inevitable unhappy result of these struggles is the maintenance of a climate in which cooperation is difficult and coexistence is more the norm.

I do not claim that all virtue in such discussion and contest is on the union's side but only want to point out that what the Pope takes for granted as a right of association freely exercised, guaranteed in a democratic society, is often trampled upon in my country and others. And one must conclude that it is trampled upon in pursuit of the profit motive and in an effort to exclude workers from any voice in ownership, or management, or, indeed, from any effective participation in the fixing of the conditions under which they will labor.

The struggle of our unions is, as the Pope points out, a "struggle for the good which corresponds to the needs and merits of working people" (*Laborem Exercens,* n. 20). We do not see it as a struggle against others but a struggle against their ignorance and their pursuit of the ultimate maximization of profit. It is never, for us, a struggle "for the sake of 'struggle' " or "in order to eliminate an opponent," (*ibid.*) since the first is wasteful of human effort and the latter carries with it the elimination of the opportunity for employment—always too scarce in our country.

This part of the struggle can only end for us when our employers fully accept the teachings of the Encyclical, and perceive the worker as a true partner in the process and not as some element of production to be managed, placated and supervised. That would require first and foremost, and at a minimum, absolute non-interference in a worker's choice to be represented by a union and a willingness to negotiate a fair contract in good faith.

U.S. COLLECTIVE BARGAINING SYSTEM

The U.S. labor movement has long insisted on a written collective bargaining agreement with each employer as the fundamental protection of workers on the job and has always regarded our collective bargaining system as the cornerstone of labor-management relations and hopefully, as the basis for labor-management cooperation.

We believe in a conflict theory of collective bargaining as the soundest basis for worker representation, worker participation and worker gains, in the current labor-management climate because we see no real or broad evidence of acceptance by U.S. employers of the concepts of just remuneration, protection of worker interests or of the participation of workers in the ownership, management or profits of the enterprise.

We accept fully the view that all capital is the product of past labor, that labor is not a commodity and that nothing has been created in the human realm except through labor. Consequently, we seek a redistribution of the wealth of our nation and an enlarged share in future wealth. Workers properly want, and are entitled to, a larger share of the wealth they produce. It is our almost universal experience that the employer—individual, corporate or non-profit organization (both secular and religious)—doesn't want to give workers their fair share, and we are therefore in essential conflict over this issue. It is, hopefully, a conflict which always "aims at the good of social justice."

Since our relationship with our employers remains at this primitive level of struggle, it has always been difficult for us to regard seriously, for ourselves, the forms of participation in the enterprise generally grouped under the heading of co-determination.

For so long as the attitudes of U.S. employers remain unchanged, we shall continue to advance a theory of collective bargaining rooted in the conflict between trade union efforts to advance social justice and what we regard as the employers' efforts to maximize profits and maintain "management prerogatives" (an euphemism for unadulterated control of work rules or work process with the least possible "participation" of workers in management).

I would note, however, that we do believe that our adversarial role, appropriate to the conflict of collective bargaining, should be limited to the period of negotiation. During the lifetime of a contract so arrived at, it ought to be replaced by a period of cooperation aimed at maximizing the potential of the joint enterprise to advance the company's business and the workers' satisfaction.

For that reason and on that premise, many U.S. unions are participating in "labor-management committees" and other cooperative programs, where those programs have their base in collective bargaining. Much attention is now being paid in our country to the question of worker satisfaction on the job and the quantity and quality of his or her work output. These two subjects have been joined under the title of "quality of work-life" and a great deal of experimentation is now going on, seeking to find new and better ways to give to workers a sense of pride in their work, a sense of their involvement in the production process, and through this sense of involvement, to draw forth from workers a greater personal interest in the quantity and quality of the product of work. All of this effort is to the good and is an implementation of the Encyclical's view that through work man achieves fulfillment as a human being and, indeed, in a sense becomes "more a human being."

Unfortunately, in many instances non-union employers are introducing such programs or giving the appearance of real participation to their employees in an effort to dissuade those employees from joining together in a union. For the most part, such programs will fail in the long run since while they appear to manifest a real concern for worker fulfillment they are, in fact, based on a less admirable desire to maximize profits, and when a conflict between the two eventually arises, as inevitably it will, that conflict will be decided in favor of maximizing profits.

The Dignity of Work

In our country, as in so many other industrialized nations, there has been a drifting away in recent years from the long accepted view that work is necessary, noble and fulfilling, and that the virtues of work are to be enjoyed. As our society focused more on the individual and his comfort, as materialism has grown, and as the perception has become more widespread that hard work is neither any longer necessary nor desirable, there has been a wandering among ideas in search of some value.

For some—generally, the young of the middle and upper economic class—this became a more personalized search for an elusive self-centered fulfillment, or, the pursuit of radicalism in search of some seemingly more noble goal. For others, there has been a confusion and a bitterness about a "work ethic" they don't share. *Laborem Exercens* statements that work must provide *"fulfillment* as a human being" and must be arranged so that it is not only worthy of man but also "corresponds to man's dignity . . . expresses this dignity and increases it," (n. 9) challenge us to spread this view of work and ensure that it prevails.

Worker Solidarity

The Encyclical's emphasis on greater worker solidarity gives trade unionists great heart. We were pleased with the call for the extension of workers' solidarity to "social groups not previously included in such movements" which are "undergoing *what is in effect 'proletarianization'* ," and the note that this can be true "of certain categories or groups of the working 'intelligentsia' " (n. 8). This call for extending worker solidarity to new groups parallels our recent efforts to bring the benefits of trade union organization to scientists and engineers, teachers and nurses, as well as to agricultural, service and industrial workers.

The call for new movements of solidarity on an international level is a call for the labor movement to "go to the poor" in various parts of the world and assist in their development. We note proudly that our recent return to the International Confederation of Free Trade Unions is an expression of our solidarity with workers throughout the world and a reflection of our belief that we can best work with, and cooperate with, other unions through such an international organization.

Worker Rights as Human Rights

The Encyclical examines workers' rights within the broad context of human rights and notes that "respect for this broad range of human rights constitutes the fundamental condition for peace in the modern world" (n. 16). U.S. unions have argued unceasingly in international labor forums and international political forums that respect by any nation for the right of association of its workers is critical to the exercise of all other rights in that society and can be used as the yardstick for the measurement of other rights. Convention 87 of the International Labor Organization (ILO) sets forth this right of workers to freely associate in their own interests, but it is violated with impunity in the Soviet Union, Poland, Czechoslovakia, Chile, South Africa, and dozens of other nations, while nations (including my own) which respect that right mount feeble protests but draw back from the application of trade sanctions or embargoes which might make that right a reality.

The AFL-CIO has always been in the forefront of those who argue for the application of the strongest sanctions against those nations which trample on the right of association, or any other right, and we intend to continue in that course. Because we do so, we are in conflict with our government at this time over its failure to take the strongest sanctions against the Soviet bloc for its role in the crushing of free trade unionism in Poland and to embargo the export of grain, goods and factories to the Soviet Union.

THE INDIRECT EMPLOYER

The concept, first introduced in this Encyclical, of considering "all of the agents at the national and international level that are responsible for the whole orientation of labor policy" as "the indirect employer" (n. 18) is startling in its imaginativeness and brilliant as a way of grouping all these forces and thereby forcing upon us a recognition of the need for national and international planning. Such planning would require a level of national selflessness and international interest and cooperation which we are currently incapable of reaching. But, it nonetheless provides the concept as a goal and the term "indirect employer" as a helpful and informative shorthand phrase for describing those "persons and institutions of various kinds and also collective labor contracts and the *principles* of conduct which are laid down by those persons and institutions and which determine the whole socio-economic *system* or are its result" (n. 17).

The efforts of the Organization for Economic Cooperation and Development (OECD) deserve mention here as one entity on the international scene which is endeavoring to deal with some of the many facets of the "indirect employer" and to enlarge the degree of international cooperation in economic affairs, production, employment and trade matters.

The Trade Union Advisory Committee of the OECD, in which the AFL-CIO participates along with all the other democratic trade unions of OECD member-nations, has been a constant goad to OECD and its members, urging the development of economic policies which will benefit workers of all nations.

The International Labor Organization, and the efforts of governments to arrive at international trade agreements and understandings, also deserve mention—though in too many cases the latter efforts are more marked by advantage-seeking than by selflessness. Nonetheless, some progress in these directions has been made and these efforts continue.

The AFL-CIO has been in the forefront of those national labor movements which supported the establishment of the ILO and fought for its importance as an international agency dedicated to a concern for workers and for employment, and for the protection of workers' rights.

The Federation also has been active in giving aid and support through financial, staff and educational assistance, to developing free trade unions in countries throughout the world, because we believe deeply that strong and democratic trade unions are a positive force which will act on the indirect employer-government to encourage it to meet its obligation to provide employment.

"To Act Against Unemployment"

The section of the Encyclical on "The Employment Issue" is central to the Document and central to the solution of the current problems faced by the industrialized nations.

"The role of the agents included under the title of indirect employer is *to act against unemployment,* which in all cases is an evil and which, when it reaches a certain level, can become a real social disaster" (n. 18). In my country, with a current unemployment level at 8.8%, or 9.5 million workers unemployed, with an additional 1.5 million no longer counted because they are too discouraged to seek work and with 5 million workers working only part-time, we believe that we have already achieved the level of a real social disaster, with the economic, social and moral consequences becoming more apparent daily.

In the United States, the indirect employer-government is not acting against unemployment and, in fact, has made it clear that it sees unemployment as an essential element, if not a tool, in bringing down inflation and reordering the distribution of national wealth. Our government, like other governments which describe themselves as conservative, is determined to avoid any degree of central planning or coordination on employment issues and leave these matters to the so-called "free markets" which have failed us so badly in the past. In addition to failing to act against unemployment, the current Administration is also, by reducing the role of the national government in education and employment and training matters, failing to make provision for the "*overall planning*" the Encyclical urges "with regard to the different kinds of work by which not only the economic but also the cultural life of a given society is shaped . . . and to organizing that work in a correct and rational way" (*ibid.*).

The "just and rational coordination" which the Encyclical calls for would require a degree of national and international planning which "conservative" (i.e., liberal capitalist) governments reject. Nonetheless, that national and international planning is essential if the good which we pursue is to be achieved.

ON WORK AND OWNERSHIP

In an earlier section of the Encyclical, "On Work and Ownership," the Pope affirms the Church's support for "various *proposals* for *joint ownership of the means of work,* sharing by workers in the management and/or profits of businesses, so-called shareholding by labor, etc." (n. 14). He continues then to note that "merely taking these means of production (capital) out of the hands of their private owners is not enough to ensure their satisfactory socialization" (*ibid.*).

The further suggestion that a way toward the goal of "socializing" property "could be found by associating labor with the ownership of capital, and by producing a wide range of intermediate bodies with economic, social and cultural purposes . . . enjoying real autonomy with regard to the public powers and pursuing their specific aims in honest collaboration with each other and in subordination to the demands of the common good,'' (*ibid.*) seems, in the context of current conflicts between contending forces in society, a wildly utopian dream—but perhaps there are mechanisms in current society which at least lead in that direction.

To some extent labor-management committees which have been formed at plant or industry level can be regarded as resembling these "intermediate bodies." In cases where these committees deal with the problems of a national industry they have enjoyed a certain autonomy and have pursued aims jointly shared by the two parties.

In exploring the employment issue, the Pope returns to this theme in speaking of the need for just and rational coordination, within the framework of which the initiative of individuals is respected, in bringing about a measure of overall planning.

For us, the labor-management committee is a natural vehicle for problem resolution or for the advancement of common interests. At various times in our history both labor and management in the United States have joined together with government to try to bring about some "overall planning" or to meet some special problem of the time. During World War II, the National War Labor Board enjoyed this status. At several points in the last twenty years Presidents have called labor and management to work together with government. Most recently, in the United States, during 1979, we negotiated with the government a "National Accord" establishing a mechanism to provide for labor's involvement and cooperation with the government on important national issues. Out of that Accord developed consultation and agreement on an incomes policy and a good deal of participation by labor in the overall planning process. Business leadership didn't formalize its relationship with the process in a written accord but they were party to the same discussions with the Administration. For a time it appeared to the American labor movement that we might be able to develop and hold together the kind of cooperative approach to national economic issues which is essential if we are to succeed on the employment issue. In the last months of 1980, as the Carter Administration's term was ending, the President established a joint labor-management government committee on the revitalization of American industry, with a broad mandate for "overall planning."

Unfortunately, our elections interceded and President Reagan's election ended the process because his Administration's deeply held conviction is that no overall planning is necessary or appropriate in our country and that free market forces will produce economic success and insure employment.

We obviously do not agree with this theory and continue to be available for the consultation with business and government which is necessary if we are to have an agreed set of goals for our society and for our economy, and if we are to be able to relate those goals to international economic conditions.

UNIONS' POLITICAL ACTIVITIES

The papal analysis of political activities of unions seems to require particular consideration in terms of its relation to this need for governments "to act against unemployment" and to carry out some role in the "overall planning" for work.

We in the AFL-CIO are quite comfortable with the formulation that "unions do not have the character of political parties struggling for power; they should not be subjected to political parties or have too close ties with them," (*Laborem Exercens,* n. 20) but we are equally sure that it is only our involvement in politics that enables us to work for a government which will "act against unemployment" and plan for providing work for all.

The Encyclical's treatment of this subject is obviously far too short to warrant too much speculation about its application in individual countries. It would give substantial discomfort to the trade union movements or political parties of a number of industrialized nations if it were literally applied, and some writers have questioned its pertinence as a moral issue.

In the United States, on the other hand, it fits our present and past policies very comfortably. We have always insisted upon our independence of government and of political party, while maintaining a strong involvement in the political process. We have seen our role as one of encouraging the participation of union members in political activity and we have always insisted on being guided by the instruction of the first President of our federation to "reward your friends and defeat your enemies" in politics. In the past year, while we have undertaken an enlarged role in the Democratic Party we have made clear that we are trade unionists first and party members second and that we would be guided accordingly. We have specifically reserved our right as trade unionists to support candidates of other parties where we deem it to be in the best interest of our members to do so. Similarly, we have made clear to the Republican Party our willingness to provide the same sort of coordinating role among those of our members who are adherents of that party.

The concept of a Labor Party or of a political party dominated by the labor movement has never had strong attraction for U.S. trade unionists. It has been raised from time to time as an expression of frustration with the extant parties and there have been some efforts to create such a party at various past times but each has foundered in a relatively short period.

Nonetheless, it is our participation in politics and in the political process, which is the only sure protection of those interests of workers which are dealt with by "the indirect employer." Consequently every success which we have in increasing and enlarging our political power enlarges our ability to defend workers' interests.

THE RIGHT TO STRIKE

That small section of the Encyclical which deals with the protection by government of the workers' right to strike, and the injunction that essential community services must be ensured, received a great deal of attention in the United States because of the coincidence of the issuance of the Encyclical with the nationwide strike of air traffic controllers whose right to strike had been infringed upon by government legislation. While the section was obviously not intended to have that effect, it was much-cited as defending the actions of the President in discharging all of the striking employees.

Aside from abrogating government responsibilities, disrupting government functions and demoralizing government employees, the Administration, by its intemperate and vindictive response to the strike of the air traffic controllers, established a climate of fear and resentment that puts unreasonable strains on public employees at every level.

The fact is that workers, as a last resort, after all other avenues of redress have failed, will strike even where that action is regarded by the state as a form of civil disobedience. And what is needed is the legal recognition of that right to strike along with special provision for the maintenance of essential services on an emergency basis.

The Encyclical, while forthrightly noting that essential community services must be ensured, does not state the need for substitute mechanisms to ensure fair treatment of workers who, on the theory that there is no other way to insure essential services, may be deprived of their right to strike. It may be argued that that concept is included within the phrase "appropriate legislation" or that "appropriate legislation" includes the concept of mediation, cooling-off periods, the availability of binding arbitration, or the specification of certain categories of workers as "essential" while protecting the right to strike of others in the work unit. However, in the circumstances of the current debate on this issue in the United States, the concentration on ensuring essential services seems unfortunate and may give the impression that no special consideration is due to workers whose right to strike the state seeks to abridge. This point will depend upon the exposition and enlargement of this theme by commentators.

THE IMMIGRANT WORKER

The Encyclical's examination of the position of the immigrant worker is a particularly timely one when some nations, in recession, must determine how to treat the immigrant or guest workers they once needed and when other nations are beset either by illegal immigration or by the necessity to receive large numbers of economic or political refugees—often with the additional difficulties attendant on making that distinction.

While the Encyclical limits its instruction to the point that the immigrant worker, seasonal or permanent, "should not be *placed at a disadvantage* in comparison with the other workers in that society in the matter of working rights," (n. 23) it is interesting that this section and the sections on national planning are grounded in a respect for national boundaries and national identities and thereby avoid the pitfalls that await those who pretend that we have achieved some sort of world society.

If we are to deal realistically and rationally with immigration planning and with the need of nations to periodically accept the unexpected refugees from another nation's inhumanity, we must first recognize the serious employment effects of immigration and factor in those effects. The effort is not assisted by those who would pretend either that there is no need for immigration controls or that any nation can hold itself apart from necessary international efforts to accommodate refugees.

The AFL-CIO has always supported a rational immigration policy and, even in difficult economic times, has consistently urged the U.S. to be generous in admitting refugees.

It is also obvious that increased international and national planning by "the indirect employer" must include assistance and aid to Third World nations so that the underdeveloped and less developed countries can grow and provide food and jobs for their own people with the resultant diminution of the pressures to emigrate.

WOMEN WORKERS

Many people in the United States were particularly pleased with papal support for the theories of recompense for women who stay at home to care for children. There have been some efforts over the past few years to obtain social security (old age pension) coverage for homemakers because keeping a home and raising children are a form of work and should be recognized as such. The social re-evaluation of the mother's role advocated by the Encyclical will support that effort.

Similarly, the thought that "the advancement of women requires that labor should be restructured in such a way that women do not have to pay for their advancement by abandoning what is specific to them and at the expense of the family," (*Laborem Exercens*, n. 19) will provide additional support for those who have advocated flexitime and part-time work for women who seek such work.

Coming from a nation where a large number of women are the principal or sole supporters of families, I hope that commentators on the Encyclical will place an additional emphasis on the equality of women in the workplace and on the impropriety of the historical low-rating of job classifications which have been regarded as "female jobs." Much attention has been given in my country to the question of equal pay for equal work and the re-evaluation of jobs so that those historically female occupations might be given equal status with jobs of "comparable worth" to society.

I hasten to note that I am not one of those who finds the tone of the Encyclical, or its use of the male pronoun, somehow anti-feminist, although that criticism has been made in my country. I believe a more careful reading belies that description. This is not to deny that a greater emphasis on the need for equal treatment of women, on the problems of women workers who are heads of families, and on the "comparable worth" issue, would have commended the Encyclical even more highly to feminist leaders in the United States.

Profit Sharing

Profit sharing has never been a major factor in the remuneration of U.S. workers and unions have accepted the concept only when considered as a supplement to, rather than a substitute for, that "living, saving, family wage." In recent years there has been some renewed interest in profit sharing but the fact is that in good times most employers have shown no disposition to share profits and it has been most often advanced as a substitute for a normal wage. Now that difficult days are upon industry there has been more employer and less union interest in it. However, in some of our most depressed industries where workers have agreed to pay reductions or to stand-still contracts, the promise of future profit-sharing has had renewed consideration.

Implications for Corporate Policy

The most immediate challenge posed by the Encyclical in the United States is the challenge to the holders and managers of capital. The national, transnational or multinational corporation based in any of the western industrialized nations, is a corporation organized around the profit motive, seeking to pay the cheapest price for labor, the cheapest price for raw materials and to obtain the highest price for its product. The measure of success is "the bottom line" in accounting terms, the amount of profit returned to the shareholders.

In *Laborem Exercens* the Pope forthrightly states that the entire structure must be revised, the principle of the priority of labor over capital must be respected, and the employment process must be recast in the service of man. When he speaks of joint ownership and profit sharing or shareholding by labor, he notes that even if these "proposals cannot be applied concretely, it is clear that recognition of the proper position of labor and the worker in the production process demands various adaptations in the sphere of the right to ownership" (n. 14).

How much more then, does that recognition require adaptations of corporate policy to workers? Is it not required that a corporate balance sheet give at least as much attention to the number and quality of jobs it has provided during the year as it does to profits? Is it not required—if the worker is to be the center of corporate planning and thought—that allowing one facility to deteriorate through inadequate reinvestment, and closing that facility with resultant unemployment, be considered a wrong that must be avoided and redressed? Is it not required that greater attention must be given to safety and health measures than to increased output—where that increase is achieved by diluting those measures? Is it not required that the transnational corporation be a force for social improvement in Third World nations, bringing with it a willingness to pay not just the going rate of an underdeveloped wage system but rather installing itself as a leading employer not only in pay and conditions but equally in terms of its management and its recognition of the dignity of its workers?

* * *

The Encyclical has given both comfort and challenge to United States unions, employers, to political and economic analysts and to the Church itself. The condemnation of rigid capitalism and of collectivism presses us toward some middle course as yet insufficiently defined.

The applications which flow from the recognition of the proper position of capital and labor are considerable. They are surely immediately present for the non-profit institution, and particularly the religious non-profit institution, as employer.

If unions are "indispensable," what Catholic institution, as employer, can fail to instruct its employees on the need for them to seek legitimate union affiliation and representation? What Catholic institution, as employer, can fail to initiate legitimate participation in management, based on collective bargaining agreement, for its employees?

For corporations or other employers who accept the concepts of the Encyclical, the same consequences flow, but only time will tell how many of such employers and corporations will accept. There is, undoubtedly, a major teaching role ahead for the Church and its institutions, particularly in industrialized nations—an uphill struggle to re-educate those who have too long accepted the view that capital has priority, that capital buys labor, and that without a profit motive there can be no industry.

In such quarters, the Encyclical's instructions that the means of production cannot be isolated "as a separate property . . . set up in the form of 'capital' in opposition to 'labor,' " that they "cannot be *possessed against labor*" and "must *serve labor,* and thus, by serving labor make possible the achievement of the first principle of this order, namely the universal destination of goods and the right to common use of them," (n. 14) will find tough going.

Consequently, the teaching role of the Church in this matter ought to be organized by the Justice and Peace Commissions in each nation, and the National Conferences of Bishops in each country ought to take a new look at its responsibility to insure the teaching of this and of all the social encyclicals and to work for the adherence of all to this body of Catholic thought.

For our part, as trade unionists we will go on pressing for the individual elements of worker rights that the Pope has defined and worry not at all about the system's appropriate title. We will continue to struggle for workers' rights, for fair compensation and all that goes with it, and above all to struggle for the recognition of worker dignity that flows from employment, under decent conditions, in a fulfilling toil about which the worker has a say and through which he participates fully in the management, ownership and profits of the enterprise.

Feminist Themes and Laborem Exercens

Andrea Lee, I.H.M. and Amata Miller, I.H.M.

This article originally appeared in *Co-Creation and Capitalism,* 1983.

The scope of a symposium on the recent encyclical of John Paul II on human work, *Laborem Exercens,* is likely to be sweeping and diverse given the centrality of work in human experience and its multiple facets. From the myriad of possible areas of analysis, we have chosen a micro-analytic one which not only springs from our own identity and experience as women, but also reflects the evolution of a phenomenon which has already wrought significant change upon world economic, social and political structures—the increasing presence of women in the world of work outside of the home. Some analysts claim that this phenomenon embodies the potential for changes equal in degree and scope to those evident during the transition from an agricultural to an industrial society.[1] The reality and implications of an exponential growth in the number of women who work outside the home are of immediate concern and interest to economists and social scientists, as well as to the controllers of work environments. Eli Ginzburg, chairman of the National Commission for Manpower says:

> This (women working outside the home) is the single most outstanding phenomenon of this century. It is a worldwide phenomenon, an integral part of the changing economy, and a changing society. Its secondary and tertiary consequences are really unchartable.[2]

It is our conviction that bringing the feminist lens to bear upon the discussion at this predominantly male symposium will raise some useful questions about the realities of women in the workplace, the intersection of thought themes in feminist theory and the encyclical and, in the original language of the symposium title, to pose a ''religious challenge to corporate power.''

It is our hope that by focusing on the centrality of economic issues within the women's movement and the seriousness of the economic injustices facing women in the workplace, we may contribute toward a more full understanding of the true nature and societal implications of women's struggle at this time in history. (Too often, Catholic Church members and leaders dismiss the women's question as trivial or focus on the particular areas of dissonance between the feminist struggle and Church teaching, e.g., ordination or abortion issues, rather than on the fundamental areas of agreement between feminist principles and Catholic social teaching.)

Our topic then will be to explore the implications of the encyclical, *Laborem Exercens,* in terms of its congruence within feminist principles on work and its implications for the humanization of the world of work for women as well as for men. Some limitations in scope and design are presented in order to clarify the dimensions of this paper. Our discussion has evolved as a reflection on data and informed experience rather than as a formal research treatise. This reflective stance is built upon several years of monitoring the experience of women at work from our particular disciplines. We have attempted to outline the most pertinent themes without concluding that these are the only themes which might be developed. Our focus is on women as a marginalized group, but this focus is not meant to signify any less concern for workers in other marginalized groups. In addition, our emphasis on women working outside the home in no way lessens our regard for women's work within the home.

Finally, it is acknowledged that, for many feminists, a Church built on patriarchal exclusivity can have nothing credible to say to women or to other social institutions in need of reform of their treatment of women. There is sharp disagreement on this point, and it must be acknowledged that the authors are not in full agreement on whether the Church can speak credibly to corporations in this regard. However, our Christian hope encourages us to search for possible linkages, to point out alliances in thought and to place trust in the growing congruence of thought among diverse groups. While acknowledging that a defensible focus on the points of divergence could be quite reasonably drawn, our emphasis is rather on the points of intersection.

The perspective of any writer has a significant impact on the outcome of an exploration and analysis. The authors of this paper share a socio-political perspective which places credence in the possibility and desirability of an evolutionary transformation of social realities from within institutions and other social organizations. The two disciplines of economics and organizational theory offer at least the possibility that our reflections will transcend a single focus or mode of analysis. We will also address the question of women's work—what the encyclical says or does not say about it, and the implications for corporate powers were the encyclical vision to become reality for women—from a feminist perspective, a point of view which will be more thoroughly developed in the first major section of this paper.

Another perspective which, because of its ties with the design and theme of this symposium, must be discussed more fully at the outset is our view concerning the role, scope, and power of corporations within contemporary society. It is presented here as a prelude to our discussion of our selected topic and as a framework within which that discussion can occur.

PERSPECTIVE ON CORPORATIONS

We are not among those who see corporations as the incarnation of evil, solely responsible for all society's ills, incapable of any good. Rather we count ourselves among those who see corporations as key institutions exercising social, economic, and political power within our society and thus also extending their influence to many other parts of the world.

Though corporations originated as primarily economic structures, it can no longer be maintained that they have solely an economic function in our society, so central have many corporations and groups of corporations become to the life of local communities, individual states, and indeed, the whole nation. Thus, they can no longer hide behind the view that their sole responsibility is to their stockholders. With the increasing scope of their influence has come an increased scope of responsibility. The economic function of corporations now extends far beyond the provision of the products they produce. Because of the magnitude of the employment and income effects of their activities, the fate of local, regional, national and international economies is dramatically influenced by decisions made in corporate board rooms. In some cases these linkages are very clear—as in Youngstown, Ohio, or in Flint, Pontiac or Detroit, Michigan. In other cases the linkages are more obscure. But there is no escape from the responsibilities of power.

Another aspect of our view is that corporations are *one* institution among many in our society, thus they are part of the system which expresses the cultural values and the historic experiences of the American people who have, over time, created the economic system we have today. Economists describe it as a ''Mixed Economy.'' (Some might perceive it today as a ''Mixed-up Economy!'') This connotes a combination of market and political decision-making processes to mobilize our resources in order to satisfy our needs and wants and to allocate the outcomes in accord with our societally determined standards of what makes a ''good society.''

Among the participants in this symposium, as among the American population, there are varying views of whether our present degree of ''mix'' is the preferred one to accomplish our purposes. Nevertheless it seems clear that social, economic, and political power are in fact shared, however uneasily, among private and public institutions today. The continual effort to develop societal processes which embody our deepest democratic principles in effective decision-making within all aspects of our communal life is one of the most challenging of pursuits. Corporations cannot by themselves create the ''good society'' as envisioned by the encyclical, but they *can* hinder its realization insofar as they seek to maintain myopic and antiquated views of their responsibility—views which do not reflect today's reality.

From the perspective of the authors, Catholic social tradition calls for a view of society as more than a collection of individuals whose pursuit of their own goals will realize the ''greatest good for the greatest number.'' Our tradition as described once again in *Laborem Exercens* sees society as more than the sum of its parts, rather as having a life of its own which must be nurtured and guided by institutions with societal scope, seeking the *common good*. Corporations are called by Catholic social teaching, as are individuals and other economic institutions, to help to develop democratic means whereby the good of *all* the people can be achieved. It calls for specific recognition that the market is not democratic in its allocation of either resources or products, and so must be complemented by other socio-economic-political institutions.

A third aspect of our view of corporations which we would like to present at the outset is that we view corporations as cross-cultural institutions with vast resources, experience, power, and capability which can be used as instruments for building community world-wide. In international circles multinational corporations are usually called "transnational enterprises" (TNE's). This connotes a broader perspective on their influence and their potential for constructive contributions to the building of a new world order—a perspective which the authors share.

Finally, it is important to state that we recognize the variety among corporations in their style, structure, policy, practice, and philosophy. Since they are human institutions there is rich diversity among them. Some are enlightened in their approach to human and societal concerns, while others seek to retain a nineteenth century "Robber Baron" perspective of management prerogatives and responsibility. The data presented here is the result of the operation of corporate structures as a whole and, as in any aggregation, individual variations are masked.

The remainder of this paper will be organized in three specific sections:

1. The Vision: An outline of feminist themes and threads of congruence and dissonance between selected themes in *Laborem Exercens* and the feminist principles.
2. The Reality: Current issues for women in the workplace.
3. Closing the Gap between Vision and Reality: Toward a transformed world: Areas for action.

These three sections will attempt to delineate the parameters and suggest some approaches to answers for the following questions: Where are the points of congruence between the feminist principles elucidated and those gleaned from the encyclical? Are there points of divergence and, if so, do they carry the capacity to neutralize the strength derived from points of congruence? If the discovery of congruent themes related to work in feminist theory and the encyclical, *Laborem Exercens,* suggest a credible vision of a preferred future for women in the work world, what are the dimensions of the present reality and the challenges they pose which look to this vision as worthy of our best human striving? If we have a glimpse of the vision and a clear grasp on our present reality, what concrete steps are possible in order to reduce the gap between vision and reality? Does the strength derived from the discovery of congruent themes offer any real hope for the transformation of the work realities of women? What is the "responsible response" of corporate powers to the growing convergence of value frameworks and principles among diverse social groupings?

Despite some initial anxiety that attempting to uncover points of congruence within a papal encyclical and the body of feminist ideology would prove to be an ill-advised procrustean adventure at best, there appear to be some areas of thought congruence as well as a few notes of stark dissonance. While the specific focus of this symposium, as well as the limits of space and time, do not permit a thorough analysis of themes in both, several surface as fruitful areas for exploration.

If one searches within the encyclical for a prescriptive plan of action toward transformation of the work world, disappointment is the most probable result. In the same way, a hope that feminist ideology will reflect undeniable unanimity, such that it embodies a single well-defined political strategy, is likely to go unfulfilled. The most that can be hoped for—and this is not necessarily an inferior outcome—is an heuristic guide for action and decision-making.

Most recently, the papal encyclicals have been precisely that—less pietistic, more prophetic; less a prescriptive or algorithmic approach to human activity than a statement of broad principle and a framework within which responsible action may occur and which is open to divergent descriptions for a preferred future. It could be argued successfully that the encyclical's "success" might be measured in terms of its force and power in guiding decisions, initiating positive change and innovation, and encouraging attitudinal and behavioral shifts. By avoiding inappropriate expectations of specificity and prescriptive accuracy, the reader encounters the freedom to explore the encyclical themes and their relevance as guides for action within particular nations, cultures, communities, and work environments.

A similar statement may be made with respect to feminist ideology. The prospect of condensing the complex and nuanced reality of feminism into a manageable set of principles is an unwieldy one. Even in the inner circles of the women's movement, there is no concise, thoroughly accepted definition for feminism. Even the word itself sparks a disparate pool of responses.

Somewhere in the blur of elementary school, most of us learned that suffixes were little syllables tagged onto the end of words. They created subtle rather than substantive changes in meaning and certainly held no capacity to evoke strong emotion, crystallize beliefs, spawn political activity, or separate persons into "we's" and "they's." It soon became apparent, however, that "ism" or "ist" added to "femin" connoted a vastly different meaning than did "ine." In traditional circles, *feminine* was acceptable, desirable, and appropriate—a truly proper adjective; *feminist* and *feminism* raised eyebrows, stirred up unrest, and muddied the waters of social acceptability, having quickly become somewhat suspect nouns.

As an expression of human struggle, feminism is simultaneously a subject for rich description and sparse definition. Reflecting this as ideological diversity in their book, *Feminist Frameworks,* Jagger and Rothenburg-Struhl outline four basic feminist perspectives:

1) *liberal feminism*—seeks opportunities for the advancement of women within the existing society through substantive changes in the worlds of education, work and other social and political structures.
2) *Marxist feminism*—centers the source of women's oppression in the single, evil core of a capitalist economy and regards the remedy as its dissolution.
3) *radical feminism*—locates the source of women's oppression in the socio-economics of gender and not in a particular economic system.
4) *socialist feminism*—a synthesis of radical and Marxist feminism which looks to both economic systems and gender peculiarities (childbirth) as the root causes of structural misogyny.[3]

In reality, the delineations may not be so neat and the majority of feminists view the roots of women's oppression as a complex aggregate of social, political, economic and religious realities. It is true, however, that the transformational perspective adopted in the introduction to this paper would suggest that the liberal feminist perspective is most closely identified with that of the writers.

FEMINIST THEMES

Even within the diverse pool of what stands in the shade of the "feminists' umbrella," several themes surface and dominate. These themes become more focused and compelling when viewed in a Christian context. If space constraints lead us to put forth these themes with the verbal austerity of axioms, it must be left to the rich stores of women's collective history to flesh out these abstract principles. The selected themes are outlined here:

1) Feminism is one of the fundamental movements toward human liberation. In that sense, it both derives strength from other primary struggles against classist and racist oppression and enters the energizing stream of solidarity with its own particularized focus and perspective.

2) If feminism is a primary movement toward human liberation, Christian feminists approach the struggle from a critical stance of awareness, analysis, and action amid enduring beliefs about the action of God in human life, and the meaning of the Gospel in the light of human experience (in this case, women's experience).

3) Feminism is not of "recent design;" it has spanned centuries of both conscious and unconscious struggles of women to achieve full personhood. Feminism has embodied the exhilaration of victory and the numbing effect of defeat; it has experienced periods of paralysis and of apparently boundless energy and drive. Viewed as a continuous, although diversely expressed, whole, feminism lays claim to a rich heritage despite the obliteration of its history by socially induced amnesia. Viewing feminism as a fad or isolated pockets of activism distorts and shrinks a bigger reality which embraces a startling continuity of issues and themes.

4) The feminist struggle centers on the right to and achievement of excellence, i.e., full personhood, by women in their private and professional lives, in political, social, religious, and economic spheres.

5) Systemic and systematic devaluation of women's abilities and

aspirations has seriously diluted the potential of humankind to create a just and humane earth.

6) Feminists struggle against systemic economic oppression of women, pointing to the sharply disproportionate number of women and children among the world's poor. Across generations of feminist activity, the ruts which trap women in poverty have engaged the compassion as well as the creative energies of feminists. They regard poverty as a systemic, and indeed epidemic, "social disease" affecting primarily women. As a result, eradication of the roots of economic oppression assumes a position of primacy in the feminist movement.

7) Social institutions embody a source of power able to effect social change, i.e., institutionalize emerging or shifting norms, and therefore are a logical target for action by feminists.

These are several of the most predominant feminists themes, ones which span at least several of the ideological perspectives outlined earlier. They establish a context within which to examine the rich variety of feminist thought and some points of congruence with selected themes in the encyclical *Laborem Exercens*. Certainly they pivot on the axial premise of the struggle for quality of life for women and, indeed, for all human persons.

SELECTED ENCYCLICAL THEMES

Quality of life and its pursuit through work is also a theme which threads through John Paul II's encyclical. In addition, several other predominant themes relevant to our discussion here may be mentioned:

1) The dignity of the human person is what gives value to work and, conversely, the work of human persons should contribute to the development of quality of life[4] (6,9,10,15,26).

2) There is not a hierarchy of types of work, i.e., the varying kinds of work do not carry different degrees of worth or value. There is no hierarchy of work in terms of intrinsic value (6,12).

3) Organizational styles of decision-making should reflect, in a positive manner, the eradication of value being assigned to

work on the basis of position in the hierarchical structure (14,15,18,20).

4) Human persons deserve work environments wherein they can conceive of themselves as co-creditors or partners in the total human effort toward wholeness and excellence (24,25,26,15).

5) Compensation is a pivotal issue in the world of work—both the level and the mode of determining it; a level of support equal to need is demanded by justice principles (19).

INTERSECTION OF IDEAS IN FEMINIST THEORY AND ENCYCLICAL THEMES

1. Centrality of Work in Human Experience

The search for points of congruence between the selected themes from *Laborem Exercens* and the pivotal feminist principles yielded some serendipitous results. From the outset it seems appropriate to view feminist ideology as a vital subset of the great movements of human struggle toward liberation. Within organized efforts to shrink and obliterate classist, racist, and sexist oppression of human beings in order that they may be free to stretch to the edges of their God-given potential for human excellence, there may be derived critical and primary relationships between these struggles and the struggle of human persons within the common and unifying arenas of human work. Certainly the encyclical reinforces the primacy of work within the domain of human experience, not only as a means of maintenance and survival, but also, ideally, as a means by which human persons participate in the ongoing creative activity of God in the universe. As clearly as John Paul II stated that "the Church finds in the first pages of the Book of Genesis the source of her conviction that work is a fundamental dimension of human existence on earth" (4), feminists focus a remarkable percentage of their efforts on transforming or revolutionizing the workplace for women, so central is it perceived to be within the reality of human existence.

During the 1970's, the feminist focus on the workplace, and other centers of economic reality, intensified. The proliferation of economic themes in women's liberation circles—feminist literature highlighting the Equal Rights Amendment as an economic or 'bread and butter' issue; the now-famous 59¢ button blitz (women in the United States make an average of 59 cents for every dollar a man makes); disturbing data on the feminization of poverty; the principle of equal pay for work of comparable value; the sharp increase in the number of households headed by women and in the number of women in the workforce—attempted to shift the public image of "women's liberation" from the faddish fancy of bored middle-class white women to one which was developing increasingly sophisticated political strategies. The feminist effort sought to force United States business, political and economic powers to come to grips with the presence, forced stagnation, and mounting discontent of women in the workplace.

Work became the focus and few stones were left unturned in the effort—the under-representation of female energy and creativity in the upper echelons of corporate monoliths in both policy-making and administrative positions; the over representation of women in low-paying, dead-end support positions within corporate structures; schedule rigidity and unsatisfactory programs for child care; unequal access to training and education programs; the complex dilemmas which surface with the increase in female labor in third-world countries housing U.S. corporate enterprises—all these areas have engaged feminist energies.

2. The Value of Work Is Derived from the Dignity of the Person

In outlining a "gospel of work," John Paul II establishes a framework of analysis wherein these and similar problems of working persons may be examined when he says that the "basis for determining the value of human work is not primarily the kind of work being done, but the fact that the one who is doing it is a person" (5). He also makes reference to the collective reaction to work conditions which do not permit the attainment of full personhood or even, in some cases, the minimal needs for survival which ". . . gave rise to a just social reaction and caused the impetuous emergence of a great burst of solidarity between workers," and that this reaction "united the working world in a community marked by great solidarity" (8). Perhaps unknowingly hinting at the escalation of efforts on behalf of women workers, John Paul II asserts that "movements of solidarity in the sphere of work . . . can be necessary also with reference to the condition of social groups that were not previously included in such movements'' (8). He goes on to state that ''this solidarity must be present whenever it is called for by the social degrading of the subject of work, by exploitation of the workers and by the growing areas of poverty and hunger'' (8).

All of the above appears to lend credence to the delineation of links between recent feminist efforts in the domain of work and the pivotal themes of the encyclical, *Laborem Exercens,* regarding the integral worth of the human person as the value qualifier of work, a qualifier which equalizes the value of work by upgrading the social worth of all human labor to a discernible and dignified level rather than by equalizing downward to a common level of mediocre acceptability.

It appears, then, that viewing work within the full scope of the human struggle toward liberation, i.e., the unleashing of opportunities for development of full human potential, holds meaning both within the context of feminist frameworks and the encyclical, *Laborem Exercens.*

3. Appropriateness of Action on Behalf of Self and Others

The feminist principles which address the struggle and activity of women within a Christian context call for an approach which embodies a critical stance of awareness, analysis, and action within the context of deeply-held beliefs about the action of God in human life and the Gospel imperatives for a contemporary world. Certainly this approach is proactive rather than reactive and would seem to suggest that responsible action on one's own behalf, as well as that of others, is appropriate for women in the work force. In his discussion on workers' rights, John Paul II reiterates this principle regarding collective and worker-initiated action as was suggested in the above mentioned quotes from the encyclicals. This emphasis on self-initiated action, decisive movement toward the attainment of human rights, and social organizing in order to achieve these goals suggests a departure from the traditional mode of ''suffering servant Christianity.'' It stands in contrast to a mode of Christianity which deceives persons into believing that strong action toward achievement of liberation or quality of life, or, in a more limited sense, the achievement of a just and humane work environment is somehow incongruent with the model of Jesus Christ as the ''lamb led silently to slaughter.'' Feminist refusal to bear such a burden which replaces creative energy with guilt is congruent with the papal affirmation of legitimate (in light of Christian principles) social action toward justice in the workplace, where justice is defined as the creation of an environment where all workers have an opportunity to attain the social fruits of the God-given human dignity. ''This entirely positive and creative, educational and meritorious character of man's [woman's] work must be the basis for the judgments and decisions made today in this regard in spheres that include human rights'' (11).

4. Significant History of Feminist and Church Involvement in Labor Issues

The encyclical reinforces the establishment of the dignity of human labor within the framework of divinely-bestowed intrinsic human worth. If Leo XIII's *Rerum Novarum* introduced a new player into the drama of social criticism of the world of work, it was surely not a player who dramatized an as yet undiscovered theme. John Paul II's repeated return to the ''Genesis roots'' of work as a human activity and his assertion that the Church has always been an advocate for the vision of work as co-creation would lend credence to this statement. In the same way as some look to the Church's involvement in the social aspects of labor as a nineteenth and twentieth century phenomenon, there is a prevailing social perception that feminist activism is of recent origin.

There is clear evidence to the contrary. The women's suffrage movement is known to many; a fewer number are aware of the strong feminist presence in the nineteenth century abolitionist movement and the strong history of female presence in labor struggles. A sampling of quotes points to a persistent thread of feminist concern for justice in the world of work:

The flour merchant, the house builder and the postman charge us no less on account of our sex; but when we endeavor to earn money to pay all these, then indeed, do we find the difference. (Lucy Stone, 1855)[5]

Wherever, on the face of the globe or on the pages of history, you show me a disenfranchised class, I will show you a degraded class of labor. Disenfranchisement means inability to make, shape or control one's own circumstances. The disenfranchised must always do the work, accept the wages, and occupy the position which the franchised assign to them. This is exactly the position of women in the world of work today. (Susan B. Anthony)[6]

Working women, throw your needles to the winds; press yourselves into employments where you can get better pay; be conductors in our cars; drive hacks. If your petticoats stand in the way of bread, virtue, and freedom, cut them off. (American Equal Rights Association, 1868)[7]

Women, you must work out your own deliverance with fear and trembling, and with the direction and blessing of God, you can do it. (Angelina Grinke, 1842)[8]

5. The Talents and Abilities of Women Are Underutilized

The impact which a transformed work reality for women would have may be viewed from several perspectives. Were the papal call toward the value of work being determined by the intrinsic worth of the person accomplishing it to be transplanted into practice, compensation levels for millions of women in low-paying service and support positions would rise, at considerable cost to the employing agencies. There are not a few corporate critics, including some feminists, who believe that corporate profit is built on a foundation of a cheap, available labor pool, frequently female, which has been socialized to the point that barriers to promotion, low pay, and lack of voice in determining policy do not surface as stimuli which engender dissent and action in the direction of change. There is evidence of congruence between the encyclical's echo of the Church's teaching on the rights of workers to organize, although feminists have adopted a more aggressive stance in raising the consciousness of women to recognize their plight and act to change it.

This struggle of women and other marginalized groups to improve their status and levels of compensation is the most visible focus of organized action. It is equally possible, however, to view the underutilization of female energy and abilities within corporate endeavors as both related to compensation and promotion inequities and, more importantly, as an unfortunate and unprofitable waste of human resources.

Feminist effort to document the magnitude of this reality has been both consistent and frustrating. One wonders what the result might be if the full scope of women's potential were made available in the workplace. Even the most sterile fiscal analysis by a corporation addressed the question: "What resources have we not tapped which are available to us?" In nearly every area of human endeavor, the feminist response would be "women's resources:" their intellectual capacity, ingenuity and creative energy, their perspective and outlook. Certainly in the competitive marketplace effective use of available resources is a principal consideration. One can only conclude that the full spectrum of women's potential has not yet been viewed as an undeveloped resource by corporations bent on leaving no "profit-generating" stone unturned or that the price or risk of turning this stone over is still too high. This point bears an interesting relationship to the Pope's focus on co-creation or "work as a sharing in the activity of the Creator" (25).

In the same paragraph, John Paul II continues with an assertion that:

> The word of God's revelation is profoundly marked by the fundamental trust that man, created in the image of God, shares by his work in the activity of the creator and that, within the limits of his own human capabilities, man in a sense continues to develop that activity, and perfects it as he advances further and further in the discovery of resources and values contained in the whole of creation (25).

Even if we concede that the papal reference to "man" is generic and inclusive, the marginalized experience of women leads to the unfortunate conclusion that, in the world of work, the papal "man" is both sex-specific and exclusionary, to the mutual detriment of women and the world. God's creative work is stifled and limited; our ability to create a just and humane earth is weakened. Pifer comments on this reality in a recent article: ". . . more and more Americans are beginning to see full employment of women's abilities as a social and political imperative. Not only is it a national moral obligation stemming from our country's basic principles, but, more pragmatically, we are beginning to realize that the safety and prosperity of the nation will increasingly depend on the maximum use of our entire stock of human talents."[9]

6. *Systemic Economic Injustices Are a Primary Stimulus Toward Transformation of the World of Work*

It has been mentioned earlier that, despite public belief to the contrary, the major focus of feminist effort has been on the uncovering and eradication of economic injustices related to work. In his reiteration of the Church's teaching on the rights of workers, John Paul II points to several areas which have also been the subject of feminist attention: the right to "suitable employment for all who are capable of it" (18); the right to unemployment and other work benefits as "a duty springing from the fundamental principle . . . of the common use of goods, or . . . the right to life and subsistence" (18); the right to "just remuneration for work done" (19).

The feminist struggle for justice in the workplace is also centered on these principles of justice. Efforts to enable legislation to correct inequities; establishment of regulatory agencies (however slow-moving and ineffectual); efforts to present the facts on levels of compensation, unequal pay for equal work, unequal access to pension and social security benefits, lack of job security and unemployment statistics as well as the plight of displaced homemakers all have captured the attention and energies of feminists with a goal of transformation. A further discussion of data related to women's work and economic injustices will be developed in the next section of this paper.

POINTS OF DISSONANCE

The search for points of congruence between the papal encyclical and the feminist focus on work surfaced some clear points of agreement. It would be a mistake and perhaps a curious manifestation of wishful thinking to conclude, however, that the papal documents and the feminist effort to reform the work world move in full synchrony. There are some undeniably dissonant notes. A brief mention of them will deter the inclination toward haste in making unwarranted assumptions on the practical implications of this alliance of thought. Three points appear particularly deserving of mention.

1) Most women work because of economic need. Some women, however, work because their work is a positive contributor toward the development of themselves as human persons. Many women work for a combination of the above reasons, albeit in varying proportions. With the publishing of the encyclical, *Laborem Exercens,* an immediate flurry of comment ensued relative to what the Pope said or did not say about women working "outside the home." It is not within the scope of this paper to discuss whether or not married women should work outside the home when economic necessity does not demand it, but rather to point out that when the Pope refers to a "single salary given to the head of the family for his (in this case the "his" is clearly not intended to be generic) work sufficient for the needs of the family without the spouse having to take up gainful employment outside the home" (19), he assumes a stance in sharp contrast to that of feminists. The Pope's statements are clearly related to earlier pronouncements of his regarding the proper and principal role of women as motherhood. While the concept of a "social re-evaluation of the mother's role" would meet with agreement by feminists, few would agree that the primary "mission of a mother" is to stay at home. The feminist view holds as inviolable the principle of woman as a human person with needs, wants, rights, and responsibilities independent of her relationship to husband and children. Even as we began with the assertion that "quality of life" was a common goal articulated by both feminists and the papal encyclical, the Pope's idea that, in most cases, quality of life for women is attained by being wife and mother is resisted by feminists. They, on the other hand, hold that while this may well be true for some women, for many others quality of life is enhanced by their working productively outside the home and sharing more equitably with their husbands the responsibilities, burdens and joys of parenting.

2) The feminist idea of "equal pay for work of comparable value" stands in uneasy juxtaposition to the encyclical focus on compensation based on need. It may be unrealistic to conceive of a marginalized group relinquishing its acquisitive striving for the same visible signs of "success" as those possessed by the power groups. There is ambivalence within feminist ranks on this point and certainly the analysis invades the socialist/capitalist debate, exceeding the scope of our discussion here.

428 / Andrea Lee, I.H.M. and Amata Miller, I.H.M.

Efforts within feminist groups to "level-out" the hierarchies of position and status, to seek out and hear the stories of working women, to search for common threads of experience have been significant. No less significant, however, has been the emergence of the "queen-bee syndrome" among women who have "made it" and the prevailing feminist belief that the values of various works differ, can be evaluated, and should be assigned levels of compensation accordingly. Ellen Cantarow highlights the dimensions of this dilemma when she says that:

> Such questions are double-edged. On the one hand they have the kernel of momentous potential; redefining the value of scorned work could lead to questioning the competitive bases for valuing human worth that characterized most of American life. But they could also just advance the "me first" ethic, encouraging the thought that secretarial work is intrinsically "better" than maintenance work. (It would hardly be the first time workers near the bottom had been pitted against each other).[10]

3) Finally, the whole issue of credibility alluded to in the introduction must be addressed. There are certainly significant hurdles to be overcome before feminists could be led to believe that the patriarchal church is championing their right to develop as full human persons. If the rhetoric suggests that the striving for "quality of life" and human excellence is a proper task for all, the policy and practice of the Church demonstrates that the parameters of what determines "quality" for women is narrowly defined and carefully prescribed. The Pope appears to counter his own logic in arguing that motherhood is what gives worth and value to women, since the original principle as stated by the Pope placed the source of worth or value within the person and not within other relationships to human persons or social institutions.

There is the clear possibility that the Church cannot speak credibly to corporations or any other social institutions on the issues of justice regarding women in the workplace. While this possibility is acknowledged, our choice has been to proceed as if a productive intersection of thought is possible. We keep in mind, however, the warning of Thelma McCormack that "normative theories dignify lost causes, comfort the victims, and feed their fantasies of wish fulfillment; they touch a chord within all of us, winners as well as losers.''[11]

Even with this sobering awareness, the hope for transformation encourages many women to move forward.[12]

THE REALITY: CURRENT ISSUES FOR WOMEN IN THE WORKPLACE

In this second part of the paper we will focus on the workplace from the perspective of the women who are counted as part of the ''labor force.'' This does not imply uncritical acceptance of the market-determined definition of ''work'' as exclusively that which enters into market transactions. Within the limits of time and space and the scope of this symposium we will focus only on work outside the home, and the realities facing the women who make part or all of their social contribution in this arena.

What does the recent encyclical have to say to the corporate world, in particular, in relation to policies and practices as they affect women? In the light of current realities, what challenges do the normative principles restated by John Paul II pose to the policy makers and administrators in corporations? What guidance do they give to those who seek to influence the corporate institutions as workers or stockholders or citizens?

While there are many aspects of the economic oppression of women which could in some sense be said to be beyond the control of the corporations, as dominant economic institutions they both embody prevailing social patterns and originate or foster changes in those patterns. Thus, it *is* appropriate to look at the present realities for women and pose challenges to corporate decision-makers in their regard.

In this section the *data* will present the challenges. The facts, drawn together in one place, placed alongside the normative vision of the encyclical, contain a clear call for change. This section will present first a brief overview of the economic realities of women in the labor force. This will give a perspective on the magnitude and importance of the economic realities facing women today and thus the urgency for society of resolving these issues.

WOMEN IN THE WORKPLACE—OVERVIEW

One of the most profound societal changes in the 1970's, a decade of marked change in American society, was the increasing presence of women in the work force. Bureau of Labor Statistics data indicate that as of June, 1980, 51% of all women over 16 were in the labor force, and 42% of all jobs were held by women. In 1950, 34% of U.S. women were in the work force.[13] Focusing on married women reveals that 52% of all married women were in the work force, and that 47% of married couple families have both husbands and wife working. Only 37% have the husband only working. By 1980 almost half of the children in two-parent families had working mothers, up from 38% in 1970. Fifty-seven percent of all women with children under 18 were in the labor force in 1980.[14] Clearly, the type of family envisioned by John Paul II in *Laborem Exercens* (19) and other statements is becoming less and less typical in the United States. That the American public also is largely ignorant of the scope of change that has occurred in family patterns partially explains that failure of private and public policy makers to deal with the consequent realities.

What of the myth that women work only for "pin money" and that their labor market status is thus less significant in economic terms than that of men? Again the facts bely the myth. Bureau of Labor Statistics data show that 20% of the mothers in the labor force in 1980 (3.8 million women) were heads of their households. Analysis of data on married women whose husbands also work showed that women are most likely to work if their husbands have incomes slightly below the national median (i.e., in the $10,000 to $15,000 range in 1977). That is, women whose husbands are teachers, technicians, small proprietors, mechanics, construction workers, police, or fire fighters are most likely to be in the work force. This corroborates other data that indicate that the ability of lower income families to live at a working class standard was dependent on the earnings of the wife. In 1979, nearly two out of three women in the work force were either single, widowed, divorced or separated, or had husbands who earned less than $10,000 per year.[15] These facts should be sufficient to show that most of the women in the work force today are there because *they* are increasingly the breadwinners for themselves and others. Economic necessity born of the rising divorce rate; the recurring high levels of unemployment, national and regional; increasing consumer indebtedness; persisting inflation; and lengthening life span for women drove many women into the labor force even while others chose to pursue careers for personal reasons.

Increasing attention is being drawn to the "feminization of poverty." Again the facts attest to the reality. Bureau of Labor Statistics and Census Bureau data indicate that 79% of the poor in the U.S. today are women and children. Over 12 million full-time workers are eligible for some form of public assistance—67% of them are women. Forty-two percent of all female single-parent households with children under 18 live in poverty and 50% of all minority single-parent households with children under 18 live in poverty. Between 1969 and 1976 the entire increase in the number of families living in poverty was among female-headed households.[16] This presence of women among the poor in disproportionate numbers indicates the institutionalized sexism that permeates the socio-economic system. In the words of *Laborem Exercens* (8):

> And the "poor" appear under various forms: they appear in various places and at various times; in many cases they appear as a *result of the violation of the dignity of human work*: either because the opportunities for human work are limited as a result of the scourge of unemployment, or because a low value is put on work and the rights that flow from it, especially the right to a just wage and to the personal security of the worker and his or her family.

This brief overview gives the data base for the scope of the problem and its seriousness. It indicates the end result of the operation of the U.S. socio-economic system, of which corporations are but one part. There are some specific aspects of the economic problems of women which are particularly traceable to corporate actions, however. Data on a few of these can be presented here.

WOMEN IN THE CLERICAL OCCUPATIONS

In its 1979 publication, "Women Still in Poverty," the U.S. Civil Rights Commission observed:

> Traditional ideas of where women belong in the economy and patterns of employment discrimination have nearly excluded women from certain areas of employment . . . and from the skilled crafts, which have been traditionally male-dominated. Women have often been channelled (regardless of their inclinations) into lower paying, lower status jobs that men have not wanted, such as clerical and household work.[17]

Clerical work has the largest percentage of women in the work force—it is the largest female ghetto; it is also the lowest paid. After World War II women saw clerical work as a step-up from blue collar work. In 1950 62% of clerical workers were women; by 1979, 80% were.

Median usual weekly earnings of full-time clerical workers in 1979 show the usual gap between male and female earnings. Even in this field where women predominate so markedly their earnings are only 64% of those of men.[18]

The U.S. Civil Rights Commission found that employment agencies steer women into clerical jobs, and that they are classified by employers into jobs with little promotion potential. An example from the insurance industry cited a woman who rated ''very high'' on all the tests during the training period, and was assigned to be a ''direct correspondent''—a clerical employee who handles inquiries from individual subscribers, while male, non-minority trainees were assigned to be ''group subscribers,'' positions which proved to have more responsibility and much more rapid promotion.[19] Such subtle forms of discrimination are difficult to eradicate, but they demonstrate the systemic violation of the principles of human dignity and of work as a means for self-actualization outlined in *Laborem Exercens* (9,15,26).

Harris Shrank and John Riley studied a large bureaucratic corporation with 14,000 employees in home and field offices. They observed that there are certain families of jobs defined as appropriately male or female and that all jobs within large organizations tend to have some position within a hierarchy. That means that each job tends to be pegged at certain salary and status levels. Some jobs, however, such as secretarial jobs, are hierarchical only within specified limits. ''There is, for example, a hierarchy of secretarial jobs, but it has an upper limit well below the highest level of jobs within the corporation.''[20] They concluded,

An occupant in the female pool of jobs has for the most part been precluded from the same sort of hierarchical movement that is found in the male pool of jobs. Of course there has been some potential for upward mobility within the female pool, but change, if it occurred, was slower and more limited in range. The upper limit for the male pool is the president's position. The comparable upper limit job within the female pool is often secretary to the president.[21]

This is but one example of what has been documented in many places. Harris and Shrank found that in the 1970's some changes were taking place which point the way to future action.

As new types of jobs were opened up gender-free pools developed in areas where there was no cultural tradition to reserve the roles to one sex or the other (e.g., computer programming, systems analyst). Also affirmative action programs have widened opportunity for women at all job levels.[22] The development of new jobs or job families may well provide the opportunity to upgrade the employment status of women within the corporate structures.

WOMEN IN MANAGEMENT

It is commonplace that women do not generally hold positions of power and authority in American corporations. Where women are in management they tend to be concentrated in lower-paying positions, in selected fields, and in staff rather than line positions, and in less powerful, less prestigious organizations.[23] In 1979 women were 25% of managerial/administrative workers overall, up from 14% in 1950 and 17% in 1970. The heaviest concentration was in sales managers and department heads in retail trade where 39% are women. Louise Kapp Howe notes that women tend to be concentrated in apparel areas but are rarely found in furniture departments where the pay is higher.[24]

If we look more closely at the data we find that women are only 5% of middle management and 1% of top management in the largest companies. A 1978 FORTUNE survey of the 1,500 largest companies in the U.S. found only 10 women among the 6,400 corporate officers and directors.[25] There is evident disparity between male and female executives in salary patterns. In 1975 BUSINESS WEEK reported that only 3% of managers and administrators earning over $25,000 were women, and only 15 women (compared to 2,500 men) headed major corporations and earned more than $100,000.[26]

Some change is occurring, however, since even 15 years ago in the mid-1960's only 1% of entering managerial trainees were women, while in the mid-1970's the entry figure was 15%. Linda Kellner Brown comments on the significance of this, noting that the presence of even a few women in the executive suites reinforces women's aspirations to achieve success in a previously male field. She notes that many investigators have argued that so-called problems of women in management would evaporate if only there were more of them.[27]

The Civil Rights Commission indicated that management representatives at their hearings did not deny that women are underutilized or concentrated at low-level jobs, but they did deny any deliberate discrimination in their practices. Most large corporations have personnel practices which allow wide latitude at each supervisory level. It is here that the informal, "secondary labor market" phenomenon comes into play, where attitudes and stereotypes and personal preferences rather than objective qualifications influence promotion paths.

The pernicious effect of all this is to restrict women to lower-paying jobs, contributing to the phenomena of economic distress outlined at the beginning of this section. Enlightened corporate policy and attitudes on the part of managers responsible for personnel at each level can be significant in upgrading the positions of women in the corporate hierarchy. As corporate executives encounter managerial couples each with their own career goals, the old resistance will tend to break down. Interestingly it has been found that older executives are less likely to have stereotypes about managers than are younger persons, probably because of their experiences with working wives and peers.[28] Principles regarding dignity of persons and work like those outlined in *Laborem Exercens* can provide support for more opportunity for women in the corporate structures.

WORK HAZARDS FOR WOMEN

Another area where corporate practice contradicts the principles regarding work outlined in the encyclical concerns hazardous working conditions. In specifying the rights of workers is included "the right to a working environment and to manufacturing processes which are not harmful to the workers' physical health . . ." (19). At the present time there are three particular occupations in which women are particularly victimized by corporate practice. These are the emerging occupational health and safety issues.

First, with the increasing use of word processing equipment in offices there is increasing documentation about hazards of eyestrain from watching video display screens and stress from the noise and speed of the work. There is some evidence that there are potential harmful cumulative effects of X-rays from the cathode ray picture tubes. All of these problems can be limited by relatively simple changes in work patterns and office equipment design. Eyestrain can be reduced to a significant degree by allowing hourly breaks, and installing anti-glare screens and adjustable lighting. Noise can be diminished by placing the high speed printers at a distance in soundproof enclosures. Encasing in metal rather than plastic can reduce radiation emissions.[29]

Second, in the electronics industry concentrated in Santa Clara County's Silicon Valley where 80% of the employees are women there has been recent documentation of chemical hazards. The trade uses 10% of all the chemicals in the U.S., including some of the most dangerous corrosives, toxic solvents, poisons and carcinogens. Area physicians are beginning to voice their concern over rising medical problems, and the death rate has risen 20% in the last eight years. Investigators have found that the chemicals in combination may have geometrically greater impact than each of them separately. The fact that most of the employees are Asians or Mexicans who have been brought in by the corporations from successful overseas operations makes organization of the workers more difficult. In addition, some manufacturers have found it profitable to encourage home assembly of the silicon chips. Reports have been received of vats of dangerous substances boiling on the kitchen stoves of women who work without any protection of minimum wages, social security, or workers' compensation.[30]

A third area of exploitation of women is in the garment industry where the competitive nature of the assembly process gives incentive to cut costs in every conceivable way. The industry is organized into "inside shops" with production facilities of the firms that design and merchandise the garments and into "outside shops," small contractors who do the sewing and assembly of the garments for the "inside shops" whenever they have an overflow of orders and for "jobbers" who contract out all of their assembly work. Because of the vulnerability and availability of immigrant women, a new generation of sweatshops with all the conditions of the nineteenth century variety has sprung up in New York's Chinatown and in the South Bronx. It is estimated that there are 500 in each of these locations. These employ mainly Hispanic and Asian women who work at piecework rates as low as 75¢ a dress. In weekly terms it is not unusual for one of these women to work a 60-hour week and take home the equivalent of $1.30 an hour (in comparison to the $4.00–$5.00 an hour usually made by ILGWU members). In hopes of making a little extra money the women also often take work home. Again, lack of education, language barriers, and immigrant status often makes it difficult to determine the extent of violations.

Sociologist Roger Wadinger has noted that what is happening is the internationalization of production for labor as well as capital. "The same people who are making clothes abroad under conditions that violate international labor codes come here to make them under relatively similar conditions."[31]

It is difficult for consumers to identify the manufacturers and contractors involved in making the clothes they buy, since retailers sew their own labels into the clothes they sell. But corporate managers know who their suppliers are.

In these areas of blatant disregard for human health, clear responsibility is apparent and women's lives are at risk. The old battles keep returning in new forms. Perhaps enlightened corporate executives can be enlisted in the battle this time around.

CLOSING THE GAP BETWEEN THE VISION AND THE REALITY:
TOWARD A TRANSFORMED WORLD: AREAS FOR ACTION

It is deep in our tradition that we are called to participate in the redemptive action of God in the world. Since Vatican II the call to action for social transformation has been articulated ever more clearly as a constitutive element of living the Gospel. Thus, the vision of a transformed world, outlined in the body of Catholic social teaching (as well as in other religious and secular documents) is not only for speculative discussion. It is also intended to provide an action orientation—some guiding principles for concrete steps for change. Choices are made in specific decisions in the light of a fundamental value stance. Without being prescriptive, Catholic social teaching, as part of the body of ethics, is generally normative.

The key principles of Catholic social teaching, expressed anew in *Laborem Exercens,* are finding corroboration in the work of the growing interdisciplinary body of scholars and focusing on the study of the future. These are also being joined by business leaders (such as the Italian industrialist Aurelio Peccei) and diplomats such as the UN's Robert Muller who see new value bases as essential for the survival of humankind in the next century. Values such as the fundamental dignity of the human person, stewardship of resources, human solidarity, and subsidiarity in organizations are integral to religious and secular visions of a preferred future. For example, the World Council of Churches has been sponsoring scholarly dialogues among futurists since the mid-1970's investigating the contours of and paths to a "just, sustainable, and participatory" future.

Dennis Gabor, Nobel Prize-winning physicist, has called in his book, *The Mature Society,* for application of energies to "social innovations" to create a world in which each person will work according to her/his intellectual gifts and abilities and motivation toward service. James Robertson, British economist, in his book, *The Sane Alternative: A Choice of Futures* describes three scenarios: "business as usual future;" "technological-fix future;" and the "SHE" future (sane, humane and ecological). His preferred SHE future expresses in its structures the values of socio-economic balance and harmony within persons, between persons, and with nature. All of these examples are cited to show the strength and diversity in the chorus of voices calling for transformation of the workplace along the lines outlined in feminist and papal themes.

In particular, Alan Pifer, as president of the Carnegie Corporation of New York in his 1976 Annual Statement, envisaged the nation setting in motion changes needed to build a new society, creatively responsive to the increasing presence of women in the workplace. It would be based on four principles which incorporate the values common to the feminist vision and *Laborem Exercens*:

1) the right to a job for everyone who needs/wants to work
2) equal opportunity and fair rewards for everyone in all sectors of employment
3) development and utilization of the abilities of every citizen
4) maximum flexibility for each person in the organization of his/her own pattern of life[32]

What are some of the specific action areas that would lead to such a society? In particular, what are some challenges to corporate policy and power?

What if corporations joined labor unions and citizen action groups in developing strategies for non-inflationary full employment? The negotiation of new contracts in the face of economic necessity in the auto industry and elsewhere provide some bases for hope that it is possible to take joint action which is mutually beneficial in the longer run. Perhaps the current public outcry against the nuclear arms race can provide occasion for corporations also to recognize the fundamentally harmful long-term effects of the arms build-up on the economy and join the conversion effort. (According to Employment Research Associates, the $135 billion 1980 U.S. military budget cost the jobs of nearly 1.3 million women in comparison with what would have been available if comparable funds were in the hands of consumers or state and local governments.) Unless adequate employment opportunities exist, the rest of the social justice agenda will be in vain.

What if corporations became at least gender-blind in hiring and promotion practices? The developing of new job pools in new industries or new divisions of expending companies can provide opportunities for far-sighted executives to introduce evolutionary change. And perhaps more visionary managers, recognizing latent talent in an underutilized female clerical force, might initiate personnel policies and educational opportunities enabling women to upgrade their positions.

What if corporate practice encouraged the development of small suppliers and worker-owned businesses? Through their purchasing patterns and contracting practices some large firms have encouraged the development of successful and viable specialized suppliers. Small businesses generate over two-thirds of the new jobs in the nation, and provide better advancement possibilities for women than do larger firms. Perhaps we might learn from the Japanese experience to encourage the strength of smaller enterprises.

What if corporate executives began to educate themselves and their constituencies to take a longer-run view, to recognize that development of everyone's potential is in the interests of all of us together? Perhaps new models of labor management cooperation might emerge. Perhaps the growing concern for improved productivity might lead to development of new forms of worker participation in decision-making which would bring the complementary gifts of women and men together in peer situations which would release new creativity in persons and organizations.

What if corporations tried to guarantee the maximum flexibility for each person in the organization of his/her own life? Perhaps the success many companies and 10% of the work force have had with flexible schedules might encourage others to experiment in ways that provide women and men opportunity to balance their home and work responsibilities more equitably. Perhaps the movement for job-sharing might lead to more fulfilled and less stress-laden workers and make it possible for women with children to carry on careers without interruption. Perhaps some creative approaches to child care might be developed.

What if corporations adopted the principles of participative decision-making consonant with feminist and encyclical principles? Perhaps adoption of some of the currently popular Japanese styles of management might lead to more humane and responsive workplaces that would also be more productive. Perhaps resistance to employee organization might give way to recognition of the realities of interdependence and the need for cooperation. Perhaps employees might respond in unexpected ways.

What if we gave a revolution and everybody won?[33]

Notes

1. Sheila Robbotham, *Women's Consciousness, Man's World* (Baltimore: Penguin Books, 1973).

2. Eli Ginzburg, *New York Times,* November 29, 1977, pp. 1,28.

3. Alison M. Jagger and Paula Rothenburg Struhl, ed., *Feminist Frameworks* (New York: McGraw-Hill, 1978).

4. Encyclical references are noted by paragraph numbers within the text, e.g. (8). Translation provided by United States Catholic Conference: Publication No. 825, Office of Publishing Services.

5. Lucy Stone, quoted in Papachristou, ed., *Women Together: A History of Documents of the Women's Movement in the United States* (N.Y.: Knopf, 1976), p. 33.

6. *Ibid.,* p. 21.

7. *Ibid.,* p. 61.

8. *Ibid.,* p. 13.

9. Alan Pifer, "Women Working Toward A New Society" in ed. K.W. Feinstein, *Working Women and Families* (Beverly Hills, CA: Sage Publications, 1979), p. 17.

10. Ellen Cantarow, "Workers Not Wives", *In These Times,* December 9–15, 1981, p. 12.

11. Thelma McCormack, "Toward a Nonsexist Perspective on Social and Political Change" in Millman and Kanter, *Another Voice* (New York: Anchor Books, 1975), p. 4.

12. *Woman's Declaration of Rights* in Papachristou, ed., *op. cit.,* p. 24.

13. Bureau of Labor Statistics, *Perspective on Working Women: A Databook,* Bulletin 2080, October, 1980, pp. 6–7; Riley, Maria, "Women Between Work and Family: Between Myth and Reality", *Center Focus,* Issue 42, March, 1981, pp. 1–3.

14. *Ibid.*

15. *Ibid.*

16. cf. "Wealth and Women", *Dollars and Sense,* No. 71, November, 1981, pp. 12–14; "Poverty: A Women's Issue", *National Organization for Women,* 1979; Pearce, Diana, "Women, Work, and Welfare: "The Feminization of Poverty" in ed., K.T. Feinstein, *Working Women and Families,* (Beverly Hills, CA: Sage Publications, 1979).

17. US Civil Rights Commission, Clearinghouse Publication 60, July, 1979, p. 19.

18. BLS Bulletin 2080, Table 49.

19. USCRC Clearinghouse Publication 60, July, 1979, pp. 22–25.

20. "Women in Work Organizations" in ed. Juanita Kreps, *Women and the American Economy,* (Englewood Cliffs, N.J.: Prentice-Hall, Inc. 1976), pp. 89–90.

21. *Ibid.*

22. *Ibid.,* pp. 99–100.

23. Rosabeth Moss Kanter, "Women and the Structure of Organizations: Exploration in Theory and Behavior" in Millman and Kanter, ed., *Another Voice,* (New York: Anchor Books, 1975), pp. 35–38.

24. *Pink Collar Workers,* (New York: G.P. Putnam, 1977), p. 16.

25. W. Robertson, "The Top Women in Big Business", *Fortune,* July 17, 1978, pp. 58–63.

26. "Up the Ladder—Finally", *Business Week,* November 24, 1975, pp. 58–68.

27. "Women and Business Management", *Signs,* 5 (Winter, 1979), p. 269.

28. *Ibid.,* p. 278.

29. "Word Processing and the Work Process", *Dollars and Sense,* no. 69, September, 1981, pp. 6–9.

30. Sue Martinez and Alan Ramo, "In the Valley of the Shadow of Death", *In These Times,* IV October 8–14, 1980, pp. 12–13.

31. Hardy Green and Elizabeth Weiner, "Bringing It All Back Home", *In These Times,* March 11–17, 1981, pp. 8–9; "Sweatshops Still Thriving", *Dollars and Sense,* no. 52, December, 1979, pp. 8–9.

32. "Women Working: Toward a New Society" in K.W. Feinstein, ed., *Working Women and Families* (Beverly Hills, CA: Sage Publications, 1979), pp. 26–33.

33. Eric Mount, *The Feminine Factor* (New York: John Knox Press, 1973), p. 178.

Major Differences: Liberation Theology and Current Church Teaching

Christine E. Gudorf

This article originally appeared in *Catholic Social Teaching on Liberation Themes,* 1980.

The first difference, though not the primary one, between liberation theology and traditional Catholic theology concerns the definition of theology. The accepted definition of theology among liberation theologians is Gustavo Gutierrez': theology is critical reflection on praxis in the light of the Word.[1] Praxis itself is the primary difference between liberation theology and the theology current in the Church. Praxis is not merely "practice," in the sense of applying in action the principles of one's belief in whatever one happens to do. Praxis is the commitment of oneself to the struggle for liberation. The relationship of theology and praxis is a spiral one in liberation theology. Theology is critical reflection on praxis in the light of faith. This reflection is then used to guide continuing praxis in new channels. Further reflection on this altered praxis results in new theology, which then continues to correct and guide praxis.

Latin American liberation theologians understand Christian praxis to aim at liberation. This Christian praxis is liberative insofar as it involves commitment to and action on behalf of the poor and oppressed of the world.[2] This commitment to action on behalf of the poor and oppressed of the world entails both striving to eliminate poverty in the world, and adopting the "poverty perspective."[3] Striving to eliminate poverty in the world is not enough. The presidents of multinational corporations maintain that they do this by working for a new economic order controlled by these corporations, which will break down national barriers preventing progress. Some evangelists claim to work for the end of poverty and oppression by the preaching of charity and brotherhood. Real, effective striving to eliminate poverty is, say the liberation theologians, linked to the "poverty perspective." Affluent liberals who speak of the perspective of the poor have not, according to liberation theologians, adopted the poverty perspective.

Gutierrez and others maintain that the poverty perspective is the perspective *of the poor engaged in the struggle for liberation.* They claim that it is the Christian perspective.[4] The poor who are engaged in the struggle for liberation have a clear understanding of the faith and of the world—a truer interpretation of what faith means and what the world is really like.[5] This is one reason why the poverty perspective is the perspective of those *within* the movement of the poor for liberation—only the poor within the struggle can see what needs to be struggled against, and what faith really means clearly enough to give shape to real liberation.

Poverty is an integral part of the method of liberation theology. It is the inescapable presence of overwhelming poverty in the Latin American context which causes the liberation movement to use social class analysis. Since liberation theology is critical reflection on the praxis of this liberation movement, social class analysis is also a part of the method of liberation theology. In the Latin American context social class analysis is necessary to prevent the cooptation of the term "oppressed"—to insure that the liberation to be won is *real* liberation from the real oppression, material poverty. The use of social class analysis from within engagement in the liberation struggle therefore prevents the "spiritualization" of the term "poverty" and the deflection of the liberation movement.

Liberation theologians deny that theology can be done apart from liberative action and commitment to political struggle.[6] This political struggle, praxis, is toward the construction of a new "historical project" indicated by Christian faith.[7] This historical project is not identical with the Kingdom of God, in that the Kingdom cannot be completed or finally realized through human efforts alone. But through construction of the historical project we do participate in the creation of the Kingdom by bringing about the liberation of humanity in history. This is a necessary part of and precondition for a liberation of humanity from sin and for the communion of humanity with God which will signal the existence of the Kingdom of God.

This historical project, in which humanity moves from social and political liberation to liberation in history, that is, to psychological liberation to self-creation and responsibility, is utopia, the creation of a new type of human being.[8] One of the Latin American liberation theologians wrote of this utopia:

> We must remember that Jesus' project is a utopia. But 'utopia,' according to modern sociology, psychology, and anthropology, does not have the negative meaning of illusion or flight from the conflictive reality of the world. It possesses a positive depth and signifies the capacity to transcend, a creative fantasy, the dialectical reason of man. Man can rise above his own historical construction and project a not-yet-experienced but still possible reality. From this moment on, historical expressions are relativized, criticized, and placed in a process of liberating conquest. The utopia of the kingdom of God does not mean the construction of a particular kind of world and a certain kind of future. Rather it surpasses the totality of the concrete forms of the world in function of another, more human and more open to the coming of God. Jesus, with the announcement of the Kingdom of God did not postulate another world, but rather a new world; this old and broken world would be totally transfigured.[9]

Liberation theology views the commitment of the Christian to the building of the historical project, utopia, through action in solidarity with the poor as the initial step. Theology, critical reflection on this praxis, is the second step, dependent not only upon theological commitment but upon this political commitment.[10]

The implications of such an understanding of theology are critical for the Church. Understanding theology as liberation theologians do, as moments of critical reflection in a life of action in faith, entails new visions. The Latin American vision of a liberative God, acting throughout history in the political struggles of the oppressed—a God of conflict—challenges the Church's view of God. The Church's traditional view of salvation is challenged by liberation theology's rejection of a split between the spiritual and the material. Salvation can no longer refer to another realm, separate and distinct from the material world.[11] The human person is seen to be both material and spiritual. A distinction is made between the spiritual and the spiritualistic,[12] a term used to refer to a false level of abstraction divorced from the real material conditions of human life. The spiritual is another dimension of real lived life, the dimension of "religious experience." Salvation, then, in liberation theology, begins here on earth in the construction of the historical project.[13] The implications for sacramental theology and for Christology are also a distinct challenge to the tradition, as is the understanding of sin which results from this conception of the human condition and the mission of the Church. The liberation theologians' understanding of theology also diverges from the traditional understanding in the matter of religious authority. A more traditional Catholic definition of theology would stress reflection on revealed truths as interpreted by the Church. Not only does the liberation definition move the spotlight to the world of action, away from an understanding of faith as dogmatic, but in so doing the traditional emphasis upon the Church as the interpreter of faith and overseer of all Catholic praxis has been omitted. Presumably it is the individual Catholic who now does his/her *own* critical reflection on his/her praxis in the light of his/her experience of the Word. This is not to deny the importance of the Church in structuring and informing that individual's experience of the Word. However, there is no room here for the kind of total control the popes claimed for the hierarchy in the various forms of Catholic Action.

It is important to note that even in this instance of departure from the traditional emphasis on the Church as sole interpreter of the faith and overseer of all praxis, the liberation theologians are critical. They do stress a measure of individualism in the understanding of praxis and theology, but they also stress that praxis entails joining with others in action, and advocate using the social weight of the Church to attack social problems rather than simply the efforts of individual Christians. It is, therefore, a selective individualism.

Traditionally the Church has understood her mission in terms of calling humanity to salvation in another world. If life on earth and salvation are no longer distinct, but rather intimately connected, then the Church's view of the appropriate approach to social and political entities of the world must be re-evaluated. The Church cannot ignore the world and its events in her concentration on the next life, but must recast herself as an agent in the political struggle in the world. To this end she requires a new set of tools for working in the world.

For there is a leap between faith and the commitment to the historical project. That leap is bridged by the use of the tools of social science—of sociology, economics, psychology, and political science—to analyze the world in order to determine how God is acting in the world and where lies the appropriate commitment which puts us on the side God has chosen. The historical project is to be built in the world for, by, and with human beings. Therefore the real world and its people need to be understood by all Christians who face commitment to the historical project. It is not enough to understand the Church's concept of unchanging human nature. Political struggle involves concrete conditions which work on human nature and create differing situations which need to be understood in their differentness. This requires social scientific analysis.

Because these tools of social science, so necessary for determining particular praxis, do not always lead to the same analysis of reality, the political options of Christians, even of Christians committed to liberation, may not be identical.[14] Hugo Assman writes that since human experience is the starting point for theology, and the secular (social) sciences have the first word about it, liberation theology takes a decisive step toward these sciences.[15]

Juan Luis Segundo distinguishes between the sciences of the past, which theology has embraced, and the sciences of the present, from which theology asserts its independence.[16] Though it is true that traditionally theology has preferred the sciences of the past, this statement of Segundo's is misleading. Even in its use of the sciences of the past the Church has resisted and refused to develop a scientific mentality. She has rejected the idea that the results of social scientific endeavor could call into question any of her past understanding of theology or society or require some new understanding of either. In short, she has not been open to changes indicated by social scientific work. Her refusal to allow the socialist political option is one example, say liberation theologians, of her refusal to use the social sciences to analyze reality which is often criticized by liberation theologians.

Thus it is clear that there are many points at which liberation theology contests the method of traditional Church theology. Some of these contested issues are: the mission of the Church, the definition of theology, the relation of the Church to the world, the character of God, the nature of truth, and many others. . . .

Paul VI made many changes in the emphasis put on the various areas of the content of the social teaching, but retained the traditional view of theology and the task of the Church. In *Libentissimo sane animo* (October 1, 1966) his address to the International Congress on the Theology of Vatican II, he said:

> Both theology and the magisterium seek to further the same purpose: to preserve the sacred deposit of revelation; to look more deeply into it; to explain it, to teach it, and to defend it. In short, they both seek to shed the light of divine truth on the life of the Church and mankind, so that all men might be led to eternal salvation.
>
> But theology and the magisterium have different duties and are endowed with different gifts. Sacred theology uses reason enlightened by faith; and it receives no little light from the divine paraclete, to which the theologian must pay heed. Its duty is to examine and comprehend the truths of revelation more thoroughly, to bring the fruits of its labor to the attention of the Christian Community, and in particular, to the attention of the magisterium itself, so that the whole Christian people may be enlightened by the doctrine which the ecclesiastical authority hands down; and finally to lend its efforts to the spreading, clarifying, confirming and defending of the truth which the magisterium authoritatively propounds.[17]

An examination of this passage makes clear that in seeking to "shed the light of divine truth on the life of the Church and mankind" theology and theologians use *only* reason and the enlightenment of the paraclete to examine and comprehend the truth of revelation. They do not look to the life of the Church and humankind; rather they come to their conclusion in the abstract, at the conceptual level. The theory is to be imposed on practice, not developed through and in the light of the successes and failures of that practice. This implies an understanding of "the truths of revelation" which does *not* recognize the possibility of present revelation in history. Without a sense of ongoing revelation, the Church will not look to present history to determine where her liberative action should be.

At no time in this statement did Paul intimate that the Church's purpose ever goes beyond the task of enlightening people as to doctrine. And yet five years later, only ten years after John's *Mater et Magistra* insisted on the three steps for the application of social principles, Paul wrote:

> In the face of such widely varying situations it is difficult for Us to utter a unified message and to put forward a solution which has universal validity. Such is not Our ambition, nor is it Our mission. It is up to the various Christian communities to analyse with objectivity the situation which is proper to their own country, to shed on it the light of the Gospel's inalterable words, and to draw principles of reflection, norms of judgement, and directives for action from the social teaching of the Catholic Church. This social teaching has been worked out in the course of history and notably, in this industrial era, since the historic date of the message of Pope Leo XIII on 'the condition of the workers' and it is an honor and a joy for us to celebrate today the anniversary of that message. It is up to these Christian communities, with the help of the Holy Spirit, in communion with the bishops who hold responsibility and in dialogue with other Christian brethren and all men of good will, to discern the options and commitments which are called for in order to bring about the social, political, and economic changes seen in many cases to be urgently needed.[18]

The language of this statement from *Octogesima adveniens* signals a shift in papal thinking. No longer did Paul refer to obedience to the decisions of the hierarchy as the required action, or stress applying principles from the social teaching to concrete situations. Instead he spoke of Christian communities coming to decision (in communion with the bishops and the paraclete), and of the need to analyze the concrete situation objectively. This, especially, is a far cry from previous teaching, which called more for obedience than analysis and judgment.

Octogesima adveniens represents a break in the tradition on a wide number of issues. The context in which Christian communities exist has assumed some importance between John's time and Paul's. It was no longer assumed that the principles always lead to the same response regardless of the context, or that the method to be followed is only to impose the principle on the individual situation.

Octogesima adveniens is interesting on several counts. There is a break between this statement and previous commemorations of *Rerum novarum* not only in terms of papal purpose, but in the type of document used. In 1941 Pius XII had excused himself for giving only a short radio broadcast rather than a major document on the grounds that the war took up most of his attention, and because Pius XI had given a complete treatment of the issue only ten years previously. Both Pius XI and John XXIII had issued encyclical letters. Paul's document, though roughly similar in size and scope, did not carry this same force because it was, for unknown reasons, issued as an apostolic letter and not as an encyclical.[19]

The change in the form of *Octogesima adveniens* was matched by a significant change in style. *Octogesima adveniens* did not attempt to set forth principles and solutions in the authoritarian style of earlier teaching. It discussed the current issues at stake in the economic, political, and social problems of the day rather than setting forth papal conclusions. Paul indicated the direction in which the Church teaching moved and the Church's general understanding of human nature and the social situation in present history. The "principles" with which he dealt are much more general than those of which his predecessors spoke. Where they referred to more or less hard and fast regulations (that Catholics were forbidden to join or work for Marxist organizations, that all Catholic Action activity be controlled by the hierarchy, or that use of violence was forbidden in all social justice struggles within a society)—Paul, in contrast, referred to the general principles of past social teaching. He found it important, for example, that John had insisted on the right to participate in decision-making as a human right. Paul emphasized not the particular conclusions to which John had come, but rather the general principle which had implications far beyond the labor situation John discussed. All of this may signal a shift away from the classic social teaching.

Paul might have written *Octogesima adveniens* to liberation theologians. In it he took up many of the major themes of liberation theology without, however, mentioning liberation theology by name. Paragraphs 7 through 21 dealt with the problems of modern society, especially as these relate to the Third World. In paragraph 22 Paul stated: "legislation is necessary but is not sufficient for setting up true relationships of justice and equality." This was certainly a shift for a tradition which relied on "action through the word."[20]

Paul then spoke of two human aspirations, to equality and to participation, which "seek to promote democratic society."[21] Political society should be, he said, "the projection of a plan of society which is consistent with its concrete means and in its inspiration, and which springs from a complete conception of the total vocation of human beings and of their differing social expressions." The question here arises: how similar is this "projection of a plan of society" to the historical project of liberation theology?

Next Paul took up the idea of utopia so important in liberation theology. Previous references to utopia in papal writings of the twentieth century had been pejorative, dismissing utopian thought as unrealistic. Some examples of this are found in *Quadragesimo anno, Divini Redemptoris,* and *Populorum progressio.*[22] In *Octogesima adveniens* Paul condemned those who adopt utopia as a convenient excuse to escape from concrete tasks to refuge in an imaginary world. But he recognized the power of utopia to "provoke imagination, to direct the world to a fresh future, and to sustain social dynamism."[23]

When Paul turned to the subject of the role of the human sciences in Christian understanding, he stated that the human sciences give promise of a positive function which the Church recognizes and so urged Christians to play an active part in scientific work. Science could assist Christian morality, he said, which

> will no doubt see its field restricted when it comes to suggesting certain models of society, while its function of making a critical judgment and taking an overall view will be strengthened by its showing the relative character of the behavior and values presented by such and such a society as definitive and inherent in the very nature of humanity.[24]

Paul maintained that these sciences are a condition at once indispensable and inadequate for a better discovery of what is human.[25] This was a giant step toward the position occupied by liberation theology. Nevertheless, recognizing the importance of the social sciences for the information they provide is not the same as recognizing that ultimately the social sciences lead to conclusions which influence and shape the very theological principles from which Paul assumed that social teaching and decision-making in the world proceed.

Perhaps the passage in *Octogesima adveniens* which most clearly revealed the influence of liberation theology was that concerning the dynamism of the Church's social teaching. Here Paul clearly adapted elements (especially language) of the liberation message. In paragraph 42 of *Octogesima adveniens* he wrote:

> It is with all its own dynamism that the social teaching of the Church accompanies men in their search. If it does not intervene to authenticate a given structure or to propose a ready made model, it does not thereby limit itself to recalling general principles. It develops through reflection applied to the changing situations of the world, under the driving force of the gospel as the source of renewal, when its message is accepted in its totality and with all its demands.[26]

For liberation theologians, however, this must be seen as an adaptation of their position, not yet an adoption. In fact, some liberation theologians might label this a *co-optation* of their position. Paul did not read the Gospel as they do, to demand commitment first. Only from the other side of active commitment, say the liberation theologians, can the Gospel be understood. For Paul, the Church possessed the truthful message regardless of its commitment.

Similarly, while Paul claimed that the social teaching develops through reflection applied to the changing situations of the world, he did not suggest that this reflection must be upon participation in the liberation struggle. Paul spoke as if the development of the social teaching comes through passive reflection on something happening "out there." For liberation theology the problem with the social teaching, and with theology in general, is misunderstanding the demands of true praxis.

When the report on liberation theology was made in September 1977 by Paul's hand-picked[27] International Commission on Theology, this misunderstanding of praxis was still very much the case. Though the report did agree that liberation was the true message of the Bible and of the Christian tradition, and did not condemn liberation theology in any way, it issued many warnings as to the dangers of theology which was too political, and involved the Church too far in the workings of the world.[28]

> Ainsi donc la pratique de la foi ne saurait se reduire à l'effort d'amelioration de la société humaine. Cette pratique de la foi comporte, en effet, à côté de la dénonciation de l'injustice, la formation de la conscience, la conversion des dispositions intimes, l'adoration du vrai Dieu et de Jésus-Christ Notre Sauveur en opposition à toutes les formes d'idolâtrie. Aussi la 'foi comme praxis' ne doit-elle pas être comprise de telle façon que l'engagement en matière politique embrasse et dirige de façon totalitaire et 'radicale' toutes les activités de l'homme.[29]

FINAL CONCLUSIONS

This survey of papal teaching brings us to two conclusions. The first is that the size of the gaps remaining between papal teaching and the minimum requirements of a liberation stance is very different depending on the particular issue at hand. The second is that the pace of the development in the papal teaching also differs a great deal depending upon the particular issue.

Within the issues of racism and Third World culture we find a continuing development of the papal teaching over the period studied. Though there remain significant differences between the Third World theologians and the official teaching on these issues, the differences have substantively narrowed under most of the last few popes.

The gap between Third World liberation theology and the papal teaching is perhaps smallest regarding private property; this issue is also one in which the papal teaching has made steady progress since Leo XIII. On the issues of Marxism and the use of violence the pontificates of John XXIII and Paul VI have touched off a minor revolution in papal teaching; the gaps between the two sides are still significant, but the logjam has been broken.

The issue on which papal teaching and Third World liberation theologians remain oceans apart is that of theological method. There are, in the Vatican refusal to break with the traditional theological method, elements of both continuity and discontinuity. There is a sense in which the *continuity* with the past on this point is to be expected. In liberation theology, theology is the second step, dependent upon prior commitment to the liberation struggle. Until the Church resolves sufficient of its other differences with liberation theology, or gets unwillingly drawn into the political struggle by the partisans of liberation theology in the clergy, the Church will not begin to take up the theological task from within engagement in the liberation struggle, and therefore will continue its traditional view as to how theology is done. The element of discontinuity in the papal stance on theological method concerns the sense in which the papal tradition of the last century was critical of both the liberal ideology and the reality of the modern world. Liberation theologians maintain that they are carrying on this tradition of radical critique of the world, and that if the *papacy* is to maintain this former critical stance it must engage the Church in praxis, thus altering its understanding of theological method.

Though the papal teaching, especially from Leo XIII to Pius XII, often confused the critique of modernity and capitalist ideology with concern for its own declining power and prestige, most of the religious values upon which that critique was based are still viewed as pertinent by the liberation theologians. Respect for the dignity and freedom of human life yet call the Church to a radical critique of the modern world and to a stance against those forces and ideologies which restrict and deny such values. This is not a time, say the liberation theologians, for the Church to make peace with the modern world; it is a time which calls for careful discrimination and critique, and for praxis on the part of the Church. Continuity in the critical stance toward the world seems to require discontinuity in theological method.

The attitude of Paul VI toward liberation theology, seemingly reversed in the years after *Octogesima adveniens,* hardened into clearcut opposition. Powerful segments of the Church in the First World joined Latin America ecclesial opponents of the theology of liberation. Not only is liberation theology today menaced by this powerful coalition of ecclesial forces, but it is also persecuted by the civil and economic powers it threatens. Beyond the question of the survival of the Latin American theology of liberation there is a question as to whether papal sensitivity to the Third World and its theologies—never before so acute as under the first years of Paul's papacy—was dulled by Paul's unsuccessful attempt to overcome fear of civil repression and political involvement in pushing the Church to become the Church of the poor. John Paul II's intention to attend the Latin American episcopal meeting in Puebla in January, 1979 demonstrates his interest in these questions. It is difficult to predict before Puebla what attitude this new pope will adopt in these questions.

Though Paul's earlier statements favorable to liberation theology did not reflect the actual practice of the Church, *Octogesima adveniens* and *Populorum progressio* were not mere rhetoric, either. They were rather an attempt to push the Church's position in the liberation theology direction. It is always necessary to consider papal teachings in the light of current Church practice, rather than as pronouncements of accepted Church stands, for such teaching may either reflect Church practice or be an attempt to alter it in one direction or another. The power of the papacy and the weight of papal statements in general prevent papal teaching from being solely rhetoric.

The issue of women—their nature, role, and place in the Church—is one on which there has been virtually no papal movement, in which the present gap between the official Church and the goals of liberation movement is very wide, and on which hopes for progress seem most bleak. On the whole it seems clear that papal accommodation to Third World liberation theology—stalled or reversing though it may now be—has not been matched by similar accommodation to the women's liberation movement or its theology. The very fact that Third World liberation theology has been taken up by segments of the clergy and even of the hierarchy has meant that the issues of that movement are somewhat heard in the Vatican and debated in the Church. Women have no such access to positions of power within the Church from which to force a hearing of their issues. Episcopal meetings, such as the Synod of 1971 and the regional meetings of CELAM in Medellin and Puebla, offer a forum in which liberation theology can be heard and comprehended. Without minimizing the powerful episcopal, papal and civil forces locked in a conspiracy to destroy the theology of liberation in Latin America, one can maintain, I think, that such forums offer a hope that the Vatican and conservative hierarchy can yet be influenced on the remaining issues—a hope that has no such basis in the case of women.

The situation of women in papal teaching, however, cannot be explained merely by the absence of women in the hierarchy, or even in the clergy. New national and racial groups have gained access to the Church, and become influential within it, from exactly the same outsider position that women occupy. For example, the modern creation of a black hierarchy only began with Pius XII, and yet the Church made continual progress before and after this in recognizing the equality and rights of black people. Today we must ask how it is that the Church can maintain the contradictions between its position on women and its position on human beings in general. The papal teaching on the rights of all human beings to equality, freedom, decision-making and participation in all aspects of life contrasts vividly with the exclusion of women from decision-making in the Church and from participation in the offices of the liturgy. These rights of all human beings contrast as well with the limited social roles deemed fit for women in the papal teaching: those which can accommodate the primary domestic vocation she is assigned, and concerning which she is given little choice.

It is impossible to accurately probe the motives of any individual pope as to the reasons for the impasse on the woman question. But the overall pattern is so clear that we are left little option but to assume that in the woman question there is something more deeply rooted than in these other areas. For the crucial sticking points in papal teaching for black and Latin American liberation theology has concerned the posture that the Church takes toward events in the world; the question as to the place of these peoples within the *Church* has not been at issue for at least decades, and in some instances centuries. With regard to women, the primary issue now is not the Church's advocacy of women's rights in the world, but the simple recognition of equal rights in the Church. It can only be assumed that the recognition of such rights presents a vital threat to the Church's understanding of herself, upon which her structure and teaching rest.

Only the high level of threat that the women's movement poses to the Church explains the stubborn clinging to the tradition of exclusion originally based upon such outdated concepts as the defilement of the altar by menstrual blood, feminine sinfulness, and the belief in female inferiority. The extent of the threat results from the fact that women are a clear majority within the Church. Their empowerment would endanger conceptions of authority and patterns of hierarchy, as well as challenge the vestigial aspects of the medieval worldview still operative in the

Church: soul/body dualism, the harmony model of the world, and the understanding of Christian love as sacrificial and vertical. Many of these changes are indeed implied in the Third World challenges to the Vatican. But the centrality of the traditional understanding of the male/female relationship to the papal view of harmony and authority, body and soul, love and hierarchy, assures that a revolution in the male/female relationship could not but call these into question also.

The challenge liberation theologies pose to the papacy, and indeed to the present Church leadership, must be, then, perceived in terms of major alterations not only in praxis, in the way in which the Church responds to the world, but in the structure, personnel and theology of the Church itself.

Notes

1. Gustavo Gutierrez, *A Theology of Liberation* (New York: Orbis, 1973), p. 13. See also Juan Luis Segundo, *The Liberation of Theology* (New York: Orbis, 1976), pp. 71–81 and Hugo Assman, *Theology for a Nomad Church* (New York: Orbis, 1975), p. 59.

2. *Theology for a Nomad Church*, pp. 53–54.

3. *A Theology of Liberation*, pp. 287–308.

4. *A Theology of Liberation*, pp. 287–308; *The Liberation of Theology*, pp. 83–87.

5. *The Liberation of Theology*, pp. 83–87; Gustavo Gutierrez, "Freedom and Salvation," in *Liberation and Change*, by Gustavo Gutierrez and Richard Shaull (Atlanta: John Knox Press, 1977), p. 75.

6. *The Liberation of Theology*, pp. 98–101; *Theology for a Nomad Church*, p. 83.

7. *Theology of Liberation*, p. 236.

8. *Theology of Liberation*, p. 236; *Theology for a Nomad Church*, pp. 67–68.

9. Leonardo Boff, "Statement of Leonardo Boff," *Theology in the Americas*, ed. by Sergio Torres and John Eagleson (New York: Orbis, 1976), p. 295.

10. *A Theology of Liberation*, pp. 11–13; *The Liberation of Theology*, pp. 75–90; *Theology for a Nomad Church*, pp. 74–83.

11. *A Theology of Liberation*, pp. 71–72.

12. Ibid., p. 290.

13. "Freedom and Salvation," p. 86; *Theology for a Nomad Church*, p. 67.

14. This is why Gutierrez in an April 1977 article in *The Witness* said: "my personal option for the socialist way is not a conclusion drawn from Evangelical premises. It comes from my socio-political analysis, which is the starting point for this option." "Terrorism, Liberation and Sexuality," *The Witness*, April 1977, p. 11.

15. *Theology for a Nomad Church*, p. 64.

16. *The Liberation of Theology*, p. 7.

17. *Osservatore Romano*, October 2, 1966; translation: *The Pope Speaks*, Vol. II, p. 345.

18. *AAS* 63 (1971): 403–404, para. 4; translation: *Renewing the Earth*, pp. 353–354.

19. In the classification of papal documents by content *litterae encyclicae* rank first. *Epistulae encyclicae* are second, and *epistulae apostolicae* (the category of *Octogesima adveniens*) rank third. (Index Documentorum of *Acta Apostolicae Sedis*.) This ranking of the documents is explained by Thomas Harte, in *Papal Social Principles* (Gloucester, Mass.: Peter Smith, 1960), p. 7; he described apostolic letters as concerning affairs of the executive or administrative order, and encyclicals as teaching instruments which explain, instruct, or admonish.

20. *Theology of a Nomad Church*, p. 47.

21. Here Paul demonstrated the new attitude toward participation and democracy which John began in *Mater et Magistra*, para. 82–99, *AAS* 53 (1961): 421–425.

22. *Quadragesimo anno*, *AAS* 23 (1931): 180, para. 14; *Divini Redemptoris*, *AAS* 29 (1937): 69, para. 8; and *Populorum progressio*, *AAS* 59 (1967): 295–296, para. 79.

23. *AAS* 63 (1971): 426–427, para. 37.

24. Ibid., pp. 428–429, para. 40; translation: *Renewing the Earth*, p. 373.

25. Ibid.

26. Ibid., p. 431; translation: *Renewing the Earth*, p. 375.

27. *Le Monde*, 7 Septembre, 1977.

28. Commission Theologique Internationale, *Declaration Sur Le Promotion Humaine et Le Salut Chretien*, *La Documentation Catholique*, Septembre 4–8, 1977, No. 1726, pp. 762 (b,2); 763 (c); and 765 (4,b).

29. Ibid., p. 762, 2a.

Biographical Notes

Gregory Baum is a professor of religious studies at St. Michael's College in the University of Toronto.

Edward Cahill was an Irish Jesuit Professor of Social Science in Milltown Park, Dublin.

Richard L. Camp is professor of history and coordinator of the Interdisciplinary Humanities Program at the California State University at Northridge.

John Coleman is professor of Christian social ethics at the Jesuit School of Theology at Berkeley.

John F. Cronin worked for many years with the American Bishops' Conference and wrote extensively in the area of social ethics.

Charles E. Curran is a professor of moral theology at the Catholic University of America in Washington, DC.

Thomas Sieger Derr is a professor of religion at Smith College.

Thomas R. Donahue is the secretary-treasurer of the AFL-CIO.

Donal Dorr is an Irish missionary priest and author of *Option for the Poor: A Hundred Years of Vatican Social Teaching*.

Denis Goulet is the William and Dorothy O'Neill professor of Education for Justice at the University of Notre Dame.

Christine E. Gudorf is assistant professor of theological ethics at Xavier University in Cincinnati, OH.

Peter Hebblethwaite is a journalist whose latest book is *John XXIII: Pope of the Council*.

J. Bryan Hehir is the secretary of the Department of Social Development and World Peace at the United States Catholic Conference in Washington, DC.

George G. Higgins worked for the American Catholic Bishops' Conference for almost forty years and is now a professorial lecturer at the Catholic University of America in Washington, DC.

David Hollenbach is an associate professor of theological ethics at Weston School of Theology at Cambridge, MA.

John Langan is a senior fellow at the Woodstock Theological Center, Georgetown University, Washington, D.C.

Andrea Lee is the dean of Continuing Education at Marygrove College in Detroit, MI.

József Lukács is professor of philosophy at the Eötuös Lorand University in Budapest.

Richard A. McCormick is the Rose F. Kennedy Professor of Christian Ethics at the Kennedy Institute of Ethics at Georgetown University.

Amata Miller is the financial vice-president of the I.H.M. sisters of Monroe, MI.

Charles M. Murphy is a priest of the diocese of Portland, ME and the former rector of the North American College in Rome.

Oswald von Nell-Breuning is emeritus professor of social ethics at Sankt Georgen, Frankfurt, West Germany.

Michael Novak is Resident Scholar in Philosophy, Religion and Public Policy at the American Enterprise Institute in Washington, DC.

James V. Schall is associate professor of government at Georgetown University.

Bartolomeo Sorge is the editor of the well-known Italian Jesuit publication *Civiltà Cattolica*.

The late Barbara Ward was a world-renowned economist and author of *The Rich Nations and the Poor Nations*.

READINGS IN
MORAL THEOLOGY NO. 4
The Use of Scripture
in Moral Theology

CONTENTS

READINGS IN
MORAL THEOLOGY NO.1
MORAL NORMS AND CATHOLIC TRADITION

CONTENTS

READINGS IN
MORAL THEOLOGY NO.2
THE DISTINCTIVENESS OF CHRISTIAN ETHICS

CONTENTS